ExamMatrix
CPA Review Textbook

REG

Regulation

SECTIONS 4000–4600

YEAR 2011

Matrix Learning Systems CPA Review Production Staff
Vice President of Accounting & Editorial/Controller: Pearl Zeiler, MBA
Coordinating Editor: James O'Leary
Desktop Publishing: Kimberli Mullen

Software Development Group:
Vice President of IT: Delmur Mayhak, Jr., CISA
Testing Supervisor: Randy Morrow, MIS
Graphic Artist: Barry Schapiro

This book contains material copyrighted © 1953 through 2011 by the American Institute of Certified Public Accountants, Inc., and is used or adapted with permission.

Portions of various FAF documents, copyright © by the Financial Accounting Foundation, 401 Merritt 7, P.O. Box 5116, Norwalk, CT 06856-5116, are reprinted with permission. Complete copies of these documents are available from the FASB and GASB.

This book contains material from Freeman/Shoulders/Allison, *Governmental & Nonprofit Accounting: Theory & Practice*. Reprinted by permission of Prentice Hall, Inc., Englewood Cliffs, NJ.

Material from Uniform CPA Examination Questions and Unofficial Answers, copyright © 1976 through 2010, American Institute of Certified Public Accountants, Inc., is used or adapted with permission.

The databanks contain material from Welsch/Newman/Zlatkovich, *Intermediate Accounting*. Reprinted by permission of Richard D. Irwin, Inc., Homewood, IL.

The databanks and textbooks contain quotations from *Governmental Accounting, Auditing, and Financial Reporting*, copyright © 2005 Government Finance Officers Association of the United States and Canada. Reprinted with permission.

This book is written to provide accurate and authoritative information concerning the covered topics. It is not meant to take the place of professional advice. **The content of this book has been updated to reflect relevant legislative and governing body modifications as of January 2011.**

Software copyright 2011, Matrix Learning Systems, Inc.

No part of this work may be reproduced or transmitted in any form or by any means, electronic or mechanical, including photocopying and recording, or by any information storage or retrieval system, except as may be expressly permitted by the 1976 Copyright Act or in writing by the Publisher. Requests for permission should be addressed in writing to Editor, Matrix Learning Systems, Inc; 7991 Shaffer Parkway, #100, Littleton, CO 80127.

Printed in the United States of America.

Preface

Congratulations on purchasing the ExamMatrix CPA Review. This powerful course is a complete system for success. It will teach you what you need to know, validate your readiness, and allow you to face the CPA Exams with confidence. It will guide you efficiently through your studies and help you achieve what thousands of other ExamMatrix accounting students and professionals before you have achieved—passing scores on the CPA Examination.

We use the power of your computer and our software to do the following:

- Provide you with your own personal instructor, who guides your customized study program.
- Prepare you for what to expect on the examination so there is no guesswork about what you need to know to pass.
- Coach you on ways to be physically, emotionally, and intellectually ready for the examination.
- Provide full printed text of examination preparation materials for you to study.
- Simulate the examination for you, drilling you with thousands of questions, weighted in accordance with the most current examination outlines.
- Give you instant help and guidance on every question, every step of the way, referring you back to the printed study materials when you need remedial help.
- Provide you with an Editorial Support Line to answer any questions that may arise while studying—call 877-272-7277.
- Provide a Pass Update or Pass Refund guarantee.
- Validate your readiness to pass each part of your examination.

You will pass with confidence.

The ExamMatrix CPA Review system components will help you reach that goal. The software portion of the ExamMatrix CPA Review is composed of the following:

- A database of over 4,000 categorized objective questions with immediate feedback to teach and review the points covered in the CPA testing process generated by the published weights from the AICPA Content Specification Outlines.
- Questions in the task-based simulation format are contained in all four exam sections.
- The ExamMatrix CPA Review textbooks, which accompany your software, utilize a unique cross-referencing system to sections and paragraphs. The software targets your weak areas and, through the cross-referencing system, guides you directly to the section in the textbook that covers that material. Each Review textbook contains the following:

- Concise reviews of authoritative pronouncements needed to pass the CPA Examination in easy-to-understand paragraph form
- Learning aids such as charts, tables, and flowcharts to aid in remembering concepts and procedures

The Review textbooks are categorized as follows:
- Section 2000 Financial Accounting & Reporting (FAR)
- Section 3000 Auditing & Attestation (AUD)
- Section 4000 Regulation (REG)
- Section 5000 Business Environment & Concepts (BEC)

Our software and our CPA Review textbooks reflect all legislative changes and are in accordance with the AICPA Content Specification Outlines.

Thinking about achieving an additional designation? Matrix Learning Systems carries reviews for the following exams:
- Certified Management Accountant
- Certified Internal Auditor
- Certified Information Systems Auditor
- Chartered Financial Analyst
- Enrolled Agent

Matrix Learning Systems will be at your side throughout your professional career, meeting your educational needs every step of the way.

Acknowledgments

The ExamMatrix CPA Review was developed and written by a team of professionals who are experts in the fields of accounting, business law, and computer science, and are also experienced teachers in CPA Review programs and continuing professional education courses.

Matrix Learning Systems expresses its sincere appreciation to the many individual candidates, as well as accounting instructors, who took time to write to us about previous editions. The improvements in this edition are attributable to all of these individuals. Of course, any deficiencies are the responsibilities of the editors and authors. We very much appreciate and solicit your comments and suggestions about this year's edition.

The editors and authors are also indebted to the American Institute of Certified Public Accountants, the Financial Accounting Standards Board, and the Governmental Accounting Standards Board for permission to quote from their pronouncements. In addition, the AICPA granted us permission to use material from previous Uniform CPA Examination Questions and Answers. AICPA codification numbers are used throughout the Review to indicate the source of materials.

We recognize the work and dedication of our team of software designers and developers. Their vision has made this the best product possible. They contributed countless hours to deliver this package and are each fully dedicated to helping you pass the exam. Our thanks go out to the many individuals who have made contributions to both the software and textbook portions of the CPA Review. We extend our gratitude to our team of software testers who ensure that you receive only the highest quality product. Finally, we express appreciation to the editorial teams who have devoted their time to review this product. They have provided invaluable aid in the writing and production of the ExamMatrix CPA Review.

Good luck on the exam!

Matrix Learning Systems

ExamMatrix CPA Review Textbook Authors

Raymond J. Clay, Jr., DBA, CPA, holds the Internal Audit Professorship in Accounting at the University of North Texas. Prior to joining the University of North Texas, he served as Director of Professional Development at Union Pacific Corporation. Dr. Clay has held faculty positions in accounting at Indiana State University and Texas Tech University. He received his bachelor's and master's degrees from Northern Illinois University and his doctorate from the University of Kentucky. He has held significant committee appointments with professional organizations, including serving as a member of the AICPA Accounting and Review Services Committee for seven years. Dr. Clay is the author of 4 books, 10 continuing professional education courses, and numerous articles appearing in professional journals.

Ennis M. Hawkins, DBA, CPA, CMA, CIA, was a Professor of Accounting at Sam Houston State University in Huntsville, Texas. His teaching and research interests include environmental and cost accounting. Dr. Hawkins has served as the Program Co-Chairman and Vice President of the Southwest Region American Accounting Association. He is also a member of the AICPA, IMA, and IIA.

Jill Hazelbauer-Von der Ohe, MBA, CPA, CMA, CFM, CVA, has her MBA from Rockford College and is currently a professor at Keller University, where she teaches accounting. In addition to a CPA, she holds CMA and CFM certifications, having received the Gold Award for the CFM exam during the 1997-98 winter exam cycle. She also holds a CVA (Certified Valuation Analyst) through NACVA, a professional organization that focuses on the valuation of closely held business for tax, estate, and other purposes. She has worked on accounting projects in Uganda and Poland.

David G. Jaeger, JD, MST, MBA, is currently Associate Professor of Accounting and Taxation at the University of North Florida. He has taught numerous courses in taxation and business law at the undergraduate, MBA, Executive MBA, and Master of Accountancy levels, as well as in continuing education courses. His research has been published in such journals as *The Tax Advisor, TAXES, Tax Notes,* the *Journal of Accountancy,* and *Research in Accounting Regulation.* His work has also been cited by the U.S. Tax Court and several U.S. Federal Courts of Appeal.

Tabitha McCormick, CPA, CFE, is the owner of Cornerstone Accounting in Millville, Pennsylvania. Cornerstone Accounting concentrates on training small business owners and financial employees to keep accurate accounting records, create efficient and effective policies and procedures, and institute strong internal controls. Cornerstone also assists businesses with implementing accounting software packages. She is a Certified Advanced QuickBooks® and QuickBooks Point of Sale® ProAdvisor and enjoys teaching QuickBooks classes for Bloomsburg University's Magee Center and other training institutions. Tabitha is also the author of two CPE courses on Identity Theft for MicroMash. She is a member of the Pennsylvania Institute of Certified Public Accountants (PICPA) and the Association of Certified Fraud Examiners (ACFE).

Darlene A. Pulliam, PhD, CPA, joined the faculty of West Texas A&M in 1997. A native of eastern New Mexico, Dr. Pulliam received a BS in Mathematics in 1976 and an MBA in 1978 from Eastern New Mexico University and joined the accounting firm of Peat Marwick and Mitchell and Co. (now KPMG) in Albuquerque. After five years in public accounting, she completed her PhD at the University of North Texas and joined the faculty of the University of Tulsa in 1987. During her 10 years in Tulsa, she taught primarily in the University of Tulsa's Master of Taxation program. Her publications include many articles appearing in *Tax Advisor*; the *Journal of Accountancy; Practical Tax Strategies; Oil, Gas and Energy Quarterly*; and the *Journal of Forensic Accounting* as an author or coauthor.

Craig D. Shoulders, PhD, joined the faculty at the University of North Carolina at Pembroke in 2004 after serving over 20 years on the accounting faculty at Virginia Tech. Dr. Shoulders has received the Cornelius E. Tierney/Ernst & Young Research Award from the Association of Government Accountants and has been recognized twice by the AICPA as an Outstanding Discussion Leader. He has recently completed a major research study on the financial reporting entity for the Governmental Accounting Standards Board and coauthors a Prentice Hall textbook on state and local government accounting as well as several continuing education courses on governmental accounting and financial reporting. Dr. Shoulders received his bachelor's degree from Campbellsville University, his master's degree from the University of Missouri-Columbia, and his PhD from Texas Tech University.

Strategic Solutions for Business (SSB) is a management consulting firm based in Denver, Colorado, specializing in accounting and information technology. **Bryan Smith, CPA,** is a managing partner of SSB with over eleven years of experience assisting clients with business intelligence, data conversions, revenue/cost assurance, data and process analytics, internal audit, operational metrics, mergers and acquisitions, and financial and regulatory compliance. **Cary Lopez, CPA, PMP,** previously a staff accountant at one of the Big Four, has worked in consulting for over five years. She has worked in various industries including oil and gas, telecommunications, financial services, software, and healthcare. Cary's focus is on business analysis and project management with an emphasis on IT and accounting projects. She has written numerous training and certification guides.

Matrix Learning Systems

ExamMatrix CPA Review Question Database Contributors

Paul N. Brown, CPA, is the Director of Technical Services for the Florida Institute of CPAs (FICPA). One of his main duties is to serve as the technical reviewer in Florida for the AICPA Peer Review Program, which administers approximately 600 reviews annually in Florida. Paul has previously been an instructor for the AICPA Advanced Reviewers Training Course and writes and instructs his own course in Florida on peer review called Peer Review Forum for Reviewers, for which he has received several outstanding discussion leader and author awards. He has also served on the AICPA's Technical Reviewers Advisory Task Force to the Peer Review Board and serves as staff liaison to various committees of the Florida Institute of CPAs. Prior to joining the FICPA, Paul was an audit manager with a regional firm in Florida. He holds a BS in Accounting and Finance from Florida State University.

Annhenrie Campbell, PhD, CPA, CMA, CGFM, is a Professor of Accounting at California State University, Stanislaus. While working as a municipal accountant, Dr. Campbell taught governmental and not-for-profit accounting as an adjunct lecturer for several years. She completed her MBA at Humboldt State University in California and her PhD at the University of Colorado in Boulder. After earning a CPA and CMA and starting her university career, Dr. Campbell became a Certified Government Financial Manager at the start of the CGFM program. She has maintained her interest in students' professional preparation for governmental and not-for-profit careers, starting with her MBA thesis topic and a joint publication on the topic in the *Government Accountants' Journal,* and continuing now in teaching both graduate and undergraduate students. In addition to numerous presentations, Dr. Campbell and her colleagues have published additional articles on educational issues in the *Journal of Business and Management, The Accounting Educators' Journal, Accounting Perspectives,* and the *Journal of the Academy of Business Education* (forthcoming).

Anthony P. Curatola, PhD, is the Joseph F. Ford Professor of Accounting at Drexel University. He holds a BS in Accounting and an MBA in Finance from Drexel University, an MA in Accounting from the Wharton Graduate School of the University of Pennsylvania, and a PhD in Accounting from Texas A&M University. Dr. Curatola joined the faculty of Louisiana State University in 1981 and returned to Drexel University in 1989 by accepting the appointment to the Joseph F. Ford Professor of Accounting Chair. Dr. Curatola's findings have appeared in media such as *Forbes,* the *Washington Post, Money* magazine, the *Wall Street Journal,* and the *New York Times,* to name a few. Currently he serves on the Foundation of Academic Research. Most recently, he was awarded the R. Lee Brummet Award in Academic Excellence from the IMA.

Jill Hazelbauer-Von der Ohe, MBA, CPA, CMA, CFM, CVA, has her MBA from Rockford College and is currently a professor at Keller University, where she teaches accounting. In addition to a CPA, she holds CMA and CFM certifications, having received the Gold Award for the CFM exam during the 1997-98 winter exam cycle. She also holds a CVA (Certified Valuation Analyst) through NACVA, a professional organization that focuses on the valuation of closely held business for tax, estate, and other purposes. She has worked on accounting projects in Uganda and Poland.

Taylor S. Klett, CPA, JD, is of counsel for the firm of Havins & Associates, LLP. He is currently an Associate Professor at Sam Houston State University and was an administrator and on the adjunct faculty there. His teaching and research interests include taxation, estate planning, ethics, and business law. He is an attorney and CPA in Texas and a member of the American Bar Association, Texas Bar Association, and AICPA. He graduated from the University of Texas and attended law school at the University of Houston Law Center (JD, with honors).

Tabitha McCormick, CPA, CFE, is the owner of Cornerstone Accounting in Millville, Pennsylvania. Cornerstone Accounting concentrates on training small business owners and financial employees to keep accurate accounting records, create efficient and effective policies and procedures, and institute strong internal controls. Cornerstone also assists businesses with implementing accounting software packages. She is a Certified Advanced QuickBooks® and QuickBooks Point of Sale® ProAdvisor and enjoys teaching QuickBooks classes for Bloomsburg University's Magee Center and other training institutions. Tabitha is also the author of two CPE courses on Identity Theft for MicroMash. She is a member of the Pennsylvania Institute of Certified Public Accountants (PICPA) and the Association of Certified Fraud Examiners (ACFE).

Robert J. Nieschwietz, a Visiting Assistant Professor at Seattle University, received his PhD in Accountancy from Arizona State University in 2001. He received a BBA and MS in Accounting from Texas A&M University in 1991 and 1996, respectively. Dr. Nieschwietz's primary research and teaching interests are within the area of auditing. His research has been published in various journals, including the *Journal of Accounting Literature, International Journal of Accounting Information Systems, International Journal of Auditing, Journal of Accounting Education, Journal of Applied Business Research, Academy of Accounting and Financial Studies Journal,* and *Journal of Risk Research.*

Paul Pierson is Director of Technical Services for the Illinois CPA Society. In this capacity, he oversees the administration of the AICPA Peer Review Program for approximately 1,300 CPA firms in Illinois. Paul has served as a discussion leader at the AICPA's Annual Peer Review Conference and its Advanced Reviewer Training Course, and is editor for the Society's peer review newsletter. He is also responsible for monitoring the continuing professional education and licensing rules in the state and responding to member inquiries regarding those matters. He currently serves on the Technical Reviewers' Advisory Task Force of the AICPA, having previously served a three-year term, and is the staff liaison for the Illinois CPA Society's Peer Review Report Acceptance and Governmental Accounting Executive Committees. Paul graduated from Illinois State University with a BS in Accounting and was an audit manager with a large, local CPA firm in East Peoria, Illinois, prior to joining the Society.

Darlene A. Pulliam, PhD, CPA, joined the faculty of West Texas A&M in 1997. A native of eastern New Mexico, Dr. Pulliam received a BS in Mathematics in 1976 and an MBA in 1978 from Eastern New Mexico University and joined the accounting firm of Peat Marwick and Mitchell and Co. (now KPMG) in Albuquerque. After five years in public accounting, she completed her PhD at the University of North Texas and joined the faculty of the University of Tulsa in 1987. During her 10 years in Tulsa, she taught primarily in the University of Tulsa's Master of Taxation program. Her publications include many articles appearing in *Tax Advisor*; the *Journal of Accountancy; Practical Tax Strategies; Oil, Gas and Energy Quarterly*; and the *Journal of Forensic Accounting* as an author or coauthor.

Marianne Rexer, PhD, CPA, is currently an Associate Professor of Accounting at Wilkes University. She has also taught at Drexel University and Johnson & Wales University. She received her PhD in Accounting at Drexel in 1997, her MS in Taxation at Bryant College in 1989, and her BS in Accounting from Wilkes University in 1985. Dr. Rexer has worked at a national CPA firm. She is a member of the American Accounting Association, the AICPA, the AICPA Audit Division, and the Pennsylvania Institute of CPAs.

Reg Rezac, PhD, MS, BS, is a Professor of Accounting at Texas Woman's University. He received his bachelor's from Jamestown College, his master's degree from the University of North Dakota, and his doctorate from the University of Northern Colorado. He has written tax material for numerous continuing professional education courses, as well as CPA review courses and chapters of taxation texts. Rezac both developed and was the first director of the Master of Taxation program at the American University. He teaches an online tax research course at TWU for undergraduate, graduate, and continuing education credit.

Strategic Solutions for Business (SSB) is a management consulting firm based in Denver, Colorado, specializing in accounting and information technology. **Bryan Smith, CPA,** is a managing partner of SSB with over eleven years of experience assisting clients with business intelligence, data conversions, revenue/cost assurance, data and process analytics, internal audit, operational metrics, mergers and acquisitions, and financial and regulatory compliance. **Cary Lopez, CPA, PMP,** previously a staff accountant at one of the Big Four, has worked in consulting for over five years. She has worked in various industries including oil and gas, telecommunications, financial services, software, and healthcare. Cary's focus is on business analysis and project management with an emphasis on IT and accounting projects. She has written numerous training and certification guides.

Kevin D. Zeiler, JD, MBA, is an Assistant Professor of Health Care Management at the Metropolitan State College of Denver. Professor Zeiler holds a BS in Health Care Management from the Metropolitan State College of Denver, an MBA from Regis University, and a Juris Doctorate from the University of Denver College of Law. Prior to becoming a faculty member, he worked for several years as a Denver Paramedic and continues to maintain his certification in the State of Colorado. Professor Zeiler teaches upper-level management courses in finance, health disparities, management, and law.

Table of Contents

Regulation

Section 4000	Overview of the Regulation Examination	1
Section 4100	Ethics, Professional, and Legal Responsibilities	5
Section 4200	Business Law	27
Section 4300	Federal Tax Process, Procedures, Accounting, and Planning	253
Section 4400	Federal Taxation of Property Transactions	283
Section 4500	Federal Taxation of Individuals	307
Section 4600	Federal Taxation of Entities	357
	Index	401

This page intentionally left blank.

Section 4000
Overview of the Regulation Examination

4010 The Regulation Section of the CPA Examination
    4011 Purpose of the Regulation Examination
    4012 Study Suggestions
    4013 Self-Evaluation
    4014 Index to the U.C.C.
    4015 Suggested Readings and References

4010 The Regulation Section of the CPA Examination

4011 Purpose of the Regulation Examination

4011.01 The Regulation section tests a candidate's knowledge of federal taxation, ethics, professional and legal responsibilities, and business law and the skills needed to apply that knowledge. The scope of the Regulation section includes professional responsibilities, agency, contracts, debtor-creditor relationships, government regulation of business, the Uniform Commercial Code, property, and federal taxation. Many of the subjects on the Examination are normally covered in standard textbooks on business law, auditing, taxation, and accounting; however, some subjects either are not included in such texts or are not covered in adequate depth. Important recent developments that candidates are expected to be familiar with may not yet be reflected in some texts. Candidates are expected to recognize the existence of legal implications and the applicable basic legal principles, and they are usually asked to indicate the probable result of the application of such basic principles.

4011.02 **Ethics, Professional and Legal Responsibilities, and Business Law.** This portion of the Regulation examination covers the knowledge of a CPA's professional and legal responsibilities and the legal implications of business transactions, particularly as they relate to accounting and auditing, and the skills needed to apply that knowledge.

4011.03 This Examination section deals with either federal or widely adopted uniform laws. Where there is no federal or appropriate uniform law on a subject, the questions are intended principally to test knowledge of the majority rules. Federal tax elements (income, estate, or gift) may be covered where appropriate in the overall context of a question.

4012 Study Suggestions

4012.01 The AICPA Content Specification Outline is presented as follows. It appears that the content of future exams will basically follow this outline. All of the topics are covered in this review. For your convenience, this text is organized according to these topics:

4012.02 **Ethics, Professional, and Legal Responsibilities 4100**

    A. Ethics and Responsibilities in Tax Practice

    B. Licensing and Disciplinary Systems

    C. Legal Duties and Responsibilities

4014.03   **Business Law 4200**

       A. Agency

       B. Contracts

       C. Uniform Commercial Code

       D. Debtor-Creditor Relationships

       E. Government Regulation of Business

       F. Business Structure (Selection of a Business Entity)

4014.04   **Federal Tax Process, Procedures, Accounting, and Planning 4300**

       A. Federal Tax Legislative Process

       B. Federal Tax Procedures

       C. Accounting Periods

       D. Accounting Methods

       E. Tax Return Elections, Including Federal Status Elections, Alternative Treatment Elections, or Other Types of Elections Applicable to an Individual or Entity's Tax Return

       F. Tax Planning

       G. Impact of Multijurisdictional Tax Issues on Federal Taxation (Including Consideration of Local, State, and Multinational Tax Issues)

       H. Tax Research and Communication

4014.05   **Federal Taxation of Property Transactions 4400**

       A. Types of Assets Estate and Gift Taxation

       B. Basis and Holding Period of Assets

       C. Cost Recovery (Depreciation, Depletion, and Amortization)

       D. Taxable and Nontaxable Sales and Exchanges

       E. Amount and Character of Gains and Losses, and Netting Process

       F. Related Party Transactions

       G. Estate and Gift Taxation

4014.06   **Federal Taxation of Individuals 4500**

       A. Gross Income

       B. Reporting of Items from Pass-Through Entities

       C. Adjustments and Deductions to Arrive at Taxable Income

       D. Passive Activity Losses

       E. Loss Limitations

       F. Taxation of Retirement Plan Benefits

       G. Filing Status and Exemptions

       H. Tax Computations and Credits

       I. Alternative Minimum Tax

4014.07   Federal Taxation of Entities 4600

    A. Similarities and Distinctions in Tax Reporting Among Business Entities

    B. Differences Between Tax and Financial Accounting

    C. C Corporations

    D. S Corporations

    E. Partnerships

    F. Trusts and Estates

    G. Tax-Exempt Organizations

4013   Self-Evaluation

4013.01 The amount of time you should spend on each of the topics depends on a number of factors.

    a. How well was the topic covered in your college business law course(s)?

    b. How long has it been since you had the course?

    c. How much did you study?

    d. Other factors, for example, including the following:

        (1) Personal experience in that topic

        (2) Additional study in that topic

4014   Index to the U.C.C.

4014.01 The Uniform Commercial Code (U.C.C.) has been adopted by all the states except Louisiana, but even Louisiana has adopted Articles 1, 3, 4, and 5.

4014.02 The U.C.C. is divided into the following articles:

    1. General Provisions

    2. Sales

    2A. Leases

    3. Negotiable Instruments

    4. Bank Deposits and Collections

    4A. Funds Transfers

    5. Letters of Credit

    6. Bulk Transfers

    7. Warehouse Receipts, Bills of Lading, and Other Documents of Title

    8. Investment Securities

    9. Secured Transactions

4014.03 Remember that the U.C.C. governs transactions involving goods (personal property). It does not cover transactions dealing with real property and services.

4014.04 These are the most important sections of the U.C.C. for the CPA Exams:

2-201	9-303	2-401
2-205	9-304	2-509
2-207	9-305	9-307
3-104	1-107	3-302
2-313	1-206	9-203
2-314	6-104	9-302
2-315	2-210	

These 20 code sections should be read by the candidate. They are ranked in the order of importance.

4015 Suggested Readings and References

4015.01 In addition to the study of the ExamMatrix CPA Review, CPA candidates should also refer to other literature resources when necessary. Candidates should consult current textbooks covering business law, auditing, and accounting.

Section 4100
Ethics, Professional, and Legal Responsibilities

4110 Ethics and Responsibilities in Tax Practice
    4111   Treasury Department Circular 230
    4112   AICPA Statements on Standards for Tax Services
    4113   Internal Revenue Code of 1986, as Amended, and Regulations Related to Tax Return Preparers

4120 Licensing and Disciplinary Systems
    4121   Liability Generally
    4122   Role of State Boards of Accountancy
    4123   Requirements of Regulatory Agencies

4130 Legal Duties and Responsibilities
    4131   Common Law Duties and Liability to Clients and Third Parties
    4132   Federal Statutory Liability
    4133   Privileged Communications, Confidentiality, and Privacy Acts

4110 Ethics and Responsibilities in Tax Practice

4111 Treasury Department Circular 230

Note: This section highlights important material in Circular 230. Circular 230 itself should be consulted for more detailed information on some topics.

Rules Governing Authority to Practice

4111.01 The Secretary of the Treasury has the power to prescribe rules and regulations regarding the conduct of tax practitioners who represent taxpayers before the IRS. These rules are in Title 31 of the Code of Federal Regulations and are commonly referred to as "Circular 230."

4111.02 The Secretary of the Treasury also has the power to appoint a director of practice under Circular 230. The director's duties include:

    a. acting upon applications for enrollment to practice before the IRS,

    b. instituting and conducting disciplinary hearings,

    c. making inquiries as to matters under his jurisdiction, and

    d. other duties that are necessary to carry out his functions.

4111.03 Practice before the IRS is defined in Circular 230 as involving all matters connected with a presentation to the IRS, or any of its officers or employees, relating to a taxpayer's rights, privileges, or liabilities under laws or regulations administered by the IRS. This includes:

    a. preparing and filing documents,

    b. corresponding and communicating with the IRS,

c. rendering written advice with respect to any entity, transaction, plan, or arrangement, and

d. representing a client at conferences, hearings, and meetings.

4111.04 Certified public accountants (CPAs) and attorneys may practice before the IRS provided they are not under suspension or disbarment from practice before the IRS. A CPA is any person duly qualified to practice as a CPA in any state, possession, territory, commonwealth, or the District of Columbia. An attorney is a person who is a member in good standing of the bar of the highest court of any state, possession, territory, commonwealth, or the District of Columbia. CPAs and attorneys must file a written declaration that they are currently qualified as a CPA or attorney and that they are authorized to represent the taxpayer in question.

4111.05 Individuals may also practice before the IRS if they qualify as an enrolled agent. An application for enrollment must be filed with the Director of Practice. The applicant must then demonstrate competence in tax matters by passing a written examination.

4111.06 An individual who is enrolled as an actuary by the Joint Board for the Enrollment of Actuaries may also practice before the IRS. Practice by an enrolled actuary is limited by Circular 230 to issues concerning pension and employee benefit plans.

4111.07 An individual may also practice before the IRS as an enrolled retirement plan agent (practice is limited to certain issues and programs involving retirement plans). Enrollment as a retirement plan agent is granted after the individual passes a written examination that demonstrates special competence in qualified retirement plan matters.

4111.08 Former IRS employees may be granted enrollment as an enrolled agent or enrolled retirement plan agent by virtue of their past service and technical experience gained as an IRS employee.

4111.09 Circular 230 allows individuals who are not CPAs, attorneys, or enrolled agents to engage in limited practice before the IRS. As a result, an individual can represent themselves before the IRS provided they present satisfactory identification.

4111.10 An individual may also engage in limited practice before the IRS even if the taxpayer is not present, in the following situations:

a. An individual may represent a member of their immediate family.

b. A regular, full-time employee of an individual employer may represent the employer.

c. A general partner or a regular full-time employee of a partnership may represent the partnership.

d. A bona fide officer or regular full-time employee of a corporation (including a parent, subsidiary, or other affiliated corporation), association, or organized group may represent the corporation, association, or organized group.

e. A regular full-time employee of a trust, receivership, guardianship, or estate may represent the trust.

f. An officer or a regular employee of a government unit, agency, or authority may represent the governmental unit, agency, or authority in the course of his or her official duties.

g. An individual may represent any individual or entity who is outside the United States, when the representation takes place outside the United States.

h. An individual who signs the taxpayer's return as the preparer (or who prepares a return but is not required to sign the tax return) may represent the taxpayer before IRS employees of the examination division regarding the tax liability of the taxpayer for the period covered by the return.

Duties and Restrictions

4111.11   A practitioner has a duty to promptly submit records or information to the IRS upon proper request. Also, there is a duty not to interfere with any lawful effort of the IRS to obtain such records or information. These duties exist unless the practitioner in good faith and on reasonable grounds believes the record or information is privileged.

4111.12   A practitioner has a duty to provide the director of practice with any requested information regarding violations of any regulations dealing with practice before the IRS.

4111.13   A practitioner who knows that a client has not complied with the revenue laws of the United States, or has made an error in or omission from any return, document, affidavit, or other paper, has a duty to advise the client promptly of such noncompliance, error, or omission.

4111.14   A practitioner must exercise due diligence in the following situations:

   a.   In preparing or assisting in the preparation of, approving, and filing returns, documents, affidavits, and other papers relating to IRS matter

   b.   In determining the correctness of oral or written representation made by the practitioner to the Department of the Treasury

   c.   In determining the correctness of oral or written representations made by the practitioner to clients with reference to any matters administered by the IRS

   A practitioner will be presumed to have exercised due diligence if the practitioner relies on the work product of another person.

4111.15   A practitioner may not unreasonably delay prompt disposition of any matter before the IRS.

4111.16   A practitioner may not knowingly and directly or indirectly accept assistance from or assist any person who is under disbarment or suspension from practice before the IRS. The practitioner must also not accept assistance from any former government employee disqualified from practice under any rule or U.S. law.

4111.17   A practitioner may not act as a notary public with respect to any matter administered by the IRS for which the practitioner is employed as counsel, attorney, or agent, or in which the practitioner may in any way be interested.

4111.18   A practitioner may not charge an unconscionable fee in connection with any matter before the IRS.

4111.19   A practitioner generally may not charge a contingent fee for services rendered in connection with any matter before the IRS. However, a practitioner may charge a contingent fee for services rendered in connection with the IRS's examination of or challenge to:

   a.   an original return or

   b.   an amended return or claim for refund or credit where the amended return or claim for refund or credit was filed within 120 days of the taxpayer receiving a written notice of the examination of or a written challenge to the original return.

   A practitioner may charge a contingent fee for services rendered in connection with a claim for credit or refund filed solely in connection with the determination of statutory interest or penalties assessed by the IRS. A practitioner can charge a contingent fee for services rendered in connection with any judicial proceeding arising under the Internal Revenue Code.

4111.20 In general, a practitioner must, at the request of the client, promptly return any and all records of the client that are necessary for the client to comply with his or her federal tax obligations.

4111.21 Generally, a practitioner is not allowed to represent conflicting interests in his or her practice before the IRS. However, the practitioner may represent conflicting interests provided each affected client waives the conflict of interest by informed, written consent.

4111.22 Practitioners are subject to various duties and restrictions regarding advertising and solicitation. For example, a practitioner may not use any form of public communication that contains any statement or claim that is false, fraudulent, unduly influencing, coercive, unfair, misleading, or deceptive. Also, a practitioner may not make any uninvited written or oral solicitation of employment in matters before the IRS if the solicitation violates federal or state law or other applicable rule.

4111.23 A practitioner who prepares tax returns may not endorse or otherwise negotiate any check issued to a client by the government in respect of a federal tax liability.

4111.24 A practitioner may not advise a client to take a position on a document, affidavit, or other paper submitted to the IRS unless the position is not frivolous.

4111.25 A practitioner may not advise a client to submit a document, affidavit, or other paper to the IRS:

    a. the purpose of which is to delay or impede the administration of the federal tax law,

    b. that is frivolous, or

    c. that contains or omits information in a manner that demonstrates an intentional disregard of a rule or regulation, unless the practitioner also advises the client to submit a document that evidences a good faith challenge to the rule or regulation.

4111.26 A practitioner must inform a client of any penalties that are reasonably likely to apply to the client with respect to a position taken on a tax return if the practitioner advised the client with respect to the position or the practitioner prepared or signed the return. Also, a practitioner must inform the client of any penalties reasonably likely to apply regarding any document, affidavit, or other paper submitted to the IRS. A practitioner must inform the client of the opportunity to avoid any penalties by disclosure, if relevant, and of the requirements for adequate disclosure.

4111.27 A practitioner can generally rely on information furnished by a client without verification. However, a practitioner cannot ignore information which is actually known and must make reasonable inquiries if the information furnished by the client appears incorrect, inconsistent, or incomplete.

4111.28 A practitioner must not give written advice (including electronic communication) concerning federal tax issues if the practitioner:

    a. bases the written advice on unreasonable factual or legal assumptions,

    b. unreasonably relies upon representations, statements, findings, or agreements of the taxpayer or any other person,

    c. does not consider all the relevant facts the practitioner knows or should know, or

    d. in evaluating a federal tax issue, takes into account the possibility that a tax return will not be audited, that an issue will not be raised on audit, or that an issue will be resolved through settlement if raised.

Sanctions for Violation of the Regulations

4111.29 The Secretary of the Treasury, after notice and an opportunity for a proceeding, may censure (a public reprimand), suspend, or disbar any practitioner from practice before the IRS if the practitioner:

    a. is shown to be incompetent, or disreputable,

    b. refuses to comply with any rules in Circular 230, or

    c. with intent to defraud, willfully and knowingly misleads or threatens a client or prospective client.

4111.30 Incompetence and disreputable conduct for which a practitioner may be sanctioned includes, but is not limited to, the following:

    a. Conviction of any criminal offense under the federal tax laws

    b. Conviction of any criminal offense involving dishonesty or breach of trust

    c. Conviction of any felony under federal or state law for which the conduct involved renders the practitioner unfit to practice before the IRS

    d. Giving false or misleading information, or participating in any way in the giving of false or misleading information to the Department of the Treasury or any officer or employee thereof, or to any tribunal authorized to pass upon federal tax matters, in connection with any matter pending or likely to be pending before them, knowing the information to be false or misleading. Facts or other matters contained in testimony, federal tax returns, financial statements, applications for enrollment, affidavits, declarations, and any other document or statement, written or oral, are included in the term "information."

    e. Solicitation of employment as prohibited under Circular 230, the use of false or misleading representations with intent to deceive a client or prospective client in order to procure employment, or intimating that the practitioner is able improperly to obtain special consideration or action from the IRS or any officer or employee thereof

    f. Willfully failing to make a federal tax return in violation of the federal tax laws, or willfully evading, attempting to evade, or participating in any way in evading or attempting to evade any assessment or payment of any federal tax

    g. Willfully assisting, counseling, encouraging a client or prospective client in violating, or suggesting to a client or prospective client to violate, any federal tax law, or knowingly counseling or suggesting to a client or prospective client an illegal plan to evade federal taxes or payment thereof

    h. Misappropriation of, or failure properly or promptly to remit, funds received from a client for the purpose of payment of taxes or other obligations due the United States

    i. Directly or indirectly attempting to influence, or offering or agreeing to attempt to influence, the official action of any officer or employee of the IRS by the use of threats, false accusations, duress or coercion, by the offer of any special inducement or promise of an advantage or by the bestowing of any gift, favor or thing of value

    j. Disbarment or suspension from practice as an attorney, certified public accountant, public accountant, or actuary by any duly constituted authority of any state, territory, or possession of the United States, including a commonwealth, or the District of Columbia, any federal court of record or any federal agency, body, or board

    k. Knowingly aiding and abetting another person to practice before the IRS during a period of suspension, disbarment, or ineligibility of such other person

- **l.** Contemptuous conduct in connection with practice before the IRS, including the use of abusive language, making false accusations or statements, knowing them to be false, or circulating or publishing malicious or libelous matter
- **m.** Giving a false opinion, knowingly, recklessly, or through gross incompetence, including an opinion which is intentionally or recklessly misleading, or engaging in a pattern of providing incompetent opinions on questions arising under the federal tax laws
- **n.** Willfully failing to sign a tax return prepared by the practitioner when the practitioner's signature is required by federal tax laws unless the failure is due to reasonable cause and not due to willful neglect
- **o.** Willfully disclosing or otherwise using a tax return or tax return information in a manner not authorized by the Internal Revenue Code, contrary to the order of a court of competent jurisdiction, or contrary to the order of an administrative law judge in a disciplinary proceeding

4111.31 A practitioner may also be disbarred or suspended from practice for:
- **a.** willfully violating the regulations in Circular 230 or
- **b.** through recklessness or gross incompetence, violating the standards in Circular 230 with respect to tax returns, documents, affidavits, and other written advice.

4111.32 Rules Applicable to Disciplinary Proceedings
- **a.** Circular 230 contains detailed rules regarding the process to be followed in disciplinary hearings regarding a practitioner's violation of any of the rules.
- **b.** Proceedings are held before an administrative law judge following procedures specified in Circular 230. The judge files his or her decision with the Director of Practice.
- **c.** An appeal of the decision of the administrative law judge can be made to the Secretary of the Treasury within 30 days of the decision.
- **d.** If a practitioner is suspended as a result of the proceedings, they are prohibited from practicing before the IRS during the period of the suspension.
- **e.** If a practitioner is disbarred, they are not allowed to practice before the IRS until authorized to do so by the Director of Practice. A practitioner who is disbarred may petition for reinstatement after five years from the date of disbarment. Reinstatement is only granted if the Director of Practice believes that the petitioner is not likely to conduct themselves in violation of the rules and that granting reinstatement is not contrary to public policy.

4112 AICPA Statements on Standards for Tax Services

4112.01 **Tax Practice.** The AICPA has issued a series of ethical tax practice standards called Statements on Standards for Tax Services (SSTSs). The SSTSs have their origin in a series of Statements on Responsibilities in Tax Practice (SRTPs) which were issued from 1964 through 1977 and provided a body of advisory opinions on good tax practice. The SSTSs supersede and replace the SRTPs effective October 31, 2000. The SSTSs and interpretations issued under the SSTSs are outlined starting at section **4112.02**. However, the candidate is encouraged to refer to the complete text of the standards and interpretations for a more complete explanation and detailed illustrations.

4112.02 Tax Return Positions (SSTS 1)

a. A CPA should determine and comply with the standards, if any, that are imposed by the applicable taxing authority with respect to recommending a tax return position, or preparing or signing a tax return.

b. If the applicable taxing authority has no written standards with respect to recommending a tax return position or preparing or signing a tax return, or if the standards are lower than the standards set forth in this provision, the following standards will apply:

(1) A CPA should not recommend to a client that a position be taken with respect to the tax treatment of any item on a return unless the CPA has a good faith belief that the position has a realistic possibility of being sustained administratively or judicially on its merits if challenged.

(2) A CPA may recommend a tax return position if the CPA:

  (a) concludes that there is a reasonable basis for the position and

  (b) advises the taxpayer to appropriately disclose that position.

(3) A CPA may prepare or sign a tax return that reflects a position if:

  (a) the CPA concludes there is a reasonable basis for the position and

  (b) the position is appropriately disclosed.

(4) In recommending certain tax return positions and in signing a return on which a tax return position is taken, a CPA should, when relevant, advise the client as to the potential penalty consequences and the opportunity, if any, to avoid such penalty through disclosure.

(5) When recommending a tax return position, a CPA has both the right and responsibility to be an advocate for the taxpayer with respect to any position satisfying the aforementioned standards.

c. The CPA should not recommend a tax return position that does either of the following:

(1) Exploits the audit selection process of a taxing authority

(2) Serves as a mere "arguing" position advanced solely to obtain leverage in the bargaining process of settlement negotiation with a taxing authority

4112.03 Answers to Questions on Returns (SSTS 2). A CPA should make a reasonable effort to obtain from the client, and provide appropriate answers to, all questions on a tax return before signing as preparer.

4112.04 Certain Procedural Aspects of Preparing Returns (SSTS 3)

a. In preparing or signing a return, the CPA may in good faith rely without verification upon information furnished by the client or by third parties. The CPA should not, however, ignore the implications of information furnished and should make reasonable inquiries if the information appears to be incorrect, incomplete, or inconsistent either on its face or on the basis of other known facts. A CPA should refer to the taxpayer's returns for one or more prior years where feasible.

b. Where the tax law or regulations impose a condition to deductibility or other tax treatment of an item ..., the CPA should make appropriate inquiries to determine to his satisfaction whether such condition has been met.

c. The individual CPA who is required to sign the return should consider information actually known to that CPA from the tax return of another client when preparing a tax return if the information is relevant to that tax return, its consideration is necessary to properly prepare that tax return, and use of such information does not violate any law or rule relating to confidentiality.

4112.05 **Use of Estimates (SSTS 4).** Unless prohibited by statute or by rule, a CPA may prepare tax returns involving the use of the taxpayer's estimates if it is impracticable to obtain exact data and the estimated amounts are reasonable under the facts and circumstances known to the CPA. If the taxpayer's estimates are used, they should be presented in a manner that does not imply greater accuracy than exists.

4112.06 **Departures from a Position Previously Concluded in an Administrative Proceeding or Court Decision (SSTS 5)**

    a. The tax return position with respect to an item as determined in an administrative proceeding or court decision does not restrict a CPA from recommending a different tax position in a later year's return, unless the taxpayer is bound to a specified treatment in a later year (such as by a formal closing agreement).

    b. As provided in SSTS 1, *Tax Return Positions,* a CPA may recommend a tax return position or prepare or sign a tax return that departs from the treatment of an item as concluded in an administrative proceeding or court decision with respect to a prior return of the taxpayer.

4112.07 **Knowledge of Error: Return Preparation and Administrative Proceedings (SSTS 6)**

    a. When preparing a return or when representing a client in an administrative proceeding, the CPA should inform the client promptly upon becoming aware of an error in a previously filed return or upon becoming aware of a client's failure to file a required return. The CPA should recommend the measures to be taken. Such recommendations may be given orally. The CPA is not obligated to inform the taxing authority, and the CPA may not do so without the client's permission, except where required by law.

    b. The CPA should request the client's permission to disclose the error to the taxing authority. Lacking such agreement, or if the CPA is requested to prepare the current year's return and the client has not taken appropriate action to correct an error in a prior year's return, the CPA should consider whether to withdraw from preparing the return and whether to continue a professional relationship with the client. If the CPA does prepare such current year's return, the CPA should take reasonable steps to ensure that the error is not repeated.

4112.08 **Form and Content of Advice to Taxpayers (SSTS 7)**

    a. In providing tax advice to a taxpayer, the CPA should use judgment to ensure that the advice given reflects the professional competence and appropriately serves the taxpayer's needs. A CPA should comply with relevant taxing authorities' standards, if any, applicable to written tax advice. Professional judgment should be used regarding the need to document oral advice. The CPA is not required to follow a standard format or guidelines in communicating written or oral advice to a taxpayer.

    b. In advising or consulting with a taxpayer on tax matters, the CPA should assume that the advice will affect the manner in which the matters or transactions considered ultimately will be reported on the taxpayer's tax returns. A CPA should consider, when relevant, return reporting and disclosure standards applicable to the related tax return position and the potential penalty consequences of the return position. Thus, for all tax advice the CPA gives to a taxpayer, the CPA should follow the standards in Statement on Standards for Tax Services 1, *Tax Return Positions.*

    c. The CPA may choose to communicate with a taxpayer when subsequent developments affect advice previously provided with respect to significant matters. The CPA cannot, however, be expected to have assumed responsibility for initiating such communication except while assisting a taxpayer in implementing procedures or plans associated with the advice provided or when the CPA undertakes this obligation by specific agreement with the taxpayer.

4113 Internal Revenue Code of 1986, as Amended, and Regulations Related to Tax Return Preparers

4113.01 A compensated tax return preparer can be liable for civil and criminal penalties for negligently or intentionally understating a taxpayer's liability.

4113.02 A compensated preparer can be liable for a $1,000 or 50% penalty of income derived (first-tier penalty) for each tax return or claim for refund that understates the taxpayer's liability. There is a second-tier penalty of $5,000 or 50% penalty of income derived if the preparer willfully or recklessly understated the liability. This penalty applies if the preparer did the following:

    a. Understated tax liability by taking a position that does not have a realistic possibility of being sustained

    b. Knew or should have known of this position

    c. Did not disclose the position in the return or an attachment to the return

4113.03 The following are some of the compensated tax return preparer's requirements under the Internal Revenue Code:

    a. Sign, give address and IRS identification number of self or employer.

    b. Furnish the taxpayer a copy of the prepared return no later than the time the original return is presented for signing.

    c. Maintain a file of returns and log of all returns prepared for three years following the close of the return period. The penalty assessed for failure to comply with the requirements of sections a.–b. is $50 per occurrence. The penalty will not apply if the failure is due to reasonable cause and not to willful neglect.

    d. Do not cash another person's tax refund check. A penalty of $500 is assessable against a preparer who violates this provision.

4113.04 Criminal penalties can be imposed for the following:

    a. Tax evasion

    b. Perjury on a tax return

    c. Bribery of an IRS employee

4120 Licensing and Disciplinary Systems

4121 Liability Generally

4121.01 As an expert, the CPA must exercise due care—the ordinary skill and competence of members of his profession—and a failure to do so will subject the CPA to liability for negligence.

4121.02 The CPA is held only to the standards of reasonable care and competence and is not charged with the duty to be infallible.

4121.03 The CPA has a confidential fiduciary relationship with each client. This relationship involves varying obligations, which range from the general requirement of dealing fairly and honestly with the client to the more specific requirements of voluntarily disclosing any potential conflict of interest.

4121.04 The CPA is responsible not only to clients, but to investors, creditors, and other third parties who may rely upon the financial statements audited by the CPA. The multiple responsibility demands a standard of care that goes beyond the parochial wishes of the client.

4121.05 The CPA's liability can either arise by way of common law (judicial decision) or by statute.

4122 Role of State Boards of Accountancy

4122.01 The professional ethics division of the AICPA interprets the Code of Professional Conduct, investigates potential disciplinary matters involving members, and presents cases before the AICPA joint trial board (this board judges disciplinary charges against state CPA society and AICPA members).

4122.02 The AICPA professional ethics division's activities are performed within the joint ethics enforcement program (JEEP), in which 48 state CPA societies participate. Generally, the codes of conduct of these societies conform to the AICPA Code.

4122.03 The Institute and state societies act as agents of each other in ethics investigations. They present cases before the joint trial board according to the bylaws of each organization. For example, if the AICPA conducts an ethics investigation of a member, it does so on its own behalf and also on behalf of the state society of which the individual is a member. The same idea applies in reverse if a state society is conducting the investigation.

4122.04 Bylaws provide for the jurisdiction of the joint trial board over the membership of both the AICPA and the state societies.

4122.05 The AICPA professional ethics division is authorized to start an investigation based on information from various sources. This information of a potential disciplinary matter can come from such sources as written complaints, reports in the media, or referrals from government agencies.

4122.06 The AICPA professional ethics division works through several committees:

a. The professional ethics executive committee

b. The technical standards subcommittee (an investigative body)

c. The government technical standards subcommittee (which investigates engagements in which the clients are state or local government entities or receive federal financial assistance)

d. The independence-behavioral standards subcommittee (which investigates and interprets the Code's rules on independence, confidentiality of client information, and other behavioral concerns)

4122.07 The AICPA professional ethics division has the authority to settle cases brought before it. This enables the division to conclude investigations without the delay or expense of formal hearings.

4122.08 State boards of accountancy are generally in charge of maintaining records of all members and following up on continuing education requirements presented by licensure candidates. The candidate must attest to the state board that the continuing education requirements have been completed.

4122.09 Most jurisdictions run random audits on the candidates to determine if the reporting of the continuing education was both accurate and timely.

4122.10 Reciprocity is a recognition of licenses between states. Therefore, before a certified public accountant moves to another state, he/she must look into the reciprocity rules in the new state. The ability to transfer licensing credentials from one state to another is controlled by state boards and reciprocity is not guaranteed.

4122.11 The NASBA (National Association of State Boards of Accountancy) is the regulating department for the state boards. The NASBA Tools for Accounting Compliance give the candidate much information to inform him/her of the requirements for multiple jurisdictions.

4123 Requirements of Regulatory Agencies

4123.01 Public Company Accounting Oversight Board

a. The Sarbanes-Oxley Act establishes the Public Company Accounting Oversight Board (PCAOB or Board), which is appointed and overseen by the Securities and Exchange Commission (SEC).

b. The Board is composed of five members appointed for 5-year terms. Two of the members must be or must have been CPAs. The remaining three members must not be and cannot have been CPAs. The chair may be held by one of the CPAs provided he or she has not been engaged as a practicing CPA for five years.

c. No member of the Board may currently "share in any of the profits of, or receive payments from, a public accounting firm," other than "fixed continuing payments" such as retirement payments.

d. The duties of the Board include:

(1) Registering public accounting firms

(2) Establishing or adopting auditing, quality control, ethics, independence, and other standards relative to the preparation of audit reports for issuers

(3) Conducting inspections of accounting firms

(4) Conducting investigations and disciplinary proceedings

(5) Imposing appropriate sanctions.

e. The Board is required to issue standards or adopt standards issued by other groups or organizations. The Board has the authority to amend, modify, repeal, and reject any standards suggested by any other group. On an annual basis the Board must report on its standard setting activity to the SEC.

f. The Board will conduct annual quality reviews of firms that audit more than 100 issuers. All other firms that are registered with the Board will be reviewed every three years. The SEC and/or Board may order a special inspection of any firm at any time.

- g. Foreign accounting firms that "prepare or furnish" an audit report involving U.S. registrants are subject to the authority of the Board. This includes a foreign firm that performs some audit work (i.e. auditing a foreign subsidiary of a US company). Also, if a U.S. accounting firm relies on the opinion of a foreign accounting firm, the audit workpapers of the foreign firm must be supplied upon request to the Board or the SEC.
- h. A violation of the rules of the Board is treated as a violation of the Securities Exchange Act of 1934 and gives rise to the same penalties that may be imposed for violations of that Act.

4123.02   Sarbanes-Oxley Act Requirements for CPA Firms

- a. CPA firms that participate in the preparation or issuance of any audit report with respect to a public company are required to register with the Public Company Accounting Oversight Board.
- b. Registered accounting firms must prepare and maintain for a period of not less than seven years, audit work papers, and other information related to any audit report, in sufficient detail to support the conclusions reached in the report.
- c. The Sarbanes-Oxley Act requires a second partner review and approval of all audit reports and their issuance.
- d. The lead audit partner and audit review partner must rotate off of the audit every five years on public company engagements.
- e. A registered accounting firm is prohibited from auditing any SEC registered client if the CEO, Controller, CFO, Chief Accounting Officer, or person in an equivalent position has been employed by the auditor during the 1-year period prior to the audit.
- f. The accounting firm is required to report to the client's audit committee:
    - (1) All critical accounting policies and practices to be used
    - (2) All alternative treatments of financial information within GAAP that have been discussed with management
    - (3) The ramifications of the use of such alternative disclosures and treatments
    - (4) The treatment "preferred" by the firm
- g. The Act makes it "unlawful" for a registered public accounting firm to provide certain nonaudit services to an issuer contemporaneously with the audit. These prohibited services include:
    - (1) Bookkeeping and related services
    - (2) Design and implementation of financial information systems
    - (3) Appraisal or valuation services, fairness opinions, or contribution-in-kind reports
    - (4) Actuarial services
    - (5) Internal auditor outsourcing services
    - (6) Management or human resource services
    - (7) Broker, dealer, investment adviser, or investment banking services
    - (8) Legal or expert services unrelated to the audit
    - (9) Any other services that the Board determines by regulation are impermissible

- **h.** Firms may provide other services not listed above (i.e. tax services) provided the firm receives pre-approval by the audit committee. Pre-approval is not required provided:
  - (1) The aggregate amount of nonaudit services provided to the issuer constitutes less than 5% of the total amount of revenues paid by the issuer to its auditor,
  - (2) Such services were not recognized by the issuer at the time of the engagement to be nonaudit services, and
  - (3) Such services were promptly brought to the attention of the audit committee and approved prior to the completion of the audit.

4123.03 Sarbanes-Oxley Act Requirements for Corporations, Officers, and Board Members

- **a.** Publicly traded companies subject to the Sarbanes-Oxley Act are those defined as an "issuer" under Section 3 of the Securities Exchange Act of 1934.
- **b.** The Act requires the CEO and CFO of each issuer to certify the appropriateness of the financial statements and disclosures contained in the periodic report and that the financial statements and disclosures fairly present, in all material respects, the operations and financial condition of the issuer. Knowing and willful violations are subject to a fine of not more than $5 million and/or imprisonment of up to 20 years.
- **c.** The Act provides that it is unlawful for any officer or director of an issuer to take any action to fraudulently influence, coerce, manipulate, or mislead any auditor engaged in the performance of an audit for the purpose of rendering financial statements materially misleading.
- **d.** Under the Act, if an issuer is required to prepare a restatement due to "material noncompliance" with financial reporting requirements, the chief financial officer must reimburse the issuer for:
  - (1) Any bonus or other incentive-based or equity-based compensation received during the 12-month period following the issuance or filing of the noncompliant document.
  - (2) Any profits realized from the sale of securities of the user during that period.
- **e.** The Act prohibits the purchase or sale of stock by officers and directors and other insiders during pension fund black-out periods.
- **f.** The SEC is given the authority under the Act to:
  - (1) Prohibit an individual from serving as an officer or director if it finds that their conduct violates securities laws and "demonstrates unfitness" to serve as an officer or director.
  - (2) Freeze the payment of an extraordinary payment to any director, officer, partner, controlling person, agent, or employee of a company during an investigation of possible violations of securities laws.
- **g.** The Act provides the following requirements regarding audit committees:
  - (1) Each member of the audit committee shall be a member of the board of directors of the issuer, and shall otherwise be independent. The SEC "may make exceptions for certain individuals on a case-by-case basis."
  - (2) "Independent" is defined as not receiving, other than for service on the board, any consulting, advisory, or other compensatory fee from the issuer, and as not being an affiliated person of the issuer, or any subsidiary thereof.
  - (3) The audit committee shall be directly responsible for the appointment, compensation, and oversight of the work of any registered public accounting firm employed by that issuer.

(4) The audit committee shall establish procedures for "receipt, retention, and treatment of complaints" that are received by the issuer regarding accounting, internal controls, and auditing.

(5) The audit committee shall have authority to hire independent counsel or other advisors to carry out its duties.

4130 Legal Duties and Responsibilities

4131 Common Law Duties and Liability to Clients and Third Parties

Liability to Clients Under Common Law

4131.01 The CPA may be held liable to clients in an audit, taxation, or consulting services engagement for the following:

a. Fraud

b. Gross negligence or constructive fraud

c. Negligence (ordinary or simple)

d. Breach of contract

4131.02 **Fraud** is an *intentional* misrepresentation of a material fact with resultant harm to some party.

4131.03 **Gross negligence** (constructive fraud) is extreme, flagrant, or reckless departure from the standards of due care and competence in performing or reporting upon professional engagements.

a. There need not be actual intent to deceive (scienter).

b. Fraud may be inferred from sloppy performance (e.g., CPA omits a vital procedure such as a bank reconciliation in order to save time).

4131.04 **Negligence** (ordinary or simple) is the failure to do what an ordinary, reasonable, prudent CPA would do in similar circumstances.

a. To establish negligence, the plaintiff (client) must establish the following:

(1) The defendant (CPA) owed a legal duty.

(2) The CPA breached that duty.

(3) The CPA's action was the proximate cause of the resulting injury to the client.

(4) The CPA's actions caused damage (loss).

b. CPAs are not liable for an honest error in judgment as long as they act with reasonable care.

4131.05 The CPA's responsibility to the client is defined by GAAS and/or specific terms of the contract.

4131.06 Greater responsibility may be assumed by an expressed contract that goes beyond the standard audit engagement.

4131.07 The agreement between the CPA and the client should be expressed in writing in an engagement letter. The engagement letter, written to the client on the CPA's letterhead, should provide a place for the client to indicate agreement with the terms of the undertaking via the client's signature. An important case on this point is *1136 Tenants' Corporation*. Because the CPA firm did not have an engagement letter, it was found liable for $237,000 (relative to a $600 annual fee) of damages for failure to discover defalcations. The CPA firm contended that the engagement called for preparation of unaudited financial statements, not an audit. The plaintiff was successful in establishing that an audit was agreed upon.

4131.08 Most legal actions by clients involve claims based upon employee defalcations or fraud not discovered by the audit examination.

4131.09 Defenses available to the CPA include the following:

    a. The CPA was not negligent or fraudulent.

    b. Contributory negligence of the client caused the loss.

    c. The CPA adhered to GAAS and planned audit examination to search for material fraud.

    d. The error was immaterial.

    e. The proximate cause of loss was not the erroneous financial statements.

4131.10 **Tax return preparer liability.** A client may be able to sue the CPA who prepared a tax return that caused the client to incur penalties or other sanctions due to the CPA's wrongful action. Basis of liability could be breach of contract or the tort of negligence.

4131.11 For taxation engagements, most claims arise from the CPA's failure to meet a filing date for a tax return.

    a. The CPA may be liable for interest on late payment *plus* penalty.

    b. The CPA may be liable for interest, penalty, *and* tax if the client can prove that the transaction was primarily motivated by erroneous tax advice rendered by the CPA.

Liability to Third Parties Under Common Law: Ultramares Rule

4131.12 The CPA may be held liable to third parties for any of the following:

    a. Fraud

    b. Gross negligence

4131.13 Under common law, CPAs have not (until recently) been found liable to those not in privity on the theory of ordinary negligence.

    a. Third parties include investors and creditors.

    b. The term "privity" refers to a contractual or near contractual relationship.

4131.14 In 1931, the common law *Ultramares* rule was promulgated. The court in *Ultramares* stated that where a CPA recklessly certifies to the truth of financial statements without taking the proper procedures to determine whether or not the financial statements are in fact true, a jury might find the CPA guilty of fraud.

    a. *Ultramares* developed a concept of gross negligence or constructive fraud.

    b. According to *Ultramares*, the third party that proves gross negligence will be successful in reaching the CPA without regard to privity.

      c. Gross negligence is a deceit that involves a misrepresentation of a material fact, with lack of reasonable ground for belief, relied upon by another, which causes damage to that party.

      d. *Ultramares* refused to hold a CPA liable to third parties for simple negligence.

4131.15   *Ultramares* is still a good precedent in some jurisdictions; however, in many states substantial inroads have been made on *Ultramares* through creation of the following rules.

Liability to Third Parties Under Common Law: Third-Party Beneficiary Rule

4131.16   The CPA may be held liable for ordinary negligence by third parties when the CPA knows that the services for a client are *primarily* for the benefit of a third party.

4131.17   When the services are primarily for the benefit of a third party, the third party is, in effect, a party to the contract.

4131.18   In order for plaintiff to be a third-party beneficiary, the *aim* and *end* of the transactions must be to benefit the third party.

Liability to Third Parties Under Common Law: Foreseeability Rules

4131.19   A CPA who is negligent in issuing the report can be liable to third parties who can be foreseen as being injured.

4131.20   According to the foreseen user rule applied by some courts, if a CPA is retained by a client to perform an audit examination for purposes of obtaining a bank loan from Fourth National Bank, the bank may successfully recoup loan losses by proving that the CPA was negligent (if the bank, in fact, relied upon the audited financial statements).

4131.21   Under the foreseen class of users rule applied by some courts, *any* bank creditor in reliance upon the negligently audited financial statements in section **4131.20** proving negligence will be successful.

4131.22   On the other hand, a trade creditor or an investor is not foreseen; therefore, such third-party users in the bank loan situation in sections **4131.20** and **4131.21** would have to prove fraud or constructive fraud in order to reach the CPA. They could not recover based on simple negligence.

4131.23   According to *Restatement of Torts,* the plaintiff (third party) does not have to be identified by a specific person to the accountant but only has to be identified by class (e.g., bank credit). This follows the foreseen class of users rule. The *Restatement of Torts,* is an attempt by the American Law Institute "...to present an orderly statement of the general common law of the United States, including in that term not only the law developed solely by judicial decision, but also the law has grown from the application by the courts of statutes...." (*Restatement, Torts* viii, ix (1st ed))

4131.24   In recent years, a few courts have applied a foreseeable users test. For CPAs to be liable, it is only necessary that they generally could expect or foresee the use of their work product by the third party in question.

4131.25 The following matrix summarizes what the plaintiff (third party) must prove to successfully reach the defendant (CPA) for fraud, gross negligence, and simple negligence.

	Fraud	Gross Negligence	Simple Negligence
False representation	*	*	*
Awareness	Knowledge	Reckless disregard	Failure to exercise care
Intention to induce reliance	*	X	X
Justifiable reliance	*	*	*
Resultant damage	*	*	*

* = Plaintiff must prove
X = Not essential

4131.26 Common law varies from state to state; thus, some jurisdictions are *Ultramares* states while others apply the foreseeability doctrine. Both alternatives should be presented in responding to a CPA Examination question. An *Ultramares* state, of course, ignores the foreseeability rule and requires the third-party plaintiff to establish fraud or gross negligence.

Liability to Third Parties Under Common Law: Unaudited Financial Statement Liability

4131.27 A third party in a common-law suit involving unaudited financial statements must prove that the CPA was either fraudulent or grossly negligent in order to successfully reach the CPA.

4131.28 The concept of foreseeability has yet to be applied to unaudited financial statements.

4132 Federal Statutory Liability

Section 11(A) of the Securities Act of 1933

4132.01 The Securities Act of 1933 regulates public offerings of securities through the mails or in interstate commerce.

4132.02 The Securities Act of 1933 requires the filing of a registration statement with the SEC prior to the sale of securities. The act requires disclosure of all material facts concerning the securities to be sold.

4132.03 Section 11(A) of the Securities Act of 1933 provides the following:

a. Any person who acquires securities may sue the CPA.

b. Plaintiff may sue if the financial statements contain an untrue statement or omit a material fact.

c. Plaintiff does not have the burden of proving that the CPA was negligent or fraudulent.

d. Plaintiff does not have to prove reliance on untrue financial statements or that financial statements were the proximate cause of any loss.

e. CPA has the burden of proof to establish innocence or that the cause of the plaintiff's loss was something other than the untrue financial statement.

4132.04 Section 11(A) of the Securities Act of 1933 expands liability as follows:

    a. Privity of contract is not a necessary element.

    b. Burden of proof, beyond proving material misstatement, is shifted from the plaintiff to the CPA.

    c. The CPA owes third-party due diligence standard of care.

    d. The Plaintiff does not have to prove fraud or deceit—simple negligence is enough.

    e. The Plaintiff does not have to prove reliance.

4132.05 Defenses under Section 11(A) of the Securities Act of 1933 are the following:

    a. The financial statements are true and not misleading.

    b. The misstatement is immaterial.

    c. The plaintiff purchased securities after issuance of a generally available earnings statement and did not rely on registration statement (usually a generally available earnings statement is published 12 months after effective date of registration).

    d. The CPA exercised due diligence (i.e., that after a reasonable investigation the CPA had reason to believe that the representations contained in the financial statements were true and complete).

    e. The damage does not relate to misstatement by CPA.

    f. The plaintiff had prior knowledge of falsity.

    g. The statute of limitations (three years from securities sale) has expired.

4132.06 The CPA's duty under Section 11(A) of the Securities Act of 1933 as to the fairness of the financial statements contained in the registration statement extends to the time when the registration statement becomes effective.

Rule 10b-5 of the Securities Exchange Act of 1934

4132.07 The Securities Exchange Act of 1934 regulates securities exchanges and securities listed and traded on exchanges.

4132.08 Rule 10b-5 of the Securities Exchange Act of 1934 makes it unlawful for a person to use any instrumentality of interstate commerce to do the following:

    a. Employ any device, scheme, or artifice to defraud.

    b. Make any untrue statement or omit a material fact.

    c. Engage in any act, practice, or cause of business that operates or would operate as a fraud or deceit upon any person in connection with the *purchase* or *sale* of any security.

4132.09 Notably absent from Rule 10b-5 (SEA 1934) are the following:

    a. Statement of defenses available to CPA

    b. Definition of to whom liability may run

    c. Measures of damages

    d. Limitation upon those who may be held liable

4132.10 The United States Supreme Court has ruled in *Hochfelder* that third parties must prove *scienter* in order to reach the CPA under Rule 10b-5 (SEA 1934).

    a. **Scienter** is intent to deceive, manipulate, or defraud on the CPA's part.

    b. Simple negligence is not enough to hold the CPA responsible.

    c. Recovery under Rule 10b-5 (SEA 1934) is limited to the actual losses resulting from the fraud.

4132.11 Courts have permitted the following defenses under Rule 10b-5 (SEA 1934):

    a. The CPA is not an insurer.

    b. The CPA's conduct does not include scienter.

    c. There is a lack of reliance and materiality.

    d. The statute of limitations has expired—this defense varies from state to state since Rule 10b-5 is silent on this point and, therefore, courts look to state statutes of limitations.

Section 18 of the Securities Exchange Act of 1934

4132.12 Under Section 18 of the Securities Exchange Act of 1934, the CPA can incur liability for filing any false or misleading statement in any document required to be filed under the act.

4132.13 Section 18 (SEA 1934) applies only to documents that are required to be filed (e.g., annual 10K, proxy statements).

4132.14 The third party must prove scienter (intent) in order to hold the CPA liable. Negligence on the part of the CPA is not enough.

4132.15 Liability extends to any third party who relies on the false statement in purchasing or selling a covered security.

4132.16 In order to recover, the third party must do the following:

    a. Actually know of and rely upon the false statement

    b. Show the price of the security was affected by the false statement

    c. Show that the reliance caused the damage

4132.17 Section 18 of the Securities Exchange Act of 1934 is much narrower in scope than Rule 10b-5.

Criminal Proceedings Against CPAs

4132.18 Violations of the securities acts that give rise to civil liability also subject the CPA to criminal penalties (fine or imprisonment or both).

4132.19 The CPA may be found criminally liable for violation of Section 24 of the Securities Act of 1933 or Section 32 of the Securities Exchange Act of 1934 if the violation can be shown to be *willful* or *intentional*.

4132.20 CPAs are also exposed to criminal penalties under the federal mail fraud and conspiracy statutes.

4132.21 There have been few criminal actions against accountants.

4132.22 The consequences to the CPA of criminal prosecution are the following:

    a. Cost of defense

    b. Resultant fines and imprisonment

    c. Successful criminal case may help to establish civil liability.

    d. Convicted CPA may be unable to continue as a member of profession.

4133 Privileged Communications, Confidentiality, and Privacy Acts

CPA Privileged Communications

4133.01 In common law, there is *not* a privilege that an accountant or client may invoke to prevent disclosures.

4133.02 About 17 states have adopted statutes creating an accountant-client privilege. The statutes vary as follows:

    a. Some apply only to CPAs, while others extend to all public accountants.

    b. Some provide that the privilege is not applicable to criminal or bankruptcy actions.

    c. Some exclude certain services such as auditing.

    d. Some statutes do not state clearly whether the client or the CPA has the benefit of the privilege. Usually, the privilege belongs to the client and the client is in control of whether or not the information is disclosed by the CPA.

4133.03 There is no general *federal* accountant-client privilege.

    a. Generally, any state-created accountant-client privilege is not recognized for federal law purposes.

    b. Under Internal Revenue Code Section 7525, however, a privilege is available for communication between a federally authorized tax practitioner (e.g., a CPA, attorney, enrolled agent, or enrolled actuary) and a client or potential client.

        (1) This privilege can only be asserted in either of the following:

            (a) Noncriminal tax matters before the Internal Revenue Service

            (b) Noncriminal tax proceedings in federal court brought by or against the United States

        (2) Tax advice is advice given with respect to a matter that is within the scope of the tax practitioner's authority to practice before the IRS.

        (3) The privilege exists only to the extent the communication would be privileged under the attorney-client privilege if the communication had been made between a client and an attorney.

        (4) The privilege does not apply to any written communication between a tax practitioner and a corporate representative (including a director, shareholder, officer, employee, or agent) concerning the corporation's participation in any tax shelter (as defined in Internal Revenue Code Section 6662 (d)(c)(iii)).

4133.04 The Code of Professional Conduct mandates a *confidential relationship,* but not *privileged communication.*

CPA's Workpapers

4133.05 CPAs are independent contractors, not employees; thus, they have legal title to their workpapers. The workpapers do not belong to the client; however, the CPA's ownership of the workpapers is custodial. This means the accountant cannot generally transfer them to a third party without the client's permission. Exceptions include subpoena by a federal court or agency or inspection by an AICPA or state society quality review team.

4133.06 A seller of an accounting practice has a duty to obtain permission of the client before making workpapers available to a purchaser of the practice.

4133.07 A deceased partner can convey workpapers to copartners.

4133.08 CPAs do not have a common-law lien on client workpapers coming into their possession.

4133.09 The CPA must generally keep the information in the workpapers confidential.

This page intentionally left blank.

Section 4200
Business Law

4210 Agency
    4211 Formation and Termination
    4212 Authority of Agents and Principals
    4213 Duties and Liabilities of Agents and Principals

4220 Contracts
    4221 Formation
    4222 Performance
    4223 Third-Party Assignments
    4224 Discharge, Breach, and Remedies

4230 Uniform Commercial Code
    4231 Sales Contracts
    4232 Negotiable Instruments
    4233 Secured Transactions
    4234 Documents of Title and Title Transfer

4240 Debtor-Creditor Relationships
    4241 Rights, Duties, and Liabilities of Debtors, Creditors, and Guarantors
    4242 Bankruptcy and Insolvency

4250 Government Regulation of Business
    4251 Federal Securities Regulation
    4252 Other Federal Laws and Regulations (Antitrust, Copyright, Patents, Money-Laundering, Labor, Employment, and ERISA)

4260 Business Structure (Selection of a Business Entity)
    4261 Advantages, Disadvantages, Implications, and Constraints
    4262 Formation, Operation, and Termination
    4263 Financial Structure, Capitalization, Profit and Loss Allocation, and Distributions
    4264 Rights, Duties, Legal Obligations, and Authority of Owners and Management

4210 Agency

4211 Formation and Termination

Definition and Explanation of Agency

4211.01 An **agency** is a fiduciary relationship between two persons where one person (the agent) acts for the benefit and under the control of the other person (the principal) and has the power to affect the legal relationships of the principal.

4211.02 The word **person** is used in the legal sense. A corporation, a partnership, or an individual can be a person and can therefore act in the capacity of either a principal or an agent.

4211.03 The relationship is consensual. Both persons must consent to enter into an agency relationship. Consent can be expressed or implied from the conduct of the parties.

4211.04 The agency relationship can be shown as follows:

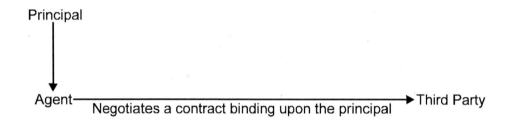

4211.05 Agency law involves the following relationships:

a. Principal and agent

b. Employer (master) and employee (servant)

c. Principal and independent contractor

4211.06 If a principal/agent relationship exists, the agent will also be viewed as either an employee or an independent contractor.

4211.07 The word *agent* is often used interchangeably with the word *employee (servant)*. However, not every employee is an agent; only an employee who is also an agent can make contracts with third parties for the principal (the employer).

4211.08 Agency is used by the principal to expand activities. A corporation, being an artificial entity created by government authorization, can act only through agents. In partnerships, each partner can act as an agent for the partnership entity. A sole proprietor hires agents so that the sole proprietor can transact more business.

4211.09 The agency relationship can be used in either business or personal situations.

4211.10 **Formalities.** No particular formalities are required to form the agency relationship. The formation can be oral, written, or the agency can be created by some conduct of the principal that may be interpreted by a third party as an intention to appoint an agent. If formed by contract, it must satisfy the requirements of a contract. The statute of frauds requires an agency contract to be in writing to be enforceable if the contract cannot be performed within one year from the time of making the contract.

Power of attorney. A power of attorney is a formal instrument, usually acknowledged by a notary public, to confer authority on an agent. The agent is referred to as an attorney-in-fact, to distinguish them from a lawyer who is an attorney-at-law.

Agency Relationships

4211.11 **Principal and agent.** The agent works for the benefit and under the control of the principal and has the right to represent the principal and make contracts with third parties on behalf of the principal.

    a. The agent must be either an employee or an independent contractor (but not all employees or independent contractors are agents).

    b. The principal is liable on contracts made by an agent if the agent has authority to act on behalf of the principal.

    c. The principal is not liable on contracts made by an employee or independent contractor unless that person is also an agent.

    d. The principal may be held liable for torts against third parties committed by agents who are employees of the principal, but not for torts committed by independent contractors.

    e. **Example:** SAS Corporation hires Gerry to sell its products as an outside salesman. Gerry calls on customers and makes sales contracts with them. SAS Corporation would be the principal, Gerry would be an agent, and the customers would be third parties. Contracts entered between Gerry and the customers would generally be binding on SAS Corporation.

4211.12 **Employer and employee.** The employee works for the benefit and under the control of the employer but does not have the right to represent the principal or make contracts with third parties. Several factors are considered in determining if an individual is an employee. The most important of these is the right of the employer to control the physical details of the employee's work. An employee can be an agent if the employee is also given the authority to enter contracts with third parties that are binding on the principal.

Example: SAS Corporation hires Lila to be a production line worker. Lila would be an employee and SAS Corporation would be the employer. Lila is not an agent because she does not have the authority to represent her principal in dealing with third parties.

4211.13 **Principal and independent contractor.** The independent contractor acts for the benefit of the principal but not under the principal's control. The principal who deals with an independent contractor is sometimes called a proprietor. The principal contracts for the end result, but the principal has no right of direction or control while the activity is being performed. The principal is not usually liable for the torts of an independent contractor even though the independent contractor is acting for the principal at the time the tort occurred.

    a. **Example:** In conducting an audit for a client, the CPA acts as an independent contractor. The client seeks an opinion, but the CPA determines what is audited and how it is audited. If the client controlled the audit, the CPA would not have professional independence.

    b. **Example:** SAS Corporation hires Williams to repave its parking lot. Williams completes the work over the weekend with no involvement by SAS Corporation. Williams would be an independent contractor as to SAS Corporation because the principal exercised no control over the physical details of the work.

c. **Example:** Williams (in the prior example) hires individuals to work for him in his repaving business. Williams tells them what to do in repaving the SAS Corporation parking lot. These individuals would be employees of Williams since he has control over the physical details of the work they perform.

It is a question of fact as to what type of relationship exists between two persons. The question arises when there is a tort while the other person is acting for the benefit of the principal. Liability of the principal is determined by the control factor.

4211.14 **Franchiser and franchisee.** This relationship is normally that of principal and independent contractor. But, the relationship could be found to be that of employer and employee if the franchiser exercises significant control over the franchisee in running the franchise. The franchiser is not liable for the torts of the franchisee if the franchisee acts as an independent contractor.

Example: Fast-food restaurants are often franchise operations. Well-known examples are Wendy's, McDonald's, and Burger King. In most chains there are stores owned by the chain (employer-employee) and franchised stores (principal-independent contractor).

Creation of an Agency

An agency can be created by the following means:

4211.15 **Contract.** Both the principal and the agent contractually agree to the relationship. This is the usual way of creating the agency relationship.

Example: Harry agrees that he will sell the products of the Doyle Corporation for a 10% commission on the sale price.

4211.16 **Agreement but not a contract.** Both the principal and the agent agree to the relationship, but the agreement is not a contract since it lacks some of the required elements. The agreement can be shown by the principal's and agent's conduct.

Since it is not necessary that the agreement be a contract, consideration is not a requirement for creation of an agency.

4211.17 **Ratification.** Ratification occurs when the principal gives approval of an act previously done by the purported agent for the principal without authority. When the act happens, it must have been done for the purported principal, not for the purported agent. The ratification must also occur within a reasonable time.

a. The principal can expressly ratify the unauthorized act by indicating the intent to be bound. Oral or written statements to either the third party or the agent can result in an express ratification.

b. An implied ratification can result if the principal retains the benefits and advantages of the contract with the third party.

c. Ratification retroactively acts as an acceptance by the principal of the unauthorized contract from the date the contract was made.

d. Ratification cannot generally be retracted once done.

e. The third party can withdraw from the contract before ratification by the principal, but not after.

f. The entire contract must be ratified by the principal. Partial ratification of the favorable parts and rejection of the unfavorable parts of the contract are not permitted.

g. Ratification is possible only when the principal knows all the important terms of the contract.

4211.18 **Estoppel.** This is called creation of agency by *apparent* authority (see section **4212.08**). This occurs when the principal leads a third party to reasonably believe that a person acts as the principal's agent. The principal is prohibited from denying the existence of an agency relationship if the third party deals with the person as the principal's agent. Technically, no agency relationship is created by estoppel, but the principal is legally liable as if there were an agency relationship. It must be the principal, not the agent, that leads the third party to believe that an agency relationship exists.

4211.19 **By operation of law.** An agency relationship can be imposed by operation of law in some unusual circumstances. These are examples:

  a. **Necessity.** This happens by operation of law when an emergency situation develops and the agent is given power to act beyond normal authority. Usually these conditions exist when the following are true:

  (1) The agent cannot contact the principal for instructions.

  (2) Failure to act will cause substantial loss to the principal.

  b. A spouse or child who purchases necessities for the family is the agent of the other spouse.

4211.20 Marriage itself does not create an agency relationship. One of the spouses can act as an agent for the other spouse, but it is not because of the marriage that the agency exists.

Example: A wife tells her husband to buy some goods from a particular store and charge the purchase price to her charge account. The husband is acting as an agent for the wife. Marriage is not the basis of the agency, rather the consent of the principal (wife) to have the husband (agent) act for her.

Classification of Agents

4211.21 **General agent.** An agent who is authorized to do a series of transactions for the principal for a continuing period of time. A general agent has much *implied authority* (see section **4212.04**).

  a. **Example:** Mildred hires Tom to operate her ice cream store. Tom is a general agent having implied authority to do many types of activities relating to the store.

  b. **Example:** A business manager of a retail store, as a general agent, has implied authority to engage in such normal activities as the following:

  (1) Buying and selling inventory

  (2) Purchasing supplies and equipment

  (3) Hiring and firing employees

  However, that manager would lack implied authority to do such things as the following:

  (1) Mortgaging the property

  (2) Borrowing money from the bank

  (3) Selling the business

  The manager would not have implied authority to do these activities because they are outside the scope of the authority that a manager of a retail store would normally have.

4211.22 **Special agent.** An agent who conducts some specific transaction for the principal over a limited period of time. A special agent has less implied authority than a general agent. Examples of special agents include the following:

    a. **Broker.** Brings the seller and buyer together. The broker is a special agent of one of the two parties and has very limited implied authority.

    b. **Factor.** A factor receives possession of some other person's property to sell for a commission. The factor is a special agent, having only that implied authority that relates to the sale of the property. The factor is sometimes called a *commission merchant*. The factor receives a commission (factorage) from the sale. The factor sells in his own name.

    c. **Lawyer.** A lawyer handles a particular case for the client. The lawyer is a special agent of the client and has only implied authority as it relates to the particular case.

    d. **Auctioneer.** Person who auctions the seller's property. Once the property has been sold, the auctioneer acts as an agent for both the seller and the buyer to transfer legal title.

4211.23 **Gratuitous agent.** Person who agrees to act as an agent without expectation of compensation. The relationship is generally the same as in the case of a compensated agent, except that a gratuitous agent has no obligation to act for the principal unless the gratuitous agent has caused the principal to reasonably rely on the agent to perform the act.

Example: Dave wants to place a bid on property being sold at auction, but is unsure that he will be able to be there in time. A friend, Bill, offers to go and place the bid on Dave's behalf. If Bill fails to go and make the bid, he may be liable to Dave since Dave reasonably relied on Bill placing the bid at the auction.

4211.24 **Compensated agent.** Person who agrees to act as an agent with expectation of compensation. This would be the assumed situation between unrelated persons.

4211.25 **Subagent.** Person appointed by an authorized agent to act for the agent. If the agent is authorized to appoint a subagent, the acts of the subagent are binding on the principal. If the agent lacks authority to appoint a subagent, the subagent's acts are not binding on the principal.

Classification of Principals

4211.26 **Disclosed principal.** A disclosed principal is a person whose existence and identity are known to the third party at the time of making the contract with the agent.

4211.27 **Partially disclosed principal.** A partially disclosed principal is a principal whose *existence* is known to the third party at the time of contracting with the agent. The specific identity of the principal, though, is unknown to the third party.

4211.28 **Undisclosed principal.** An undisclosed principal is a principal whose existence and identity are not known to the third party at the time of contracting. From the third party's point of view, the agent appears to be acting on their own behalf.

Legal Capacity of the Parties

4211.29 **Of the principal.** If the principal does not have legal capacity to enter a contract, the principal does not have the capacity to appoint an agent. In other words, if a principal cannot legally enter a contract directly, they cannot do so indirectly through an agent.

4211.30 **Of the agent.** To make a contract for the principal, an agent does not need contractual capacity; only the principal needs capacity to enter a contract. A minor can act as an agent for an adult, and contracts made by a minor agent are legally binding on the adult principal. These contracts with third parties would not be voidable by the adult principal even though the agent was a minor. The minor agent, however, could disaffirm the agency contract since this is a voidable contract to the minor agent. This would not, however, impact any contracts entered for the principal with third parties prior to the disaffirmance.

Example: Harris, a minor acting as an agent for Lynn, makes a contract with James. The contract is valid so long as both Lynn and James have legal capacity. It makes no difference that the agent was a minor with only limited capacity to contract for himself.

4211.31 Anyone who can act for himself, can act through an agent.

Purpose of the Agency

4211.32 The purpose of the agency must be legal. Any agreements lacking a legal purpose will be found to be an illegal bargain for which the courts will not adjust equities between the parties to the agreement.

Agency Coupled with an Interest

4211.33 An agency coupled with an interest is an agency relationship where the agent has an interest in the subject matter of the agency. The subject matter is a property interest or a security interest. The principal acting alone cannot terminate the agency. Death, insanity, or bankruptcy of the principal does not terminate the agency. This relationship is sometimes called an "agency power coupled with an interest" or an "agency coupled with security."

Example: Kevin loaned $5,000 to Brian, and the debt has not yet been repaid. Brian appoints Kevin as an agent to negotiate the sale of Brian's property, with Kevin receiving a part of the sale proceeds to repay the loan. This is an agency coupled with an interest.

4212 Authority of Agents and Principals

Authority of the Agent to Act for the Principal

4212.01 The authority, or power, of an agent is the capacity to change the legal status of the principal by dealing with third parties.

4212.02 The authority of the agent is determined by the principal and can come only from the principal. Authority comes from the consent of the principal.

    a. The burden of proving the agent's authority rests with the third party who deals with the agent. If authority cannot be proved, the purported principal is not liable on the contract.

    b. The agent cannot create their own authority.

    c. A third party who deals with an agent, knowing the agent exceeds their authority, does so at their own peril and will not generally be able to hold the principal liable for the agent's unauthorized act.

4212.03 **Express authority.** Authority that is stated in spoken or written words by the principal.

Example: David owns a fruit and vegetable market. He tells Jennifer to enter a contract with Acme Produce Wholesalers to purchase 10 cases of apples. Jennifer, as agent, has express authority to make this purchase.

4212.04 **Implied authority.** The authority that is commonly and customarily needed to conduct the purpose of the agency. Implied authority is needed to fill in the gaps to carry out the agent's express authority. It cannot come from words or conduct of the agent. It can vary from one location to another. It can vary among different types of businesses.

Example: Brian owns a clothing store. He hires Erin and gives her the authority to manage the store. Erin enters a contract with ABC Clothing Corporation in order to obtain clothing to sell in the store. Even though Erin did not have express authority to enter the contract with ABC, she would have implied authority to enter this contract since it is necessary to fulfill the purpose of the agency.

4212.05 **Incidental authority.** Same as implied authority.

4212.06 **Actual authority.** The combination of express and implied authority.

4212.07 **Customary authority.** The authority that comes from the customs of that type of business.

4212.08 **Apparent authority.** Apparent authority, or appearance of authority, comes from the words or actions of the principal that lead a third party to reasonably believe and act upon the belief that actual authority exists in the purported agent. Belief and reliance are shown when the third party makes a contract with the purported agent. Apparent authority is determined from the view of the third party dealing with the purported agent. The words or actions must come from the principal, not the purported agent, in order to create apparent authority.

    a. **Example:** Andrea, an outside salesperson for Mamou Corporation, called on customers, sold merchandise, delivered merchandise, and collected receivables. After being fired, Andrea collected some of the receivables from existing customers and disappeared. The existing customers will not have to pay Mamou again. The principal, Mamou, created the situation by allowing Andrea to collect the receivables previously. From the customers' point of view, Andrea had apparent authority to collect the balances due. The firing terminated actual authority, but the principal, Mamou, had led the customers to believe and act upon the belief that Andrea had actual authority. These existing customers should be informed of the firing in order to terminate the apparent authority.

    b. The following factors are sometimes considered in determining whether apparent authority exists:

        (1) The third party's knowledge of the agent's actual authority and limitations

        (2) The customs in that type of business

        (3) The principal's prior approval of similar activities by the agent

4212.09 **Ostensible authority.** Another term for apparent authority.

4212.10 **Power to appoint subagents.** As a general rule, an agent cannot appoint subagents in order to delegate the agent's duties and obligations. This is because the principal selects the agent based on personal qualifications. If the duties of the agent are purely ministerial, mechanical, or routine, an exception is allowed and the agent may appoint a subagent. If the duties require skill, discretion, or judgment, no subagent may be appointed unless the principal gives permission.

4212.11 **Financial powers.** An agent who sells goods for cash, and has possession of the goods, has the authority to collect the cash. The agent has no implied authority to accept credit in place of cash. Payment to an agent lacking authority to accept the payment does not discharge the debt. The third party would still be required to make payment to the principal.

4212.12 **Termination.** The agent's actual authority ceases when the agency is terminated; however, the agent still has apparent authority from the viewpoint of third parties with whom the agent has dealt. These third parties must be given actual notice of the termination to end the apparent authority. For those third parties who have not dealt with the agent, constructive notice is adequate to end the apparent authority. Publishing the termination in a newspaper having general circulation is adequate constructive notification as to those third parties.

Termination of the Agency

4212.13 **Revocation by the principal.** The principal acting alone can revoke the authority of the agent. This is because an agency is a consensual relationship requiring the consent of both parties.

    a. If the relationship is an agency coupled with an interest, the principal cannot revoke the agency.

    b. The principal can still be liable on the agency relationship because the agent may still have apparent authority from the view of third parties with whom the agent has previously dealt. These third parties should be given actual notice of the dismissal of the agent. This notice would eliminate the lingering apparent authority. The notice can be given in person, by letter, or by phone.

    c. If the revocation is contrary to the agency contract, the principal could be liable for breach of contract if the breach is not justified. This is because while, principals have the power to terminate the agency, they may not have the legal right to do so.

4212.14 **Renunciation by the agent.** Renunciation takes place when the agent acting alone withdraws from the agency relationship.

    a. If the renunciation is contrary to the agency contract, the agent could be liable for the breach of contract if the breach is not justified. Like the principal, the agent also has the power to terminate the agency but may not have the legal right to do so.

    b. **Example:** Dave employs Jennifer as his agent under a 3-year agency agreement. After six months, Jennifer withdraws as Dave's agent. Jennifer has the power to terminate the agency in this way, but will be liable to Dave for breach of contract.

4212.15 **Mutual agreement of both principal and agent.** If the principal and the agent mutually agree to end the agency relationship, it ends.

4212.16 **Accomplishment of the purpose of the agency.** When the purpose of the agency is done, the agency relationship terminates.

Example: The legal case given to the lawyer is settled and paid. The lawyer, a special agent, has accomplished the purpose of the agency, and the agency relationship is terminated.

4212.17 **Time period ends.** If the principal and agent have agreed that the agency relationship will end after an express period of time, the lapse of that time will terminate the agency relationship.

4212.18 **Operation of law.** Operation of law means automatically without any action needed by the parties. All authority of the agent is terminated, even apparent authority, when the termination is by operation of law. An agency relationship is terminated by operation of law without notice being required in the following circumstances:

    a. **Death of the principal or agent.** It is not necessary that the other party have knowledge of the death.

b. **Insanity of the principal or agent.** It is not necessary that the other party have knowledge of the insanity.

c. **Bankruptcy of the principal.** It is not necessary that the other party have knowledge of the bankruptcy. The agency relationship is not terminated if the agent becomes bankrupt.

d. **Impossibility of performance.** If the purpose of the agency becomes objectively impossible to perform, the agency terminates by operation of law.

Example: Caitlin is acting as agent to sell Erin's office building. If the building is destroyed by fire, the purpose of the agency becomes objectively impossible to perform. The agency therefore terminates by operation of law.

e. **The performance of the agency becomes illegal.**

Example: Brian employs Kevin as his agent to sell fireworks to third parties. If the state subsequently passes a statute making the sale of fireworks illegal, the agency would terminate by operation of law.

4212.19 **Notice to third parties**

a. Generally, the principal should give personal notice of termination of the agency to any third party who has dealt with the agent. This would eliminate any problems with the principal being bound to contracts entered by the former agent under the doctrine of apparent authority.

b. Published notice of termination of the agency is generally sufficient notice to any third parties who have not dealt with the agent previously.

c. Acts of the agent after a termination by operation of law cannot bind the principal or the principal's estate based on a theory of apparent authority.

4213 Duties and Liabilities of Agents and Principals

Agent's Duties and Obligations

4213.01 **Agent's duties and obligations to the principal.** This is a fiduciary relationship, one of trust and confidence. Some of the attributes of this fiduciary relationship are the following:

a. **Loyalty.** Undivided loyalty to the principal with no conflict with the agent's personal interests. The agent should not disclose confidential information to anyone except the principal. The agent should not act for two principals (dual agency) unless both principals know and agree. The agent may not make a secret profit on the subject matter of the agency. The agent cannot engage in self-dealing.

(1) An agent who breaches the fiduciary duty of loyalty loses any compensation, fee, or commission that would have been due to the agent.

(2) If the principal finds the agent has been self-dealing, the transaction is voidable at the principal's option.

Example: The principal employs an agent to purchase a specified piece of land. If the agent instead purchases the land for herself, this is a breach of the duty of loyalty to the principal.

b. **Obedience.** The agent should follow instructions unless they are criminal or illegal. If the agent fails to follow instructions, the agent is personally liable for any loss incurred by the disobedience. If there are no instructions, the agent is not disobedient if the agent uses judgment in discretionary or emergency situations.

Example: The principal tells the agent not to give goods to Kevin until Kevin pays. Kevin promises the agent that he will pay in three days if the agent gives him the goods now. If the agent hands over the goods and Kevin does not pay, the agent is liable to the principal for the contract price.

c. **Accounting.** The agent must keep records for examination by the principal. The agent must not commingle the principal's property with his own. The agent is legally liable if commingling causes a loss.

If the agent uses the principal's funds for their own purpose, the principal can sue the agent for the return of the funds. If the agent has purchased property with the funds, the principal can generally elect to take the property even if it is of greater value.

Example: An agent uses the principal's funds ($500) to purchase a painting. The principal can recover either the $500 or the painting, even if the painting has appreciated in value.

d. **Due care.** The agent must use reasonable care and not be negligent in carrying out the agency. Reasonable care is that care a reasonably prudent person would use in like or similar circumstances. The agent may be liable to the principal if the agent is negligent in carrying out the agency.

e. **Give notice of information.** The agent must transmit important information to the principal. Failure to do this could be costly to the principal because notice to the agent is legally equivalent to notice to the principal. The agent can be held liable for any damages that result from the failure to give notice.

f. **Indemnification.** The agent must indemnify the principal if the principal pays damages in a legal action for the wrongful acts of the agent.

g. **Competition.** The agent must not compete with the business activity of the principal.

h. **Termination.** After the agency relationship is terminated, the former agent cannot continue to act as the principal's agent. The duty not to disclose confidential information regarding the agency continues, however, even after the agency is terminated.

4213.02 **Agent's duties and obligations to employees.** Unless they are also agents, employees do not act in a fiduciary relationship to their employer.

Principal's Duties and Obligations

4213.03 The principal's duties and obligations to the agent are not fiduciary. The agent owes a fiduciary duty to the principal, but the principal does not owe a fiduciary duty to the agent.

4213.04 These are the duties and obligations that the principal owes to the agent:

a. **Compensation.** The principal generally owes to the agent the duty of compensation. If the amount is expressly mentioned in the contract, that will be the amount. If no amount is expressly mentioned, it will be the reasonable amount as determined by the court. The compensation may be on a contingent fee basis. A person may act as a gratuitous agent, but the normal assumption is that a person expects to be compensated for activities done for the benefit of some other person.

b. **Reimbursement.** The principal must reimburse the agent if the agent spends their own funds to carry out the agency.

Example: Erin, acting as agent for Jennifer, delivers goods to a customer of Jennifer. The customer refuses to accept the goods and Erin incurs costs to store the goods. Erin is entitled to reimbursement from Jennifer for the storage costs.

c. **Indemnity.** The principal must indemnify the agent if the agent suffers expenses from a legal action resulting from carrying out the agency.

Example: Erin, acting as agent for Jennifer, her undisclosed principal, enters into a contract with Emily. The contract is breached and Emily sues Erin, collecting a judgment of $5,000. Jennifer must indemnify Erin for the $5,000 loss.

d. **Contractual.** The principal must perform all the terms of the agency contract or be legally liable for breach of contract.

e. **Warnings.** The principal must warn the agent of any dangers and unreasonable risks involved in the employment.

Third Party's Duties and Obligations

4213.05　The third party is liable for all the duties and obligations that arise from the contract.

Agent's Rights

4213.06　**Agent's rights against the principal.** The principal's duties and obligations are the rights of the agent. The agent has the following rights:

a. **Have the principal perform the agency contract.** If the principal breaches this contract, the agent can sue the principal.

b. **Compensation.** Unless it is agreed otherwise, it is assumed that the principal should compensate the agent for the work. The amount will be the contract amount. If no amount is given in the contract, it will be the reasonable value of the services.

c. **Reimbursement.** If the agent expends their own funds in carrying out the agency, the principal must repay the agent.

d. **Indemnity.** If the agent pays damages from a legal action based on carrying out the agency, the principal must indemnify the agent.

4213.07　**Agent's rights against the third party.** For the usual situation involving a disclosed principal and a contract, the agent has no rights against the third party because the agent is not a party to the contract. If the agent is liable on the contract due to the fact the principal is undisclosed or partially disclosed, the agent has whatever rights come from the contract. The presence or absence of the agency relationship does not affect the rights of the agent on the contract.

Principal's Rights

4213.08　**Principal's rights against the agent.** The principal has the following rights:

a. Performance of the agency contract by the agent.

b. Indemnification from the agent/employee if obligated to pay damages for the torts of the agent/employee in a suit by a third party based upon the doctrine of *respondeat superior*.

Example: Agent/employee negligently operates the employer's delivery truck while working and injures a pedestrian. Under the doctrine of *respondeat superior*, the injured pedestrian sues the employer and collects $25,000. The employee must indemnify the employer for the amount of $25,000.

c. In addition to the rights that the principal has by virtue of the agency relationship, the principal also has the right to expect the agent to act as a fiduciary. This fiduciary relationship requires the agent to place the interests of the principal above their own interests. The principal has the right to sue the agent for breach of this fiduciary duty.

4213.09 The principal has the right to expect performance of contracts made with third parties regardless of whether the contract was made personally or by an agent. If the third party has committed a tort against the principal, the principal has a right to sue for damages.

4213.10 The principal can enforce their rights in the following ways:

    a. By suing for the legal remedy of damages

    b. By seeking an equitable remedy, such as an injunction, specific performance, rescission of the contract, or an accounting

    c. By revoking the agency. This would involve discharging the agent.

Third Party's Rights

4213.11 **Third party's rights against the principal**

    a. For contracts. The third party has the rights that arise from the contract. If the principal breaches the contract, the third party can sue the principal for breach of contract.

    b. For torts of the agent/employee. The third party can sue the principal for torts of the agent if the agent/employee was acting in the scope and course of the agency when the tort happened. This is called the doctrine of *respondeat superior*.

4213.12 **Third party's rights against the agent**

    a. For contracts. If the principal was undisclosed or partially disclosed, the agent can be sued on the contract. If the principal was disclosed at the time of making the contract, the agent cannot be sued on the contract.

    b. For torts of the agent. The agent, like everyone else, is responsible for her own torts. The third party can sue the agent for the agent's torts against the third party.

Agent's Liability

4213.13 **Agent's liability on contracts**

    a. As a general rule, the agent is not personally liable on contracts the agent makes for the principal.

    b. With a disclosed principal. When the third party knows that the agent is acting as an agent and also knows the identity of the principal, the agent is not liable on the contract. This is the usual and most common situation.

    c. With a partially disclosed principal. A partially disclosed principal exists when the third party knows the agent is acting for a principal, but the third party does not know the principal's identity. The agent is liable on the contract. Once the identity of the principal is discovered, the third party could also sue the principal but cannot recover from both.

    d. With an undisclosed principal. An undisclosed principal exists when the third party, at the time of contracting, does not know the person is acting as an agent. The agent is liable on the contract. Once discovered, the third party can also sue the principal but cannot recover from both.

    e. With a nonexistent principal. The agent is personally liable on the contract if the agent contracts with a third person by representing that the agent acts for a fictitious or nonexistent principal. The agent would be breaching the implied warranty of authority that is made to the third party.

- **f.** The agent is personally liable to the third party on a contract in the following instances:
    (1) The agent makes the contract in her own name. The principal would be either undisclosed or partially disclosed.
    (2) The agent guarantees the performance of the principal, and the principal fails to perform.
    (3) The agent contracts for a nonexistent principal and makes no guarantees.
    (4) The agent acts without authorization from the principal in making the contract.
- **g.** The agent is *not* liable on a contract in the following instances:
    (1) The agent contracts for a disclosed principal.
    (2) The principal ratifies an unauthorized contract made by the agent for the principal. In this case, the action of the agent is treated as if it were authorized from the beginning.
    (3) The third party elects to hold the newly discovered principal liable on a contract made by the agent for an undisclosed or partially disclosed principal.

4213.14 Agent's liability for torts. An agent/employee, like any individual, is liable for his own torts. This liability exists even though the agent/employee is working for the principal when the tort occurs. If the injured third party sues the principal under the doctrine of *respondeat superior* and collects, the agent/employee has the legal duty to indemnify the principal since this is a breach of the duty to carry out the agency using due care.

4213.15 Agent's liability for crimes. The agent/employee, like any individual, is liable for her crimes. The fact that the agent/employee is working for a principal when the crime is committed is no defense for committing the crime.

4213.16 Agent's liability on negotiable instruments. An agent will be liable on a negotiable instrument if the agent signs his own name without indicating the existence and the identity of the principal.

- **a.** If the act is authorized, the agent can expect reimbursement from the principal for the amount paid on the negotiable instrument.
- **b.** To avoid liability on the instrument, the agent must indicate that the signing is in a representative capacity (as an agent for another party).

    Example: The agent is not liable on the instrument if agent Ann Addley signs for SAS Corporation like this:

    SAS Corporation
    by Ann Addley, Agent

- **c.** The agent will also be liable on a negotiable instrument if the agent signs the principal's name without authority. This is forgery.

Principal's Liability

4213.17 Principal's liability for contracts

- **a.** Where the agent had actual (express or implied) authority, the principal is liable on the contract.
- **b.** Where the agent did not have authority but the act was later ratified by the principal, the principal is liable on the contract.

- c. Where the purported agent had apparent authority to make the contract, the principal is liable on the contract.
- d. The principal is not liable even if the purported agent represents that she acts for the principal if the act is unauthorized.
- e. **Settlement before discovery.** If an undisclosed principal settles with the agent after the contract is made, after the goods are delivered, and before discovery by the third party, the principal is not liable on the contract. The agent would be liable.
- f. **Settlement after discovery.** If an undisclosed principal settles with the agent after the contract is made, after the goods are delivered, and after discovery by the third party, the principal is liable on the contract.
- g. **Notice to agent.** Notice to the agent or knowledge obtained by the agent within the scope of the agency binds the principal. The principal need not have actual knowledge to be held liable.
- h. The principal is directly liable on all contracts he makes with other persons.
- i. The principal is vicariously liable on contracts made by authorized acts of agents.
- j. The principal can use the usual defenses to deny liability on a contract. The principal cannot use the defenses that are personal to the agent.

4213.18 **Principal's liability for torts of the agent/employee.** The principal is liable for torts of the agent if the agent was acting in the scope of and in the course of the agency when the tort happened. This vicarious liability is called the doctrine of *respondeat superior*. The term "vicarious" means a substitute. The principal is liable as a substitute for the agent. The principal is liable whether the tort was authorized or unauthorized. The principal is liable whether the tort was defined as intentional, negligence, or liability without fault.

- a. The trend is to expand the doctrine of *respondeat superior* to make the principal legally liable in more circumstances.
- b. If the agent/employee is not acting for the principal, the agent is on a detour or on a "frolic of their own" and is the only person liable for the tort.

4213.19 **Principal's liability for torts of an independent contractor.** As a general rule, the principal is not legally liable for the torts of an independent contractor. Only the independent contractor is liable for the torts. The exceptions to this rule are as follows:

- a. **Work that is inherently dangerous.** It would be contrary to public policy to allow a person to avoid liability by hiring an independent contractor to do inherently dangerous work.
- b. **Work that is illegal.** A principal cannot avoid liability by hiring an independent contractor to perform illegal work that will benefit the principal.
- c. **Work that is inseparable from the principal's operation.** If the work is so integrated into the business operation that it cannot be delegated, the principal is liable.

    Example: A hotel could not hire an independent contractor to operate the elevator system because operation of the elevator is essential to a multistory hotel's operation. If the independent contractor committed a tort while operating the elevator, the hotel, in addition to the independent contractor, would be liable.

- d. **Work that cannot be delegated.** Some duties imposed by law are nondelegable.

4213.20 **Principal's liability for crimes of the agent.** The principal is not liable for the crimes of the agent unless the principal actually participated in the crime.

Example: Jim, acting as an agent, was making a delivery for his principal, Susan. While driving the truck he was given a ticket for speeding and reckless driving. Speeding and reckless driving are crimes. Susan, the principal, is not liable for the crimes of speeding and reckless driving.

4213.21 **Principal's liability on negotiable instruments.** A principal will be liable on a negotiable instrument if either of the following is true:

    a. An agent with authority signs the principal's name.

    b. The principal signs his own name.

Third Party's Liability

4213.22 The third party is liable on contracts that they make. The agency relationship on the other end of the contract does not affect the liability of the third party. The third party is liable even if the principal is undisclosed or partially disclosed.

4220 Contracts
4221 Formation

4221.01 A *contract* is a legally enforceable agreement.

Classifications of Contracts

4221.02 **Express contract:** The parties manifest their agreement by spoken or written words.

4221.03 **Implied contract:** Implied in fact. The agreement is manifest, not by direct words, but from the conduct of the parties.

4221.04 **Quasi contract:** Implied in law. One party is unjustly enriched at the expense of the other party such that the court will impose an obligation on the enriched party to pay the other party. No quasi contract will be imposed if there is an express or implied contract existing between the parties. The court implies a contractual obligation without regard to the agreement of the parties in order to prevent the unjust enrichment from occurring.

4221.05 **Formal contract:** Under seal. Consideration is conclusively presumed. A notary public's imprint on a document is not a seal.

4221.06 **Informal contract:** Without a seal. Most contracts are informal and do not require a seal to be legally enforceable.

4221.07 **Divisible contract:** Promises that are not dependent on each other. Partial performance of the contract is allowed.

4221.08 **Indivisible contract:** Interdependent promises that cannot be separated.

4221.09 **Unilateral contract:** A promise in exchange for an act.

4221.10 **Bilateral contract:** Promise in exchange for a promise.

4221.11 **Executory contract:** Something remains to be completed on the contract.

4221.12 **Executed contract:** All parties to the contract have done all that they are obligated to do.

4221.13 **Unenforceable contract:** A contract that will not be enforced by the court. Valid when made but made unenforceable by some later event, such as the running of the statute of limitations or discharge of the contract in bankruptcy.

4221.14 **Valid contract:** Binding and enforceable.

4221.15 **Void contract:** Never had legal effect because of the lack of an essential element.

4221.16 **Voidable contract:** Valid until one party exercises a right to avoid the contract.

Parties to a Contract

4221.17 Parties to a contract may be diagrammed as follows:

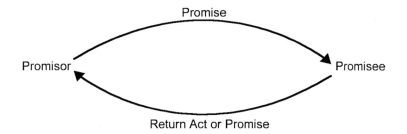

Laws Governing Contracts

4221.18 **Laws governing contracts for sale of goods** (personal property): Uniform Commercial Code (U.C.C.). If no specific U.C.C. rule applies, common law applies.

4221.19 **Laws governing contracts for sale of real property:** Common law rules apply.

4221.20 **Laws governing contracts for services** (employment): Common law rules apply.

Elements of a Contract

4221.21 There are four **elements** necessary to have a valid contract:

1. Agreement: Manifestation of mutual assent,
2. Consideration,
3. Legal purpose, and
4. Competent parties.

Agreement

4221.22 An *agreement* is a mutual understanding between two or more persons.

4221.23 There must be a manifestation of mutual assent for the parties to be legally obligated on the contract.

4221.24 Objective standard is used to determine agreement. This means what persons show by their conduct, not necessarily what is thought.

4221.25 Normally, an agreement is reached by an offer and an acceptance of that offer.

Offer

4221.26 An *offer* is a promise to do or refrain from doing something in the future provided the other party complies with the stated conditions.

4221.27 Parties to an offer may be diagrammed as follows:

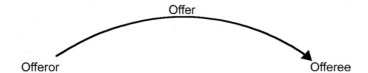

4221.28 The offer is always a promise.

4221.29 To have a valid offer, the following must be true:

    a. There must be contractual intent. Use the reasonable person objective standard. Ask, "Would a reasonable person based on the circumstances believe that an offer had been made?" An offer is not any of the following:

        (1) A social invitation. "If you promise to come over to my house tonight, I promise to cook you a steak dinner." This creates a social, not a legal, obligation.

        (2) A statement made in obvious jest. "I will give a million dollars to anyone who will tell me the name of that song."

        (3) A statement made in anger, rage, or excitement. "I will give a million dollars to anyone who tells me the name of the person who stole that bike from me."

        (4) An invitation to negotiate further.

    b. The offer must be definite and have a certainty of terms. Courts cannot enforce what cannot be determined. It need not be with absolute certainty but must be capable of determination with reasonable certainty.

        (1) Usually need time of performance, price, what is to be done, and subject matter of the contract identified.

        (2) Output contracts are OK. An *output contract* promises to sell all of a person's production over a set period of time.

        (3) Requirements contracts are OK. A *requirements contract* promises to buy all of a person's requirements for the product over a set period of time.

        (4) Failure to state a specific dollar price is OK, if the price can be objectively determined.

        Example: I promise to sell you 1,000 bushels of corn at the market price next Thursday.

    c. The offer must be communicated to the offeree. It may be to an individual or to a group.

4221.30 Advertisements: Attempts to solicit an offer from the reader. Advertisements are not definite enough to be an offer, even if it contains a stated price.

4221.31 Quote: Invitation to make an offer—not an offer.

4221.32 Bid: An offer.

4221.33 Preliminary negotiations: Dickering before a final contract—not an offer.

4221.34 An offer may be withdrawn (revoked) by notifying the offeree anytime before acceptance.

4221.35 Revocation of an offer by the offeror is effective when received by the offeree.

4221.36 Rejection of an offer by the offeree is effective when received by the offeror.

4221.37 An offer may not be assigned to anyone else.

4221.38 **Option contract:** A contract entered to keep an offer open; the offer cannot be withdrawn without breach of contract during the agreed-upon time period.

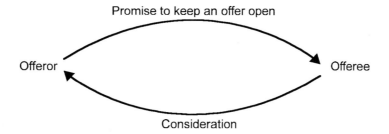

4221.39 An offer may be terminated by the following:
   a. Expiration of the time specified in the offer or a reasonable time if no time is mentioned
   b. Revocation received by offeree before acceptance
   c. Rejection by the offeree (a counteroffer is a rejection combined with a new offer to the original offeror)
   d. Death of offeror or offeree
   e. Insanity of offeror or offeree
   f. Destruction of the subject matter relating to the offer without the fault of either party
   g. Intervening illegality—subsequent legislation making the offer or the resulting contract illegal (e.g., an offer to sell bourbon just before prohibition became effective)

4221.40 **Irrevocable offers** are exceptions to the general rule that offers are revocable. These are some examples of irrevocable offers:
   a. Option contract—made irrevocable by a contract between the parties in which the offeror agrees to keep the offer open in return for some consideration from the offeree.
   b. Unilateral contract when the offeree has begun substantially to perform the contract. Revocation would be unfair to the party who has begun performance.
   c. Stated time of a written offer signed by a merchant even though there is no return consideration received in exchange for the promise. This is from U.C.C. 2-205.

Acceptance

4221.41 Acceptance is assent of the offeree to the terms of the offer.

4221.42 Offer + acceptance = mutual assent.

4221.43 The acceptance must conform to the terms of the offer. An acceptance that adds terms to the original offer is a counteroffer. See U.C.C. 2-207 for an exception for nonmaterial terms for contracts between merchants.

4221.44 The acceptance must be communicated to the offeror. Acceptance is effective when dispatched if an authorized method is used even if it is not received by the offeror.

    a. Dispatch means to send.

    b. If the method of acceptance is specified, that is the only authorized method.

    c. If the method of acceptance is not specified, the following would be authorized methods:

        (1) Same as the offeror used to convey the offer

        (2) Customary method used in this type of transaction

        (3) Prior method used between the parties in question

4221.45 The offeree must have knowledge of the offer for there to be an acceptance. You cannot accept what you do not know about. (This comes up in reward cases.)

4221.46 Silence does not constitute acceptance unless justified by prior dealings, or the parties agree that silence will operate as an acceptance.

4221.47 Acceptance may be by making a return promise (bilateral contract) or completion of an act (unilateral contract).

Creation of a Contract

4221.48 To create a contract, mutual assent (agreement) must be given. Real assent is lacking if a party is induced to contract by mistake, fraud, duress, or undue influence, in which case the wronged party can avoid the contract. A contract obtained by mistake, fraud, duress, or undue influence is voidable.

Fraud in the Inducement

4221.49 **Fraud in the inducement** is a false representation of a material fact intentionally made, justifiably relied upon, and resulting in injury.

4221.50 **Definitions**

    a. **Fact:** It is not an opinion or a prediction of what will happen in the future. An opinion by an expert may be considered a fact. A fact is something that can reasonably be subject to exact knowledge.

    b. **Material:** It must be related to something of substance and must be important.

    c. **Intentionally:** Known by the speaker to be false.

    d. **Justifiably:** No better information available. If the party knows the statement is false, or could easily and should reasonably have checked the statement, the reliance is not justifiable.

    e. **Injury:** Some damages result from the wrong.

4221.51 Fraud may be an act, an omission, a concealment, or a nondisclosure.

4221.52 Silence alone is not fraud unless there is a duty to speak based on the relationship between the parties.

4221.53 If the misrepresentation is innocent and not made with the intent to deceive, the injured party may rescind the contract, but cannot obtain damages for the tort of deceit. Deceit is the tort equivalent to *fraud in the inducement* for contracts.

Fraud in the Execution

4221.54 **Fraud in the execution** results from the substitution of one document for another. The contract so executed is void because there is no consent to contract.

4221.55 The person signing either does not intend the signature to show agreement to a contract or is misled, through no negligence of their own, as to the contents of the writing.

Duress

4221.56 **Duress** is a wrongful act that compels contractual agreement through fear.

4221.57 Duress is subjective (what a person thinks), not objective (what a person shows). Age, sex, experience, intelligence, and relation of the parties must be considered.

4221.58 The acts leading to duress need not be illegal, although they often are.

4221.59 The threats can be against the individual, someone closely related to the individual, or their property.

4221.60 Threat of a civil suit is not duress. A person has the right to file a civil suit.

4221.61 Threat of criminal suit may be duress.

4221.62 Mere argument, advice, persuasion, or annoyance is not duress.

4221.63 Duress makes the contract voidable.

Undue Influence

4221.64 **Undue influence** is unlawful control exercised by the dominant party, which is a substitute for the free will of the dependent party.

4221.65 It is similar to duress but is generally applied to persons in a close confidential relationship, such as the following:

   a. Husband and wife
   b. Parent and child
   c. Guardian and ward
   d. Trustee and beneficiary

4221.66 Courts are not strict in determining what is a confidential relationship.

4221.67 If there is a transaction where the dominant party has gained at the expense of the dependent party, the undue influence is presumed, and the burden of proof is upon the dominant party to prove otherwise.

Mistakes

4221.68 **Mutual mistake.** If both parties are mistaken as to a material fact (neither at fault or both at fault equally), there is no contract. It is void because there has been no agreement.

Example: The parties enter a contract for the sale of a horse, both believing the horse is alive at the time. If the horse in fact has died before the agreement is entered, the contract is voidable by either party based on mutual mistake.

4221.69 **Unilateral mistake.** One party is mistaken. There is a good contract so long as the other party is not aware of the mistake and has not entered the contract to take advantage of the mistaken party.

4221.70 A mistake as to value is an ordinary risk in the normal business transaction. A contract cannot generally be avoided for a mistake in value.

4221.71 A mistake of law as to the parties' legal rights under the contract is not grounds for rescission.

4221.72 If a person knowingly and voluntarily signs a document, the person conclusively presumed to know its contents and assent to them. The person cannot avoid the contract for mistake.

Unconscionable Contract

4221.73 If the court finds as a matter of law that a contract is unconscionable, it may reform the contract to serve justice (see U.C.C. 2-302).

4221.74 If the parties are in unequal bargaining positions, the courts are more likely to find an unconscionable contract and will allow the party in the inferior position to avoid the obligation.

4221.75 An unconscionable contract is a contract that no rational person would enter into and no ethical person would want to impose on another person.

4222 Performance

Consideration

4222.01 **Consideration:** A bargained-for exchange in which there is legal detriment to the promisee or legal benefit to the promisor.

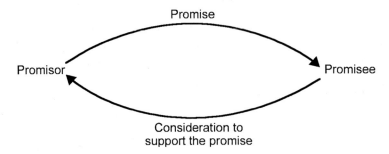

4222.02 Consideration is the inducement to enter the contract. Most people would not enter into a contract unless they received something in return.

4222.03 Consideration must be bargained for. It cannot have already happened. Past consideration is not valid consideration.

4222.04 A contract must be supported by consideration to be valid and enforceable. It is one of the four elements of a contract.

4222.05 Relative value differs from legally sufficient consideration. The two considerations need not be of approximately the same value. Generally, courts do not look at the adequacy of the consideration.

4222.06 Consideration applies only to executory contracts, not executed contracts. If the contract is already completed, there is no longer a question of the contract being enforceable.

4222.07 The following are not good considerations:

a. **Illusory promise:** A promise in form but not in substance.

(1) A promise to buy whatever gasoline I want for the next year. This is a promise in form but really obligates me to do nothing. I could buy nothing or I could buy 500 gallons of gasoline and still not break my promise.

(2) Output and requirement contracts are not illusory.

b. **Doing what one is already legally bound to do by previous contract or statutory duty**—for instance, paying a police officer to catch criminals. This is a preexisting duty.

c. **Past consideration**—cannot be consideration for a new contract.

d. **Moral consideration**—a person may feel morally obligated, but this does not mean legally obligated.

4222.08 Consideration may be any of the following:

a. A return promise to do something the promisee is not legally obligated to do

b. An act other than a return promise that the promisee is not legally obligated to do

c. A forbearance—promising not to do something that the promisee has a legal right to do

4222.09 **Liquidated debt:** Debt for a sum that both parties agree as to amount. Payment of a lesser sum will not discharge the balance since the debtor has a preexisting duty to pay the agreed amount. Some additional consideration is needed to support a promise to forget about collecting the remaining amount. Paying before the due date would be such additional consideration if both parties agree. This is because prior to this agreement the party is not legally obligated to pay early.

4222.10 **Unliquidated debt:** Amount is disputed in good faith by the parties. Payment of a sum less than the amount suggested by one of the parties discharges the obligation if the other party accepts the lesser amount as full payment.

4222.11 **Promissory estoppel**

a. A substitute for consideration

b. Three elements must exist for promissory estoppel to apply:

(1) A promise by the promisor that is reasonably expected to be relied upon by the promisee

(2) The promisee does in fact detrimentally rely on the promise

(3) Injustice can be avoided only by enforcing the promise

c. A promise that induces action is binding without return consideration if justice is served.

d. **Example:** A promise of a donation to a charity where the charity makes expenditures in anticipation of the donation but does not give return consideration to support the promise to donate. Promissory estoppel could be used to enforce the promise to donate to the charity even though the promise is not supported by consideration.

4222.12 **Seals.** If a document has a seal, consideration is conclusively presumed. The U.C.C. negates the effect of seals for sale of goods contracts. A seal can be the word *seal* on the contract.

4222.13 Promises that do not require consideration under the U.C.C.

    a. A claim for breach of contract for sale of goods can be discharged without consideration if a written waiver is signed and delivered.

    b. A written offer (promise) by a merchant to buy or sell goods cannot be withdrawn for the time stated, even though the offeree has not given return consideration to be binding.

4222.14 A promise that does not require consideration under the common law.

A renewed promise to pay a debt that cannot be enforced, because of the statute of limitations, needs no new consideration.

Illegal Bargains

4222.15 An agreement whose formation or performance is a tort, a crime, or is opposed to public policy constitutes an illegal bargain.

4222.16 The court will not enforce an illegal bargain, generally leaving the parties where the court finds them. This means the court will not adjust the equities between the parties. The courts will sometimes grant relief to the following persons even though they are involved in an illegal bargain:

    a. A party that the violated law intended to protect. States have laws that require all physicians to be licensed by the state. An unlicensed physician who contracts with a patient has violated the licensing statute making the agreement an illegal bargain. The courts will help the patient, but not the physician. The licensing statute was enacted to protect patients from unlicensed physicians.

    b. A party that is not in a good bargaining position when making the agreement. This party is said to be not equally at fault (not *in pari delecto*). Courts will sometimes grant relief to this type of party.

    c. A party who seeks to back out of an illegal bargain before execution.

    d. A party to an agreement where part is legal and part is illegal. Sometimes the courts will grant relief if the obligations are severable. This means the courts will separate the agreement to make an enforceable portion and an unenforceable illegal bargain.

4222.17 Violation of statutes

    a. Criminal statutes: The bargain is always illegal and unenforceable. The following are examples:

        (1) Bribing a government employee to get a contract

        (2) An agreement to commit any statutory crime, such as hiring a hit man to kill someone

    b. Licensing statutes: Illegal and unenforceable only if licensing is for regulatory purposes.

        (1) **Regulatory:** The purpose is to protect the public against unqualified persons, for instance, a lawyer, physician, CPA, or real estate broker. The professional could not recover on the agreement if they were not properly licensed.

        (2) **Revenue-producing:** The purpose is to raise money, for instance, a salesperson's license or driver's license. Failure to have a license required by a revenue-producing statute does not make the contract illegal. Either party could recover on the contract.

    c. Wagering or gambling agreements: The agreement is not enforceable. A gambling agreement results when the parties bet on the outcome of an uncertain event in which the parties have no interest other than the bet.

d. **Usury:** Charging an interest rate in excess of the maximum allowed by statute for the loan of money.

   (1) Remedy for violation:

   (a) Lender collects principal but not interest in the majority of states.

   (b) Lender collects principal and interest up to the lawful rate.

   (c) Lender loses both principal and interest.

   (2) The following are permissible and are not usury violations:

   (a) Collecting a legal maximum interest in advance

   (b) Adding a reasonable service fee to cover incidental cost of inspection, service, and recording

   (c) Having a credit price and a cash price for the sale of goods

   (3) Statutory exceptions allowing higher interest rates exist for the following:

   (a) Pawnshops

   (b) Small loan companies

   (c) Credit unions

   (4) Usury does not apply to time payment differential on the sale of goods, only to lending money.

   (5) Many states have enacted consumer credit laws to make consumer credit sales, revolving charge accounts, and interest on credit card sales subject to maximum percentages of interest. In effect, the loan of money and these consumer transactions are both subject to a maximum interest rate.

4222.18 **Bargains contrary to public policy are also illegal and unenforceable.**

   a. **Restraint of trade**

   (1) Society looks with disfavor on any agreement that unnecessarily restrains a person from exercising their trade, business, or profession.

   (2) Contracts in total restraint of trade are always illegal. A contract in total restraint of trade has as its prime purpose the establishment of a monopoly through price fixing, division of sales territories, and limitations on production.

   (3) A contract in partial restraint of trade, if the restraint is secondary to the main purpose of the contract (ancillary in nature).

   (a) It is enforceable if the following are true:

   i. The restraint is necessary to protect the purchaser, the remaining members of the business, or the employer.

   ii. The restraint is reasonable as to time and geographic area.

   iii. The restraint does not place an undue burden on the promisor.

   iv. It occurs in the sale of a business or profession, the sale of property, or the termination of employment.

   (b) This type of agreement is referred to as a covenant not to compete.

   (4) Courts will enforce the remainder of the contract without the restraint of trade clause.

   b. Obstructing the administration of justice, such as bribing a judge or juror

   c. Corrupting public officials

d. **Exculpatory clause:** Provision of a contract which relieves a person of liability for his own negligence. Attempts to do this are sometimes seen on signs in parking lots, such as "Not responsible for damage done to your car." Courts do not enforce exculpatory clauses that are determined to be contrary to public policy.

e. Unduly influencing legislative or executive action

Contractual Capacity

4222.19 Every party to a contract is presumed to have contractual capacity until shown otherwise.

4222.20 **Minors**

    a. A minor's contract is voidable at their option, but the other party to the contract may not avoid the contract.

    b. Generally, the age of majority, when the individual is no longer a minor, is the age of 18.

    c. Contracts by a minor for necessities:

        (1) A minor will still have to pay the reasonable value of necessities. This may or may not be the same as the contract price. This is a quasi-contractual obligation imposed by the courts to prevent unjust enrichment.

        (2) What is a necessity is a question of fact. Necessities have always been considered food, clothing, lodging, and medical services not supplied by a parent. Items for health, education, and transportation may be necessities in some cases.

        (3) In order to recover, the burden of proof as to what is a necessity rests with the adult seller.

    d. **Disaffirmance**—getting out of the contract.

        (1) A minor may disaffirm contracts while still a minor and for a reasonable time after reaching majority.

        (2) It may be an express or an implied disaffirmance.

        (3) If a minor has the goods, the minor must return them to the seller to disaffirm a contract for the sale of the goods. The goods can be in any condition. The right to disaffirm is not conditioned on being able to return the goods.

        (4) A disaffirmance of a conveyance of land can only be done after the minor reaches majority; however, the minor who sold land and disaffirmed the contract can retake the land before reaching the age of majority.

        (5) A minor who has sold goods may not be able to regain the goods even if they disaffirm. The U.C.C. allows a person with a voidable title to transfer good title to a good-faith purchaser for value. If the adult has sold the goods to someone else in good faith and for value, the minor cannot get them back. The minor can get the money equivalent to the value of the goods.

        (6) A minor is liable for torts if the torts are independent of the contract. Misrepresentation of age is a good example of a tort that precedes, and is independent of, the contract of sale.

        (7) Contracts a minor may not be able to disaffirm include the following (it varies by state):

            (a) Educational loans

            (b) Court-approved contract (court has already checked to see that the contract is fair)

- (c) Enlistment contract
- (d) Insurance contract
- (e) Medical care
- (f) Bank account
- (g) Stock transfer
- (h) Business contract
- (i) Marriage contract

    e. **Ratification**

       (1) A person is liable on a contract made during their minority if they ratify the contract. A minor can ratify a contract only after reaching the age of majority.

       (2) Ratification may be expressed in words or implied by actions.

       (3) Retention of goods for an unreasonable time after reaching majority age can amount to ratification of the contract.

    f. A parent is not liable for the minor's contracts unless the minor is acting as the parent's agent.

    g. A minor's contracts are voidable, not void.

4222.21 Insane persons

    a. A mentally incompetent person may avoid liability on contracts. Test: "Is the person unable to understand the effect and nature of the act?"

    b. It is not necessary to be adjudicated insane to be mentally incompetent.

    c. If a person is adjudicated insane, their agreements are void. If a person can show that they are mentally incompetent without prior adjudication of insanity, their contracts are voidable.

4222.22 Intoxicated persons

    a. A contract made by a person so intoxicated so as not to be able to comprehend the nature and effect of the transaction may be voidable. This is allowed very rarely since courts may view the intoxicated person as being at least partly responsible for their condition.

    b. Being drunk is not a good excuse to disaffirm a contract.

4222.23 Private corporations

    a. A private corporation exceeding its scope of power is held liable on its contracts.

    b. *Ultra vires*: Beyond the corporation power.

4222.24 Public corporations

    a. A city or a town is an example of a public corporation.

    b. There is generally no recovery against a public corporation that exceeds its legal limits in making a contract.

Statute of Frauds

4222.25 Certain contracts must be in writing and signed by the party to be charged or the contract is unenforceable if the statute of frauds is raised as a defense.

4222.26 The party to be charged is the party that is being sued to be held liable on the contract.

4222.27 The writing may be a note, a memorandum, an informal notification, or more than one writing. The writing must meet the test of reasonable certainty and should contain the name of the parties, subject matter, and material terms and conditions.

4222.28 **Sale of goods**

    a. A contract for the sale of goods for a price of $500 or more must be in writing to be enforceable.

    b. **Exceptions** (see U.C.C. 2-201):

        (1) Between merchants, an oral contract is enforceable if one of the merchants sends a written confirmation to the other and receives no objection within 10 days after sending it. Both merchants are bound on the oral contract.

        (2) If the goods are specially manufactured (for a unique purpose and cannot be resold as shelf items), the oral contract is enforceable if the manufacturer has made a substantial start on their manufacture before the other party tries to withdraw from the contract.

        (3) If the goods have been paid for and accepted or received and accepted, the oral contract is enforceable. If there has been only a partial acceptance of the goods or a partial payment, the contract is enforceable only to that extent.

        (4) If the person admits in court to have contracted with the plaintiff, the contract is enforceable to the quantity admitted.

4222.29 **Securities.** Any contract for the sale of securities must be in writing to be enforceable.

4222.30 Sale of intangible personal property (e.g., a patent, copyright, or royalty right) for more than $5,000 must be in writing.

4222.31 **Transfer of an interest in land**

    a. Transfer of any interest in real property must generally be in writing.

    b. This provision would include sale of real estate, giving a lien (mortgage) on the real estate, certain leases of real estate, and granting an easement.

    c. Agreements to build on real estate, do other work such as landscaping, or to lend money to buy real estate do not generally have to be in writing to be enforceable.

    d. **Exception:** An oral contract for the sale of real property is enforceable if the buyer takes possession and/or makes valuable improvements on the land. This is called the doctrine of part performance. A valuable improvement might be building a house on the land.

4222.32 **Contracts that cannot be performed within one year**

    a. An executory, bilateral contract that cannot be performed within one year of making the contract is not enforceable unless it is in writing.

    b. Time starts from the time of making the contract, not from the time of expected performance.

    c. If it is possible to perform the contract within one year, no matter how improbable, an oral contract is enforceable.

4222.33 **A promise to pay the debt of another must be in writing to be enforceable.**

    a. This is called *suretyship* (see also section **4241**).

b. The person making the promise to pay the debt of another is called a surety or a guarantor.

c. The promise must be to the creditor. This is referred to as a collateral promise rather than an original promise.

d. An oral promise to the debtor to pay the debtor's debt is enforceable even if oral. It was not made to the creditor and is considered an original promise.

e. **Exception:** An oral promise made to the creditor to pay the debt of the debtor made solely to benefit the person making the promise. It is called the main purpose doctrine or the leading objective rule.

4222.34 **Promise where one and only one of the promises is a promise to marry**

a. Must be in writing to be enforceable.

b. Mutual promises to marry may be oral and still be enforceable.

c. **Example:** Father promises boy $10,000 if he promises to marry daughter. Boy will not get the $10,000 if father does not want to pay if it was an oral promise.

Parol Evidence Rule

4222.35 **Parol-extrinsic:** Evidence about the agreement that is not in the written agreement. It is outside the agreement and usually oral.

4222.36 **Parol evidence rule.** Extrinsic (oral or written) evidence is not admissible to add to, alter, or vary the terms of a written contract. The reason is that all preliminary negotiations are merged into the writing.

4222.37 It is all right to make an oral contract and a written contract at the same time if the subjects of the contracts are different.

4222.38 It is not a violation of the parol evidence rule to admit oral testimony to prove or explain the following:

a. The contract was obtained by fraud, misrepresentation, duress, or undue influence.

b. The contract was illegal.

c. An oral condition precedent to the contract. Until the condition precedent happens, the contract does not come into existence.

d. A subsequent modification has been made to the contract. This could be oral or written.

e. Ambiguous terms in the written contract. Oral testimony would clear it up.

f. The contract is voidable due to a party being a minor or being insane.

g. Fill in blank spaces regarding nonmaterial terms if the written contract is incomplete. These terms cannot vary, alter, or contradict the written contract.

Interpretation of Contracts

4222.39 If the terms of a contract are unclear or conflict, the court will apply principles of construction and interpretation.

4222.40 Under rules of interpretation and construction for contracts:

a. > means "control."

- b. The contract is construed as a whole, not in parts. The whole contract is read with all words and sentences taken in context.
- c. Written > typed > printed. Written provisions of a contract are more likely to be current than printed words on a preprinted contract.
- d. Specific > general. If there is an inconsistency, the specific provisions control and qualify the meaning of the general provisions.
- e. Lawful > unlawful. If a provision can be interpreted in both a lawful and unlawful manner, it is assumed that the parties intended a lawful purpose.
- f. Words > figures to determine amount or quantity.

    Example: A check says "$467.88" and "Four hundred seventy-six dollars and eighty-eight cents." The amount the bank will pay is $476.88 (words) instead of $467.88 (figures). Figures are easier to transpose than are quantities written in words.

- g. Public > private. Where the public interest is affected, an interpretation is preferred that favors the public interest over any private interests of the parties.
- h. Nondrafter > drafter. Since the drafter wrote the contract, he has already had the opportunity to clear up any ambiguity. Therefore, any ambiguity will be resolved in favor of the nondrafter by construing the contract language most strongly against the drafter.

Assignments of Contracts

4222.41 **Assignment of Contracts**

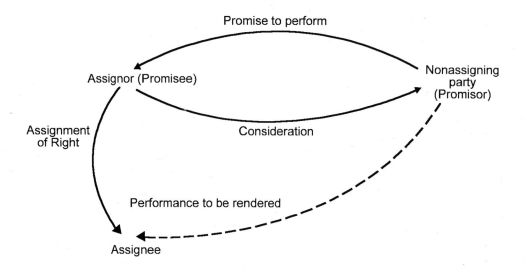

- a. An assignment involves a transfer by one party to a contract of some or all of the rights to another person who is not a party to the original contract.
- b. Agreement or consent of the nonassigning party is not needed.
- c. **Assignor:** Transferor. The party that transfers the rights.
- d. **Assignee:** Transferee. The party that gets the rights from the transfer.
- e. No special language is necessary to make an assignment.
- f. May be a total transfer or partial transfer of the contract by the assignor.
- g. No consideration is necessary. The assignment may be part of another contract or it may be gratuitous.

        h.   When a right is assigned, the assignor normally no longer has any interest in the right.

4222.42   **Contracts ordinarily are assignable.**

        a.   An offer to enter into a contract is not assignable.

        b.   Rights (legal ability to get something from the other party) are almost always assignable.

4222.43   **Contracts not assignable**

        a.   Contracts involving personal services, such as an employment contract.

              Example: Your employer could not assign your employment contract to the local garbage department to work on the garbage truck.

        b.   Contracts that involve the personal satisfaction of one of the parties.

              Example: An artist tells you that you need not pay the $100 fee for painting your portrait unless you are personally satisfied. You could not assign the contract to someone else who might be more critical of any painting.

        c.   Contract that states the contract is not assignable can generally not be assigned.

            (1)   A person may assign the right to sue the other party for damages even though the contract prohibits assignment.

            (2)   A creditor may assign the contract of an account debtor even though the contract prohibits assignment.

        d.   Contracts where the assignment would treat the nonassigning party unfairly by doing the following:

            (1)   Materially changing the duties under the contract

            (2)   Materially increasing the burden or risk under the contract

            (3)   Materially impairing the chance of obtaining return performance

4222.44   **Effect of assignment**

        a.   **Liability of assignor:** Still liable to the nonassigning party on the contract for the promised consideration.

        b.   **Liability of assignee:** Not liable just because of receiving the assignment. The nonassigning party may be able to sue the assignee if the nonassigning party is a creditor beneficiary of the contract between the assignor and assignee.

        c.   **Rights of assignee:** Assignee gets all the rights of the assignor. Any defenses the nonassigning party has against the assignor can be asserted against the assignee (up to the amount of the assignment).

        d.   To protect the right to receive performance, the assignee should notify the nonassigning party of the assignment. If there is no notice and the nonassigning party performs for the assignor, their duty under the contract is discharged.

        e.   If no notice is given and the nonassigning party performs for the assignor, the assignee can sue the assignor for damages.

4222.45   **Priorities among successive assignees where the assignor assigns the same rights to more than one assignee**

        a.   **American rule:** First assignee in point of time prevails. Once the assignment is made, the assignor has nothing left to assign.

        b.   **English rule:** First assignee to give notice to the nonassigning party prevails.

Delegation of Duties

4222.46 **Delegation of duties** (legal obligations to do something for another party)

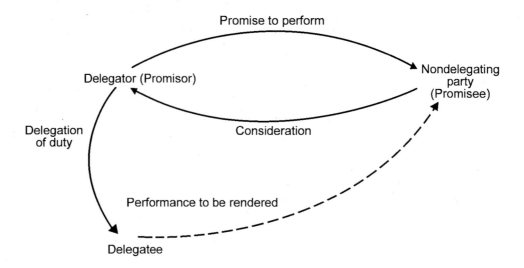

4222.47 Delegation involves the appointment by the delegator of the delegatee to render performance on the delegator's behalf.

4222.48 Though the terms are often used interchangeably, assignment and delegation are the flip sides of the coin. Rights are assigned. Duties are delegated.

4222.49 When a duty is delegated, the delegator is still liable to the nondelegating party for any defective performance by the delegatee. The delegator is relieved from liability only if the nondelegating party agrees to release by way of a novation (see section **4224.13**).

4222.50 **Nondelegable duties**

    a. A duty is nondelegable when performance by the delegate would vary materially from performance by the delegator.

    b. If the contract is based on the artistic skill or unique ability of the delegator, the duty to perform is nondelegable.

    c. If the duties under the contract simply call for mechanical skills, which can be tested by objective standards, the duty to perform is delegable.

    d. **Examples:**

        (1) A contract duty to paint a portrait would generally be nondelegable, because it involves unique abilities and artistic skill.

        (2) A contract duty to install a concrete driveway would generally be delegable, because this usually would involve only mechanical skills that can be tested by objective standards.

4223 Third-Party Assignments

4223.01 Third-party beneficiary

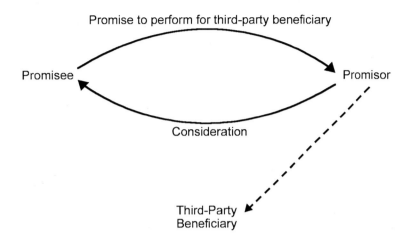

4223.02 A contract where a party promises to render a performance for a third party is a third-party beneficiary contract.

4223.03 **Donee beneficiary:** Promisee's purpose was to make a gift to the third-party donee beneficiary. There is no legal duty owed to the beneficiary by the promisee.

4223.04 **Creditor beneficiary:** Promisee's purpose was to satisfy a legal duty owing from the promisee to the third party.

4223.05 **Incidental beneficiary:** Person who benefits from a contract being carried out, but who the makers of the contract did not intend to benefit.

4223.06 A third-party intended beneficiary (creditor or donee) can sue to enforce the contract.

4223.07 A donee beneficiary can sue only the promisor to enforce the third-party beneficiary contract. A creditor beneficiary can sue either the promisor or the promisee to enforce the third-party beneficiary contract.

4223.08 An incidental beneficiary cannot sue to enforce a contract.

4224 Discharge, Breach, and Remedies

Remedies for Breach of Contract

4224.01 Contract remedies are intended to put the injured party in the same position as if the contract had been performed insofar as possible. If the legal remedy of damages is not adequate, the equitable remedies of specific performance, rescission, or injunction may be used.

4224.02 **Compensatory damages**

    a. **For sale of goods contracts**

        (1) If buyer has the goods and title has transferred to buyer— the contract price.

(2) If seller has the goods and no title has transferred—the difference between the contract price and the fair market value. If not a stock item, the seller will have to sell the goods in a good faith transaction (not to a related party) to determine the fair market value.

(3) Seller will not deliver the goods—the difference between the contract price and the fair market value. Buyer will have to buy identical item from another seller (called covering) to establish the fair market value. If the buyer is able to get the goods from another seller at a price that is lower than the contract price, the buyer need not refund the savings. There would be no compensatory damages.

b. For sale of services

(1) Seller will not perform—difference between fair market value of getting the services done and the contract price.

(2) Buyer refuses to accept the services—profit that would have been made by the seller.

c. Damages include any expense that is reasonably foreseeable with whatever knowledge the breaching party has.

4224.03 Nominal damages

a. A small sum, like $1, would be awarded for breach of contract either:

(1) with no compensatory damages or

(2) when unable to prove damages with reasonable certainty.

b. No logical person would sue if they expected to collect only nominal damages. They would still have to pay attorney fees and would actually lose money by bringing the suit. In awarding nominal damages, the court merely pats the winner on the back, says they were in the right and awards them a small amount.

4224.04 Special damages

a. These are damages that would not be foreseen unless a person has some special information about the circumstances.

b. The wronged party can recover these special damages only if the breaching party has this special information. With this specific information the damages would be foreseeable.

4224.05 Liquidated damages

a. Amount of damages agreed upon in advance and included in the contract.

b. Used where the actual compensatory damages would be difficult to determine (e.g., breach of construction contracts).

c. Court will enforce liquidated damage provisions in a contract if they were a reasonable estimate of the probable loss when made and are not a penalty used to prevent a breach.

d. If the courts find the liquidated damage provision to be a penalty, they will disregard the provision and make the party try to prove compensatory damages.

4224.06 Mitigation of damages. After a breach, the injured party must take steps to minimize further loss. The injured party failing to take this action will not be able to collect the additional portion of the damages that could have been prevented.

4224.07 Restitution

a. An equitable remedy available only if damages would be inadequate to make the nonbreaching party whole.

       b. Also called *rescission.*

       c. Restitution involves return to the injured party of the consideration given or its value.

4224.08   **Specific performance**

       a. An equitable remedy available only if damages would be an inadequate remedy for breach of the agreement.

       b. Two common examples of specific performance:

           (1) **Contract to buy (not sell) land.** Each piece of land is unique unto itself. The buyer could not go into the marketplace and buy an exact equivalent.

           (2) **Purchases of unique personal property.** These are one-of-a-kind items. They would also include items like the controlling interest stock of a corporation. The buyer could not go into the marketplace and buy the same thing.

       c. The promise must be clear and relate to a specific identifiable item.

       d. No specific performance for the following:

           (1) **Building contract.** Too difficult for the court to supervise.

           (2) **Personal services.** This would be involuntary servitude prohibited by the Thirteenth Amendment. Courts will enforce a negative injunction to prohibit the individual from doing that type of work during the period of the contract. This has happened when a professional basketball player jumped to a new league but still had a contract with the old team.

Discharge of a Contract

4224.09   **Discharge:** End of a contractual obligation.

4224.10   **Discharge related to conditions**

       a. Condition precedent not happening

           (1) A condition precedent must occur before a contractual obligation comes into existence.

           (2) **Example:** Buyer agrees to purchase a house on condition that he can obtain a $90,000 loan at 7.75% or lower within the next 30 days. Being able to get the loan is a condition precedent to being obligated to purchase the house.

       b. Condition subsequent happening

           (1) A condition subsequent ends an existing contractual obligation.

           (2) **Example:** Returning the goods in 10 days and getting a full refund if you are not satisfied. This is a condition subsequent that terminates the promise to pay a refund for the goods after 10 days have passed.

4224.11   **Performance of the contract**

       a. Complete performance

           (1) Discharges the contract.

           (2) Must be exactly as agreed.

       b. Substantial performance

           (1) Slightly less than complete performance where there is technically a breach, but it is not material.

(2) Allows the person to recover the contract price less the amount needed to complete the contract.

(3) Usually applies to construction contracts where it is an oversight rather than intentional.

    c. Partial performance

        (1) Less than substantial performance.

        (2) Allows the person to recover only by a quasi-contract (contract implied in law) for the value of the services rendered. A quasi-contract is imposed only when unjust enrichment would result.

4224.12 Payment

    a. Full payment discharges the obligation.

    b. Payment by check is conditional upon the check being paid by the bank.

    c. Partial payment:

        (1) Must be applied as directed by the debtor.

        (2) If the debtor does not specify, the creditor may apply it in any way.

        (3) It may even be applied to a debt which would be unenforceable because the statute of limitations has run out.

    d. Consumer credit statutes may give the priorities of application to the creditor for some types of transactions.

4224.13 Novation: A three-party agreement where the creditor agrees to release the debtor and take some third party as a substitute. The novation discharges the contractual obligation of the original debtor.

4224.14 Accord and satisfaction

    a. **Accord:** Agreement between the two contracting parties where some different performance will replace the original performance. An accord by itself does not discharge the contractual obligation.

    b. **Satisfaction:** Carrying out the accord.

    c. An accord and satisfaction discharges the contractual obligation.

4224.15 Impossibility of performance

    a. **Subjective impossibility**—it is inconvenient or too expensive to carry out the contract—does not discharge the contract.

    b. **Objective impossibility**—discharges the contractual obligation.

        (1) Nobody could carry out the contract. This is real impossibility.

        (2) Either of the following would be objective impossibility:

            (a) Subject matter of the contract is destroyed after making the contract but before performance is due.

            (b) The person who is to perform a personal services contract dies after making the contract but before the performance is due.

      c. Doctrine of commercial frustration—excuses contractual performance if both parties contemplated the happening of some event that does not occur.

      Example: Coronation case in England. People rented apartments to see the parade, but the king got sick and the parade was canceled.

4224.16 Release

    a. Give up the legal right to sue the other party on a contract.

    b. It discharges the other party.

    c. A release of one joint obligor releases all other joint obligors.

4224.17 Covenant not to sue

    a. Promise not to sue a person, discharges that person.

    b. Promise not to sue does not affect other joint obligors.

4224.18 Operation of law

    a. The statute of limitations runs out so that a lawsuit can no longer be filed to enforce the contract.

    b. The person is discharged of the debt through bankruptcy proceedings.

4224.19 Breach

    a. Failure to perform without a valid reason.

    b. Breach by one party discharges the duty of performance by the other party.

4224.20 Anticipatory breach

    a. Repudiation of the contract by informing the other party that the contract will be breached when performance is due.

    b. Other party may do either of the following:

      (1) Wait and do nothing until the time for performance passes.

      (2) Sue immediately for the breach even though the time for performance has not yet arrived; however, damages may be difficult to establish.

Joint and Several Contracts

4224.21 Joint contracts

    a. Two or more persons jointly promise to perform an obligation.

    b. Suit must be brought against all joint promisors.

    c. Judgment may be levied against one of the joint promisors.

    d. A release of one joint obligor releases all of them.

    e. If one joint promisor dies, the remaining promisors remain obligated to perform.

    f. A promise by two or more persons is presumed to be joint.

    g. "We jointly promise" is a joint contract.

4224.22 Several contracts

a. Severally = individually.

b. Two or more persons who separately agree to perform the same obligation may be sued individually.

c. If one of several obligors dies, his estate is liable on the obligation.

d. A release of one obligor has no effect on the other.

e. "Each of us promises" or "We severally promise" is a several contract.

4224.23 Joint and several contracts

a. Two or more persons are bound both jointly and severally.

b. "We, and each of us, promise" are joint and several contracts.

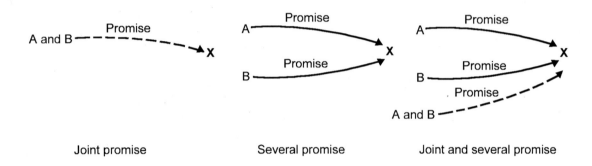

Joint promise   Several promise   Joint and several promise

4230 Uniform Commercial Code

4231 Sales Contracts

Goods

4231.01 Definition of goods. Tangible personal property that is movable at the time of identification to the sales contract:

a. Including unborn young of animals, growing crops, or timber and minerals or structures if they are severed from the real estate by the seller

b. Not including money, investment securities (stocks and bonds), or the right to sue (Money treated as a piece of property, such as a collectible coin, would be a good. Taken from U.C.C. 2-105.)

4231.02 Why classification as goods is important. Article 2 of the U.C.C. only applies to goods. If the subject of the sale is something other than goods, Article 2 of the U.C.C. will not apply. If real property or services are the subject of the contract, common law rules will be used.

4231.03 Real versus personal property. If a contract calls for the severing of property, the law of the U.C.C. applies if the seller is the person who will sever the property from the land. If the buyer severs the property, the law of real property will apply to the contract.

4231.04 **Tangible versus intangible property.** Tangible property is property that has physical existence. Intangible property has value but has no physical existence. A patent or a copyright is an example of intangible property.

4231.05 **Goods and services in the same transaction.** The predominant feature of the contract controls which law is used.

4231.06 **Goods and real property in the same transaction.** If goods and real property are a part of the same contract, use the U.C.C. for the goods and the real property law of the state where the real property is located for the real estate portion of the contract. Different laws can apply to different parts of the same contract.

4231.07 **Future goods.** Future goods are goods that are not in existence or not identified to the sales contract (U.C.C. 2-105(2)). If goods are classified as future goods, neither title nor risk of loss can pass from the seller to the buyer. The agreement would be a contract to sell rather than a contract of sale. This diagram helps explain future goods.

	Do the goods exist?	
	Yes	No
Are the goods identified to the particular sales contract? — Yes	Goods	Future Goods
Are the goods identified to the particular sales contract? — No	Future Goods	Future Goods

4231.08 **Fungible goods.** Fungible goods are goods where any unit is the equivalent to any other unit. Goods can be fungible by nature, such as bulk wheat, bulk corn, and oil; or fungible by usage, such as bales of cotton and cases of canned goods. Fungible goods are an exception to the requirement that the portion that the buyer is purchasing must be separated from the mass and identified to the contract. Instead, the buyer gets a fractional interest in the undivided whole. The buyer can get title, risk of loss, and an insurable interest in the buyer's fraction of the undivided whole.

Merchants

4231.09 **Definition of merchant (from U.C.C. 2-104):**

a. Deals in that kind of goods

b. Holds himself out as a merchant

c. Employs an agent or broker who is a merchant in that kind of goods

4231.10 Classification as a merchant is important because the U.C.C. places higher standards on merchants than on nonmerchants. Also, special rules may apply to the transaction if either one or both of the parties are merchants.

4231.11 The standard for merchant versus nonmerchant is good faith. For a merchant, good faith means honesty in fact and observing commercial standards of fair dealing in the trade. For a nonmerchant, good faith means honesty in fact. From U.C.C. 2-103(1)(b) and 1-201(19).

Laws That Apply to Contracts for the Sale of Goods

4231.12 **Laws that apply to contracts for the sale of goods:**

a. **English common law.** The law relating to the sale of goods came mostly from the portion of the English common law called the Law Merchant.

    b. **American common law.** This law was transported from England to the United States by the colonists. With only minor modifications, it is the same as the English common law.

    c. **English Sales of Goods Act in 1893.** This was a codification of the existing English common law of that date.

    d. **Uniform Sales Act of 1906.** This was a codification of the existing American common law of that date. It was adopted by virtually all of the states.

    e. **Article 2 of the Uniform Commercial Code promulgated in 1952.** This has been adopted by all states except Louisiana. It incorporated many of the modern commercial practices in actual use and supersedes the prior laws that affected the sale of goods.

General Principles of the U.C.C.

4231.13   General principles of the U.C.C.

    a. The U.C.C. is to be liberally construed to promote its purpose rather than be a technical law.

    b. The U.C.C. simplifies, clarifies, and modernizes the law pertaining to the sale of goods.

    c. The U.C.C. permits expansion of the law through custom, usage, and agreement.

    d. The U.C.C. provides a uniform law regarding the sale of goods in all the states.

    e. Unless expressly disallowed, the contracting parties may vary the provisions of the U.C.C. by agreement.

    f. Contracting parties must act in good faith in performing their obligations under the U.C.C.

    g. Merchants are held to a higher standard of conduct than are nonmerchants.

U.C.C. Changes in the Common Law Regarding Contracts for the Sale of Goods

4231.14   Irrevocable offers

    a. **From U.C.C. 2-205.** A written offer signed by a merchant:

        (1) is irrevocable:

            (a) for the stated time period in the offer.

            (b) for a reasonable time if there is no stated time.

            (c) but the "stated" or "reasonable" time cannot exceed three months.

        (2) does not require consideration to be irrevocable. These are called firm offers. This section applies only to offers made by merchants.

    b. **Common law.** Unless the offer is part of an option contract with consideration being given in exchange for the promise to keep the offer open, an offer can be revoked any time before acceptance.

4231.15   How definite the agreement must be to be a contract

    a. **U.C.C.** An agreement is enforceable as a contract even if terms are not specified, as long as the court feels the parties intended to make a contract and there is a reasonable basis for giving a remedy. From U.C.C. 2-204(3).

    b. **Common law.** An agreement is not enforceable as a contract unless it is definite in all material terms.

4231.16 **Price not contained in agreement**

    a. **U.C.C.** If the parties intend to be bound by their agreement that fails to state a price, it is enforceable as a contract as long as the parties identify the goods and the quantity to be delivered. The price will be the reasonable price at the time for delivery if no other way of determining the price was stated in the contract. This situation is described as an open price provision. From U.C.C. 2-305.

    b. **Common law.** Material terms such as price must be agreed upon or the agreement is too indefinite to be enforced as a contract.

4231.17 **Time not contained in agreement**

    a. **U.C.C.** If time is not stated in the agreement, it will be the reasonable time as determined from the circumstances. This situation is described as an open time provision. From U.C.C. 2-309 and 2-310.

    b. **Common law.** Material terms such as time must be agreed upon or the agreement is too indefinite to be enforced as a contract.

4231.18 **Delivery provision not contained in agreement**

    a. **U.C.C.** If the terms of delivery are not stated, the goods are delivered to the buyer at the seller's place of business or at the seller's residence. If both parties know that specifically identified goods are at some other place, that place will be the location where the seller will deliver the goods to the buyer. From U.C.C. 2-308. If the agreement contemplates shipping the goods but does not mention the arrangements, the seller has the right to make the arrangements as long as they are done in good faith and within commercial reasonableness. From U.C.C. 2-311 and 2-307.

    b. **Common law.** Material items such as delivery terms must be agreed upon or the agreement is too indefinite to be enforced as a contract.

4231.19 **Method by which an offer can be accepted**

    a. **U.C.C.** The acceptance can be communicated in any reasonable manner under the circumstances in order to be effective when it is dispatched. From U.C.C. 2-206(1).

    b. **Common law.** The acceptance must be communicated in the same manner as the offer or in the manner in which the offer is received in order to be effective when dispatched.

4231.20 **Accepting an offer to buy goods**

    a. **U.C.C.** A seller can accept an offer to buy goods for prompt shipment by either of the following:

        (1) Prompt shipment

        (2) Prompt promise to ship

    From U.C.C. 2-206(1)

    b. **Common law.** If the offer proposes a unilateral contract (a promise for an act), acceptance can only be by the act of shipping the goods. If the offer proposes a bilateral contract (a promise for a promise), acceptance can only be by promising to ship the goods.

4231.21 **Accepting an offer by promising to ship the goods**

    a. **U.C.C.** From U.C.C. 2-206(2). Allows acceptance of an order by shipping the goods.

    b. **Common law.** Not recognized under the common law.

4231.22 Additional or different terms in acceptance or confirmation

a. **U.C.C.** If an acceptance or confirmation contains additional or different terms, it is an acceptance of the offer and a contract is formed unless either of the following is true:

(1) It was not sent within a reasonable time.

(2) Acceptance is expressly made conditional on the offeror's agreement to the additional or different terms.

b. The additional or different terms are proposals for addition to the contract. If both parties are merchants, the additional or different terms become a part of the contract, unless any of the following are true:

(1) The original offer prohibited any additional or different terms.

(2) They materially alter the offer.

(3) The offeror gives notice of objection within a reasonable time. From U.C.C. 2-207. This is referred to as the "Battle of the Forms Provision."

c. **Common law.** An acceptance cannot contain added terms and must agree exactly with the offer. If there are additional or different terms, the communication is a counteroffer and not an acceptance.

4231.23 Formation of contract by conduct of the parties

a. **U.C.C.** If the parties act as if they have made a contract, they have a contract, even if material terms are not agreed upon. The U.C.C. is used to fill in the missing terms. From U.C.C. 2-207(3).

b. **Common law.** If the terms of the agreement are not definite, there is no contract, even if the parties act as though there was a contract.

4231.24 Modification of a contract

a. **U.C.C.** An agreement modifying a contract for the sale of goods needs no consideration to be enforceable. The modification must be in writing only if either of the following is true:

(1) The original contract said it could only be modified by a writing.

(2) The modified contract is within the statute of frauds. From U.C.C. 2-209(1).

b. **Common law.** A promise to modify a contract needs new consideration to make the promise enforceable. Prior consideration will not support a new promise to modify an enforceable contract.

4231.25 Statute of frauds

a. **U.C.C.** Contracts for the sale of goods for $500 or more must be evidenced by a writing signed by the party to be charged. An oral agreement between merchants is enforceable if one of the parties sends a confirmation of the oral agreement to the other party, and the recipient does not object within 10 days after receipt. An oral agreement for the sale of goods is enforceable if it involves specially manufactured goods, the defendant admits in court that the contract was made, the goods were received and accepted, or the goods were paid for and accepted. From U.C.C. 2-201.

b. **Common law.** Certain types of contracts are not enforceable unless there is a writing signed by the party against whom enforcement is sought.

4231.26 **Sufficiency of the writing as related to the statute of frauds.** To be enforceable, agreements within the statute of frauds must be evidenced by a writing sufficient to show that a contract was made between the parties and must be signed by the person against whom enforcement is sought.

    a. U.C.C. The requirement of a writing is liberally construed and need only contain the quantity of the goods since the contract is not enforced beyond the quantity stated. From U.C.C. 2-201.

    b. Common law. The writing must contain all the material terms of the agreement. These include price, quantity, and terms of payment.

4231.27 **Confirmation of an oral agreement**

    a. U.C.C. An oral agreement between merchants is enforceable if one of the parties sends a written confirmation of the oral agreement to the other, and the recipient does not object within 10 days after receipt. From U.C.C. 2-201.

    b. Common law. Oral agreements over the statutory amount are not enforceable. There are no provisions for a confirmation.

4231.28 **Specially manufactured goods (as related to the statute of frauds)**

    a. U.C.C. An oral contract for the sale of specially manufactured goods for $500 or more is enforceable if the seller has made the goods or made substantial commitments for their manufacture before the buyer tries to revoke the contract. From U.C.C. 2-201.

    b. Common law. There are no provisions for specially manufactured goods.

4231.29 **Admitting an oral contract was made (as related to the statute of frauds)**

    a. U.C.C. If a party admits in court that an oral contract was made, it is enforceable to the extent of the admission. From U.C.C. 2-201.

    b. Common law. Admitting in court that an oral contract was made would not make the oral contract enforceable.

4231.30 **Oral contract when payment is made and accepted**

    a. U.C.C. An oral agreement where payment for the goods was made and accepted is enforceable for the amount of goods paid for. Additional amounts in the oral agreement are not enforceable. From U.C.C. 2-201.

    b. Common law. There are no provisions for payments made and accepted.

4231.31 **Oral contract when goods are received and accepted**

    a. U.C.C. An oral agreement where goods are received and accepted is enforceable for the amount of the goods received and accepted. Additional amounts in the oral agreement are not enforceable. From U.C.C. 2-201.

    b. Common law. There are no provisions for goods received and accepted.

4231.32 **Seals**

    a. U.C.C. A seal is totally inoperative and has no effect on contracts or offers dealing with the sale of goods.

    b. Common law. A contract containing a seal is conclusively presumed to have consideration. The seal is an impression made on wax on the document, the word "seal," or the letters "L.S." (meaning *locus siglli*) in place of the seal.

Interpretation of Sales Contracts

4231.33 **Interpretation of sales contracts:** If language in a contract is unclear, the courts will consider these factors in interpreting a contract:

    a. **Course of performance.** What the parties have done previously when dealing with each other. One occasion cannot establish a course of performance. From U.C.C. 2-208(1).

    b. **Course of dealing.** Sequence of previous conduct between the parties to a particular transaction that establishes a common basis of understanding for interpreting their expressions and conduct. A single occasion cannot create a course of dealing. From U.C.C. 1-205.

    c. **Usage of trade.** Practice that is regularly observed in the trade so as to justify the expectation that it will be observed in future transactions of the same kind.

    d. The course of performance controls the course of dealing, which controls the usage of trade.

4231.34 **Unconscionable agreement**

    a. *Unconscionable* means grossly unfair and oppressive.

    b. A court can refuse to enforce part or all of a contract if the court finds the contract or any of its terms to be unconscionable. From U.C.C. 2-302.

4231.35 **Ownership rights in goods**

    a. Whomever owns goods has the rights of ownership.

    b. The owner of the goods can do any of the following:

        (1) Use the goods.

        (2) Give the goods to someone else.

        (3) Sell the goods to someone else.

    c. If the owner sells the goods, the ownership rights may not all transfer to the buyer at the same time.

    d. When there is a sale, *ownership rights* can be divided into three categories:

        (1) Legal title

        (2) Risk of loss

        (3) Right to insure the goods

    e. The parties can agree when legal title and risk of loss will pass from the seller to the buyer. This is almost never done.

    f. If the seller and buyer do not agree when title and risk of loss will pass, they may specify the terms of how the goods are to be delivered. The U.C.C. has default conditions based on the delivery terms that specify when title and risk of loss will pass.

4231.36 **When title to goods is important:**

    a. **Taxation of goods.** Whomever has legal title to the goods can be taxed.

    b. **Inventory.** Whomever has legal title will include the goods in their inventory.

    c. **Judicial seizure.** Goods may be judicially seized by a creditor from a debtor if the debtor has legal title to those goods. If the goods are merely in the possession of the debtor, with legal title in some other person, the goods may not be seized to satisfy the debts of the debtor.

Passage of Title from the Seller to the Buyer

4231.37 Title passes from the seller to the buyer when there is a sale of goods.

4231.38 Title can pass from the seller to the buyer only if the goods exist. No title can pass on goods that do not yet exist, called future goods. See U.C.C. 2-105.

4231.39 Title can pass from the seller to the buyer only if the goods are identified to the particular sales contract. Identification occurs when the seller identifies goods held in inventory as belonging to the particular sales contract in question. See U.C.C. 2-401.

4231.40 If the goods are existing and identified, title passes when the seller and buyer specify in the sales contract. If there is no agreement between the parties, the following rules apply:

    a. If the contract is a shipment contract, title passes when the seller delivers the goods to the carrier.

    b. If the contract is a destination contract, title passes when the goods are offered for delivery at the destination. The destination is usually the city where the buyer is located.

    c. If existing and identified goods are to be delivered without physical movement of the goods and:

        (1) there is a document of title that the seller must deliver, title passes when the document of title is delivered.

        (2) there is no document of title, title passes when the sales contract is made.

Imperfect or Defective Title in the Goods

4231.41 There are three degrees of title:

    1. Perfect. Good and valid title to the goods.

    2. Voidable. Valid until someone exercises a right to invalidate that title.

    3. Void. No title rights were ever obtained. In other words, a void title is no title at all.

4231.42 A purported seller with void title cannot pass any title to a purported buyer. A thief has a void title to the goods that were stolen and cannot pass any title to the person buying from the thief.

4231.43 A seller possessing a perfect or voidable title in goods can pass title to a buyer. If the title to the goods is perfect, the seller cannot dispute the buyer's title. If the title is voidable, the seller can always reclaim the goods directly from the buyer. The following are situations when the seller could void the buyer's title and reclaim the goods. But the party who has voidable title can convey title to a third person.

    a. The buyer used fraud in the inducement to influence the seller to enter the contract.

    b. The buyer's check in payment for the goods is returned from the bank "NSF."

    c. The buyer is insolvent when the goods are purchased on credit. The seller can void the buyer's title and reclaim the goods within 10 days after the buyer receives the goods. If the buyer misrepresents the solvency in writing within three months before delivery, the seller can void the title and reclaim the goods even after the 10-day limit. See U.C.C. 2-702.

    d. The seller is a minor. A minor may void a contract for the sale of goods, void the buyer's title, and reclaim the goods.

  e. The seller delivered the goods to a person who was impersonating the buyer.

  f. The seller and buyer agree that title will pass only when the seller is paid, but the buyer gets possession of the goods before he pays the seller.

4231.44 The seller's right to reclaim the goods from the buyer is absolute, but this right does not extend to certain third parties who take perfect title to the goods. The owner cannot reclaim the goods from either of the following:

  a. A good faith purchaser from a buyer with voidable title

  b. Buyers in the ordinary course of business who purchase from a merchant to whom the goods were entrusted

4231.45 **Good faith purchaser from a buyer with voidable title.** A good faith purchaser must give value. Any contractual consideration is value.

4231.46 **Entrustment.** The entrustment is usually a mutual benefit bailment. The most common examples are so the merchant could sell the goods for the entruster, for repair of the goods, or goods simply left with the merchant after purchase until they are picked up.

  Example: Sam entrusts his watch to a jewelry shop for repair. The jeweler, a merchant, could sell the watch to a buyer in the ordinary course of business who would obtain perfect title.

4231.47 **When risk of loss is important:**

  a. Risk of loss is important when the goods are damaged or destroyed during the time period of the sale.

  b. Whomever has risk of loss for the goods when they are damaged or destroyed will suffer the economic loss.

  c. Only the seller or the buyer can have risk of loss. A bailee, common carrier, or warehouseman never has risk of loss. They might be, however, liable for negligence that causes damage to the goods while the goods are in their possession.

Risk of Loss

4231.48 Risk of loss is the attribute of ownership that makes the person liable for damage to or destruction of the goods. Risk of loss is with either the seller or the buyer; there is no other possibility.

4231.49 Legal title and risk of loss often pass together but not always.

4231.50 Risk of loss will pass from the seller to the buyer when they mutually agree. Rarely is this done. If there is no agreement, the U.C.C. specifies default times that will be used depending on how the buyer is to obtain possession of the goods.

4231.51 Insurance owned by the buyer or seller has no effect on risk of loss. If risk of loss is with the buyer, the buyer's insurance company will indemnify the loss. If risk of loss is with the seller, the seller's insurance company will indemnify the loss.

4231.52 **Splitting risk of loss.** The parties may agree that the risk of loss will be split between the parties.

4231.53 Risk of loss is not important unless the goods are damaged or destroyed. Only then are the parties concerned as to who has risk of loss.

4231.54 If there is no breach and there is a shipment contract, risk of loss passes to the buyer when the goods are delivered to the carrier. The seller must also contract with the carrier for transportation to the buyer and notify the buyer of the shipment. See U.C.C. 2-509.

4231.55 If there is no breach and there is a destination contract, risk of loss passes when the seller tenders delivery of the goods at their destination. See U.C.C. 2-509.

4231.56 When a carrier is involved, title and risk of loss pass at the same time.

4231.57 If there is no breach, the goods are held by a bailee (usually a warehouse), and:

  a. there is a negotiable document of title (warehouse receipt), risk of loss passes when the buyer gets the negotiable document of title.

  b. there is a nonnegotiable document of title, risk of loss passes when the document is presented to the bailee. If no presentation is made, it passes after the buyer has a reasonable time to present it. If the bailee fails to honor the document, risk of loss does not pass.

  c. there is no document of title, risk of loss passes when the bailee acknowledges the buyer's right to the goods.

4231.58 If there is no breach, no carrier, and:

  a. the seller is a merchant, risk of loss passes when the buyer receives the goods. This could happen when the merchant seller delivers the goods to the buyer or when the buyer picks up the goods at the merchant seller's place of business.

  b. the seller is a nonmerchant, risk of loss passes when the seller tenders (offers) delivery to the buyer.

4231.59 If the seller sends nonconforming goods that the buyer rejects, risk of loss stays with the seller until the seller cures the defect.

4231.60 If the seller sends nonconforming goods that the buyer accepts knowing of the defect, the risk of loss passes to the buyer.

4231.61 If the seller sends nonconforming goods that the buyer accepts not knowing of the defect but then revokes the acceptance once the defect is discovered, risk of loss stays with the seller from the beginning. The seller's risk of loss is only to the amount that the buyer's insurance fails to cover the loss.

4231.62 If the buyer breaches the contract, risk of loss shifts to the buyer for existing and identified goods for a reasonable time and only to the extent that the seller's insurance fails to cover the loss. Title to the goods would remain with the seller.

4231.63 Study the following chart of transfer of title and risk of loss:

Type of Delivery or Sale	When Title Passes	When Risk of Loss Passes
Transfer of Title and Risk of Loss Chart		
Delivery by Movement of Goods		
Physical delivery by carrier:		
Shipment contract (unusual type of sale between merchants)	Delivery of goods to carrier	Delivery of goods to carrier
Destination contract	Tender of goods at destination	Tender of goods at destination while in possession of carrier
Other contracts requiring physical delivery by seller:		
Merchant seller	Completion of seller's duties of delivery	Buyer's taking physical possession of goods
Nonmerchant seller	Completion of seller's duties of delivery	Tender of delivery
Delivery Without Movement of Goods		
Goods in seller's possession:		
Merchant seller (usual type of sale between merchant and nonmerchant)	Identification of goods or making sales contract, whichever is later	Buyer's taking physical possession of goods
Nonmerchant seller	Identification of goods or making sales contract, whichever is later	Tender of delivery
Goods in bailee's possession:		
Delivery by negotiable document of title	When buyer takes possession of document	Receipt of document of title by buyer
Delivery of nonnegotiable document of title	When buyer takes possession of document	Honoring of document by bailee or buyer's inaction after receipt
Delivery by procuring acknowledgment without document of title	Identification of goods or making of contract, whichever is later	Bailee's acknowledgment of buyer's right
Delivery by giving buyer written directions to bailee	Identification of goods or making of contract, whichever is later	Honoring of document by bailee or buyer inaction after receipt
Sale on approval	Acceptance by the buyer	Acceptance by the buyer
Sale or return	Pursuant to above rules	Pursuant to above rules

4231.64 Role of the carrier in the sales contract

a. Carriers are parties that transport goods. They can be common carriers who must offer their services without discrimination to all who seek their services and are regulated by the government. They can be private carriers who can serve whom they wish and are not regulated by the government.

b. Carriers are not a party to the sales contract. Carriers may contract with the seller or buyer to transport the goods from the seller's location to the buyer's location.

c. Carriers do not own the goods at any time. They are bailees who have possession and control of the goods while they are in transit or in temporary storage. Carriers do not have title or risk of loss. Only the seller and buyer can have title and risk of loss.

d. Carriers can be liable for loss or damage to the goods. The carrier is liable to the seller or buyer depending upon who has risk of loss when the goods were lost or damaged. Common carriers are not liable for damage or loss if it was caused by any of the following:

   (1) The shipper (seller)

   (2) The inherent nature of the goods being transported

   (3) Intervention of governmental authority

   (4) An act of war

   (5) An act of God

4231.65 Insurable interest

a. The seller has an insurable interest in the goods so long as the seller has title, risk of loss, or has a security interest in the goods.

b. The buyer has an insurable interest in the goods from the time existing goods are identified to the contract.

c. Both the seller and the buyer can have an insurable interest in the same goods at the same time.

4231.66 Sale on approval

a. The buyer has the right to return the goods even though the goods conform to the contract.

b. The purpose of delivery of the goods is for the use of the potential buyer.

c. The buyer can use the goods before any commitment to purchase the goods.

d. The time the potential buyer has to decide whether to purchase or not is specified in the contract. If no time is specified, it is a reasonable time.

e. The transaction is a bailment until the buyer decides to buy.

f. Title and risk of loss stay with the seller until the buyer decides to purchase.

g. If the potential buyer does not decide to purchase, the seller must pay for their return. Title and risk of loss would never leave the seller.

4231.67 Sale or return

a. Buyer has the right to return the goods even though the goods conform to the contract.

b. The purpose of delivery of the goods is for the buyer to resell the goods.

c. The buyer can return goods that cannot be resold.

d. Time to return the unresold goods is specified in the contract. If not specified, it is a reasonable time.

e. Title and risk of loss pass to the buyer under the same rules as other sales.

f. The buyer pays for the return of the goods not resold.

g. Title and risk of loss stay with the buyer until the goods are actually returned to and received by the seller. The return is at the buyer's risk and expense.

4231.68 **Consignment**

a. A consignment is the delivery of goods to an agent who tries to resell the goods.

b. A consignment is treated as a sale or return.

4231.69 **Seller's obligations on sales contracts**

a. **Tender delivery of the goods.** See U.C.C. 2-503(1). The seller must tender delivery of conforming goods. The tender must be at a reasonable hour of the day and goods must be held available for the buyer for a reasonable period of time.

   (1) If the sales agreement is a shipment contract, the seller tenders delivery of the goods to a carrier at the point of shipment. The seller must send any documents covering the goods to the buyer and notify the buyer of shipment.

   (2) If the sales agreement is a destination contract, the seller must tender delivery at the destination. The seller must give notice and send any necessary documents to the buyer.

b. **Delivery of the goods.** The following are the ways the seller can deliver goods to the buyer:

   (1) Buyer can pick up the goods from the seller.

   (2) Seller takes the goods to the buyer.

   (3) Seller ships the goods by a common carrier to the buyer.

   (4) Goods held by a third party are made available to the buyer without any documents of title being involved.

   (5) Goods held by a third party are made available to the buyer using a document of title.

What Happens If the Sales Contract...

4231.70 What happens if the sales contract does not specify anything about the place of delivery?

a. If a carrier is not involved, it is the seller's place of business or residence if there is no business.

b. If a carrier is to be used, the terms of shipment govern the place of delivery.

See U.C.C. 2-308.

4231.71 What happens if the sales contract specifies that the law of a particular state will be used to resolve any dispute coming from the sales contract? The law of that state will be used if the transaction is reasonably related to that state. See U.C.C. 1-105.

4231.72 What happens if the sales contract has express terms that differ with course of performance, course of dealing, and usage of the trade?

- a. Express terms control over course of performance, course of dealing, and usage of the trade.
- b. Course of performance controls over course of dealing and usage of the trade.

    See U.C.C. 2-208.
- c. Course of dealing controls over usage of the trade.

    See U.C.C. 1-205.

4231.73 **What happens if the sales contract is performed by a person with a reservation, using the words "under protest" or "without prejudice"?** The person's rights are not prejudiced by such performance.

4231.74 **What happens if the sales contract is indefinite?** If the parties have intended to make a contract and there is a reasonably certain basis for an appropriate remedy, the contract is enforceable.

4231.75 **What happens if the sales contract offer does not specify the method of acceptance?** The offer can be accepted in any reasonable way. See U.C.C. 2-206.

4231.76 **What happens if the sales contract offer is to buy goods for prompt shipment?** The offer can be accepted by a prompt shipment or by a prompt promise to ship. See U.C.C. 2-206.

4231.77 **What happens if the sales contract acceptance contains added or different terms from those in the offer?**
- a. A contract is formed unless the acceptance is made conditional on assent by the offeror to the added or different terms.
- b. The added terms are proposals for addition to the contract.
- c. If both parties are merchants, the added terms become part of the contract unless the following are true:
    - (1) The offer states that added or different terms are not permitted.
    - (2) They materially alter the offer. Price and quantity are always material. The use of a different common carrier would probably be immaterial.
    - (3) The receiving merchant objects to the added or different terms within a reasonable time.

4231.78 **What happens if the sales contract is modified by the parties in a later agreement?**
- a. No consideration is needed for the modification to be binding.

    See U.C.C. 2-209.
- b. If the modified amount is $500 or more, the agreement must comply with the statute of frauds.
- c. If the modified amount is under $500, an oral modification agreement is enforceable.

4231.79 **What happens if the sales contract is performed by the original promisor delegating the performance to another equally competent person?** The delegation is permitted unless the following are true:
- a. The original sales contract prohibited such a delegation.
- b. The other party had a substantial interest in the original promisor performing the promise.

    See U.C.C. 2-210.

4231.80 What happens if the sales contract is performed by one of the parties assigning their right to receive performance to a third party?

    a. Rights can be assigned unless:

        (1) the original sales contract prohibited such assignments.

        (2) the assignment would materially:

            (a) change the duty of the other person,

            (b) increase the burden or risk imposed on the other person, and

            (c) impair the chance of getting return performance.

    b. A right to sue for the other person's breach can be assigned even if the original sales contract prohibited such assignments.

    See U.C.C. 2-210.

4231.81 What happens if the sales contract did not contain the price?

    a. The contract is still valid.

    b. The price will be the reasonable price at the time of delivery.

4231.82 What happens if the sales contract contains real property as the consideration for the payment of the goods?

    a. The U.C.C. applies part of the sales contract to the goods.

    See U.C.C. 2-304.

    b. The U.C.C. does not apply part of the sales contract to the real property. The real property law of the state where the property is located will be used.

4231.83 What happens if the sales contract does not mention the time for payment? Payment is due at the time and place where the buyer is to receive the goods. See U.C.C. 2-311.

4231.84 What happens if the sales contract allows one of the parties to specify some of the particulars of performance?

    a. The contract is valid and not too indefinite.

    b. The party specifying the particulars must act in good faith and within limits set by commercial reasonableness.

    See U.C.C. 2-311.

Statute of Frauds in the U.C.C.

4231.85 The statute of frauds deals with which contracts must be in writing to be enforceable. The U.C.C. incorporated some of the provisions of the statute of frauds from the common law but made significant changes. Only the statute of frauds within the U.C.C. is covered here.

4231.86 An oral contract for the sale of goods for a price of less than $500 is always enforceable.

4231.87 An oral contract for the sale of goods for a price of $500 or more is not enforceable unless the following are true:

    a. There is a writing signed by the person against whom the contract's enforcement is sought to show that the contract was made. The writing can be a written contract, a memo, or a series of writings between the parties. The U.C.C. is very liberal on what can be a writing. The only terms that must be in the writing are the quantity of the goods.

- b. The contract is between two merchants, one of the merchants sends a written confirmation to the other, and the receiving merchant does not object within 10 days after the confirmation is received. A confirmation is often sent after a telephone conversation when goods are ordered.
- c. The goods are specially manufactured for the buyer and there is no repudiation of the contract before the seller makes the goods or makes substantial commitments for their manufacture.
- d. The party admits in court that the contract was made.
- e. The goods were accepted and paid for by the buyer.
- f. The goods were received and accepted by the buyer.

See U.C.C. 2-201.

4231.88 If a contract has been modified, it is the modified contract amount that determines whether the modified contract is within the statute of frauds.

4231.89 An oral contract for the sale of securities (stocks and bonds) is not enforceable unless the following are true:
- a. There is a writing signed by the person against whom the contract's enforcement is sought to show that the contract was made for the stated quantity of described securities at a stated price.
- b. A certified security has been delivered and accepted, and the person receiving it has not sent a written objection within 10 days after receipt.
- c. An uncertified security has been registered, and the person has not sent a written objection within 10 days after receipt.
- d. Payment has been made.
- e. A written confirmation has been received by the party against whom enforcement is sought and the person has not sent a written objection within 10 days after receipt.
- f. The person admits in court that the contract was made. From U.C.C. 8-319.

4231.90 An oral contract for the sale of intangible personal property for over $5,000 is not enforceable unless there is a writing that shows the contract was made, shows the terms of the contract, and is signed by the person against whom enforcement is sought. This provision does not apply to the sale of goods or to securities. From U.C.C. 1-206.

4231.91 **Open price terms in a sales contract**
- a. A sales contract can be made without the parties agreeing on the price of the goods. At common law this would not be permitted because the agreement would be too indefinite.
- b. If the parties agree that the seller will set the price, the seller must do so in good faith.
- c. If the parties agree that the buyer will set the price, the buyer must do so in good faith.
- d. If the parties agree that one of them is to set the price, and that party fails to do so, the other party can do either of the following:
    (1) Treat the contract as canceled.
    (2) Set the reasonable price.
- e. If the parties agree to mutually set the price at some later time, that price will control.

  f. If the parties agree that the price will be set by some market standard or by some third party, that price will control.

  g. Otherwise, the price will be the reasonable price at the time for delivery.

Transfer of Contractual Rights and Duties to Third Persons

4231.92 A right is the claim to receive something from the other contracting party. A right for one contracting party is a duty for the other contracting party.

4231.93 Rights are more easily transferred to third persons than are duties.

4231.94 Transfer of a right is called assignment.

4231.95 Rights from a contract can be assigned unless either of the following is true:

  a. The contract prohibits the assignment of rights.

  b. The assignment would materially affect the other party by doing any of the following:

   (1) Changing her duty

   (2) Increasing her burden or the risk imposed on her

   (3) Impairing her chance of return performance

4231.96 The right to sue for damages for breach of contract can be assigned in all circumstances, even if the original contract prohibited such assignment.

4231.97 A duty is the obligation to do something for the other contracting party. A duty for one contracting party is a right to receive something for the other contracting party.

4231.98 Duties are more difficult to transfer to third persons than are rights.

4231.99 Transfer of a duty is called *delegation,* but the word *assignment* is sometimes used.

4231.100 Duties from a contract can be delegated unless either of the following is true:

  a. The contract prohibits the delegation of the duty.

  b. The other party has a substantial interest in having the original promisor perform the duty.

4231.101 Delegation of a duty does not contractually relieve the duty to perform or the contractual liability for a breach.

4231.102 A prohibition of assignment of the contract means that only the delegation of duties is prohibited unless circumstances indicate that rights also cannot be assigned.

4231.103 An assignment of the contract is an assignment of rights and a delegation of duties of the assignor. By assignor acceptance, the assignee promises to perform the duties under the contract. If the assignee fails to perform, the assignor or the other party to the contract can sue the assignee.

4231.104 All of the listed rules regarding the transfer of contract rights and duties to third parties are found in U.C.C. 2-210.

Terms in Sales Contracts

4231.105 F.O.B., city of shipment. F.O.B. means free on board. It is a delivery term that obligates the seller to put the goods in possession of the carrier at the expense of the seller. Title and risk of loss pass to the buyer when the carrier gets possession of the goods. The buyer must give any instructions needed for delivery. This is a shipment contract. An example would be: F.O.B., New Orleans. The seller ships from New Orleans.

4231.106 F.O.B., city of destination. F.O.B. means free on board. It is a delivery term that obligates the seller to deliver the goods to the buyer's city and tender delivery of the goods to the buyer at that location. Cost of transportation is paid by the seller. Title and risk of loss remain with the seller until tender of delivery. This is a destination contract. An example would be: F.O.B., Chicago. The buyer is in Chicago.

4231.107 F.O.B., city of shipment or destination, vessel/RR car/or other vehicle. In addition to city of shipment and destination obligations, the seller must load the goods on the vessel, railroad car, or truck at the seller's expense and risk of loss. The buyer must give instructions needed for delivery. An example would be F.O.B., New Orleans, Adabelle Lykes. Adabelle Lykes is a ship leaving the port of New Orleans. New Orleans could be the city of the buyer or seller.

4231.108 F.A.S., vessel or dock at a named port. F.A.S. means free alongside. It is a delivery term that obligates the seller to do the following:

    a. Deliver the goods to the side of the vessel or to a dock designated by the buyer.

    b. Get a bill of lading.

The buyer must give any instructions needed for delivery. An example would be F.A.S., Nashville Avenue Wharf in New Orleans.

4231.109 C.I.F. means that the price of the goods includes the cost of the goods, insurance on the goods to the place of destination, and freight cost to the place of destination. The seller is obligated to do the following:

    a. Put the goods in possession of the carrier and obtain a negotiable bill of lading to the named destination.

    b. Load the goods and get a receipt for the goods from the carrier showing that the freight has been paid for.

    c. Buy an insurance policy covering the goods during transit.

    d. Prepare an invoice for the goods and any other documents for the transportation.

    e. Promptly send all documents needed to perfect the buyer's rights.

When the seller tenders the documents, the buyer must make payment even though the goods are still in transit. The buyer has no right of inspection prior to acceptance of the documents.

4231.110 C. & F. means that the price includes cost of the goods and freight to the place of destination. Seller has the same obligations as C.I.F. except for those related to insurance.

4231.111 Ex-ship means "from the carrying vessel." Seller is obligated to have the goods unloaded from the ship at the seller's cost and have the carrier turn over the goods to the buyer. Risk of loss passes to the buyer when the goods are unloaded from the ship.

4231.112 No arrival, no sale. The seller must properly ship conforming goods. If the goods arrive, the seller must tender the goods to the buyer. If the goods are lost or deteriorate due to the seller's action, the seller is liable for breach of contract. If the goods are lost or deteriorate through no fault of the seller, the seller is not liable for breach of contract.

Warranties

4231.113 Definition. A warranty is an assurance or guarantee that goods will confirm to certain standards. Types of warranties include the following:

a. Warranty of title

b. Express warranty

c. Implied warranty:

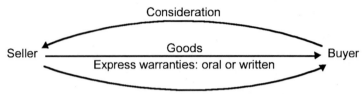

4231.114 Warranty of title. In a sales contract the seller warrants that the following are true:

a. Title is good.

b. Transfer is rightful.

c. Goods are delivered free of any security interest or lien.

The warranty of title can be excluded or modified only by specific language or by circumstances where the buyer knows that the seller does not claim clear title in the goods. A merchant in that type of goods additionally warrants that the goods are free of any infringement action by a third party. A buyer that furnishes specifications to the seller also warrants that the compliance with the specifications will not infringe on the rights of any third person.

4231.115 Express warranty. An express warranty is a warranty created by any of the following:

a. Affirmation

b. Promise

c. Description

d. Sample

e. Model

An express warranty is usually created by words. The words can be oral or in writing. The express warranty can result from the oral statements of a salesperson, descriptions of the goods in a written contract, descriptions of the goods in a catalog, and printing on the box that contains the goods. No particular words are necessary to create an express warranty. The express warranty need not be labeled and can be called a guaranty. The express warranty becomes a part of the sales contract. A warranty may be made after the transaction is complete and would require no new consideration.

4231.116 Express warranty by affirmation or promise

a. An affirmation of fact relates to existing or current situations.

b. A promise relates to future performance of the goods. See U.C.C. 2-313.

4231.117 Express warranty by description

    a. Any description of the goods creates an express warranty.

    b. An express warranty by description can result from words, pictures of the goods, drawings of the goods, blueprints, or technical specifications.

    c. The description of the goods made by a manufacturer can legally obligate the manufacturer, wholesaler, or retailer as an express warranty on the goods sold.

4231.118 Express warranty by sample or model

    a. A sample is taken from the goods to be sold.

    b. A model represents the goods to be sold, but is not taken from the quantity to be sold.

    c. The express warranty by sample or model says the goods will conform to the sample or model. See U.C.C. 2-313.

4231.119 Implied warranties. Implied warranties are imposed on the goods by operation of law. They are imposed automatically without agreement or consent of the contracting parties. The contracting parties need not even be aware of the existence of implied warranties. Implied warranties can be excluded or modified if the seller follows specified procedures.

4231.120 Implied warranty of merchantability. This warranty applies only to merchants who deal in that type of goods being sold. Nonmerchants are not subject to the implied warranty of merchantability. As a minimum to be merchantable, the goods must be as follows:

    a. Pass without objection in the trade as they are described.

    b. Be of fair, average quality as they are described (this applies only to fungible goods).

    c. Be fit for the ordinary purpose for which such goods are used.

    d. Be within the variation within each unit and among all units for type, quality, and quantity permitted by the agreement.

    e. Be adequately contained, packaged, and labeled as required by the agreement.

    f. Conform to the affirmations of fact or promises made on the container or label (if there are any).

The commercial service of food or drink for consumption on or off the premises is a sale of goods, and not a contract for services, to which warranties will apply. This warranty, like other warranties, can be excluded or modified. See U.C.C. 2-314.

4231.121 Implied warranty of fitness for a particular purpose. This implied warranty can apply to merchants or nonmerchants. It is imposed on the seller of goods if either of the following is true:

    a. The seller knows or has reason to know the particular purpose for which the goods are required.

    b. The seller knows or has reason to know that the buyer is relying on the seller's skill or judgment to select or furnish the goods.

The implied warranty of fitness for a particular purpose says the goods will be fit for that particular purpose. This warranty, like other warranties, can be excluded or modified. See U.C.C. 2-315.

4231.122 Exclusion or modification of warranty of title. This warranty can be excluded or modified by either of the following:

a. Specific language

b. Circumstances that give the buyer reason to know that the person selling the goods does not claim title or that the seller is selling only those rights of some third person

Example: A sheriff's sale of property seized from a debtor to pay a judgment creditor. See U.C.C. 2-312(2).

4231.123 Exclusion or modification of express warranty. A seller can avoid making any express warranties on the goods by careful actions and wording. The seller can claim that any statements are opinions or are sales puffing and not affirmations of fact or promises. But if a statement is deemed to create an express warranty, it generally cannot be disclaimed. See U.C.C. 2-316(1).

4231.124 Exclusion or modification of implied warranty of merchantability. A seller can disclaim orally or in writing, but it must mention "merchantability."

a. If it is in writing, it must be conspicuous.

b. Language such as "as is" or "with all faults" acts as an exclusion of this warranty.

c. If the buyer examines the goods before the sale, there is no implied warranty of merchantability for defects found or which should have been found by a proper examination.

d. If the buyer refuses to examine the goods before the sale at the request of the seller, there is no implied warranty of merchantability for defects that would have reasonably been found by the requested inspection.

e. The implied warranty of merchantability can be excluded by course of dealing, course of performance, or usage of the trade. See U.C.C. 2-316.

4231.125 Exclusion or modification of implied warranty of fitness for a particular purpose

a. Must be in writing and be conspicuous.

b. Words such as "There are no warranties that extend beyond the description on the face hereof" exclude all implied warranties, both merchantability and fitness.

c. Language such as "as is" or "with all faults" acts as an exclusion.

d. If the buyer examines the goods before the sale, there is no implied warranty of fitness for defects found or which should have been found by a proper examination.

e. If the buyer refuses to examine the goods before the sale at the request of the seller, there is no implied warranty of fitness for defects that would have reasonably been found by the requested inspection.

f. The implied warranty of fitness can be excluded by course of dealing, course of performance, or usage of the trade. See U.C.C. 2-316.

4231.126 Conflicting warranties on the same goods. Conflicting warranties are resolved in favor of the person who did not create the conflict. See U.C.C. 2-317.

4231.127 Beneficiaries of warranties. The buyer is a beneficiary of the warranties. The seller's warranty also extends to persons in the family or household or a guest of the buyer. See U.C.C. 2-318.

4231.128 Magnuson-Moss Warranty Federal Trade Commission Act

a. The Magnuson-Moss Warranty Act generally applies to written warranties given for consumer products. A consumer product is defined as personal property that is ordinarily used for personal, family, or household purposes.

b. The act is mainly enforced by the Federal Trade Commission (FTC) or an action brought by the attorney general. However, a consumer injured as a result of a violation of the act can also bring suit.

c. The provisions of the act generally apply to written warranties given by sellers on the sale of consumer products.

d. Nothing in the act requires that a seller give a written warranty. However, if a written warranty is made and the cost of the consumer goods is more than $10, the warranty must be labeled as being either a "full" or "limited" warranty.

e. If the cost of the consumer goods is more than $15 (by FTC Regulation), the warrantor is required to make certain disclosures in a full and conspicuous manner. The disclosures must be in a single document and presented in readily understood language.

f. The information that must be disclosed in the written warranty includes the following:

   (1) Who is protected by the warranty in the case where coverage is limited in some manner

   (2) What products, parts, characteristics, components, or properties are covered by the warranty

   (3) The action the warrantor will take in the case of a product defect

   (4) The time the warranty begins if it is a different date than the purchase date (also, the duration of the warranty must be stated)

   (5) What action must be taken by the consumer in order to obtain a remedy under the warranty

   (6) Any attempt by the warrantor to limit consequential damages or other remedies

g. If the seller provides a "full" written warranty, the warrantor must promise the following:

   (1) To remedy any product defect free of charge during the warranty period

   (2) To provide a refund of the purchase price or a replacement product if, after a reasonable number of attempts, the product cannot be repaired

h. A warrantor that provides a "limited" written warranty promises to do whatever is specifically stated in the warranty language.

4231.129 Chart of Warranties.

Warranties Involved When There Is a Sale of Goods Under the U.C.C.			
Made by	Type of Warranty	What Warranty Covers and When it Applies	How Excluded, Modified, or Disclaimed
Seller	Express	Can be an ad, catalog, or technical description. Relates to quality or quantity of the goods. Can be an affirmation of fact or promise, description, or sample or model. Not sales "puffing" or opinion. 2-313	By words or conduct if consistent with the written contract.
Seller	Implied	Implied by operation of law. This means it is imposed without action or knowledge of the contracting parties.	See below for merchantability and fitness for a particular purpose. Buyer inspects goods before making the contract. By course of dealing or usage of trade. 2-316(3)
Seller	Implied-Merchantability	Only applies to a merchant seller. Goods must be of average quality for that type of goods, properly packaged, and properly labeled. Does not mean perfect. 2-314 The older the goods and the more used, the less the warranty.	Must mention the word "merchantability" and any writing must be conspicuous. 2-316(2)
Seller	Implied-Fitness for a Particular Purpose	Applies to merchants and nonmerchants. Applies only if seller knows of buyer's intended application, seller knows that the buyer is relying on the seller to select the goods, and seller actually selects the goods. 2-315	Must be in writing and be conspicuous. 2-316(2)
Seller	Title	The seller owns the goods and the goods are not subject to any security interests or liens held by other persons.	Only by specific language or by circumstances that let the buyer realize the seller will not or cannot guarantee title. Like a sheriff's sale. 2-312(2)
Seller	Infringement	Applies only to a merchant. The goods will not be subject to a patent or trademark infringement suit by a third party. Does not apply if buyer supplies the specifications. 2-312(3)	Only by specific language or by circumstances that let the buyer realize the seller will not or cannot guarantee title. Like a sheriff's sale. 2-312(3)
Buyer	Infringement	Applies only to a merchant. If the buyer supplies the specifications, the buyer warrants that the seller will not be subject to a patent or trademark infringement suit by a third party due to the seller's manufacturing. 2-312(3)	Only by specific language or by circumstance that lets the buyer realize the seller will not or cannot guarantee title. Like a sheriff's sale.

Performance of the Sales Contract

4231.130 The duties of the parties to a sales contract can come from the following:

    a. **Those specified by the parties.** These are usually the most important terms. They often include the following:

        (1) Quantity of the goods

        (2) Price of the goods

        (3) Terms of payment for the goods

        (4) When delivery is to be made

    b. **Those that are customary in the trade** and between the two contracting parties from previous transactions.

    c. **Those that are determined by the U.C.C.** The U.C.C. allows the parties to the contract to agree upon any terms they wish; but if they do not agree, the U.C.C. specifies the default terms that will apply between the parties.

4231.131 **If any terms of performance are left open where one of the parties decides what or how to do something:**

    a. The party must use "good faith" and "commercial reasonableness."

    b. An objective standard is used to judge the activity.

4231.132 **Performance of the sales contract**

    a. This is a diagram of the sales contract:

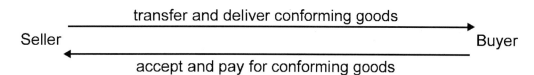

    b. These obligations are to be done concurrently (at the same time) unless the contracting parties agree otherwise.

        (1) Most of the time the parties do agree otherwise. The following are examples:

            (a) The merchant seller requires the consumer buyer to pay for the goods before delivery.

            (b) The merchant seller allows the merchant buyer to pay for the goods 30 days after the invoice is sent.

4231.133 **Legal action based on the sales contract**

    a. Neither party can sue unless they offer to perform their part of the contract. The seller must tender delivery of the goods. From U.C.C. 2-507. The buyer must tender payment. From U.C.C. 2-511.

    b. An offer to perform that is refused puts the refusing party in default.

    c. Legal action cannot be maintained unless the other party is in default on the sales contract.

d. The other party is in default if the person does any of the following:

   (1) Performs according to the contract

   (2) Tenders performance according to the contract

   (3) Is excused from tender of performance

4231.134 Seller's obligations

   a. **Tender of delivery.** Seller must make conforming goods available for the buyer and give the buyer notice so the buyer can take delivery.

   (1) Tender must be at a reasonable time and in a reasonable manner.

   (2) Delivery must be all at once (no piecemeal delivery, unless agreed upon).

   b. **Place of delivery.** The seller must perform according to the contract if the place of delivery has been agreed upon by the contracting parties. If no agreement has been made, the place of delivery depends on the circumstances and the terms of the contract.

   (1) If no carrier is involved, the place of delivery is the seller's place of business or the seller's residence if there is no business.

   (2) If both parties know the goods are located somewhere other than the seller's place of business, the place of delivery is that known location. The goods might be stored in a warehouse or held by a carrier awaiting delivery instructions. The seller must give the buyer a negotiable document of title (warehouse receipt or bill of lading) or notify the bailee of the buyer's right to receive the goods.

   (3) If it is a shipment contract involving a carrier, the contract requires the seller to ship the goods by a carrier. The seller must do the following:

   (a) Deliver the goods to a carrier.

   (b) Contract for their transportation.

   (c) Send to the buyer any transportation documents.

   (d) Notify the buyer that shipment has been made. Examples of shipment contracts involve these shipping terms:

   i. F.O.B., seller's city

   ii. F.A.S.

   iii. C.I.F.

   iv. C. & F.

   c. **Make a perfect tender.** The seller must ship or tender goods that conform exactly with the requirements of the contract.

   (1) A near-perfect tender is not sufficient.

   (2) Imperfect tender gives the buyer the right to reject all or part of the shipment.

   (3) The following are the exceptions to the requirement of a perfect tender:

   (a) The parties agree that a perfect tender is not necessary.

   (b) Cure. The seller can correct a mistake if conforming goods can be substituted for defective goods within the contract time for performance. If the contract time for performance has passed, there is no right for the seller to cure. If the seller intends to cure, the buyer must be notified of this intent.

(c) If the agreed manner of delivery becomes impractical or unavailable through no fault of either party, a commercially reasonable substitute can be utilized.

(d) A buyer in an installment contract cannot reject an installment unless the nonconformity impairs the value of the installment and cannot be cured.

(e) Commercial impracticability. Performance is excused by the happening of a contingency that both of the parties thought would not happen and was an essential part of the contract. At common law this was called "impossibility of performance" or "frustration of purpose."

(f) Destruction of identified goods. If goods identified to the contract are destroyed through no fault of either party and before risk of loss has passed to the buyer, both the seller and buyer are excused from performance.

4231.135 Buyer's obligations. These are the buyer's obligations on a sales contract.

a. **Accept goods that conform** to the contract.

(1) This acceptance can be by words or by conduct.

(2) Acceptance is presumed if the buyer had a reasonable opportunity to inspect and has not rejected the goods in a reasonable time.

(3) Using the goods for resale can be an acceptance by conduct.

b. **Pay for the goods** according to the agreed terms in the contract. If credit terms are agreed upon, the credit period usually starts on the day of shipment.

c. **Right to inspect the goods.** The buyer can inspect the goods before payment unless either of the following is true:

(1) The parties agree otherwise.

(2) The terms are C.O.D.

The time and place for inspection must be reasonable. The costs of inspection are paid by the buyer.

d. **Revocation of acceptance.** If the buyer has previously accepted nonconforming goods, the buyer can revoke that acceptance if the nonconformity substantially impairs the value of the unit or lot of the goods, and the buyer:

(1) accepted the goods on the assumption that the nonconformity would be corrected and it has not been corrected within a reasonable time.

(2) does not discover the nonconformity because it was difficult to discover before acceptance or because the seller's assurance that the goods were conforming kept the buyer from inspecting the goods. See U.C.C. 2-608(1)(a).

Notice of revocation of acceptance. The buyer must notify the seller of the revocation of acceptance. The revocation is not effective until notification is given to the seller. The notification must be within a reasonable time after discovery of the nonconformity or the buyer should have discovered the nonconformity. See U.C.C. 2-608(2).

e. **Make a partial acceptance.** The buyer can make a partial acceptance if only some of the goods are nonconforming. The buyer cannot accept less than a commercial unit.
Example: A case of canned food, not an individual can, would be a commercial unit.

f. **Rejection.** A buyer can reject the delivered goods. Rejection is proper if the goods are nonconforming to the contract. Rejection of conforming goods is a breach by the buyer.

g. **Failure to notify** the seller of a breach after delivery. If the buyer fails to notify the seller of a breach of contract due to nonconforming goods, the buyer cannot pursue any remedy against the seller.

h. Anticipatory repudiation. If the seller informs the buyer that the seller will not perform when performance is due, it is called an anticipatory repudiation (see section **4747**). The buyer can do any of the following:

(1) Wait until performance is due before resorting to remedies for breach.

(2) Resort to any other remedy for a breach immediately.

(3) Suspend performance on the contract.

Wrongful Action by the Buyer for Which the Seller Can Seek a Remedy, If the Seller and Buyer Have an Existing Sales Contract

4231.136 Buyer becomes insolvent

a. The seller can refuse further deliveries except for cash for the goods to be delivered, including payment for previously delivered goods under the contract.

b. The seller can stop delivery of goods in the hands of a common carrier or warehouse.

4231.137 Buyer has received goods on credit while insolvent

The seller can reclaim the goods by demanding their return within 10 days after the buyer receives the goods. The seller's right to reclaim the goods is subordinate to a (second) buyer in the ordinary course of business from the (first) buyer or a good-faith purchaser from the (first) buyer. Successful reclamation of the goods excludes all other remedies.

4231.138 Buyer has received goods on credit while insolvent after misrepresenting solvency to the seller in writing within three months before delivery

The seller can reclaim the goods by demanding their return. The seller's right to reclaim the goods is subordinate to a (second) buyer in the ordinary course of business from the (first) buyer or a good-faith purchaser from the (first) buyer. Successful reclamation of the goods excludes all other remedies.

4231.139 Buyer wrongfully rejects the goods

The seller can do the following:

a. Withhold delivery of additional goods.

b. Stop delivery of goods in the hands of a common carrier or a warehouse.

c. Identify goods to the remainder of the contract to determine damages.

d. Resell the goods and recover damages.

e. Recover damages for nonacceptance of the conforming goods.

f. Recover damages for the price.

g. Cancel the contract.

These actions by the seller are not mutually exclusive and the seller may utilize whichever action is appropriate under the circumstances.

4231.140 Buyer wrongfully revokes acceptance of the goods

The seller can do the following:

a. Withhold delivery of additional goods.

b. Stop delivery of goods in the hands of a common carrier or a warehouse.

c. Identify goods to the remainder of the contract to determine damages.

d. Resell the goods and recover damages.

e. Recover damages for nonacceptance of the conforming goods.

f. Recover damages for the price.

g. Cancel the contract.

These actions by the seller are not mutually exclusive and the seller may utilize whichever actions are appropriate under the circumstances.

4231.141 Buyer fails to make a payment due on or before delivery of goods

The seller can do the following:

a. Withhold delivery of additional goods.

b. Stop delivery of goods in the hands of a common carrier or a warehouse.

c. Identify goods to the remainder of the contract to determine damages.

d. Resell the goods and recover damages.

e. Recover damages for nonacceptance of the conforming goods.

f. Recover damages for the price.

g. Cancel the contract.

These actions by the seller are not mutually exclusive and the seller may utilize whichever actions are appropriate under the circumstances.

4231.142 Buyer repudiates the contract, wholly or partially

The seller can do the following:

a. Withhold delivery of additional goods.

b. Stop delivery of goods in the hands of a common carrier or a warehouse.

c. Identify goods to the remainder of the contract to determine damages.

d. Resell the goods and recover damages.

e. Recover damages for nonacceptance of the conforming goods.

f. Recover damages for the price.

g. Cancel the contract.

These actions by the seller are not mutually exclusive and the seller may utilize whichever actions are appropriate under the circumstances.

4231.143 Seller's rights on sales contracts

Arrangements for shipping. The seller has the right to arrange for shipment of the goods if these arrangements are not agreed upon. From U.C.C. 2-311.

4231.144 Buyer's rights on sales contracts

a. **Assortment of goods.** The buyer has the right to select the assortment of the goods to be purchased if the assortment is not agreed upon in the sales contract. From U.C.C. 2-311.

b. If the seller wants to deliver the goods piecemeal and the sales contract says nothing about it, the buyer may demand all goods be delivered at the same time.

c. If the seller delivers nonconforming goods, the buyer has the following options:

(1) He may reject all the goods.

(2) He may accept all the goods.

(3) He may accept some of the goods in commercial units and reject the remainder.

(4) He must notify the seller of a rejection within a reasonable time.

4231.145 Remedies. The parties to a sales contract can by agreement specify the remedies available in the event of a breach. They can by agreement do the following:

a. Limit the amount of damages that can be recovered. A court will ignore a limitation on remedies if limiting remedies "fails of its essential purpose." For example, assume a remedy is limited to repair of the good. If the goods are not repaired by the seller in a reasonable time, a court will ignore the limit.

b. Alter the amount of damages that can be recovered.

c. Provide for additional remedies.

d. Provide for remedies that act as a substitute for those already in the U.C.C. For example, the seller may state on the package that the only remedy is refund of the purchase price.

e. Limit consequential damages so long as the limit is not unconscionable.

f. Exclude the use of consequential damages so long as the limit is not unconscionable.

g. Agree on liquidated damages, a set amount to be paid in the event of a breach. A liquidated damage amount must be reasonable to be enforced by a court. Reasonableness is determined based upon the following:

(1) The anticipated loss or harm caused by the breach

(2) The difficulties of proof of loss

(3) The inconvenience of otherwise obtaining an adequate remedy

h. Agree to nothing regarding remedies and use the remedies provided in the U.C.C. See U.C.C. 2-719.

Seller's Actions and Remedies

4231.146 Seller may refuse to deliver except for cash if the buyer is insolvent. Refusal to pay cash under these circumstances is default by the buyer. From U.C.C. 2-702(1).

4231.147 Seller may reclaim goods already delivered to the buyer if either of the following is true:

a. The buyer received goods on credit while insolvent, and the seller demanded return of the goods within 10 days of the buyer receiving the goods.

b. The buyer received goods on credit while insolvent, and the buyer misrepresented his solvency in writing to the seller within three months before delivery of the goods and the seller demands return of the goods.

The seller's right to reclaim the goods is subordinate to those of a buyer in the ordinary course of business or a good-faith purchaser from the buyer. A successful reclamation of the goods excludes all other possible remedies. From U.C.C. 2-702(2) and (3).

4231.148 Seller may withhold delivery of remaining goods if the buyer did any of the following:

a. Wrongfully rejected the earlier goods

b. Wrongfully revoked an earlier acceptance of the goods

c. Failed to make a payment before delivery

d. Repudiated the contract in whole or in part

From U.C.C. 2-703

4231.149 Seller may stop delivery of the goods in transit or held by a bailee (common carrier or warehouse) if the buyer did any of the following:

a. Wrongfully rejected the earlier goods

b. Wrongfully revoked an earlier acceptance of the goods

c. Failed to make a payment before delivery

d. Repudiated the contract in whole or in part

From U.C.C. 2-705

4231.150 Seller may identify any conforming goods as belonging to the contract to make the goods available for resale if the buyer did any of the following:

a. Wrongfully rejected the earlier goods

b. Wrongfully revoked an earlier acceptance of the goods

c. Failed to make a payment before delivery

d. Repudiated the contract in whole or in part

The seller must use reasonable judgment as to completing unfinished goods.

From U.C.C. 2-704.

4231.151 Seller may resell the goods and recover damages if the buyer did any of the following:

a. Wrongfully rejected the earlier goods

b. Wrongfully revoked an earlier acceptance of the goods

c. Failed to make a payment before delivery

d. Repudiated the contract in whole or in part

From U.C.C. 2-706

4231.152 Seller may recover damages for nonacceptance of the goods if the buyer did any of the following:

a. Wrongfully rejected the earlier goods

b. Wrongfully revoked an earlier acceptance of the goods

c. Failed to make a payment before delivery

d. Repudiated the contract in whole or in part

From U.C.C. 2-708

4231.153 Seller may recover the price of the goods if the buyer did any of the following:

a. Wrongfully rejected the earlier goods

b. Wrongfully revoked an earlier acceptance of the goods

c. Failed to make a payment before delivery

d. Repudiated the contract in whole or in part

From U.C.C. 2-709

4231.154 Seller may cancel the contract if the buyer did any of the following:

    a. Wrongfully rejected the earlier goods

    b. Wrongfully revoked an earlier acceptance of the goods

    c. Failed to make a payment before delivery

    d. Repudiated the contract in whole or in part

4231.155 Seller may ask for adequate assurance of performance.

4231.156 Cure (see section **4231.170**).

Details of Seller's Remedies

4231.157 **Identifying goods as applying to the sales contract.** The seller can identify conforming goods or unfinished goods, as those that apply to the breached sales contract. For unfinished goods the seller may complete the goods or resell them for their salvage value. The seller is obligated to act with reasonable commercial judgment to minimize further loss. From U.C.C. 2-704.

4231.158 **Stop delivery of goods in transit.** The seller can order a carrier or warehouse to stop delivery of goods that are the subject of a breached sales contract. Delivery cannot be stopped if any of the following are true:

    a. The buyer has already received the goods.

    b. The warehouse has acknowledged to the buyer that the goods are being held for the buyer's disposition.

    c. The carrier has acknowledged to the buyer that the goods have been sent or are being held for the buyer.

    d. A negotiable document of title (bill of lading or warehouse receipt) has been negotiated to the buyer.

The seller must give the carrier or warehouse a reasonable time to act to stop the delivery of the goods. After notice, the goods must be held according to the seller's directions. The seller is liable for any expenses or damages to the carrier or warehouse caused by the stoppage. If a negotiable document of title covers the goods, the carrier or warehouse is not obligated to stop delivery. If a nonnegotiable document of title covers the goods, a carrier or warehouse is not obligated to respond to a stop order unless it is from the consignor.

4231.159 **Resell the goods.** The seller may resell the undelivered goods from a breached sales contract. All aspects of the resale must be in a commercially reasonable manner. The seller can recover the difference between the resale price and the contract price plus incidental damages less expenses saved. The resale can be at a public or private sale, in units or for the whole amount, at any time and place, and on any terms determined by the seller. If the resale is at a private sale, the seller must give the buyer reasonable notification of the intent to resell. If the resale is at a public sale, the following conditions apply:

    a. Only identified goods can be sold.

    b. The sale must be at the usual place or market, if one is available.

    c. The seller must give the buyer reasonable notice of the time and place of the resale unless the goods are perishable.

    d. Prospective bidders must be able to inspect the goods.

e. The seller may buy at the public sale. If these provisions are not followed, the seller cannot recover damages from the buyer based on the resale. A purchaser who buys in good faith at the resale takes the goods free of any rights of the original buyer even if the seller fails to comply with the resale requirements. The seller keeps any profit made on the resale and need not account to the original buyer.

4231.160 **Cure.** Replace nonconforming goods within the time allowed for performance under the contract.

4231.161 **Ask for adequate assurance of performance.** If the seller still has the goods and if reasonable grounds for insecurity exist, the seller can do any of the following:

    a. Suspend performance.

    b. Make a written demand for adequate assurance of performance.

    c. Wait for a reasonable time (not to exceed 30 days) for a reply.

Failure of the buyer to respond is a breach of contract by the buyer. From U.C.C. 2-609(4).

Buyer's Actions and Remedies

4231.162 As possible remedies, the buyer may do any of the following:

    a. Cancel the contract.

    b. Cover.

    c. Recover damages.

    d. Recover identified goods.

    e. Obtain specific performance. (From U.C.C. 2-716.)

    f. Utilize a security interest on goods in the buyer's possession.

    g. Deduct damages from the price to be paid the seller.

    h. Use liquidated damages if agreed upon in the contract.

Details of Buyer's Remedies

4231.163 **Cancel the contract** if any of the following occur:

    a. The seller breaches the contract by failing to deliver.

    b. The seller breaches the contract by repudiating the contract.

    c. The buyer rightfully rejects acceptance of the goods.

    d. The buyer justifiably revokes a prior acceptance of the goods.

From U.C.C. 2-711

4231.164 **Cover.** Cover is when the buyer purchases goods as a substitute for those that were to come from the seller. The buyer must act in good faith and without unreasonable delay and must purchase the goods in a commercially reasonable manner. The buyer can cover if any of the following occur:

    a. The seller breaches the contract by failing to deliver.

    b. The seller breaches the contract by repudiating the contract.

    c. The buyer rightfully rejects acceptance of the goods.

    d. The buyer justifiably revokes a prior acceptance of the goods.

The buyer's damages will be the difference between the cost of cover and the contract price plus incidental damages (e.g., additional shipping and handling) less expenses saved because of the breach.

$$\text{buyer's damages for cover} = (\text{cost of cover} - \text{contract price}) + \text{incidental damages} - \text{expenses saved}$$

A buyer is not required to cover. Failure to cover does not bar the buyer from other remedies available. From U.C.C. 2-712.

4231.165 **Damages for nondelivery or repudiation.** The buyer may recover damages for nondelivery or repudiation of the sales contract if any of the following occur:

 a. The seller breaches the contract by failing to deliver.

 b. The seller breaches the contract by repudiating the contract.

 c. The buyer rightfully rejects acceptance of the goods.

 d. The buyer justifiably revokes a prior acceptance of the goods.

$$\text{damages} = (\text{market price} - \text{contract price}) + \text{incidental damages} - \text{expenses saved}$$

The market price is measured when the buyer learned of the breach and at the location where the goods would have been tendered or the location where the goods would have arrived. From U.C.C. 2-713.

4231.166 **Recover identified goods** if any of the following occur:

 a. The seller breaches the contract by failing to deliver.

 b. The seller breaches the contract by repudiating the contract.

 c. The buyer rightfully rejects acceptance of the goods.

 d. The buyer justifiably revokes a prior acceptance of the goods.

From U.C.C. 2-502.

4231.167 **Utilize security interest** in goods in their possession that have been rightfully rejected or have been accepted then have had the acceptance revoked for any prior payments or expenses incurred for inspection, receipt, transportation, or storage by the buyer. From U.C.C. 2-716.

4231.168 **Deduct damages from the price to be paid to the seller.** If the seller has breached the contract, the buyer can deduct damages when paying the balance of the purchase price. The buyer must notify the seller of the intention to use this set-off. From U.C.C. 2-717.

4231.169 **Use the remedies in the sales contract.** The contracting parties can provide remedies as a substitute for those in the U.C.C. Typically, these contractual provisions limit the buyer's remedies to either of the following:

 a. Return of the goods and reimbursement of the price paid

 b. Repair and replacement of defective goods

4231.170 Cure

a. **Definition.** Cure is a right of the seller to replace or correct nonconforming goods received by the buyer.

b. **Right to cure.** The seller has an absolute right to cure so long as the time of performance has not been reached. After the time of performance has passed, the seller can cure only if the seller:

   (1) had reasonable grounds to think that nonconforming goods would be acceptable,

   (2) gives the buyer timely notice of the intent to cure, and

   (3) cures within a reasonable time. The reasonable grounds could result from prior dealings with the buyer or from sending a new, improved model. From U.C.C. 2-508.

c. Once the seller cures with conforming goods, the buyer loses the right to reject.

4231.171 Anticipatory repudiation

a. **Definition.** An anticipatory repudiation is a situation where one of the parties to a contract indicates that he will not perform before the time that performance is due.

b. **Action by the wronged party.** The wronged party may do any of the following:

   (1) Await performance by the repudiating party for a commercially reasonable time.

   (2) Suspend own performance on the repudiated contract.

   (3) Sue immediately for the anticipated breach using any of the remedies allowed for a regular breach of contract. It is not necessary to wait until the time when the performance is actually due. See U.C.C. 2-610.

c. **Retraction.** The party that anticipatorily repudiates the contract may retract the repudiation unless the wronged party has done any of the following:

   (1) Canceled the contract

   (2) Materially changed position

   (3) Indicated that the repudiation is considered final

d. **Assurance.** If there are reasonable grounds for insecurity for the performance of the contract, the wronged party may make written demand for assurance that the contract will be completed when performance is due. The wronged party may think that the person will repudiate again rather than perform as agreed. Between merchants, their actions must be commercially reasonable as to grounds for insecurity and suspension of performance. The recipient of a demand for adequate assurance of performance has a reasonable time, not to exceed 30 days, to provide the assurance. See U.C.C. 2-609.

e. **Damages.** Damages for an anticipatory repudiation are to be based on the market price of the goods when the wronged party learned of the repudiation.

4231.172 Liquidated damages

a. **Definition.** Liquidated damages are damages that are agreed upon by the parties at the time of contracting and are contained in the contract.

b. Liquidated damages are used instead of proving compensatory damages after a breach has occurred.

c. **Enforceability.** Liquidated damage provisions are enforceable if they are reasonable when agreed upon, considering the following:

(1) Expected damages from a breach

(2) Difficulties of proving damages

(3) Inadequacy of an adequate remedy

Unreasonably large liquidated damages are void and are unenforceable even though the parties have agreed to them. They are viewed as penalties that are used to prevent a party from breaching rather than a reasonable estimate of damages.

4231.173 Sale by auction

a. Sale of goods by auction, like other types of sale of goods, is covered by Article 2 of the U.C.C.

b. **Auction with reserve.** The auctioneer reserves the right to take the goods off the block and not sell them. This is the ordinary type of auction. The auctioneer takes the goods off the block when the bid price is lower than that set by the owner as a minimum sale price.

c. **Auction without reserve.** Once the auctioneer calls for bids on the item, the item must be sold to the highest bidder. The auctioneer cannot withdraw the item unless no bid is received within a reasonable time. An auction is without reserve only if expressly so advertised.

d. A bid at an auction is a contractual offer. A bid can be withdrawn any time prior to acceptance by the auctioneer. A bid is accepted by the auctioneer's fall of the hammer. If a bid is withdrawn, the prior bid is not revived and the auctioneer must restart by calling for new bids.

4231.174 Statute of limitations

a. **Definition.** After a breach of contract, the statute of limitations is the time period within which the wronged party must start legal action. Failure to start the legal action within the allowed time period permits the other party to have the action dismissed by the court when the affirmative defense of running of the statute of limitations is pleaded.

b. **Four years.** The statute of limitations for sale of goods contracts is four years, unless the parties agree otherwise in their contract.

c. **Agreement.** If the parties choose to modify the statute of limitations specified in the U.C.C., they may do so by agreement in their contract. The contracting parties may do either of the following:

(1) Reduce the time to not less than one year.

(2) Not extend it beyond the four years.

d. **Start.** The time period of the statute of limitations starts when the breach occurs. Knowledge of the breach by the wronged party is not important. For a warranty, the time starts when the goods are tendered for delivery unless the parties expressly state otherwise.

e. **Tolling.** Tolling means a suspension of the time period of the statute of limitations. Tolling happens when the wrongdoer is out of the state's jurisdiction. The U.C.C. does not alter a state's laws regarding the tolling of the statute of limitations.

4231.175 Parol evidence rule

    a. Definition. When there is a written contract, parol evidence is any evidence of the transaction other than the written contract. Parol evidence is also called extrinsic evidence, meaning outside of the contract.

    b. Rule. The parol evidence rule states that parol evidence from prior or contemporaneous agreements may not be admitted to contradict what is contained in the written contract. It is not a violation of the rule, and evidence can be admitted:

        (1) to explain course of dealing, usage of trade, or course of performance or

        (2) to add consistent additional terms unless the written contract is found to be a complete and exclusive statement of the agreement.

4231.176 Notice. The U.C.C. requires one party to give notice or communicate with the other party to the contract when any of the following occur:

    a. One of the parties is terminating the contract. From U.C.C. 2-309.

    b. The seller discovers a breach. From U.C.C. 2-607.

    c. The buyer is sued for breach of warranty for which the seller is liable. From U.C.C. 2-607.

    d. The buyer revokes a prior acceptance of the goods. From U.C.C. 2-608.

    e. One party has reasonable grounds for insecurity regarding the performance of the other party, and they want adequate assurance of performance. From U.C.C. 2-609.

    f. A party retracts an anticipatory breach given to the other party. From U.C.C. 2-611.

    g. A party repudiates a contract performance not yet done. From U.C.C. 2-610.

    h. A seller is reselling goods by private sale after the buyer has breached. From U.C.C. 2-706.

    i. The buyer is deducting damages from the price still due under the contract after the seller's breach. From U.C.C. 2-717.

4231.177 Inspection of goods

    a. Unless otherwise agreed, the buyer has the right to inspect the goods before being obligated to pay for the goods.

    b. When. Inspection can be made after the goods have been identified to the contract and before payment. From U.C.C. 2-513(1).

    c. Cost. The cost of inspection is paid by the buyer, but the buyer can recover the cost of inspection if the goods are nonconforming and are rejected by the buyer.

    d. Terms. If the terms of the contract are C.O.D. or C.I.F., the buyer waives the right to inspect before delivery.

    e. Inspection must be at a reasonable time and place and done in a reasonable manner.

Situations Excusing Performance

4231.178 Once the parties have entered a sales contract, the parties are obligated to perform what they have promised to do. In some situations, performance is excused when events occur that neither party could reasonably foresee. The following are the situations when performance is excused:

    a. Casualty to identified goods

    b. Failure of the manner of delivery

    c. Failure of the manner or means of payment

    d. Failure of presupposed conditions

    e. Unconscionable agreement

4231.179 **Casualty to identified goods.** If the goods are totally destroyed without fault of either party, both parties are excused from their performance obligations. From U.C.C. 2-613. The seller is excused from performance only if the following are true:

    a. Goods were identified to the contract.

    b. Destruction was total, not partial.

    c. Destruction was caused by the seller.

    d. Risk of loss did not pass to the buyer.

The seller bears the loss but is excused from having to deliver new goods.

4231.180 **Failure of the manner of delivery.** If the agreed manner of delivery becomes commercially impractical, a reasonable substitute must be tendered and accepted. From U.C.C. 2-614(1). This is a seller's excuse.

4231.181 **Failure of manner or means of payment.** If the manner or means of payment fails because of governmental regulation, the buyer may pay by some other reasonable means. From U.C.C. 2-614(2).

4231.182 **Failure of presupposed condition.** If a totally unforeseen contingency changes the essential nature of the performance obligation, the party will be excused from performance. From U.C.C. 2-615. Mere unprofitability or inconvenience is not sufficient to excuse performance.

4231.183 **Unconscionable agreement.** If the court finds an agreement to be unconscionable, it will rewrite the contract to rid it of the unconscionable portion if possible or will refuse to enforce the contract if this cannot be done.

Product Liability

4231.184 The problem of product liability is how to allocate loss for accidents rather than determining the problem of contractual liability.

4231.185 **Breach of warranty**

    a. Traditionally based on privity of contract, but the trend is to allow the user to sue remote parties.

    b. Express or implied warranties.

    c. The U.C.C. extended liability to family, household, and guests of the buyer.

4231.186 Negligence

a. Tort liability, not in contract.

b. Manufacturer is liable to persons injured when negligent in preparation or manufacture of the product when a reasonable person could foresee that such negligence would cause injury.

c. Society imposes a duty to exercise reasonable care.

d. Courts have found negligence for the following:

   (1) Failure to inspect goods

   (2) Misrepresentation as to what the goods could be used for

   (3) Failure to warn of known defects and known dangers

   (4) Failure to properly design the goods

e. It is often difficult to prove negligence. The following two legal theories have been helpful in allowing a plaintiff to recover for negligence:

   (1) *Res ipsa loquitur.* Cause of the injury was something that lay within the sole responsibility of the defendant. The court then assumes the defendant is negligent but lets the defendant rebut this presumption of negligence if they are able. It shifts the burden of proof from the plaintiff to the defendant.

   (2) Negligence *per se*. Negligence is presumed if the defendant violates a statutory duty. For instance, injury from faulty electrical wiring contrary to a building code would provide a basis for negligence per se being applied by the court.

f. Negligence = Duty owing + Breach of that duty + Injury + Proximate cause (breach is the cause of the injury). All four must be present.

4231.187 Tort of deceit

a. Deceit is the intentional misrepresentation of a material fact knowingly made, justifiably relied upon, and resulting in injury.

b. When these circumstances are used to avoid a contract, it is called fraud in the inducement.

c. For the tort of deceit, the wronged person takes the contract but sues for the improper conduct that induced him to make the contract.

d. May be by advertising or labels on the product.

4231.188 Tort of misrepresentation

a. Misrepresentation is innocently making a misrepresentation of a material fact without intending to deceive the other party, but the other party justifiably relies on the misrepresentation and it results in injury.

b. Similar to deceit, except that the wronged party can get the equitable remedy of rescission but may not sue for damages.

4231.189 Strict liability (but not absolute) in tort

a. Tort liability without considering fault if product is dangerous or defective.

b. Sellers of manufactured product (retailers and manufacturers but not wholesalers) are liable.

(1) **Dangerous product.** Dangerous + Defective + Injury + Proximate cause. Retail seller who knows or should know that the product is likely to be dangerous is liable for bodily harm caused by the product unless they warn of the danger (e.g., poison).

(2) **Defective product.** A seller of a defective product is held strictly liable to anyone injured, even innocent third parties.

c. Not accepted by all states with regard to all types of defects. Most common application is with sales of food and drink.

4232 Negotiable Instruments

4232.01 **Definition:** A negotiable instrument is a written promise or order to pay money.

4232.02 Commercial paper (which is a contract for the payment of money) can be either of the following:

a. **Negotiable.** This commercial paper can be transferred by the process of negotiation if it meets the requirements of Article 3 of the U.C.C.

b. **Nonnegotiable.** This commercial paper does not meet the requirements of Article 3 of the U.C.C. Its transfer is governed by the law of contracts. It can be transferred by assignment of the instrument, but not by negotiation.

4232.03 Negotiable instruments are governed by Article 3 of the U.C.C. Article 3 does not apply to money, documents of title (bills of lading and warehouse receipts), or investment securities.

a. Early law of commercial paper came from the law merchant, a distinct part of the common law formulated by the merchants.

b. In 1896, the Uniform Negotiable Instruments Law (NIL) was published and ultimately adopted by all the states. The U.C.C. superseded the NIL when states adopted the U.C.C.

c. In 1990, the American Law Institute and the National Conference of Commissions on Uniform State Laws created a Revised Article 3 as well as amendments to Article 1 and Article 4. Since a majority of states have adopted Revised Article 3 and the related amendments, this revised version is the basis for the following discussion.

4232.04 There are two major functions of commercial paper:

1. **Substitute for money.** There is not enough paper money and coins to transact all the business transactions. Checks, therefore, operate as a substitute for money.

2. **Extending credit.** Commercial paper can be used as a more formalized method of extending credit. Lending institutions are more likely to loan money based on commercial paper, such as a promissory note signed by the borrower, than they would be for open credit.

4232.05 **Advantages of commercial paper over ordinary contract rights**

a. **Easier to transfer.** Negotiable commercial paper is easier to transfer than an ordinary contract right because it is more readily accepted.

b. **Less risk.** Negotiable commercial paper has less risk in the possession of the transferee than does the assignment of a contract right. The reason is that the party that takes by negotiation may not be subject to personal defenses when payment is made on the instrument.

Parties to Commercial Paper

4232.06 **Acceptor.** The party that accepts a draft by obligating herself to be primarily liable for its payment.

4232.07 **Accommodation indorser.** An indorser who signs an instrument to lend credit to another party on that instrument.

4232.08 **Accommodation party.** A party that signs an instrument to lend credit to another party on the instrument.

4232.09 **Bearer.** The party in possession of an instrument that is payable to bearer or indorsed in blank.

4232.10 **Drawee.** The party that is ordered to pay a check or a draft.

4232.11 **Drawer.** The party who signs or is identified in a draft as a person ordering payment.

4232.12 **Holder.** A party that has possession of a negotiable instrument that is any of the following:
  a. Drawn to that party
  b. Issued to that party
  c. Indorsed to that party
  d. Issued to bearer
  e. Indorsed in blank

4232.13 **Holder after a holder in due course.** The party that takes an instrument after a holder in due course who acquires the rights of a holder in due course under the shelter rule.

4232.14 **Holder in due course.** A party that takes a negotiable instrument:
  a. for value,
  b. in good faith,
  c. without notice that the instrument is overdue, has been dishonored, or that there is any uncured default with respect to payment of another instrument issued as part of the same series,
  d. without notice that the instrument contains an unauthorized signature or has been altered,
  e. without notice of any claim of a property or possessory interest in it, and
  f. without notice that any party has any defense against it or claim in recoupment to it.

4232.15 **Indorsee.** Party to whom an indorsement is made on a negotiable instrument.

4232.16 **Indorser.** Party making an indorsement on a negotiable instrument.

4232.17 **Maker.** Party who signs or is identified in a note as a person undertaking to pay.

4232.18 **Payee.** Party to whom an instrument is made payable.

4232.19 **Primary party.** Party that is first liable to pay an instrument. For a note, the primary party is the maker. For an accepted draft, it is the acceptor. There is no primary party on a check or draft as issued.

4232.20 Secondary parties. Parties liable to pay on a negotiable instrument if the primary parties do not pay and if proper and timely notification is given. Secondary parties include the drawer of a check or draft and an indorser.

Types of Negotiable Instruments

4232.21 The following are the types of instruments recognized by Article 3 of the U.C.C.:

a. **Draft.** Sometimes called a bill of exchange. An instrument whereby the party creating it (drawer) orders another party (drawee) to pay money to a third party (payee).

b. **Check.** A draft drawn on a bank and payable on demand.

c. **Certificate of deposit.** An acknowledgment by a bank of the receipt of money with the return promise to repay that money. A certificate of deposit is a note of a bank.

d. **Note.** A promise whereby one party (maker) promises to pay a sum of money to another party (payee). See U.C.C. 3-104(e).

These four types of instruments are negotiable if they meet the requirements to be negotiable. If they do not meet the requirements, they are nonnegotiable instruments.

4232.22 The four types of negotiable instruments are:

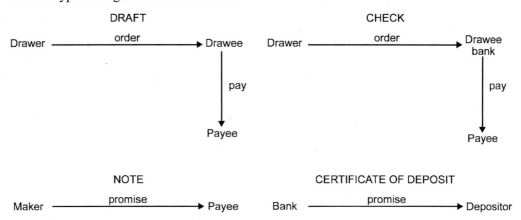

4232.23 This table compares the types of commercial paper.

Attribute	Draft	Check	Note	Certificate of Deposit
Number of parties to original instrument	3	3	2	2
Promise or order	order	order	promise	promise
Person who drafts the instrument	drawer	drawer	maker	bank
Person primarily liable when issued	no one	no one	maker	bank
Persons secondarily liable	drawer and indorsers	drawer and indorsers	indorsers	indorsers

Requisites for Negotiability

4232.24 For an instrument to be negotiable, it must be as follows:

    a. Be in writing.

    b. Be signed by the maker or the drawer.

    c. Be an unconditional promise or order to pay a fixed amount of money, with or without interest or other charges described in the promise or order.

    d. Be payable to order or to bearer at the time it is issued or first comes into possession of a holder (unless it is a check).

    e. Be payable on demand or at a definite time.

    f. Not state any other undertaking or instruction by the person promising or ordering to do any act in addition to the payment of money, but the promise or order may contain (1) an undertaking or promise relative to collateral to secure payment, (2) an authorization for confession of judgment, or (3) a waiver of benefit of any law intended for the advantage or protection of an obligor.

4232.25 If an instrument lacks any of the requirements, it is nonnegotiable. Negotiability must be determined from examining the face of the instrument when it is issued to determine if the four requisites are present. Examination of other documents or sources is not permitted. Negotiability must be within the four corners of the instrument. An indorsement cannot change a negotiable instrument into a nonnegotiable instrument. The indorsement can restrict transfer of the negotiable instrument but not its negotiability. Once negotiable, always negotiable.

Signed Writing

4232.26 For an instrument to be negotiable, it must be in writing and signed by the maker or drawer.

4232.27 To meet the requirement of a writing, the instrument can be handwritten, printed, typewritten, or in any other intentional method of reduction to tangible form. The key is that it cannot be oral.

4232.28 A writing is considered signed if it includes any symbol executed or adopted by a party with the present intention to authenticate the writing. Usually it is handwritten but could be initials, a rubber stamp, an "X" mark, or any other symbol placed on the writing to authenticate it.

Unconditional Instrument

4232.29 A promise or order is conditional and therefore not negotiable if it states any of the following:

    a. An express condition to payment

    Example: If a note provides "a promise to pay to the order of John Smith $500 provided he paints my fence," it is not negotiable because it is payable subject to an express condition.

    b. That the promise or order is subject to or governed by another writing

    c. That the rights or obligations with respect to the promise or order are stated in another writing

    Example: A note is not negotiable if it states that payment "is subject to the terms and conditions of a particular mortgage."

4232.30 A reference to another writing does not of itself make the promise or order conditional.

4232.31 A statement in the instrument that payment can be made only from a particular fund or source does not make an instrument conditional.

4232.32 A reference to another document for a statement of rights with respect to collateral, prepayment, or acceleration does not destroy negotiability of a note.

Example: A statement on the note stating that it is secured by a particular mortgage does not destroy negotiability.

4232.33 A statement of the consideration for which the instrument was given or a description of the transaction that gave rise to the instrument does not destroy negotiability.

4232.34 The requirement of a countersignature of a person whose specimen signature appears on the promise or order (e.g., a traveler's check) does not make the promise or order conditional. See U.C.C. 3-106.

Fixed Amount

4232.35 Fixed amount means an amount ascertainable from the face of the instrument.

4232.36 The fixed amount requirement applies only to the principal amount.

4232.37 If a specific rate of interest is stated on the instrument, this meets the requirement of a fixed amount because the amount can be determined at the time the instrument is payable.

4232.38 The fixed amount requirement is also satisfied if the amount of interest is calculated by reference to a formula or index stated in the instrument.

4232.39 If the amount of interest payable cannot be ascertained from the description on the instrument, interest is payable at the judgment rate in effect at the place of payment of the instrument and at the time interest first accrues.

Payable in Money

4232.40 An instrument is payable in money if it is payable in either of the following:

    a. Currency or current funds

    b. A foreign currency

See U.C.C. 3-107.

4232.41 Money is defined as a medium of exchange authorized or adopted by a domestic or foreign government as part of its currency.

4232.42 An instrument that includes a promise to perform an act other than or in addition to payment of money is nonnegotiable.

Example: "I promise to deliver 60 bushels of apples 90 days after the date of the loan" is nonnegotiable.

Example: "I promise to pay $100 and deliver 30 bushels of apples 90 days after the date of the loan" is nonnegotiable.

Example: "I promise to pay $200 or deliver 60 bushels of apples 90 days after the date of the loan" is nonnegotiable.

Payable on Demand

4232.43 An instrument is payable on demand if it is any of the following:

    a. Payable "at sight"

    b. Payable "on presentation"

    c. Payable "on demand"

    d. States no time for payment

See U.C.C. 3-108.

Payable at a Definite Time

4232.44 An instrument is payable at a definite time if it is payable by any of the following:

    a. On or before a stated date

    b. At a fixed period after a stated date

       Example: A note is dated June 24, 20X1, and states that it is payable "60 days after date."

    c. At a fixed period after sight

       Example: A draft states that it is payable "30 days after sight."

    d. At a definite time subject to acceleration

    e. At a definite time subject to extension at the option of the holder

    f. At a definite time subject to extension to a further definite time at the option of the maker or acceptor or automatically if some specified event happens (An instrument is not payable at a definite time if the uncertain event has happened. Later events cannot make the instrument payable at a definite time.)

See U.C.C. 3-108.

Payable to Order

4232.45 An instrument is payable to order if it is payable to the order of an identified person or to an identified person or order. The identified person may be one of the following:

    a. The maker

    b. The drawer

    c. The drawee

    d. The payee

    e. Two or more payees together (**Example:** "Pay to the order of Tom Smith and Bill Jones")

    f. Two or more payees in the alternative (**Example:** "Pay to the order of Tom Smith or Bill Jones")

    g. An estate (**Example:** "Pay to the order of the estate of William A. Patterson")

    h. A trust (**Example:** "Pay to the order of the William Keener Trust")

    i. A fund (**Example:** "Pay to the order of the University of New Orleans Athletic Fund")

    j. An office (**Example:** "Pay to the order of the Assessor's Office")

k. An officer (**Example:** "Pay to the order of the Assessor of Hamilton County")

l. A partnership (**Example:** "Pay to the order of the St. Charles Partnership")

m. An unincorporated association (**Example:** "Pay to the order of the Association for the Preservation of Forest Park")

4232.46 These parties can legally act for the entity:

Estate	Executor or administrator
Trust	Trustee
Fund	Representative
Office	Incumbent or successor
Partnership	Authorized person, probably a partner
Unincorporated association	Authorized person

4232.47 If an instrument (other than a check) is simply made payable to a specific payee and not payable to the payee's order, the instrument is nonnegotiable.

Example: A check that reads "Pay to John Smith" could qualify as a negotiable instrument.

If a check fails to contain the language "to the order of," it would still qualify as a negotiable instrument.

Payable to Bearer

4232.48 An instrument is payable to bearer when it is payable to the following:

a. Bearer (**Example:** "Pay to bearer")

b. The order of bearer (**Example:** "Pay to the order of bearer")

c. A named party or bearer (**Example:** "Bill Patterson or bearer")

d. Cash (**Example:** "Pay to cash")

e. The order of cash (**Example:** "Pay to the order of cash")

f. Any term that does not designate a specific payee

See U.C.C. 3-109.

Negotiability

4232.49 The following omissions, statements, promises, or terms do not affect negotiability of an instrument:

a. Lack of a statement of the consideration given for the instrument

b. Lack of the place where the instrument was drawn or payable

c. A statement that collateral was given on the transaction

d. A statement that the holder may resort to collateral in the case of default

e. A promise to maintain, protect, or give additional collateral

f. A term authorizing a confession of judgment on the instrument if it is not paid on time

g. A term waiving the benefit of a law that protects the obligor

h. A term in a draft stating that the payee acknowledges full satisfaction of an obligation of the drawer by cashing or indorsing the instrument

        i. A statement in a draft saying the order is effective only if no other part is honored

        j. The presence of a seal on the instrument

4232.50 Incomplete instrument

        a. If an instrument is signed while still incomplete, the instrument cannot be enforced until completed.

        b. If the instrument is completed in accordance with the authority given, it is effective as completed.

        c. If the completion is unauthorized, the rules of material alteration apply.

Typical Clauses in Commercial Paper

4232.51 Acceleration clause: Allows the holder of an installment time instrument to demand payment of the entire amount due with interest if one of the installments is not paid when due. See U.C.C. 1-208 and 3-108.

4232.52 Extension clause: Allows the date of maturity to be extended. If the right to extend is given to the maker, the time must be specified. If the holder has the right to extend the time, the new maturity date need not be specified because it then becomes a demand rather than a time instrument.

Transfer of Commercial Paper

4232.53 A negotiable instrument can be transferred to another party by either of the following:

        a. Negotiation

        b. Assignment

4232.54 A nonnegotiable instrument can be transferred to another party only by assignment. It can never be transferred by negotiation.

4232.55 Transfer of a negotiable instrument to another party is first done by the payee. There is no limit as to the number of transfers. In commercial practice there are very few transfers.

4232.56 If a transfer is by assignment, the rights are determined by the common law relating to contracts. The party receiving the instrument is an assignee not a holder.

4232.57 If a transfer is by negotiation, the rights are determined by Article 3 of the U.C.C. The party receiving the instrument by negotiation is a holder.

4232.58 From the viewpoint of the issuers (drawer or maker), a negotiable instrument involves more risk than a nonnegotiable instrument because personal defenses such as breach of contract are not available to avoid payment if a party that qualifies as a holder in due course (HDC) later comes into possession of the instrument.

4232.59 From the viewpoint of the payee and subsequent holders, a negotiable instrument involves less risk, is more transferable, and is more readily accepted by subsequent holders than a nonnegotiable instrument.

Negotiation of Commercial Paper

4232.60 Transfer of a negotiable instrument is anticipated because the instrument is made payable "to the order of" a named party or is made payable to "bearer." Therefore, the drawer or maker should know that payment may ultimately have to be made to someone other than the payee.

4232.61 Negotiation is the transfer of possession of a negotiable instrument (whether voluntary or involuntary) whereby the party receiving it becomes a holder.

4232.62 Negotiation of an instrument can be by either of the following:
    a. Delivery alone
    b. Delivery with the necessary indorsement

4232.63 If the instrument is order paper:
    a. it is made payable to a named party and
    b. it can be negotiated only by delivery with the necessary indorsement of the named party.

4232.64 If the instrument is bearer paper:
    a. it is made payable to bearer,
    b. it may be negotiated by delivery alone without any indorsement, and
    c. it may also be negotiated by delivery with an indorsement.

4232.65 The validity of a negotiation is determined by the form of the instrument at the time of transfer. The form can be "order paper" or "bearer paper."

Assignment of Commercial Paper

4232.66 If an instrument is nonnegotiable, it can still be transferred, but only by assignment, and not by negotiation.

4232.67 If a negotiable instrument that is order paper is transferred to a party without the necessary indorsement of the named party, the transfer is an assignment not a negotiation. The transfer can be turned into a negotiation if the named party later provides the proper indorsement.

Indorsements

4232.68 If it is order paper, a negotiable instrument can be negotiated only if the named party provides the necessary indorsement.

4232.69 If it is bearer paper, a negotiable instrument can be negotiated by delivery of the instrument with no indorsement. Bearer paper can also be negotiated by delivery of the instrument with an indorsement.

4232.70 **Types of indorsements.** All indorsements can be classified by three pairs of indorsement types:
    1. Blank indorsement or special indorsement
    2. Unqualified indorsement or qualified indorsement
    3. Nonrestrictive indorsement or restrictive indorsement

4232.71 Examples of types of indorsements:

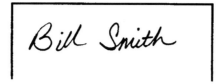

blank, unqualified, and nonrestrictive

special, unqualified, and nonrestrictive

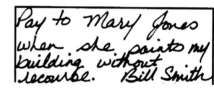

blank, qualified, and nonrestrictive

special, unqualified, and restrictive

blank, unqualified, and restrictive

special, qualified, and restrictive

4232.72 Indorsements can be handwritten, hand printed, rubber stamped, machine printed, or a combination of these.

4232.73 Indorsements are placed on the back of the instrument. There is no maximum number of indorsements. If there is no further room for indorsements, a paper can be attached to the instrument to allow further indorsements. This attached paper is called an allonge. The attachment should be by glue, paste, or staples. Use of a paper clip would not be sufficient. Allonges are used very infrequently.

4232.74 A party cannot be liable on a negotiable instrument unless that party's name appears on the instrument.

4232.75 An indorsement can be made by the holder or someone authorized to sign on behalf of the holder.

Example: A check payable to "ABC Corporation" could be indorsed "ABC Corporation by Bill Smith, President" if Bill Smith has authority.

4232.76 A party that negotiates a negotiable instrument by delivery alone cannot have liability on the instrument since their name does not appear on the instrument by way of indorsement.

4232.77 An indorsement cannot make a negotiable instrument nonnegotiable. Negotiability is determined from the face of the instrument and is not changed by any indorsement. An indorsement can state "Pay to Susan Mann" rather than "Pay to the order of Susan Mann," which would be required on the face of the instrument in order to make it negotiable. An indorsement also can contain a condition without affecting the negotiability of the instrument, whereas a condition on the face of the instrument would make the instrument nonnegotiable.

4232.78 A conditional indorsement does not impose any obligation on the maker, drawee, or acceptor to see that the condition has occurred prior to payment on the instrument.

4232.79 An indorsement must be written on the instrument or on a paper firmly affixed to the instrument, called an allonge. An indorsement on a separate document has no effect.

4232.80 An indorsement must affect the entire instrument. Any attempted fractional effort is ineffective as a negotiation. Instead, it is an assignment.

4232.81 If the holder's name is wrong or misspelled, the indorsement can be made either in the correct name or the name as stated on the instrument. Any person who pays or gives value for the instrument may require the indorser to sign both names.

Example: A check issued to Bill Smith that is payable to the order of "Bill Smyth" may generally be indorsed as "Bill Smith" or "Bill Smyth."

Blank Indorsement

4232.82 A blank indorsement is an indorsement that does not specify a further indorsee. It is normally only a signature, but it may also contain a qualified indorsement and/or a restrictive indorsement.

4232.83 A blank indorsement makes the instrument bearer paper, which can then be further negotiated by delivery alone.

4232.84 A blank indorsement turns an order instrument into a bearer instrument.

4232.85 A blank indorsement can be converted by a holder into a special indorsement by adding the words "pay to" a named party or "pay to the order of" a named party above the indorsement. Example:

[Signature: Bill Jones]

This is the original blank indorsement by Bill Jones as it was received by holder Susan Mann. The instrument is bearer paper.

[Signature: Pay to Susan Mann / Bill Jones]

The original blank indorsement has been converted into a special indorsement when the holder, Susan Mann, added the words "Pay to Susan Mann" above the signature of Bill Jones. The instrument is now order paper and must be indorsed by Susan Mann before it can be negotiated.

Special Indorsements

4232.86 A special indorsement specifies the party to whom the instrument is transferred.

4232.87 **Words of negotiability.** An indorsement need not include the same words of negotiability that are required on the front of the instrument. "Pay to" and "Pay to the order of" are equivalent as they are related to indorsements.

4232.88 Examples of special indorsements:

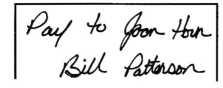

4232.89 A special indorsement makes the instrument order paper. The indorsement of the transferee is necessary to further negotiate the instrument.

Qualified Indorsements

4232.90 The words "without recourse" in an indorsement only mean that the indorser assumes no responsibility to pay the instrument if it is dishonored.

4232.91 A qualified indorser still makes the warranties of transfer. See U.C.C. 3-416.

4232.92 To totally disclaim any liability for an instrument, the indorser should use "without recourse and without warranties."

4232.93 If a party gives value and receives a negotiable instrument, that party is entitled to an unqualified indorsement of that negotiable instrument by the party receiving the value.

4232.94 A qualified indorsement requires a signature after the words. A qualified indorsement can be coupled with a blank indorsement, a special indorsement, a restrictive indorsement, or a nonrestrictive indorsement.

4232.95 Examples of a qualified indorsement:

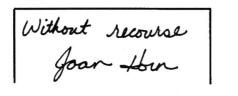

Unqualified Indorsement

4232.96 An unqualified indorsement contains no qualification.

Restrictive Indorsements

4232.97 The U.C.C. recognizes four types of restrictive indorsements:

   1. **Conditional indorsement.** This is an order to pay the instrument only if a specified event occurs. The instrument can be further negotiated before the condition occurs. An indorsement conditioning the right to receive payment does not affect the right of the indorsee to enforce the instrument. Anyone paying for or taking the instrument for value can disregard the condition. The following are examples:

      (a) Pay Susan Howell when she completes her contract.

      (b) Pay Tom Smith when he gets married.

2. **Indorsement purporting to prohibit further negotiation of the instrument.** However, this type of indorsement is not effective to restrict further negotiation. The following are examples:

    (a) Pay to the order of John Smith only.

    (b) Pay to John Smith only.

3. **Indorsement containing a term stating a purpose of deposit or collection.** This is the most common type of restrictive indorsement and is used to put the instrument into the collection process. Only a bank can acquire the rights of a holder after this type of restrictive indorsement. The following are examples:

    (a) For collection

    (b) For collection only

    (c) For deposit

    (d) For deposit only

    (e) Pay any bank

4. **Indorsement stating it is for the use or benefit of the indorser or some other party** (a trust indorsement). The following are examples:

    (a) Pay to X in trust for Y.

    (b) Pay to X for the use of Y.

4232.98 A depository bank must act consistently with any restrictive indorsement on a negotiable instrument. Failure to do so makes the depository bank liable for the tort of conversion. If an instrument is indorsed "For deposit only," the bank would not be acting consistently with the indorsement if the bank paid cash to a party that brought the instrument to the bank.

4232.99 Intermediary banks may disregard any prior restrictive indorsements and need only examine the indorsement of their immediate transferee.

4232.100 Examples of restrictive indorsements:

Nonrestrictive Indorsements

4232.101 A nonrestrictive indorsement is an indorsement that does not contain a restriction.

Holder

4232.102 **Definition.** The holder of a negotiable instrument is a party that has a negotiable instrument that is any of the following:

    a. Drawn to that party, to its order, or to bearer

    b. Issued to that party, to its order, or to bearer

    c. Indorsed to that party, to its order, or to bearer

    d. Indorsed in blank (signature without naming a party) (This is a bearer instrument.)

4232.103 A holder has the same rights as an assignee of a contractual right. The holder obtains the same rights as the party that transferred the negotiable instrument.

Holder in Due Course

4232.104 A holder in due course is a holder that takes a negotiable instrument:

    a. for value,

    b. in good faith, and

    c. without notice that:

        (1) the instrument is overdue.

        (2) the instrument has been previously dishonored (not paid).

        (3) any person has a defense against paying the instrument or a claim to it.

        (4) the instrument contains unauthorized signatures, alterations, or is so irregular or incomplete so as to call into question its authenticity.

4232.105 Status as a holder in due course is generally important only if there is a personal defense that could be used as an excuse not to pay the instrument. If there is no personal defense, a holder or a holder in due course can both collect on the instrument. If there is a real defense to payment of the negotiable instrument, neither the holder nor holder in due course could collect on the instrument.

4232.106 Personal defenses are not good against a holder in due course.

4232.107 Real defenses are good against a holder in due course.

4232.108 A party's status as a holder in due course is determined when the party acquires the instrument. Later knowledge will not affect the previously established holder in due course status. If a party reacquires an instrument, the status is determined when the party first acquires the instrument.

4232.109 A holder is considered to have taken a negotiable instrument for value by doing the following:

    a. Paying the agreed consideration of the contract for which the instrument was issued

        (1) Making a promise to pay the consideration at a future time is not giving value.

        (2) "For value" and contractual consideration are not exactly the same. A promise to do something in the future is sufficient for contractual consideration but not "for value" to determine a holder's status as a holder in due course.

    b. Acquiring a security interest in the instrument

    c. Acquiring a lien on the instrument

- d. Taking the instrument for an existing debt
- e. Taking the instrument as security for an existing debt
- f. Exchanging it for another negotiable instrument
- g. Exchanging an irrevocable commitment to pay for the instrument

    Example: A check or irrevocable letter of credit

4232.110 The above example would be "for value": X takes a negotiable instrument and pays cash for it.

4232.111 The above example would not be "for value": X takes a negotiable instrument and promises to pay for it in 30 days.

4232.112 A party cannot be a holder in due course if the instrument is any of the following:

- a. Purchased at a judicial sale
- b. Taken by legal process
- c. Taken by an estate
- d. Purchased as part of a bulk transfer

4232.113 A bank can become a holder in due course if it allows a depositor to withdraw funds based on the deposit of a check that is later returned to the bank NSF; allowing the depositor to withdraw funds based on the check is considered giving value.

4232.114 Taking in good faith

- a. This means acting honestly in getting the instrument.
- b. Taking in good faith applies to the party receiving the instrument, not the party making the transfer.

4232.115 Taking with notice

- a. A party takes with notice if any of the following occur:
    - (1) The instrument is overdue. This means past the date of maturity.
    - (2) The party knows it has been dishonored.

        Example: A check was stamped "INSUFFICIENT FUNDS."

    - (3) The party knows there is a defense against the instrument that could cause the instrument not to be paid when presented.
    - (4) The party knows there is another claim to the instrument.
- b. The party must examine the face of the instrument. Any unusual markings would give the party notice. The following are examples:
    - (1) The face of the instrument indicates a defect.
    - (2) The instrument is incomplete.
    - (3) The instrument is irregular on its face.

4232.116 A holder after a holder in due course has all the rights of the holder in due course. This is called the shelter rule. This prevents multiple lawsuits. The holder could collect from the HDC and the HDC would then be able to collect from the maker or acceptor because they are primarily liable on the instrument. If no real defense is present, a party does not need to prove HDC status.

4232.117 Generally, a person who formerly held the instrument cannot improve their rights by later reacquiring the instrument from an HDC.

Example: Jennifer, as a prior holder of the instrument, had knowledge of a claim or defense. She cannot obtain the rights of an HDC by later reacquiring the instrument from an HDC.

Defenses of the Parties

4232.118 A defense is an excuse for not performing a legal obligation. For commercial paper, this obligation is usually payment of the instrument.

4232.119 Payment of a negotiable instrument is not excused unless there is a valid defense.

Personal Defenses

4232.120 Personal defenses are valid against holders, but not against holders in due course to prevent payment on the instrument. The following are examples and explanations of personal defenses:

    a. Breach of contract or warranty

    b. Lack of consideration

    c. Failure of consideration

    d. Duress that makes a contract voidable (if it makes the contract void, it would be a real defense)

    e. Undue influence that makes a contract voidable (if it makes the contract void, it would be a real defense)

    f. Fraud in the inducement (the party knows the instrument is negotiable but is convinced to sign by fraud)

    g. Mental incapacity that makes a contract voidable (if it makes the contract void, it would be a real defense)

    h. Minority to the extent that it makes a contract voidable (if it makes the contract void, it would be a real defense)

    i. Instrument discharged by payment

    j. Instrument discharged by cancellation

    k. Unauthorized completion of an incomplete instrument

    l. Nondelivery of a completed instrument

Real Defenses

4232.121 Real defenses are valid against both holders and holders in due course to prevent payment on the instrument.

4232.122 The following are examples and explanations of real defenses:

    a. Forgery

b. Unauthorized signature

c. Fraud in the execution—the party signs a negotiable instrument but honestly believes they are signing something else.

d. Material alteration—if the amount of the instrument is raised, the real defense of material alteration can be used to keep from paying the increased amount, but the original amount must still be paid.

e. Alteration of a completed instrument

f. Illegality that would make a contract void

g. Lack of capacity due to minority that would make a contract void

h. Lack of capacity due to insanity that would make a contract void

i. Extreme duress that would make a contract void (this is a situation in which the force or threat is so overwhelming that a party loses all free will)

j. Discharge in bankruptcy

k. Party demanding payment does not own the instrument

Claims to an Instrument

4232.123 Claims to an instrument include the following:

a. A claim to ownership of the instrument by one who asserts that he is the owner and was wrongfully deprived of possession

b. A claim of a lien on the instrument

c. A claim for rescission of an indorsement

4232.124 An HDC takes free of claims that arose before they became a holder; however, they are subject to claims arising when or after they become an HDC.

Rights of the Parties

4232.125 Each of the parties to a negotiable instrument has rights by virtue of being a party to a negotiable instrument.

4232.126 These rights include the following:

a. Right of the holder to receive payment of the instrument

b. Right of the holder to seek redress from secondary parties if the instrument is not paid

c. Right of the payee or indorser to negotiate the instrument to someone else

Discharge

4232.127 Liability of parties on a negotiable instrument can be discharged in the following situations:

a. **Payment of the instrument.** An instrument should be marked paid when the instrument is paid.

b. **By cancellation of the instrument.** This could be done by the intentional destruction of the instrument or marking it paid without having received payment.

c. **By cancellation of another person's indorsement.** The party whose indorsement was canceled is discharged from liability on the instrument.

d. **By reacquisition of the instrument.** This reacquisition would discharge all the intervening indorsees.

e. **By tender of payment** of a past due instrument that is not accepted, liability for future interest, costs, and attorney's fees are discharged. Principal and accrued interest up to the date of the tender are not discharged.

f. Discharge does not require consideration to be valid.

What Happens If...

4232.128 **What happens if the date of issue does not appear on the instrument?** This would not affect negotiability unless the maturity date of the instrument can only be determined based on the issue date.

Example: A note states that it is "Payable 90 days after date of issue," but fails to state the issue date. The note would be nonnegotiable since a negotiable instrument must be either payable on demand or at a specified time that can be determined from the face of the instrument.

4232.129 **What happens if the drawee will not pay the instrument when due?** The holder can sue the drawer and any prior indorsers. The holder can sue on the signature or warranty liability.

4232.130 **What happens if the maker will not pay the instrument when due?** The holder can sue the makers on their primary liability or any prior indorsers on their secondary liability. The holder can sue on the signature or warranty liability.

4232.131 **What happens if the drawer issues a check without signing it?** The instrument is nonnegotiable if the drawer fails to sign it.

4232.132 **What happens if an instrument is made payable both to order and to bearer?** It is payable to order unless the bearer words are handwritten or typewritten. If the bearer words are handwritten or typewritten, the instrument is payable to bearer.

4232.133 **What happens if an instrument is antedated?** The negotiability of an instrument is not affected by the fact that it is antedated. The time it is payable is determined by the stated date.

4232.134 **What happens if an instrument is postdated?** The negotiability of an instrument is not affected by the fact that it is postdated. The time it is payable is determined by the stated date.

4232.135 **What happens if an instrument is payable to the order of party A and party B?** Both party A and party B must indorse to negotiate, discharge, or enforce the instrument.

4232.136 **What happens if an instrument is payable to the order of party A or party B?** Either party A or party B can indorse to negotiate, discharge, or enforce the instrument.

4232.137 **What happens if the holder cannot tell whether the instrument is a draft or a note?** The holder may treat it as either.

4232.138 **What happens if the instrument contains conflicting handwritten, typewritten, and preprinted terms?** Handwritten terms control over typewritten and preprinted terms. Typewritten terms control over preprinted terms.

4232.139 **What happens if words differ from number figures on the instrument?** Words control over number figures but if the words are ambiguous then the number figures will control over ambiguous words.

4232.140 **What happens if the instrument provides for interest but does not state the rate of interest?** The rate is the judgment rate at the place of payment, payable from the date of the instrument. If undated, it is payable from the date of issue.

Liability on a Negotiable Instrument

4232.141 Liability on a negotiable instrument is based on a signature. No party is liable on an instrument unless an authorized signature is on the instrument. See U.C.C. 3-401(a).

4232.142 **Signature**

    a. A name on an instrument

    b. Can be a trade name or an assumed name.

    c. Can be a written signature, a word or words, a mark, a stamp, or a thumbprint.

    d. Can be handwritten, typed, stamped, or printed. See U.C.C. 3-401(b).

4232.143 **Unauthorized signature**

    a. Does not bind the party named in the signature unless the party either:

        (1) later ratifies the signature or

        (2) is precluded from denying it. See U.C.C. 3-404(a).

    b. Does bind the party making the unauthorized signature. See U.C.C. 3-404 and 3-401(b).

4232.144 **Signing by an agent for a principal**

    a. An agent may legally bind the principal on a negotiable instrument.

    b. An agent cannot legally bind the principal unless the agent is authorized to sign for the principal.

    c. If an agent signs without authorization, the agent is liable on the instrument.

    d. An agent who is acting with authorization and attempting to sign for the principal can be liable if the agent does not disclose the agency relationship or the identity of the principal.

4232.145 Examples of signature liability for an indorsement on a negotiable instrument where XYZ Corp. is the principal and John A. Smith is the agent:

John A. Smith	*John A. Smith* *Agent*
Agent liable; principal not liable.	Agent liable; principal not liable.
XYZ Corporation *by John A. Smith* *Agent*	*John A. Smith* *for XYZ Corporation*
If authorized, agent not liable; principal liable.	If authorized, agent not liable; principal liable.

Liabilities of the Parties

4232.146 **Primary liability.** A party primarily liable on an instrument has absolute liability to pay.

4232.147 **Secondary liability.** A party secondarily liable on an instrument has only conditional liability (i.e., liability to pay the instrument only if parties who are primarily liable do not and certain other conditions are met).

4232.148 Liability of the various parties is as follows:

    a. **Maker.** The maker is primarily liable on a note.

    b. **Drawer.** The drawer is secondarily liable on a draft or check. After issue, no one is primarily liable. If the instrument is presented for payment (check or demand draft) or presented for acceptance (time draft) and notice is given, the drawer is liable.

    c. **Indorsers.** Indorsers of a negotiable instrument are secondarily liable if presentment is made, the instrument is dishonored, and they are notified of the dishonor.

    d. **Drawee.** The drawee who accepts a draft or check is primarily liable on the negotiable instrument. Unless the drawee accepts the negotiable instrument, there is no primary liability on the instrument.

        (1) Acceptance before payment is usually only used with drafts payable at some future date.

        (2) A check is accepted by the drawee bank if the bank certifies the check prior to payment.

        (3) For checks and drafts payable at sight or payable on demand, presentment is made for payment. The holder or holder in due course cannot compel the drawee to pay the negotiable instrument unless the drawee previously accepted the negotiable instrument.

    e. **Acceptor.** The acceptor is the drawee who signs on the instrument and agrees to pay the instrument on the due date. This is usually done with time drafts and not with instruments due on demand or at sight. The acceptor is primarily liable on the instrument.

Certification of a Check by a Bank

4232.149 A drawee bank may, but is not required to, certify a check.

4232.150 Certification makes the drawee bank the acceptor of the check. The acceptor is primarily liable for payment on the check.

Presentment

4232.151 There are two types of presentments for negotiable instruments:

    1. Presentment for acceptance

    2. Presentment for payment

4232.152 **Presentment for acceptance:** A demand for acceptance made by the holder of the instrument upon the drawee of a draft or check.

4232.153 **Presentment for payment:** A demand for payment made by the holder of the negotiable instrument upon any of the following:

    a. Drawee of a check or draft

      b. Acceptor of a check or draft

      c. Maker of a note

4232.154 If the drawee accepts the instrument, the party is called the acceptor.

4232.155 Presentment for acceptance is normally used only for time drafts. The holder of a time draft has the option to submit the instrument for acceptance prior to the date of payment. Presentment for acceptance of a time draft by the holder is necessary to hold the secondary parties (drawer and indorsers) liable. The holder of a "due on demand" instrument is entitled to immediate payment but not acceptance.

4232.156 If the instrument is payable at a bank, failure of the holder to present the instrument for payment will discharge the drawer, acceptor, or maker only to the extent that they lose funds because the drawee or payor bank becomes insolvent after the due date.

4232.157 For time instruments, presentment for payment should be on the due date.

4232.158 For demand instruments, presentment for payment must be within a reasonable time in order to hold secondary parties liable on the instrument if dishonored.

4232.159 For domestic checks, the time for presentment for payment is within 30 days after its date to hold the drawer liable and is also within 30 days from the date of an indorsement to hold the indorser liable.

Dishonor

4232.160 Dishonor is the refusal to do either of the following:

      a. Accept an instrument before the due date.

      b. Pay the instrument when due.

Notice of Dishonor

4232.161 Notice of dishonor is necessary to hold secondary parties liable on the instrument. Notice is not necessary to hold liable parties primarily liable on the instrument.

4232.162 Notice of dishonor should be given to any party that could be liable on the instrument. The notice would identify the instrument and say it has been dishonored.

4232.163 Notice can be given as follows:

      a. In any reasonable manner

      b. Orally

      c. In writing

4232.164 Written notice of dishonor is effective when sent and need not actually be received.

Liability on Transactions That Utilize a Negotiable Instrument

4232.165 There are three types of liability that can result from a transaction that involves the issue of a negotiable instrument:

      1. Contractual liability. This is the liability that is based on the contract between the parties. It has nothing to do with the use of a negotiable instrument.

2. **Signature liability** on the negotiable instrument. This is based on a person's signature on a negotiable instrument.

3. **Warranty liability** on the negotiable instrument. This liability is based on the transfer of a negotiable instrument from one party to another person.

Warranty Liability of Parties to a Negotiable Instrument

4232.166 There are two types of warranties that are imposed on parties to a negotiable instrument:

1. Presentment warranties

2. Transferee warranties

4232.167 These warranties are imposed on the parties by operation of law (automatically, without action by the parties) unless expressly waived.

Presentment Warranties

4232.168 Presentment warranties go from the presentor to the payor or acceptor.

Diagram:

```
Presentor ── instrument presented for payment ──▶ Payor
            presentment warranties

Presentor ── instrument presented for acceptance ──▶ Acceptor
            presentment warranties
```

4232.169 Parties who present the instrument for payment or acceptance warrant that they are as follows:

a. They have good title to the instrument or are authorized to act for the party that has that title.

b. They have no knowledge that the signature of the maker or drawer is unauthorized.

c. The instrument has not been materially altered.

4232.170 These warranties are made whether or not the presentor indorses the instrument.

4232.171 **Example of use.** If the presentor is a thief, he does not have good title to the instrument. By receiving payment on the instrument after presentment for payment, the presentor has breached the presentment warranty on title. The payor could sue the presentor for breach of the presentment warranty and collect the damages for his loss.

Transferee Warranties

4232.172 Transferee warranties go from the transferor to the transferee, but not to transferees that are payors or acceptors. If the transferee is a payor or acceptor, the presentment warranties apply to the transfer.

4232.173 Parties that transfer a negotiable instrument for value warrant that the following are true:

a. They have good title to the instrument or are authorized to act for the party that has title and the transfer is rightful.

b. All signatures are authentic or authorized.

c. The instrument has not been altered.

d. No defense of any party is good against the transferor.

e. They have no knowledge of any insolvency proceedings regarding the maker, acceptor, or drawer of an unaccepted instrument.

4232.174 The transferor's warranties run to the immediate transferee and all subsequent holders of the instrument if the transferor indorses the instrument.

4232.175 The transferor's warranties run only to the immediate transferee and not to subsequent holders if the transferor negotiates by delivery alone without indorsement.

4232.176 The transferor's warranties apply only to transferors who receive consideration for the transfer. The warranties are not imposed on a transferor who gives the instrument as a gift to a transferee.

Obligations of Drawee Bank to Holder of Check

4232.177 The check is not an assignment of funds in the drawer's account held by the bank.

4232.178 The holder of an uncertified check cannot legally compel the drawee bank to pay a check even if the account has sufficient funds to cover the amount of the check. The holder's only recourse is against the drawer or any prior indorsers.

4232.179 If the bank has certified a check, the bank has accepted the check and is primarily liable on the instrument. The holder can sue to compel the bank to pay the certified check.

Rights and Duties of the Drawee Bank Regarding Checks

4232.180 The drawee bank contracts with the customer and is obligated by the terms of that contract. Article 4 of the U.C.C. also imposes obligations on the drawee bank. The drawee bank and customer relationship can be as follows:

a. **Debtor and creditor.** The customer is the creditor and the bank is the debtor when the customer makes a deposit. If the bank elects to pay an overdraft of the customer, the customer drawer is the debtor and the bank is the creditor.

b. **Principal and agent.** For deposits of checks, the bank acts as an agent for the customer to collect checks.

4232.181 **Certification of a check by the bank**

a. The bank is not obligated to certify a check.

b. Banks usually will certify for one of their customers but not for a holder.

c. Refusal by a bank to certify is not a dishonor. See U.C.C. 3-409(d).

d. When a check is certified, the bank immediately withdraws the funds from the drawer's account so that the funds are available when the check is presented for payment.

e. Certification of a check can be requested by either a holder or the drawer. In either case, if the check is certified, the drawer and any prior indorsers are discharged from liability on the instrument. See U.C.C. 3-414(c) and 3-415(d).

f. If a check is altered before certification, the bank is liable for the altered amount.

g. If a check is altered after certification, the bank is liable only for the original amount.

4232.182 The bank is obligated to honor checks drawn by the customer if there are sufficient funds in the drawer's account. The bank is not obligated to a payee or holder of the check. The bank is liable to the drawer customer for a wrongful dishonor.

4232.183 If the drawer customer does not have sufficient funds to pay a check, the bank:

    a. can dishonor the check, or

    b. may pay the check and seek reimbursement from the customer drawer.

4232.184 **Stale check.** A check is stale if presented to the bank for payment more than six months after the date of issue. A bank that receives a stale check may do any of the following:

    a. Pay the check in good faith.

    b. Dishonor the check.

    c. Check with the customer for directions to pay or to dishonor. See U.C.C. 4-404.

4232.185 **Missing indorsements.** The bank can add any necessary indorsement of the customer needed to collect on a check.

4232.186 **Death of a customer.** The bank can pay checks for 10 days after the death of a customer unless an heir or executor orders the bank to stop payment on checks.

4232.187 **Stop payment orders**

    a. Only a customer can order a stop payment by the bank for outstanding checks. Payees, holders, holders in due course, and indorsers cannot compel the bank to stop payment on a check.

    b. Oral stop payment orders are good for 14 calendar days.

    c. Written stop payment orders are good for six months, but they can be renewed. A check over six months is stale, but a bank can still pay a stale check.

    d. If the bank pays a check contrary to a valid stop payment order, it must credit the customer's account. The bank will be liable to the customer for any damages suffered due to the bank's error. The bank gets whatever rights the customer had regarding the check.

4232.188 **Overdrafts.** The bank can pay or dishonor. Some banks may contract with the customer to pay automatically any overdrafts on the account.

4232.189 **Forgery** of drawer's signature on a check.

    a. The drawer is not liable.

    b. If the drawer is negligent (like not controlling access to a check-writing machine), the bank is not liable for payment of the check.

    c. The bank is not liable for a series of forgeries by the same person if the drawer does not notify the bank within 30 calendar days of when the drawer is able to examine the first check containing a forged signature. The bank would not be liable for any checks paid that contain subsequent forgeries by the same forger that it pays prior to notification.

    d. If the forgeries are not reported within one year of the receipt by the drawer, the bank is not even liable for the initial forgery.

    e. The bank cannot recover against a holder who cashes a check with the drawer's forged signature if the holder does not know of the forgery. The bank is obligated to know the signature of the drawer.

4232.190 Forged indorsement. The bank must credit the drawer's account if it pays a check containing a forged indorsement. The bank is not liable for payment on a forged indorsement unless the bank is notified of the forged indorsement within three years.

4232.191 Payment of an altered check

    a. Drawer's account can be charged only the amount of the original check before alteration.

    b. The bank can seek recovery against its transferor based on a breach of the presentment warranties.

    c. The bank is not liable to credit the drawer's account if the drawer is negligent in writing the check so that alteration is easy.

4232.192 Accept deposits. The bank is obligated to accept the deposits of the customer. The bank acts as an agent to collect on deposited checks. If a deposited check is returned NSF, the amount can be taken from the customer's account.

Banks

4232.193 These are the banks that are involved in the processing of checks:

    a. **Depository bank.** First bank to receive the deposit of a check.

    b. **Payor bank.** Bank that pays the check from the customer's account. The bank would be the drawee on the check.

    c. **Collecting bank.** All banks that help collect on the check other than the payor bank.

    d. **Intermediary bank.** All banks to which an item is transferred in the course of collection other than the payor or depository bank.

Collection Between Customers of the Same Bank

4232.194 A check is paid if not dishonored by the start of the second banking day after receipt. See U.C.C. 4-215(e)(2).

Collection Between Customers of Different Banks

4232.195 Banks must pay the check before midnight of the next banking day following receipt.

4232.196 The U.C.C. allows deferred posting. Checks received after 2:00 in the afternoon are recorded the next day.

Letters of Credit

4232.197 A letter of credit is a written instrument, usually issued by a buyer's bank, in which the issuing bank promises to honor demands for payment by a third person (the seller) according to the terms of the instrument. If the conditions of the letter of credit are met, the bank will pay the seller.

4232.198 Letters of credit are often used in international business transactions. Generally, international letters of credit are governed by the Uniform Customs and Practices for Documentary credits adopted by the International Chamber of Commerce.

4232.199 Generally in a simple letter of credit situation:

    a. The issuer, generally a bank, agrees to issue the letter of credit, determine whether a seller has performed certain required acts, and if they have made payment to the seller.

    b. In return, the buyer promises to reimburse the issuer for the amount they pay to the seller.

4232.200 Under the letter of credit, the issuer is required to pay the seller if they comply with the terms and conditions of the letter of credit. Usually, a letter of credit will require the seller to deliver a bill of lading to the issuing bank to prove that goods have been shipped to the buyer.

4232.201 If documents that conform to the terms of the letter of credit are presented, the issuing bank is obligated to pay. This would be true even if the buyer feels that the goods are defective or in the case where the buyer refuses to pay the issuing bank. This is due to the fact that the obligation of the issuing bank is independent of the sales contract between the buyer and seller. Other documents required often include an invoice listing the terms of purchase, a customs certificate showing that the goods have been cleared for export, and proof of insurance. Production of these documents provides evidence that the goods have been shipped in conformity with the letter of credit.

4232.202 A letter of credit assures the seller that they will receive payment when they comply with the conditions of the letter. It also assures the buyer that the seller will not receive payment until they fulfill the terms and conditions of the letter of credit.

4232.203 Irrevocable Letter of Credit: An irrevocable letter of credit is one under which the buyer's bank is not able to avoid its obligation to pay unless relieved of the obligation by both the buyer and seller.

4232.204 Confirmed Letter of Credit: With this type of letter of credit, the seller's bank assumes the liability on the letter of credit as follows:

    a. The buyer's bank issues a letter of credit to the seller and the seller's bank confirms the letter of credit.

    b. The seller then delivers the goods to the carrier, receives a negotiable bill of lading, and delivers the bill of lading to the seller's bank. The seller also presents a draft drawn on the buyer demanding payment for the goods.

    c. The seller's bank pays the seller for the goods and the buyer's bank reimburses the seller's bank for the payment.

    d. The buyer finally reimburses its bank for the payment.

4232.205 With a confirmed letter of credit, the payment is received by the seller before the goods actually arrive at the buyer's location.

    a. In this situation, the buyer cannot refuse to pay for the goods by claiming they are defective.

    b. The recourse available to the buyer, if in fact the goods are defective, is to file a contract action for damages against the seller based on the contract for the sale of the goods.

4232.206 Advised Letter of Credit: With this type of letter of credit, the seller's bank is an agent for the collection of the amount owed to the seller.

    a. The seller's bank simply collects the payment from the buyer's bank and then transfers the payment to the seller.

    b. The buyer then reimburses its bank.

4233 Secured Transactions

4233.01 A *secured transaction* is a transaction in which the debtor gives to the creditor an interest in specific personal property to secure the payment of the debt. If the debt is not paid, the creditor can sell the personal property and apply the proceeds to the unpaid debt. This is faster and cheaper than suing the debtor, getting a judgment, locating property owned by the debtor, seizing the property, and having it sold at public auction to satisfy the debt. The real property equivalent of a secured transaction is a mortgage. The secured transaction also gives the creditor a priority over other creditors of the debtor in the personal property used to secure the debt.

4233.02 The *secured party* is the lender, seller, or other party in whose favor the security interest arises (i.e., the creditor).

4233.03 The *debtor* is the party that owes payment or other performance of the obligation that is secured.

4233.04 The law of secured transactions comes from Article 9 of the U.C.C. A revised Article 9 has been adopted by all of the states and is the basis for the following discussion. Revised Article 9 applies to transactions that create a security interest in tangible or intangible personal property or fixtures. A fixture is personal property that is attached to real property. A central air conditioning unit that is installed in a house would be an example of a fixture.

4233.05 A *security interest* is an interest in personal property or fixtures that secures payment or performance of an obligation.

4233.06 *A security agreement* is an agreement between the debtor and secured party that the secured party shall have an interest in the debtor's property to secure payments or performance of an obligation. It creates the security interest. It may be oral or written.

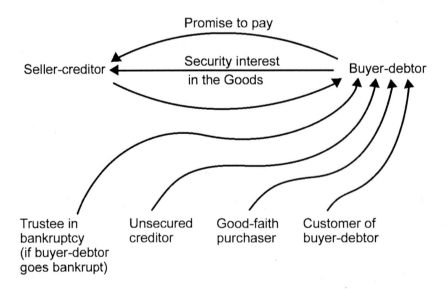

Other persons who might have rights in or compete for goods

4233.07 **Requirements of a written security agreement are as follows:**

    a. It must be "authenticated" by the debtor. This can include traditional signatures as well as "signatures" that are not handwritten on paper. This facilitates the use of electronic security agreements.

    b. It must reasonably identify the collateral. Generally, Article 9 types of property (i.e. "inventory", "accounts") can be used to identify the collateral.

4233.08 The agreement must be in writing to be enforced against the debtor and certain third parties unless the secured party has taken possession of the collateral pursuant to an agreement. The agreement must be made so that the person will have possession for purposes of security.

Attachment of a Security Interest

4233.09 **Attachment:** Creation; coming into existence of a security interest. In order for a security interest to be legally enforceable, it must attach to particular collateral.

4233.10 Before a security interest attaches, the following must occur:

    a. There must be a security agreement (oral or written) between the debtor and the secured party.

    b. The secured party must give value.

    c. The debtor must have rights in the collateral.

4233.11 The security interest cannot attach until the secured party gives value. Value is generally any consideration that would support a contract. Value also includes any security for preexisting obligations or any binding commitment to extend credit in the future (future advances).

4233.12 The debtor has no rights in an account until the account comes into existence, a contract until the contract is made, timber until the trees are cut, minerals until extracted from the ground, crops until the crops are planted, and fish until the fish are caught.

4233.13 Attachment establishes the creditor as having superior rights against the debtor, but attachment alone does not establish superior rights against a trustee in bankruptcy, unsecured creditors, other secured creditors, and good-faith purchasers from the buyer.

Classifications of Collateral

4233.14 **Collateral:** Property that is subject to a security interest.

4233.15 Revised U.C.C. Article 9 covers security interests that are created in personal property. Personal property includes that which is both tangible and intangible.

4233.16 **Tangible property:** Goods. These are classified by use. The rules applied may vary based on the category involved.

    a. **Consumer goods:** For personal use and consumption. Like buying a refrigerator for your home.

    b. **Equipment:** For business (profit or nonprofit) use. This is also the default classification if you cannot classify it anywhere else. An example would be a doctor buying a refrigerator to use in his office to store medicine.

c. **Farm products:** Used by a debtor engaged in farming as an occupation. An example would be a farmer buying a refrigerator to keep eggs cold before he sells them to a supermarket.

d. **Inventory:** Goods held for sale or lease. This includes raw materials, work-in-progress, finished goods inventory, and supplies. An example would be refrigerators held by an appliance dealer for sale to consumers.

Note that a refrigerator could be any one of the four classifications, depending on its use.

4233.17 Software "embedded" in goods so that it becomes "part of the goods" is treated as goods. If software is not "embedded" in a good it is considered a general intangible.

4233.18 **Intangible personal property:** No physical existence; a right to receive property. Classifications are as follows:

a. **Instruments:** Negotiable instruments or investment securities. Examples would be checks, drafts, promissory notes, certificates of deposit, bonds, and shares of stock.

b. **Document of title:** A document of title issued by or addressed to a bailee or covering goods in the bailee's possession. Examples are a bill of lading and a warehouse receipt.

c. **Chattel paper:** Writing that evidences both a monetary obligation and a security in or lease of specific goods. An example would be a security agreement. A security agreement held by a creditor could be used to secure a debt owed to another creditor.

d. **Accounts:** Right to receive payment for goods sold or leased not evidenced by an instrument or chattel paper. The account does not need to be due and payable. Accounts also include payment obligations arising out of the sale, lease, or license of all kinds of tangible and intangible personal property (i.e., license fees payable for use of software). Also included are credit card receivables.

e. **Contract right:** Right to payment under a contract not yet earned by performance nor evidenced by an instrument or chattel paper. These are potential accounts.

f. **General intangibles:** Whatever is not otherwise classified. Examples are goodwill, literary rights, right to performance from someone else, copyrights, trademarks, and patents. Remember that the statute of frauds says that a contract or the sale or transfer of intangible personal property for over $5,000 must be in writing to be enforceable.

Financing Statement

4233.19 A financing statement is filed to give public notice of the security interest. It provides constructive notice of the security interest. Third parties are deemed to know it exists even if they do not have actual knowledge.

4233.20 A financing statement must contain the following:

a. Names and addresses of both the secured party and the debtor. If an incorrect name of the debtor is used, the financing statement is ineffective, if a "standard" search would not find it.

b. Description of the collateral (If the collateral is a fixture, it must also include a description of the real estate to which the fixture is attached.)

c. Under Revised Article 9, signature of the debtor is not required if the secured party is authorized by the debtor to make the filing without the debtor's signature. This facilitates electronic filing of financing statements.

4233.21 Location of filing of a financing statement:

    a. Statewide only (generally the Secretary of State's office)

    b. The filing must be in the place of the debtor's "location" except for fixed time filings and filings to perfect a security interest in as-extracted collateral and timber to be cut. Location is defined as:

        (1) For "registered organizations" created by filing with a state, the state of filing.

        (2) For an entity not created by a filing, the entity's location is its chief executive offices.

        (3) For an individual, the place of their principal residence.

    c. Perfection of an agricultural lien on farm products occurs by filing centrally in the jurisdiction where the farm products are located. A fixture filing is made locally where the real estate is located.

4233.22 A filed financing statement is effective for five years.

    a. After five years, the security interest becomes unperfected.

    b. It can be continued if a continuation statement is filed. It would be good for five more years. This can be done indefinitely.

4233.23 A financing statement generally need not be filed for property subject to a state certificate of title laws. In these cases, the security interest must be noted on the title for the secured party to be protected. This rule would apply, for example, to cars, boats, and mobile homes.

Perfection of a Security Interest

4233.24 The security agreement *binds* the debtor and the secured party from the moment it is made. But generally, it does not *protect* the secured party against the rights of third parties until it is perfected.

4233.25 Perfection of a security interest can occur in various ways, but *both* attachment and perfection of the security interest must occur before the interest is good against other creditors.

4233.26 Perfection of a security interest can occur by taking the collateral into possession, public filing of a financing statement, or by attachment alone to make the security interest effective against third parties.

4233.27 **Perfection of a security interest for accounts, contract rights, and general intangibles:** Perfection by filing only.

4233.28 **Perfection of a security interest for goods:** Perfection by taking possession or filing a financial statement. No filing is needed if the secured party has possession of the collateral goods.

4233.29 **Perfection of a security interest for consumer goods:** The security interest is automatically perfected upon attachment if the purchaser buys on credit or the secured party lends to the debtor the funds that are used to make the purchase. The security interest is called a purchase money security interest (PMSI); however, this perfection by attachment is not good against a buyer of consumer goods who does any of the following:

    a. Purchases without knowledge of the security interest

    b. Gives value for the goods

c. Purchases for their own personal family or household use

d. Purchases before a financing statement if filed

Note: This buyer is an individual who bought the consumer goods from the original purchaser.

4233.30 **Perfection of a security interest for instruments, documents and chattel paper:** Perfection by possession or filing.

4233.31 **Perfection of a security interest for fixtures:** Perfection only by filing a financing statement with the office where mortgages on real estate are recorded.

4233.32 A security interest in instruments and negotiable documents is perfected by attachment alone for 21 days without filing or possession.

Rights and Duties of the Parties

4233.33 A secured party with possession of the collateral must exercise reasonable care in preserving the collateral. Legally, the secured party is a bailee in a mutual benefit bailment.

4233.34 Expenses incurred in the custody, preservation, and operating of the collateral are paid by the debtor.

4233.35 Risk of loss is with the debtor.

Priorities Among Conflicting Security Interests in the Same Collateral—Who Gets It?

4233.36 The issue of priority is important when several creditors claim interests in the same collateral.

4233.37 Where multiple security interests exist in the same collateral, the security interests rank in priority according to the time of filing of financing statements or perfection, whichever is earlier.

4233.38 If no security interests have been perfected, the interests have priority based upon the order in which they attached to the collateral.

4233.39 The holder of a purchase money security interest (PMSI) in inventory of the debtor has priority over another secured party who has a prior security agreement with the debtor that contains an "after acquired property clause" covering the debtor's inventory if either of the following is true:

a. The PMSI is perfected by filing at the time the debtor receives the inventory.

b. The PMSI secured party gives written notice to the prior secured party before the debtor gets possession of the inventory.

4233.40 The holder of a PMSI in collateral other than inventory has priority over conflicting security interests in the same collateral if the PMSI is perfected either:

a. at the time the debtor receives the collateral or

b. within 10 days.

4233.41 A buyer in the ordinary course of business from a merchant seller takes free of any security interest in the property purchased even if it is perfected and the buyer is aware of it. The purpose of this rule is to allow a consumer to buy a merchant's inventory without fear that it could be repossessed by the secured party.

4233.42 Artisans' liens have priority over any perfected security interests in the collateral.

Default

4233.43 Default is not defined in the U.C.C. The debtor and secured party are therefore able, by agreement, to define what constitutes a default in their particular case.

4233.44 The secured party may take possession of the collateral either by judicial process or without judicial process if it can be done without a breach of the peace.

4233.45 Generally, the secured party can retain the collateral in satisfaction of the debtor's obligation. Written notice of the intention to keep the collateral must be sent to the debtor and also (except for consumer goods) to any other secured party from whom written notice of a claim in the collateral is received.

4233.46 If no objection to the secured party keeping the collateral is received within 21 days, the collateral may be retained. If objection is made, the secured party must sell the collateral.

4233.47 The secured party must dispose of the collateral if the collateral is classified as consumer goods and the debtor has paid 60% or more of the purchase price. The secured party must sell the consumer goods within 90 days or be liable to the debtor.

4233.48 If the collateral is sold, the proceeds of the sale go to pay the expenses of the sale, then to satisfy the unpaid debt, then to any other debts owed by the debtor to the creditor. Any amount remaining is returned to the debtor. If there is a deficiency, the debtor can be held liable for this amount.

Floating Lien—A Security Interest in Collateral That Is Continually Changing

4233.49 **Floating lien.** This type of security interest is valid. This is often referred to as an "after acquired property clause."

4233.50 An example of a floating lien would be a security interest in the inventory of a new car dealer. The dealer sells cars daily and gets new shipments from the factory weekly. The security interest would float from the cars sold to the new cars coming into the dealer's inventory.

Common Law Lien

4233.51 A *common law lien* is given to artisans, innkeepers, and common carriers to secure payment for services rendered.

4233.52 Possessory: Lienholder has the right to keep the property until the debt is paid.

4233.53 The lien is lost if possession of the property is surrendered.

4233.54 If the lien is lost, the lienholder cannot retake possession, but she can sue the debtor for the value of the service.

Statutory Lien

4233.55 A *statutory lien* is a lien on personal property created by a statute enacted by the legislature.

4233.56 If the lien was not recognized at common law, the courts construe the language of the statute strictly.

4233.57 **Simplifies the foreclosure.** Creditor holds the property for the statutory period, notifies the person, and then sells the property for whatever they can get. There is no need to get judgment, levy on the property, and have the property sold at public auction by the sheriff. This is expensive and not worth the effort for many low-cost items.

4234 Documents of Title and Title Transfer

Documents of Title

4234.01 The rules governing documents of title are found in Article 7 of the Uniform Commercial Code.

4234.02 A warehouse receipt is a document of title to goods being stored. A bill of lading is a document of title to goods being shipped.

4234.03 A warehouseman or a common carrier is a bailee of the goods who has entered an agreement to either store or transport the goods in accordance with the owner's instructions.

4234.04 Warehouse receipts or bills of lading can be either negotiable or nonnegotiable.

4234.05 In order to be negotiable, a warehouse receipt, bill of lading, or other document of title must provide that the goods are to be delivered to bearer or to the order of a named person.

Warehouse Receipts

4234.06 To be valid, a warehouse receipt need not be in any particular form.

4234.07 However, the warehouseman will be liable to anyone injured due to the receipt not including the following:

  a. The location of the warehouse where the goods are stored
  b. The date of issue of the receipt
  c. The consecutive number of the receipt
  d. Whether the goods are to be delivered to bearer or to the order of a named person
  e. The rate of storage and handling charges
  f. A description of the goods or of the packages in which they are contained
  g. The signature of the warehouseman or agent
  h. Whether the warehouseman is the owner of the goods solely, jointly, or in common with others
  i. A statement of the amount of any advances made or liabilities incurred for which the warehouseman claims a lien or security interest

4234.08 A purchaser for value in good faith of a warehouse receipt can hold a warehouseman liable for either nonreceipt or misdescription of the goods.

4234.09 A warehouse receipt can qualify the description of the goods if it is done conspicuously by such language as "content, condition, and quantity unknown."

4234.10 A warehouseman owes the holder of the warehouse receipt the duties of a mutual benefit bailee and is required to exercise reasonable care regarding the goods.

4234.11 If the goods are ready to deteriorate or threaten other goods in the warehouse, the warehouseman may terminate the bailment through notification.

4234.12 Generally, a warehouseman must keep the goods covered by each receipt separate; however, fungible goods (e.g., grain) can be mingled.

Negotiation of Documents of Title

4234.13 Negotiable documents of title are negotiated in basically the same way as negotiable instruments. A document of title made out to bearer can be negotiated by delivery. A document of title made out to the order of a named person must be indorsed and delivered for negotiation to take place.

4234.14 If a person takes a negotiable document of title in good faith and in the regular course of business, the person becomes a bona fide holder.

4234.15 A bona fide holder has basically the same advantages given to a holder in due course of a negotiable instrument.

4234.16 A person who receives a negotiable document of title by proper negotiation acquires the following:

   a. Title to the document

   b. Title to the goods

   c. The right to the goods delivered to the bailee after the document is issued

   d. The direct obligation of the issuer to hold or deliver the goods according to the document's terms

4234.17 A transferor of a negotiable document of title warrants to the immediate transferee that the following are true:

   a. The document is genuine.

   b. They have no knowledge of any facts that would impair its validity or worth.

   c. The negotiation or transfer is rightful and fully effective with respect to the title to the document and the goods it represents.

4240 Debtor-Creditor Relationships

4241 Rights, Duties, and Liabilities of Debtors, Creditors, and Guarantors

4241.01 The rights and duties of debtors and creditors outside of bankruptcy are governed primarily by state law.

4241.02 Once a debt is past due, a creditor may file a legal action against the debtor in order to obtain a judgment and satisfy the claim out of the debtor's property.

4241.03 State law also provides a number of nonbankruptcy compromises that may be used to provide relief for a debtor.

Attachment

4241.04 Attachment is the prejudgment, court-ordered seizure of property of the debtor.

4241.05 The creditor can make use of an attachment to ensure that assets of the debtor are available to satisfy a judgment obtained by the creditor.

4241.06 The creditor's attachment rights are created by state statute.

4241.07 To make use of the remedy of attachment, the creditor generally must do the following:

    a. File an affidavit with the court showing the debtor to be in default and the statutory grounds for the attachment.

    b. Post a bond with the court to compensate the debtor for any loss suffered if the creditor fails to win the suit.

4241.08 If all of the requirements are met, the court will issue a writ of attachment ordering a court officer (sheriff) to seize property of the debtor.

4241.09 If the creditor wins the suit, the attached property can be sold to satisfy the judgment.

Writ of Execution

4241.10 If a court judgment is obtained against the debtor, the creditor may have to resort to post-judgment remedies to collect.

4241.11 If the debtor does not voluntarily pay the judgment, the creditor will have the clerk of courts issue a writ of execution.

4241.12 The writ of execution is a court order directing an officer of the court (sheriff) to levy against (seize) specific property of the debtor.

4241.13 The debtor's property is then sold at a judicial sale and the proceeds are used to pay the judgment and the costs of the sale. Any excess is returned to the debtor.

4241.14 The debtor generally has the right to redeem the seized property before the sale takes place by paying the amount of the judgment.

Exempt Property

4241.15 Most states provide for the exemption of certain property of the debtor from attachment or execution. The exact property that is exempt varies greatly from state to state.

4241.16 All states provide a homestead exemption under which either the entire family home or a specific dollar value of the home is exempt from attachment or execution by creditors. This exemption generally would not apply to a valid home mortgage lien.

4241.17 Most states also provide exemptions for certain personal property of the debtor. The most common items include the following:

    a. Household furnishings up to a specific dollar amount

    b. A motor vehicle (for a specific dollar amount)

    c. Clothing and certain personal possessions (e.g., family photos) of the debtor

    d. Equipment and tools used in the debtor's trade or business up to a specific dollar amount

4241.18 Exempt property would generally not be exempt from an IRS tax lien resulting from a failure to pay tax.

Garnishment

4241.19 Garnishment is a statutory remedy of the creditor that is directed at a third party, rather than the debtor.

4241.20 The third party (garnishee) must either owe a debt to the debtor or be holding property that belongs to the debtor.

4241.21 As a result of the garnishment, the third party is ordered to turn over the payment of the debt or the property of the debtor to satisfy the creditor's judgment.

4241.22 The most common garnishments are served on the debtor's employer to garnish the debtor's wages or upon a bank to garnish the funds in the debtor's accounts.

4241.23 Both federal and state laws limit the amount that can be garnished from the debtor's weekly wages.

Composition Agreement

4241.24 A composition agreement is an agreement between the debtor and the creditors whereby the creditors receive a pro rata portion of the debt owed them in exchange for a promise to forgive the rest of the debt.

4241.25 The agreement must meet all of the requirements of a contract.

4241.26 The consideration for the promise of each creditor to forgive the balance of the debt owed to them is the promises of the other creditors to forgive the balance of their claims against the debtor.

4241.27 The debtor is released only from the claims of the creditors who agree to the composition. Other creditors may still pursue judicial remedies such as attachment of the debtor's property.

Assignment for the Benefit of Creditors

4241.28 In an assignment for the benefit of creditors, the debtor voluntarily transfers property to a trustee. The trustee uses the property to pay the debtor's creditors on a pro rata basis.

4241.29 An assignment does not require the consent of the creditors. Each creditor may also choose to accept or reject the partial payment.

4241.30 Acceptance of partial payment from the trustee does not legally discharge the debtor from the balance of the debt. The creditors can still attempt to collect the full amount of their claims unless they agree to forgive the balance by way of a composition agreement.

Equity Receivership

4241.31 In an equity receivership, the court appoints a receiver to collect the assets and income of the debtor.

4241.32 The receiver is appointed to handle the debtor's affairs upon petition of a creditor.

4241.33 The court then orders the receiver to take such action as the following:

    a. Liquidating the debtor's assets by way of public or private sale in order to pay creditors

    b. Operating the debtor's business for a period of time in order to continue a stream of income that can be used to pay creditors' claims

Fair Debt Collection Practices Act

4241.34 The Fair Debt Collection Practices Act (FDCPA) is a federal statute that was passed to control abuses in the debt collection process.

4241.35 The Fair Debt Collection Practices Act (FDCPA) regulates the collection of consumer debt. Consumer debt is defined as debt that arises for personal, family, or household purposes.

4241.36 Commercial debt, such as debt arising from the purchase of inventory, is not covered by the Fair Debt Collection Practices Act (FDCPA).

4241.37 The Fair Debt Collection Practices Act (FDCPA) applies to debt collectors. Debt collectors are defined as third-party collectors, such as collection agencies.

4241.38 The rules of the Fair Debt Collection Practices Act (FDCPA) do not apply to original creditors collecting their own debts.

4241.39 Debt collectors must provide written verification of the debt if the debtor asks. Collectors must automatically provide written verification within five days of contacting the debtor. This writing must include the following:

    a. The amount of the debt

    b. The name of the creditor

    c. The debtor's right to dispute the debt in writing within 30 days

4241.40 Under the Fair Debt Collection Practices Act (FDCPA), if the debtor disputes the debt, the debt collector must cease all further collection efforts until it supplies the debtor with a written verification of the debt. Verification can be satisfied by either of the following:

    a. A judgment evidencing the debt

    b. A statement itemizing the debt owed by the consumer and the consideration the debtor received

4241.41 The Fair Debt Collection Practices Act (FDCPA) provides restrictions on the debt collector's contact with the debtor. Among these are the following:

    a. Debtors cannot be contacted at inconvenient times, generally before 8:00 in the morning or after 9:00 at night. Debtors who work at night cannot be disturbed during their daytime sleeping hours.

    b. Debtors cannot be contacted at their place of employment if the employer objects or has a policy prohibiting such contact.

    c. If the debtor notifies the collector in writing that the debtor wants no more contact, the collector must stop contacting the debtor and take other steps to collect the debt.

    d. If the debtor has an attorney and notifies the collector of this fact, the collector can generally contact only the attorney from that point on.

4241.42 Debt collectors are generally prohibited by the Fair Debt Collection Practices Act (FDCPA) from communicating with third parties about the debt.

    a. Third parties may be contacted only to obtain information to locate the debtor such as address, phone number, or place of employment.

    b. When contacting third parties, debt collectors are prohibited from doing the following:

        (1) Disclosing that the debtor owes a debt

        (2) Communicating with the third party (or debtor) by postcard

        (3) Disclosing in correspondence that the sender is in the debt collection business

        (4) Identifying the debt collector's employer unless expressly requested

4241.43 Other conduct is also restricted under the Fair Debt Collection Practices Act (FDCPA). For example:

    a. Collectors may not harass, oppress, or abuse the debtor.

    b. Debt collectors may not falsely misrepresent that they:

        (1) are affiliated with the government,

        (2) are attorneys,

        (3) have sold the debtor's account to another, or

        (4) will take actions that they cannot lawfully take.

4241.44 Remedies available under the Fair Debt Collection Practices Act (FDCPA):

    a. The Federal Trade Commission is responsible for enforcement of the act.

    b. Under the FDCPA, debtors can bring civil actions against collectors who violate the act. Debtors can recover damages for actual injuries suffered.

    c. Debtors can collect up to $1,000 in addition to actual damages based upon the nature of the collector's conduct.

    d. Attorneys' fees and court costs may also be recovered by debtors under the act.

Rights, Duties, and Liabilities—Guarantors

4241.45 Parties that promise a creditor that they will be liable for the principal debtor's performance are either guarantors or sureties.

4241.46 **Guaranty:** Relationship among three parties in which the guarantor promises to pay the obligation of the principal debtor that is owed to the creditor if the principal debtor defaults on the obligation.

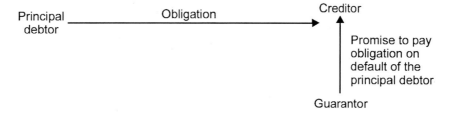

4241.47 Suretyship: Relationship among three parties in which the surety promises to pay the obligation of the principal debtor that is owed to the creditor.

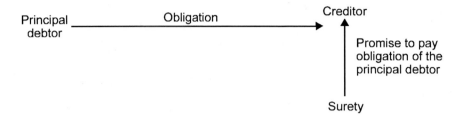

4241.48 Difference between guarantor and surety

a. **Guarantor:**

(1) Liability created in some other instrument from that of the principal debtor—often at a different time.

(2) Promise to perform if the debtor cannot perform. The guarantor is secondarily liable.

(3) "I will pay if the debtor cannot pay."

(4) Creditor needs to demand payment from the debtor and give notice of default to the guarantor to collect from the guarantor.

(5) The promise of the guarantor is said to be collateral to that of the principal debtor.

b. **Surety:**

(1) Liability created concurrently with that of the debtor.

(2) Promise to do the same thing the debtor promises. The surety is primarily liable.

(3) "I will pay if the debtor does not."

(4) Creditor does not need to demand payment from the debtor to collect from the surety.

(5) Liability established in the same instrument as the principal debtor.

The legal rights and duties of guarantors and sureties are substantially the same. The terms are often used interchangeably.

4241.49 Consideration: Legally sufficient consideration is required to make a suretyship or guaranty contract enforceable.

4241.50 Statute of frauds

a. Any promise to pay the debt of another person is unenforceable unless there is a writing signed by the party to be charged.

b. The statute of frauds applies only to guaranty contracts since they involve secondary promises. Surety contracts, which involve primary promises to pay, do not fall under the statute of frauds.

c. Promise must be made to the creditor to fall within the statute of frauds. If the promise is made to the principal debtor, the promise is valid and enforceable even if oral.

4241.51 Main purpose doctrine: This is an exception to the statute of frauds when the promise is made for the primary benefit of the promisor. This means that an oral promise to pay the debt of another is enforceable if the oral promise was made primarily to benefit the promisor.

4241.52 Classification of guarantors and sureties:

    a. **Unconditional or absolute**

        (1) Binds the guarantor unconditionally to perform the obligation.

        (2) Absolute guarantor becomes liable when debtor defaults. Nothing else is needed.

        (3) Suretyship contracts are unconditional unless a condition is present.

    b. **Conditional**

        (1) Binds the guarantor only after the performance of some act by the creditor.

        (2) Typical acts that make liability conditional include the following:

            (a) Unsuccessful attempt to collect from the debtor

            (b) Unpaid judgment

            (c) Showing it would be futile to proceed to a judgment against the debtor

    c. **General**

        (1) Addressed "To whom it may concern"

        (2) Any creditor who has knowledge of the guaranty and extends credit may enforce the guaranty.

    d. **Special:** Addressed to a particular person.

    e. **Temporary** (or limited or single): Limited to a single transaction, a specified period of time, or a specified maximum amount.

    f. **Continuing**

        (1) Contemplates a transaction of indefinite time.

        (2) May be a series of credits or a credit line.

    g. **Compensated:** Person who agrees to serve as a surety and receives compensation (usually money) for undertaking the risk. An example would be a bonding company.

    h. **Noncompensated** (also called accommodation): Person who agrees to serve as a surety without compensation. Courts tend to discharge the noncompensated surety from an obligation for any change the creditor makes in the contract with the principal debtor.

4241.53 **Rights of creditor:** A creditor may proceed against the principal debtor alone, the surety alone, the surety and the principal debtor, or foreclose on any security interest furnished by the principal debtor, or against the guarantor after default by the principal debtor.

4241.54 Defenses available to the principal debtor:

    a. **Discharge in bankruptcy.** This is a personal defense available only to the principal debtor. This defense may not be used by the guarantor or surety to avoid paying the creditor.

    b. **Minority of the principal debtor.** This is a personal defense available only to the principal debtor. (Minority generally refers to being under the age of 18.) This defense may not be used by the guarantor or surety to avoid paying the creditor.

c. **Performance of the obligation.** If the principal debtor has done what was promised, the creditor or the surety cannot insist that the debtor do it again.

d. **Breach of contract by the creditor.** Like any other contract, the wrongdoer cannot insist on performance if the wrongdoer has not done what they promised to do.

4241.55 Defenses available to the guarantor or surety to avoid liability to the creditor:

a. **All nonpersonal defenses** of the principal debtor are available. Remember that bankruptcy and minority of the debtor are personal defenses not available to the guarantor or surety.

b. **Minority or bankruptcy of the guarantor or surety is a defense.** Minors can avoid liability on all contracts, even guarantor or suretyship contracts.

c. **Creditor's fraud or nondisclosure of something important.** For example, the creditor does not tell the surety that one of the principal debtor's employees was embezzling money.

d. **Creditor modifying principal debtor's contract.** For example, the creditor extends the time for the principal debtor to repay.

e. Creditor's release of security or co-guarantors or co-sureties.

f. Creditor's release of the principal debtor.

g. Anything the creditor does that will hurt the guarantor's or surety's chance of coming out whole will discharge the surety from the obligation to the creditor.

   (1) Courts tend to release the noncompensated guarantor or surety for any change in the contract.

   (2) For a compensated guarantor or surety, only the amount lost due to the change will be excused.

4241.56 Remedies of the guarantor or surety:

a. **Defense:** Use a defense to avoid payment to the creditor.

b. **Reimbursement or indemnity:** Get the principal debtor to pay the guarantor or surety for the amount the guarantor or surety had to pay the creditor.

c. **Subrogation:** When the guarantor or surety discharges the principal debtor's obligation to the creditor, the guarantor or surety gets all the creditor's rights regarding the obligation.

d. **Contribution:** From co-guarantor or co-sureties for paying more than legally obligated.

4241.57 **Surety bonds:** These bonds are an acknowledgment of an obligation to make good the performance by another of some act or duty.

a. **Common-law bonds:** No law requiring them.

b. **Statutory bonds:** Required by statute.

c. **Construction bonds** (performance bonds)

   (1) Cover the performance of a contract.

   (2) Often used in construction contracts and supply contracts.

   (3) May cover laborers and materialmen as third-party intended beneficiaries to the contract between the creditor and the surety. Remember that third-party intended beneficiaries can sue to enforce the contract.

(4) Subclassifications

    (a) Performance bonds—For performance of work

    (b) Payment bond—For payment of laborers and materialmen

(5) Miller Act

    (a) Federal act that requires a performance and payment bond on all construction contracts for the federal government for more than $2,000.

    (b) Not required for construction that is only financed by the federal government (e.g., Federal Housing Administration).

d. **Fidelity bonds**

  (1) These bonds indemnify the employer against loss from dishonesty of an employee.

  (2) Surety gets right of subrogation against a wrongdoing employee.

e. **Official bond:** Required on some public officials that have custody of public funds.

f. **Judicial bonds**

  (1) Required in connection with judicial proceedings to indemnify the other party against damages resulting from the proceedings.

  (2) Examples:

    (a) Bail bond

    (b) Appeal bond

    (c) Injunction bond

    (d) Attachment bond

4242 Bankruptcy and Insolvency

4242.01 Bankruptcy results when the intended performance of the debtor becomes impossible due to excessive debt. The solution is to take the debtor's property and distribute it to the unpaid creditors through a uniform process.

4242.02 The Constitution contains an express provision allowing Congress to enact uniform bankruptcy laws. Major bankruptcy laws were enacted in 1898, 1938, 1978, and 2005. The most recent major revision is the Bankruptcy Prevention and Consumer Protection Act of 2005.

4242.03 Reasons for a bankruptcy law

a. Fair distribution of the debtor's property so that there is equal treatment of unsecured creditors

b. To give honest but overextended debtors a fresh start through discharge of debts or postponement of the time for payment

4242.04 The chapters on topics of the Bankruptcy Law are as follows:

Chapter	Topic
1	General Provisions
3	Case Administration (Bringing a Bankruptcy Case)
5	Creditors and Their Claims, the Debtor's Duties and Discharge, and the Handling of the Debtor's Estate
7	Liquidation of the Debtor's Estate to Pay Creditors
9	Adjustment of Debt of a Municipality (Like a City)
11	Reorganization of Debt (Primarily Businesses)
12	Adjustment of Debts for Family Farmers
13	Adjustment of Debts of an Individual with Regular Income
15	U.S. Trustees

Written Notice to Consumer Debtor

4242.05 Before a bankruptcy case is commenced by an individual whose debts are primarily consumer debts, the bankruptcy clerk must give the individual written notice containing the following:

(1) A brief description of:

(a) Chapters 7, 11, 12, and 13 and the general purpose, benefits, and costs of proceeding under each of those chapters and

(b) the types of services available from credit counseling agencies

(2) Statements specifying that:

(a) a person who knowingly and fraudulently conceals assets or makes a false oath or statement under penalty of perjury in connection with a bankruptcy case will be subject to fine, imprisonment, or both, and

(b) all information supplied by a debtor in connection with a bankruptcy case is subject to examination by the attorney general

Who May Be a Debtor Under Chapter 7

4242.06 A debtor under Chapter 7 must reside in the United States and have a domicile, a place of business, or property in the United States.

4242.07 The debtor in a proceeding under Chapter 7 cannot be any of the following:

a. A railroad

b. An insurance company

c. A domestic bank

d. Any other lending institution (like a credit union or a savings and loan association)

e. A governmental unit

4242.08 Debtors under Chapter 7 are not eligible for bankruptcy relief. These organizations are covered by special statutes, and their liquidations are supervised by certain regulatory agencies.

Voluntary Petition

4242.09 A voluntary petition is filed by the debtor.

4242.10 A voluntary petition may be done jointly by husband and wife if both consent.

4242.11 Filing automatically subjects debtors and their property to jurisdiction of the bankruptcy court.

4242.12 In a voluntary petition, the debtors need not be insolvent. They only need to show that they have debts.

4242.13 An individual must receive credit counseling from an approved nonprofit budget and credit counseling agency within 180 days before filing a voluntary bankruptcy petition.

    a. The debtor must participate in either individual or group sessions that outline opportunities for available credit counseling and assist the individual in related budget analysis.

    b. A certificate of compliance from the nonprofit budget and credit counseling agency must be filed with the petition.

    c. Exception may be made to the budget and credit counseling requirement:

        (1) in districts where the bankruptcy trustee (or bankruptcy administrator, if any) determines that adequate budget and credit counseling services are not available.

        (2) for debtors who are unable to complete the requirement due to incapacity (impairment by reason of mental illness or mental deficiency), disability (physical impairment), or active military duty in a military combat zone.

4242.14 The bankruptcy court may dismiss a voluntary bankruptcy petition for several reasons. These include:

    a. unreasonable delay by the debtor that is prejudicial to creditors,

    b. nonpayment of any fees or charges,

    c. failure of the debtor to file required documents and information within required time periods,

    d. the debtor has income above the average median family income for the state where the bankruptcy petition is filed,

    e. the debtor fails to pay post-petition alimony or child support,

    f. the debtor was convicted of a drug trafficking crime and the victim files a motion to dismiss the petition, or

    g. the debtor was convicted of a violent crime and the victim files a motion to dismiss the petition.

Involuntary Petition

4242.15 An involuntary petition is filed by the debtor's creditors.

    a. If there are 12 or more creditors, three or more must file against a debtor if their total unsecured claims are at least $14,425. (Insiders or employees are not creditors.)

    b. If there are fewer than 12 creditors, one or more creditors must file if their total unsecured claims are at least $14,425.

4242.16 Involuntary petitions are allowed only for Chapter 7 (Liquidation) and Chapter 11 (Reorganization). There is no involuntary petition for Chapter 9 (Adjustment of Debt for a City) or Chapter 13 (Adjustment of Debt for an Individual with Regular Income). These last two types of bankruptcy proceedings are initiated only by a voluntary petition filed by the debtor.

4242.17 Involuntary petitions cannot be filed against any of the following:
- a. Farmer
- b. Wage earner
- c. Railroad, insurance, or banking corporation
- d. Building and loan association
- e. Nonprofit corporation

4242.18 When the involuntary petition is filed, the debtor and their property automatically come under the jurisdiction of the bankruptcy court if no challenge is made by the debtor.

4242.19 If the debtor contests the involuntary petition, the creditors must prove either of the following:
- a. The debtor has not been paying debts as they come due.
- b. The debtor's property has been placed in a receivership or an assignment for the benefit of creditors within 120 days before the involuntary petition was filed.

4242.20 The filing of the petition stays all pending actions by creditors against the debtor.

Estate

4242.21 The debtor's estate consists of all tangible and intangible property of the debtor, unless specifically exempted.

4242.22 The estate has the same interest as did the debtor in the property.

4242.23 The debtor's estate includes certain after-acquired property. Specifically, the estate includes any type of property that the debtor acquires, or becomes entitled to acquire, within 180 days after the petition filing date:
- a. by inheritance,
- b. as a beneficiary of a life insurance policy, or
- c. as the result of a divorce decree or a property settlement agreement with the debtor's spouse.

4242.24 Earnings from services performed by the individual debtor after the filing of the petition are not included in the estate.

Exempt Property

4242.25 A debtor who is an individual (*not* a partnership or corporation) can claim certain exemptions. This exempt property is not included in the debtor's estate and is therefore not liquidated to pay the debts.

4242.26 Exemptions are established by either state or federal law.

4242.27 The debtor may choose to keep certain property either exempted by state law, or exempt under federal law, unless state law specifically disallows use of the federal exemptions.

4242.28 Federal exemptions from the bankruptcy law, if allowed by state law, include the following:
- a. Up to $21,625 of the debtor's interest in a homestead (this may be either a house or trailer of the debtor used as a residence) or in a burial plot for the debtor or a dependent of the debtor

b. Up to $3,450 of the debtor's interest in one motor vehicle—the equity in the motor vehicle is based on the motor vehicle's market value.

c. Up to $550 for each item of furniture, household goods, wearing apparel, appliances, books, animals, crops, or musical instruments held for personal, family, or household use of debtor or dependent of debtor—this exemption applies up to a maximum total of $11,525

   The following items are not considered to be household goods:

   (1) Works of art (unless by or of the debtor, or any relative of the debtor)

   (2) Electronic entertainment equipment with a fair market value of more than $600 in the aggregate (except one television, one radio, and one VCR)

   (3) Items acquired as antiques with a fair market value of more than $600 in the aggregate

   (4) Jewelry with a fair market value of more than $600 in the aggregate (except wedding rings)

   (5) A computer (except as otherwise provided), motor vehicle (including a tractor or lawn tractor), boat, or a motorized recreational device, conveyance, vehicle, water craft, or aircraft

d. Up to $1,450 in jewelry for personal use

e. Up to $1,150 plus up to $10,825 of any unused homestead exemption in any other property that the debtor chooses

f. Up to $2,175 in implements, professional books, or tools of the trade

g. Any unmatured life insurance owned by the debtor other than a credit life insurance contract

h. Up to $11,525 in any accrued dividend or interest under, or loan value of, any unmatured life insurance contract owned by the debtor under which the insured is the debtor or an individual of whom the debtor is a dependent

i. Right to receive Social Security, veterans', unemployment, or disability benefits, reasonable alimony, support, or separate maintenance payments

j. Professionally prescribed health aids for the debtor or dependent of the debtor

k. The debtor's right to receive, or property that is traceable to:

   (1) an award under a crime victim's reparation law;

   (2) a payment on account of the wrongful death of an individual of whom the debtor was a dependent, to the extent reasonably necessary for the support of the debtor and any dependent of the debtor;

   (3) a payment under a life insurance contract that insured the life of an individual of whom the debtor was a dependent on the date of such individual's death, to the extent reasonably necessary for the support of the debtor and any dependent of the debtor;

   (4) a payment, not to exceed $21,625, on account of personal bodily injury, not including pain and suffering or compensation for actual pecuniary loss, of the debtor or an individual of whom the debtor is a dependent; or

   (5) a payment in compensation of loss of future earnings of the debtor or an individual of whom the debtor is or was a dependent, to the extent reasonably necessary for the support of the debtor and any dependent of the debtor.

- **l.** Retirement accounts which are tax exempt under the Internal Revenue Code. However, there is a cap on the exemption amount for IRAs of $1,171,650. This limit may be increased if "the interests of justice so require."

- **m.** Certain contributions to qualified education savings accounts. To be excludible, the designated beneficiary must be a child, stepchild, grandchild, or stepgrandchild of the debtor for the tax year in which the funds were placed into the account. (Adopted and foster children also qualify.)

  Funds that qualify for exclusion from the bankruptcy estate are those placed in the qualified education account within a year of the petition date as long as they are not excess statutory contributions and are not pledged or promised to any entity in connection with any extension of credit. For contributions placed in an account having the same beneficiary within 365 to 720 days before filing, the exemption limit is $5,850.

- **n.** Contributions to qualified state tuition programs. These are excluded from the bankruptcy estate under the same monetary limits stated previously for contributions to qualified education savings accounts.

4242.29 State law often gives debtors exemptions for assets that differ from those allowed under the Bankruptcy Code. In some states, a debtor can choose federal or state exemptions. In other states, debtors are required to use state exemptions.

Current bankruptcy law prevents a debtor from moving to a more generous exemption state shortly before filing in order to protect a greater amount of their assets. A debtor must have resided in the state for two years (730 days) in order to use that state's exemption law. If this time requirement is not met, the exemption rules of the debtor's prior state of residency apply.

Also, state homestead exemptions can vary from the federal amount, with some states allowing a homestead exemption of an unlimited dollar amount. To prevent abuse in this area, a debtor cannot claim a state homestead exemption of more than $146,450 unless they have acquired the home more than 40 months (3-1/3 years, or 1,215 days) prior to filing for bankruptcy.

Regardless of how long the debtor has lived in the state, the debtor is not entitled to any homestead exemption that exceeds $146,450 if the debtor owes a debt arising from a federal or state securities law violation or from any criminal act, intentional tort, or willful or reckless misconduct that caused serious physical injury or death to another individual in the preceding five years.

Right to Setoff

4242.30 **Setoff:** Subtracting receivables from payables to see how much is owed; subtracting payables from receivables to see how much is due.

4242.31 Setoff is always an advantage to creditors, since without setoff they would have to pay the full amount on payables but would get only a percentage of the receivables in the bankruptcy proceeding.

4242.32 A person who is both a debtor and a creditor of the debtor has the right to setoff.

Administration

4242.33 Debtor must file a list of creditors, schedule of assets and liabilities, statement of financial affairs, and list of property claimed as exempt.

4242.34 Debtor must cooperate with the trustee. If not, the court may not discharge the debtor.

4242.35 Debtor must appear at a meeting of creditors and answer questions.

4242.36 Trustee may operate the debtor's business.

4242.37 Trustee may void preferential or fraudulent transfers made by the debtor within 90 days of filing.

Possible Defenses to the Trustee's Effort to Challenge a Particular Transfer as Being a Voidable Preference

4242.38 There are five general *requirements,* all of which must be present for the trustee to void a potential transfer:

1. Transfer goes to a creditor.
2. It must be in payment for a previous debt owed by the debtor.
3. It must have been made while the debtor was insolvent.
4. It must have been made within 90 days of filing the petition (one year if the creditor was an insider or had reason to think the debtor was insolvent). An insider is someone with a special relation to the debtor—a relative, a partner, etc.
5. Creditor got more than they would have received had the transfer not been made (usually considered to be the creditor's share of a Chapter 7 liquidation).

4242.39 The trustee cannot void the transfer under the following circumstances:

a. If credit transactions are exchanges of equal value done at the same time (this is because the transfer does not reduce the value of the debtor's estate)

b. If the creditor is acting in the ordinary course of business or in accordance with ordinary business terms

c. If security interest is given in goods the debtor buys from the seller (called purchase money security interest)

d. If the creditor gives new value to the debtor to offset the prior transfer by the debtor

e. If creditors are holding a security interest in inventory or receivables

f. For statutory liens that cannot be voided

g. To the extent the transfer was a bona fide payment of a debt for a domestic support obligation

h. In a case filed by an individual debtor, whose debts are primarily consumer debts, where the aggregate value of all property that constitutes or is affected by the transfer is less than $600

i. In a case filed by a debtor whose debts are not primarily consumer debts, where the aggregate value of all property that constitutes or is affected by such transfers is less than $5,850

Transfers by a Debtor

4242.40 Transfers by a debtor that defraud creditors are always voidable.

4242.41 Transfers by the debtor can be voided by the trustee if made as follows:

a. Within two years of filing with actual intent of defrauding creditors or

b. Within two years of filing, and the debtor received much less than an equal exchange, and:

(1) was insolvent at the time of the transfer, or became insolvent because of the transfer,

(2) was left with an unreasonably small amount of capital, or

(3) intended or believed the debts would be beyond their ability to repay.

Types of Transactions Entered by the Debtor That Can Be Voided by the Trustee

4242.42 **Preferential transfers:** One creditor preferred over other creditors.

4242.43 **Fraudulent transfers:** Defrauds all creditors.

Trustee Can Void Transfers

4242.44 **Transfer voids made before the filing of the bankruptcy petition:** The trustee can void fraudulent transfers made within two years prior to filing of the petition.

4242.45 **Transfer voids made after the filing:** (Remember, the debtor can continue to run the business even after filing unless the court orders the debtor not to.) The trustee must exercise this power within two years after the transfer is made or before the bankruptcy case is closed—whichever comes first.

4242.46 The trustee can cancel any contracts of the debtor based on any defenses that are available to the debtor (e.g., duress, undue influence, fraud, failure of consideration).

Proof of Claim

4242.47 Creditors present their claims to the court by filing a proof of claim against the debtor.

4242.48 A debtor or trustee may file a proof of claim for the creditor if the creditor does not file.

Allowed Claims

4242.49 Only allowed claims share in the distribution of the debtor's assets.

4242.50 Only unsecured creditors must file a proof of claim to recover.

4242.51 Secured creditors are not required to file a proof of claim. However, to the extent the claim exceeds the value of the collateral securing the claim, the creditor is treated as an unsecured creditor. A proof of claim must be filed in order to recover any of this amount.

4242.52 Any interested party can object to a filed claim. If an objection is made, a court hearing is held to decide the amount or the validity of the claim.

Disallowed Claims

4242.53 The following are disallowed claims that are not paid through the bankruptcy proceeding:

  a. Unmatured interest

  b. Claims already offset by a receivable by the creditor (this prevents double payment)

  c. Tax due on property where the tax exceeds the value of the property (in this case, the property is forfeited)

  d. Excess charges for services by an insider or attorney of the debtor

  e. Alimony and child support not yet due—the debtor still owes these even after the discharge in bankruptcy

    f. Claims by a lessor for a broken lease that exceeds the larger of either of the following:

        (1) One year's rent

        (2) 15% of total lease payments, but not more than three years' rent

    g. Claims by employees for a broken employment contract that exceeded one year after filing

Priority in Distribution to Secured and Unsecured Creditors

4242.54 The claim of a secured creditor to the debtor's property has priority to the claims of all unsecured creditors.

4242.55 The secured creditor has three choices to satisfy the debt that is owed:

    a. Accept the collateral as full payment of the debt.

    b. Foreclose on the collateral and apply the proceeds from sale of the property to offset the debt.

    c. Allow the trustee to dispose of the collateral and remit the proceeds from the sale of the property to the secured creditor.

4242.56 The secured creditor generally may also recover any reasonable fees and costs that result from the debtor's default on the secured debt.

4242.57 Any part of the value of the collateral that exceeds the secured interest is available to satisfy claims of unsecured creditors.

4242.58 If the value of the collateral is less than the amount of the secured debt, the secured creditor can file a proof of claim for this deficiency. The secured creditor is considered an unsecured creditor as to this amount.

4242.59 The priority in distribution to unsecured creditors is as follows:

    a. Administrative expenses, court costs, and fees

    b. Debts owed for domestic support obligations (alimony, maintenance, child support)

    c. Unsecured debts incurred during the involuntary gap (between filing of involuntary suit and order for relief and trustee appointment) arising in the ordinary course of the debtor's business

    d. Wages, salaries, or commissions earned within 180 days of filing, up to $11,725 for each individual

    e. Contributions to employee benefit plans for services within 180 days of filing. Cannot exceed $11,725 times number of employees. This amount is reduced by the aggregate amount paid to employees for wages, salaries, or commissions (see item (d.) above) and by the aggregate amount paid by the estate on behalf of such employees to any other employee benefit plan.

    f. Certain unsecured claims of persons engaged in the production of grain or engaged as U.S. fishermen to the extent of $5,775 for each individual

    g. Deposits of money by individuals with the debtor for purchase or rental of property or personal services for personal or household use up to $2,600 each (like a layaway plan or security deposit)

    h. Federal, state, or local taxes (like income taxes, property taxes, or withholding taxes)

      i. Allowed unsecured claims based upon any commitments by the debtor to a federal depository institution's regulatory agency

      j. Claims for death of personal injury resulting from operation of a motor vehicle or vessel if such operation was unlawful because the debtor was intoxicated from using alcohol, a drug, or another substance

Plan

4242.60 A plan is required in bankruptcy Chapters 9, 11, and 13.

4242.61 The plan can specify the following:

      a. How much creditors will be paid (may be partial or full)

      b. In what form creditor will be paid

      c. Other necessary details

4242.62 During the repayment period, the debtor is protected from creditor pressure.

4242.63 The plan often classifies claims and interest into classes.

4242.64 The plan must consider all classes and treat all members of a class equally.

4242.65 The plan must be confirmed by the court. The debtor, trustee, creditors, SEC, and others may raise objections.

Debts Not Discharged by Bankruptcy (Debtor Still Owes Even After Bankruptcy Discharge)

4242.66 The following are among the debts not discharged by bankruptcy:

      a. Taxes

      b. A debt obtained by false representation

      c. Debts not listed on the schedule of debts submitted by the debtor

      d. Obligations resulting from breach of fiduciary duty

      e. Judgments for embezzlement or larceny

      f. Debts owed for alimony or child support

      g. Judgments for intentional injury by debtor to a person or property of another (called intentional torts)

      h. Amounts for fines and penalties due to a governmental unit

      i. Amounts owed on educational loans unless this would impose an undue hardship on the debtor and the debtor's dependents

      j. Debts that survived a previous bankruptcy

      k. Consumer debt owed to a single creditor of more than $600 for "luxury goods or services" incurred by an individual debtor on or within 90 days before the filing of the bankruptcy petition (luxury goods or services do not include goods or services reasonably acquired for the support or maintenance of the debtor or a dependent of the debtor)

      l. Cash advances of more than $875 that are extensions of consumer credit under an open-end credit plan (as defined in the Consumer Credit Protection Act) that are obtained on or within 70 days before the filing of the bankruptcy petition

- m. Amounts owed for death or personal injury caused by the debtor's operation of a motor vehicle, vessel, or aircraft if such operation was unlawful because the debtor was intoxicated from using alcohol, a drug, or another substance
- n. Fines or penalties imposed under federal election law

Discharge of Debtor

4242.67 A discharge can be given to individuals only.

4242.68 Discharge will generally be given unless the individual debtor did any of the following within one year prior to filing or during the bankruptcy proceedings:

- a. Destroyed or concealed property in order to defraud creditors
- b. Destroyed, falsified, or concealed records
- c. Failed to cooperate (lied, withheld information, made false claim)
- d. Refused to obey lawful order of court
- e. Refused to testify in answering questions approved by the court

The Trustee

4242.69 Once the debtor becomes subject to bankruptcy proceedings, the court appoints an interim trustee to take over the debtor's property or business.

4242.70 Shortly, a permanent trustee takes over. Usually, the permanent trustee is elected by the creditors at a creditor's meeting.

4242.71 The trustee is an individual or a corporation who, under court supervision, represents the debtor's estate.

4242.72 The basic duties of the trustee are the following:

- a. Investigate the financial affairs of the debtor.
- b. Collect the debtor's assets and any claims owed to the debtor.
- c. Temporarily operate the debtor's business if necessary.
- d. Reduce the debtor's assets to cash.
- e. Receive and examine claims of creditors. The trustee will challenge in bankruptcy court any claims that are questionable.
- f. Oppose the discharge of the debtor if the trustee feels there are legal reasons why the debtor should not be discharged.
- g. Render a detailed accounting to the bankruptcy court of all assets disposed of and received.
- h. Make a final report to the bankruptcy court when administration of the debtor's estate is completed.

4242.73 The trustee is paid from the estate.

4242.74 Compensation cannot exceed the following amounts of the debtor's estate under the Bankruptcy Reform Act of 1994.

Amount			Percentage
$ 0	to	$ 5,000	25
$ 5,001	to	$ 50,000	10
$ 50,001	to	$ 1,000,000	5
	Over	$ 1,000,000	3

(or reasonable compensation if less)

4242.75 The trustee can employ attorneys, accountants, appraisers, and other individuals with prior court approval.

4242.76 The trustee can also sue and be sued as trustee.

Chapter 7 Bankruptcy

4242.77 A Chapter 7 bankruptcy can be voluntary or involuntary.

4242.78 A Chapter 7 bankruptcy has special provisions for stockholders and commodities brokers.

4242.79 A Chapter 7 bankruptcy can apply to a business debtor or a nonbusiness debtor (like an individual).

4242.80 The attorney for the debtor in a Chapter 7 bankruptcy has certain specified obligations, including:

    a. filing an affidavit with the bankruptcy court stating that they have informed the debtor of the various forms of bankruptcy and their details and

    b. reasonably verifying the information contained in the bankruptcy petition and the supporting schedules.

4242.81 Individual debtors with income below the median for their state of residency can generally receive the protection of a Chapter 7 proceeding. In contrast, an individual debtor with income above the state median income must submit to a means test that measures the extent to which the debtor can repay general unsecured claims.

4242.82 A Chapter 7 case will be dismissed or, with the debtor's consent, converted to a Chapter 13 case if it is found that there is abuse by an individual debtor with primarily consumer debt. Abuse can be found in the following two ways:

    1. Abuse can be found due to bad faith or fraud on the part of the debtor.

    2. Abuse is presumed if a debtor has sufficient income to pay back a portion of their debts as determined under the means test.

4242.83 Under the Chapter 7 means test, abuse is presumed to exist if net monthly income (current monthly income less the deduction listed below) multiplied by 60 is not less than the lesser of:

    a. 25% of the debtor's nonpriority unsecured claims in the case, or $6,000, whichever is greater; or

    b. $10,000.

4242.84 In a Chapter 7 bankruptcy, the presumption of abuse can only be rebutted if the debtor presents detailed documentation of "special circumstances." Special circumstances include a debtor having a serious medical condition or being on active duty in the military. These special circumstances must justify adjustments to income or expenses.

4242.85 The debtor's net monthly income is determined by deducting two major categories of expenses:

    a. Reasonable living and other expenses allowed in the Internal Revenue Service Financial Analysis Handbook as "necessary expenses" and

    b. The following expenses authorized under the Bankruptcy Code:

        (1) Expenses to maintain the safety of the debtor and the debtor's family from domestic violence

        (2) Payments to secured creditors that will become due in the five years after filing, divided by 60 (past due payments may be included only if the collateral is necessary for the support of the debtor and the debtor's dependents)

        (3) Alimony, child support, and other priority claims such as unpaid taxes divided by 60

        (4) Expenses that are reasonable and necessary for the care and support of an elderly, disabled, or chronically ill family member

        (5) Actual expenses for grade and high school up to $1,500 per child annually, if the expenses are not covered by applicable IRS standards and the debtor documents that they are reasonable and necessary

        (6) Actual expenses for household utility services, if the expenses are not covered by the IRS Local Standards and the debtor documents that they are reasonable and necessary

4242.86 In Chapter 7, an interim trustee can be appointed after the case is filed. He or she serves until the regular trustee is elected or designated and is appointed from a panel of private trustees.

4242.87 A Chapter 7 proceeding may be converted (one change only) to Chapter 11 or Chapter 13.

4242.88 The court can order a Chapter 7 bankruptcy case to Chapter 11 (but not Chapter 13).

4242.89 Under current law, a debtor who obtains relief under Chapter 7 must wait eight years before filing under Chapter 7 again.

Chapter 9 Bankruptcy

4242.90 Chapter 9 bankruptcy is available only to municipalities.

4242.91 A Chapter 9 bankruptcy applies only to a municipality that:

    a. is insolvent or not able to meet debts as it matures,

    b. wants a plan to adjust debts, and

    c. has obtained creditor agreement, has negotiated in good faith with creditors but has not reached agreement, or is unable to negotiate with creditors because it is impractical.

4242.92 A Chapter 9 bankruptcy must be voluntary, not involuntary.

4242.93 There is no trustee under a Chapter 9 bankruptcy.

4242.94 For a Chapter 9 bankruptcy, a proof of claim need not be filed by creditors because a list of creditors is required to be filed by the debtor.

4242.95 A municipality cannot liquidate. Chapter 9 bankruptcy allows the city to operate while it adjusts or refinances its creditor claims.

4242.96 A Chapter 9 bankruptcy must end up with an approved plan.

Chapter 11 Bankruptcy

4242.97 A Chapter 11 bankruptcy is used if it is felt continuing the business is preferred to a liquidation.

4242.98 A Chapter 11 bankruptcy applies only to those who could be a debtor under Chapter 7 and railroads.

4242.99 A Chapter 11 bankruptcy can be voluntary or involuntary. The same requirements apply for filing an involuntary petition as in a Chapter 7 proceeding.

4242.100 Chapter 11 contains special provisions for reorganization of railroads.

4242.101 Chapter 11 is primarily for businesses. Individuals can use this Chapter, but it would probably be too burdensome and expensive.

4242.102 In a Chapter 11 bankruptcy, a trustee may or may not be appointed. The debtor may remain in possession of property at the court's discretion. If a trustee is appointed, they take over the business and have the same basic powers as in a liquidation proceeding.

4242.103 Railroads can only be in Chapter 11 reorganization.

4242.104 In a Chapter 11 bankruptcy, a proof of claim need not be filed by creditors because a list of creditors is required to be filed by the debtor.

4242.105 A Chapter 11 bankruptcy may be converted (one conversion only) to Chapter 7.

4242.106 The purpose of a Chapter 11 bankruptcy is to restructure finances so the debtor can continue to operate. It binds nonconsenting creditors, while a common-law composition does not.

4242.107 A Chapter 11 bankruptcy must end up with an approved plan.

4242.108 Where the debtor is an individual, unless the bankruptcy court orders otherwise for cause, confirmation of a Chapter 11 plan does not discharge any debts provided for in the plan until the court grants a discharge on completion of all payments under the plan.

4242.109 If the debtor is an individual, earnings from personal services performed by the debtor after the commencement of the case or other future income of the debtor can be used to pay creditors for execution of a Chapter 11 plan.

4242.110 A Chapter 11 bankruptcy plan can divide creditors into classes (claims of employees, bondholders, etc.), but all creditors in each class must be treated equally.

4242.111 The court will approve a Chapter 11 reorganization plan if one of the following is true:

    a. Each class has approved the plan or

    b. The court rules that the plan is "fair and equitable" to all classes (even if creditors object to the plan).

4242.112 In a Chapter 11 bankruptcy, if the parties involved cannot produce an acceptable plan or if the plan does not work, the court can dismiss the case or convert it into a liquidation proceeding (Chapter 7).

4242.113 After a Chapter 11 bankruptcy plan is confirmed, the debtor is discharged from those claims not provided for in the plan. Nondischargeable debts are the same in Chapter 11 as in Chapter 7.

Chapter 13 Bankruptcy

4242.114 A Chapter 13 bankruptcy applies only to an individual (or individual and spouse) with regular income who owes unsecured debts of less than $360,475 and secured debts of less than $1,081,400.

4242.115 A Chapter 13 proceeding must be voluntary. The creditors cannot institute an involuntary Chapter 13 bankruptcy.

4242.116 A Chapter 13 bankruptcy can only be used by individuals (not partnerships or corporations). A small sole proprietorship can qualify as an individual if the other requirements are met.

4242.117 A Chapter 13 bankruptcy requires a trustee whose main function is to receive and distribute the debtor's income on a periodic basis.

4242.118 A Chapter 13 bankruptcy may be converted (one conversion only) to Chapter 7.

4242.119 A Chapter 13 bankruptcy must end up with an approved plan.

4242.120 A Chapter 13 bankruptcy plan must do the following:

    a. State the portion of the debtor's future income that will be turned over to the trustee for distribution to creditors. In determining the disposable income of the debtor, exclusions are made for numerous items, including up to 15% of the debtor's gross income for charitable contributions and the reasonable cost of health insurance for the debtor and their family.

    b. Describe how creditors will be paid.

    c. Generally, the plan may not provide for payments over a period that is longer than three years. However, the bankruptcy court for good cause (based on a specified computation of family income) may approve a period that is not longer than five years.

4242.121 A Chapter 13 bankruptcy plan can separate creditors into classes, but creditors in a class must be treated equally.

4242.122 A Chapter 13 bankruptcy plan can provide for partial payment of debts, but must provide for full payment of any claims that are given priority in a Chapter 7 proceeding.

4242.123 A Chapter 13 bankruptcy protects the debtor's credit standing better than Chapter 7 liquidation.

4242.124 The court will confirm a Chapter 13 bankruptcy plan if the following are true:

    a. The debtor proposes it in good faith.

    b. All secured creditors accept the plan.

4242.125 A hearing on confirmation of a Chapter 13 bankruptcy plan may be held not earlier than 20 days and not later than 45 days after the required creditors meeting. The hearing may be held earlier only if the bankruptcy court determines that it is in the best interests of the creditors and the estate and there is no objection to the earlier date.

4242.126 Unsecured creditors are bound by a Chapter 13 bankruptcy plan if it is confirmed by the court, even if the plan modifies their claims.

4242.127 Anytime before or after confirmation of a Chapter 13 plan, the debtor can convert the proceedings to a liquidation case.

4242.128 The court can convert the proceedings of a Chapter 13 bankruptcy to a liquidation case or dismiss the case if the debtor fails to perform according to the plan.

4242.129 In a Chapter 13 bankruptcy, before a debtor can receive a discharge, they must complete a financial management course.

4242.130 A debtor who fully performs a Chapter 13 bankruptcy plan will generally be granted a discharge upon completion. In certain cases, debtors can be discharged even if they do not complete the plan, provided the failure is due to circumstances beyond their control.

4242.131 In a Chapter 13 bankruptcy, discharge can be revoked within one year if it is discovered that the discharge was obtained by fraud.

4250 Government Regulation of Business

4251 Federal Securities Regulation

State Regulation of Securities

4251.01 Securities transactions can be subject to state law as well as federal law.

4251.02 Compliance with both sets of laws governing the securities transaction is necessary.

4251.03 The state regulatory laws, like the federal laws, are designed to protect the investing public from the fraudulent schemes of unscrupulous promoters.

4251.04 There are three types of state laws that regulate securities:

    1. Antifraud laws impose sanctions if fraud has been used in the sale of securities. These include civil and criminal penalties as well as the issuance of injunctions to prevent continuation of the fraudulent acts.

    2. Registration of dealers and brokers makes it unlawful for dealers and brokers to engage in securities transactions unless they register with the state.

    3. Disclosure of information by registration of securities using one of these three methods:

        (a) **Notification:** Quick method for companies with a proven record of earnings.

(b) **Qualification:** Detailed and time-consuming registration process where state officials judge the merits of the securities.

(c) **Coordination:** Accept a copy of the documents filed with the SEC to meet federal requirements under the Securities Act of 1933.

4251.05 State regulation was not effective for various reasons, including the following:

a. Differences among the states regarding their securities laws. Some had no legislation and some had inadequate laws. The laws could often be avoided by operating across state lines.

b. States failed to provide proper enforcement of the laws.

c. Unjustified exemptions in the state laws.

4251.06 State laws are called *blue-sky* laws. This was based on the feeling that some promoters would attempt to sell the blue sky to unwary investors.

4251.07 In 1911, Kansas was the first state to enact a law to regulate the sale of securities. By 1913, a total of 22 other states had enacted such laws. Today, all states have such laws.

4251.08 State laws often parallel the federal laws by allowing the same classes of securities to be exempt from registration. Some state laws exempt securities that are listed on a national stock exchange.

4251.09 State laws are not uniform. The 1956 effort of the National Conference of Commissioners on Uniform State Laws to get their Uniform Securities Act adopted in all states has not been successful. About two-thirds of the states have adopted the act, but many have made significant changes to it.

General Information About Regulation of Securities

4251.10 Typical abuses during the 1920s that led to the enactment of the federal securities laws included the following:

a. **Price manipulation.** Brokers and dealers used wash sales or matched orders to create a false impression of activity to force prices up.

b. **Deceit.** False and misleading statements were used to induce persons to invest in questionable schemes.

c. **Excessive use of credit.** There was no limit to the amount of credit a broker could extend to a customer.

d. **Misuse of corporate information.** Insiders took advantage of fluctuations in stock prices to make a personal profit.

4251.11 The objective of securities regulation is to protect innocent persons from investing their funds in speculative investments over which they have little control.

4251.12 The 1933 and 1934 acts were enacted in response to the great stock market crash of 1929.

Definitions

4251.13 **Accredited investor:** Accredited investors are banks, insurance companies, and persons with a net worth of over $1 million, persons with an annual income of over $200,000 for the last two years, or persons making purchases of more than $150,000 where the purchase price is not more than 20% of the person's net worth at the time of sale. Accredited investors would not be wiped out by an unsuccessful investment. (From SEC Rule 505)

4251.14 **Broker:** A person who serves as the agent of the investor (principal) in buying or selling the securities of the investor. The broker acts as an agent and owes a fiduciary duty to the investor.

4251.15 **Buying stock on margin:** Using credit to buy and hold stock. The percentage of credit allowed is controlled by the Federal Reserve Board and enforced by the SEC.

4251.16 **Controlling person:** A person who controls or is controlled by the issuer. The person could be a major stockholder, a director, or an officer. An offer to sell securities to the public made by a controlling person is subject to the registration requirements of the 1933 act.

4251.17 **Dealer:** A person who acts for himself and buys securities from or sells securities to the investor. The dealer does not act as an agent in the transaction.

4251.18 **Disclosure:** Providing all material facts. Full disclosure is required in many aspects of the 1933 and 1934 acts.

4251.19 **Due diligence:** The reasonable professional standard of care that would relieve a person of liability under the 1933 act on a registration statement that contained untrue statements of a material fact or omissions of a material fact.

4251.20 **Exemption:** Release from the legal obligation. Certain types of securities and certain types of securities transactions are exempt from the registration requirements of new securities.

4251.21 **Expert:** A person whose professional statement or report is used in a registration statement. Accountants, engineers, and appraisers are examples of experts acting in their professional capacity. Such experts are liable if a registration statement contains untrue statements of a material fact or omissions of a material fact unless the expert acted with "due diligence."

4251.22 **Insider:** A director, an officer, or a person who owns more than 10% of the class of securities registered under Section 12 of the 1934 act. Insiders must register with the SEC their initial ownership of securities of the company and subsequent changes in their ownership. The stock ownership of 10% includes direct and indirect ownership. Insiders are covered in the 1934 act.

4251.23 **Issuer:** The person who issues securities. The person can be a corporation, partnership, or other organization.

Example: The SAS Corporation decides to sell two million new shares of its common stock. SAS would be an issuer.

4251.24 **Matched orders:** A sale of securities by one party and a purchase by another party to manipulate price and give the appearance of active trading. A matched order is a violation of the antitrust provisions of the 1934 act.

4251.25 **Offering circular:** A legal offering document describing and offering a security for sale. Compared to a prospectus, the offering circular is less detailed and unaudited. An offering circular is filed with the SEC before issuance of the securities and is used with low-dollar Regulation A issues. The offering circular must be given to all offerees of the security.

4251.26 **Primary offering:** New securities initially offered by the issuer to the underwriters, then to the general public. Offerings are either primary or secondary.

4251.27 **Prospectus:** A legal offering document describing and offering a security for sale. The prospectus must be given to all persons who are offered the opportunity to buy securities. The prospectus is a summary of the registration statement. The prospectus can be a notice, circular, advertisement, TV or radio production, or a letter.

4251.28 **Proxy:** A shareholder's written assignment of the right to vote the shares owned by the shareholder.

4251.29 **Proxy statement:** A document that contains detailed information and must be included in a proxy solicitation. Before being sent to shareholders, the proxy statement must be submitted to the SEC, which reviews it to ensure that full disclosure is made.

4251.30 **Registration statement:** The formal document that must be filed with the SEC before a company can undertake a primary offering of securities. Registration statements are public information.

4251.31 **Restricted security:** A security purchased from the issuer in a nonpublic offering that is subject to restrictions on resale. A restricted security must be registered before resale unless SEC Rule 144 exempts it.

4251.32 **Scienter:** Intentional misconduct; intent to deceive, manipulate, or defraud. Scienter is required for a Rule 10b-5 violation.

4251.33 **Secondary offering:** Securities that are purchased and sold through a stock exchange or over-the-counter sales. Securities issued in a secondary offering were previously issued by the corporation and held by an investor.

4251.34 **Securities exchange:** Same as stock exchange. An organized secondary market where investors can buy and sell securities. The best-known example is the New York Stock Exchange.

4251.35 **Security:** A stock, bond, investment contract, or plans to make profits by the efforts of other persons. For the federal securities law, a security is more than just stock of a corporation. A security includes both equity and debt interests. A security is an investment of money in a common enterprise with an expectation of profits from the efforts of others. Under this broad definition, courts have found securities to include the following:

- **a.** Sale of a limited partnership interest
- **b.** Sale of live cattle with contracts to care for them
- **c.** Sale of a citrus grove with a management contract
- **d.** Sale of condominiums
- **e.** Sale of fractional undivided interest in gas, oil, or mineral rights
- **f.** Sale of a franchise

4251.36 **Short-swing profit:** A profit made by the purchase and sale of a security within a 6-month period of time. Insiders cannot keep short-swing profits.

4251.37 **Stock exchange:** Same as securities exchange. An organized secondary market where investors can buy and sell securities. The best-known example is the New York Stock Exchange.

4251.38 **Tender offer:** An offer to buy shares of a company. Usually, the tender offer is part of an effort to gain control of a company and is made to existing shareholders. The tender offer may contain conditions regarding the offer. A typical condition is that at least 50% of the shareholders must accept the offer before the shares will be purchased.

4251.39 **Tippee:** Person to whom material nonpublic information, called a tip, is transmitted. If the tippee uses the information to buy or sell securities, the tippee is liable under SEC Rule 10b-5.

4251.40 **Underwriter:** Person or organization, usually an investment banker, who buys securities from the issuer for resale to the general public. For large offerings of stock, the underwriters often form a syndicate. The underwriters buy all the securities offered and own what they cannot resell to the public. A dealer who sells securities for an underwriter for a commission is not considered an underwriter.

4251.41 **Wash sale:** A sale and a purchase of a security by the same person. The wash sale manipulates price and gives the appearance of active trading. A wash sale violates the antifraud provisions of the 1934 act.

Securities Act of 1933

4251.42 The purpose of the Securities Act of 1933 is to protect the unsophisticated investing public. The protection is accomplished by enforcing antifraud provisions and requiring that new issues of securities be registered with the SEC prior to issuance. Registration requires full disclosure of all important information. The act applies to situations in which the securities are sold to the general public by the issuer, an underwriter, or a controlling person. There are some exempt securities and exempt transactions that do not require the registration of the securities. Each investor or potential investor must be given a prospectus. The prospectus discloses important information summarized from the registration statement that allows the investor to make informed investment decisions.

4251.43 **Registration.** Any security that is not exempt must be registered with the SEC before it can be sold to the general public in interstate commerce by the issuer, by an underwriter(s), or by a controlling person. The company that issues the securities must file a registration statement with the SEC and give potential investors a prospectus.

    a. The registration statement contains the following:

       (1) Information about the planned offering and distribution of the securities

       (2) Names of officers of the company and their salaries

       (3) Names of persons who control the company

       (4) Information about the securities to be offered

       (5) Information about the issuing company, including audited financial statements

       (6) How the company will use the proceeds of the sale

       (7) A description of pending or threatened lawsuits

       (8) The prospectus that will be given to investors

(9) Risks involved with the securities

b. The SEC has 20 days to examine the registration statement. In actual practice, the time can be much longer since the SEC can require an amendment that will require a new 20-day waiting period. The SEC cannot rule on the merits of the issue, but it can compel complete disclosure of information.

c. During the 20-day period:

(1) Securities cannot be sold.

(2) The seller of the securities (issuer, underwriter, or controlling person) can distribute a "red herring" prospectus. This preliminary prospectus contains a statement in red ink that a registration statement has been filed, but is not yet effective.

(3) The seller of the securities can publish tombstone advertisements that announce the participating underwriters and the number of securities and their price. A tombstone ad must state that the ad is not an offer to sell, nor a solicitation of a buy offer, since any offer must be made by means of a prospectus.

(4) Oral, but not written, offers to buy can be received.

d. After the 20-day period:

(1) The registration statement is effective.

(2) The securities can be sold. Investors must be given the prospectus before purchase of the securities.

e. Simplified registration

(1) **SEC Regulation A** exempts securities issues of up to $5 million within a 12-month period from registration but not from antifraud provisions. The filing can include no more than $1.5 million offered by all selling security holders. The issuer must file an offering circular with the SEC. This is not a total exemption but is an exemption from the filing of the most costly and time-consuming registration statement. The offerees have no restrictions on resale.

(2) **SEC Rule 240** exempts securities issues of up to $100,000 within a 12-month period from registration but not from antifraud provisions. Sales to full-time employees are excluded from the $100,000, but there cannot be more than 100 holders of the securities and no solicitation of the general public. The issuer must file a short form with the SEC. This is not a total exemption but is an exemption from the filing of the more costly and time-consuming registration statement.

(3) **SEC Rule 246.** All offerees of a Regulation A issue of securities must be given an offering circular.

f. The following diagram shows how the registration statement is integrated into the process of issuing securities.

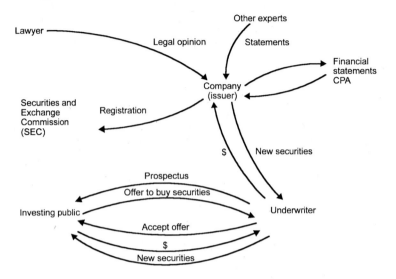

g. SEC Rule 415—Shelf Registration

(1) This rule provides for shelf registration. This involves registration of securities that are registered for an offering to be made on a continuous (i.e., an employee stock benefit plan) or a delayed basis in the future (i.e., market conditions become more favorable to issuance of the securities).

(2) Rule 415 provides that shelf registration applies only to certain types of offerings, including the following:

(a) Securities offered pursuant to a dividend or interest reinvestment plan or an employee benefit plan

(b) Securities issued upon the exercise of outstanding options, warrants, or rights

(c) Securities that are to be issued upon conversion of other outstanding securities

(d) Securities that are pledged as collateral

(e) Mortgage-related securities

(f) Securities that are to be issued in connection with business combination transactions

(g) Securities of certain large, publicly traded companies eligible to use short-form registration procedures

(3) A post-effective amendment to the registration statement must be made to reflect in the prospectus any facts or events arising after the effective date of the registration statement that, individually or in the aggregate, represent a fundamental change in the information set forth.

(4) Amendments must also be made to the registration statement to include any material information regarding the plan of distribution not previously disclosed in the registration statement or any material change to such information.

(5) Also, a post-effective amendment must be made to remove from registration any of the securities being registered that remain unsold at the termination of the offering.

4251.44 **Exempt securities.** These securities are exempt from registration (but not from the antifraud provisions):

    a. **Commercial paper.** Commercial paper that matures within nine months of issue that is used for current business operations is exempt from registration. Any commercial paper used for capital projects is not exempt.

    b. **Securities of the government.** Securities issued by or guaranteed by the government are exempt from registration. An example would be the bonds of a local government to expand an airport.

    c. **Securities of banks.** Because banks are already regulated by the Federal Reserve Board, their securities are exempt from registration.

    d. **Securities of nonprofit organizations.** Securities issued by religious, educational, or charitable nonprofit organizations are exempt from registration.

    e. **Securities of savings and loan associations.** Because these associations are already regulated by other state and local administrative agencies, their securities are exempt from registration.

    f. **Securities of common carriers or contract carriers.** Carriers include railroads and truckers. They are already regulated by the Interstate Commerce Commission, so their securities are exempt from registration.

    g. **Insurance, annuity, and endowment policies.** Insurance, annuity, and endowment policies issued by an insurance company are not considered securities within the meaning of the 1933 act. Insurance policies are not subject to the registration process. Stock and other securities issued by insurance companies are subject to registration.

    h. **Exchange securities issued in bankruptcy reorganizations.** These would be from Chapter 11 of the bankruptcy law and issued by a trustee in bankruptcy.

    i. **Securities exchanged with existing security holders.** Securities that are exchanged with current holders by the issuer are exempt from registration if no commissions are given. An example would be when a corporation gives a stock dividend, has a stock split, or exchanges one class of stock for another class.

4251.45 **Exempt transactions.** The following transactions are exempt from registration (but not from the antifraud provisions):

    a. **Private placement:** A transaction by an issuer not involving any public offering. The following factors are important in determining if there has been a nonpublic offering:

        (1) The number of offerees—the smaller the number, the more likely the offering is private.

        (2) The relationship of the offerees to each other

        (3) The relationship of the offerees to the issuer

        (4) The number of shares offered—the lower the number, the more likely the offering is private.

        (5) The total dollar size of the offering

        (6) The manner of offering

            (a) Direct offers to the buyers are more likely to be considered as private offerings.

            (b) Use of the channels of public distribution to attract offerees is less likely to be considered a private offering.

            (c) A public advertisement cannot be considered a private offering.

(7) **SEC Rule 146** establishes these factors to qualify as a private offering:

    (a) Around 35 persons

    (b) No general advertisements

    (c) The offerees are sophisticated investors.

    (d) The offerees have access to or disclosure of company information. This could be by employment or bargaining power.

    (e) Purchase of the stock is made for investment and not for resale.

Resale of securities purchased in a private placement is severely restricted. Initial purchasers must hold the securities for a minimum time period (typically two years) and thereafter sell only small amounts (such as no more than 1% in any quarter). Quick resale by the investor would make the investor liable as an underwriter selling securities without registration. See SEC Rules 144 and 237.

b. **Intrastate offerings. SEC Rule 147** allows corporations to sell their securities within the state without registration if all of the following criteria are met:

    (1) The corporation is incorporated and doing business in that state.

    (2) The corporation derives at least 80% of its gross revenues from within the registration state and has at least 80% of its assets located in the state.

    (3) 80% or more of the proceeds from the offering will be used in the state.

    (4) All of the corporation's officers are residents of the state.

    (5) The stock contains a provision that it cannot be resold to nonresidents for nine months. Resale of the stock to residents of the state is not restricted.

These restrictions make exemption based on intrastate offerings extremely difficult.

c. **Small issues of securities.**

    (1) **SEC Rule 242** exempts securities issues of up to $2 million within any 6-month period if sold to accredited persons. Accredited persons are institutional investors, buyers of $100,000 or more in securities, and the issuer's officers and directors. The issuer can sell to up to 35 non-accredited investors but must furnish a simplified prospectus to all purchasers, even if they are accredited persons.

    (2) Simplified registration for small issues under Regulation A and SEC Rule 240 is discussed in section **4514.02**.

d. **Casual sales.** Sales by investors of securities they own are an exempt transaction. The investor cannot also be an issuer, underwriter, dealer, or controlling person. The sale is typically done by a broker on the investor's order.

e. **Regulation D.** This regulation is a combination of the private placement and small issue exemptions. Issuers must file Form D, which lists minimal information, with the SEC. Regulation D has three separate thresholds with differing requirements:

    (1) **SEC Rule 504.** This rule can only be used by companies not reporting to the SEC, usually closely-held companies. No registration is required if no more than $1 million of securities are sold within a 12-month period with the following:

        (a) No limit on the number of investors

        (b) No general public offering or advertising

        (c) No restrictions on resale by the investor

(d) If the securities are registered exclusively under a state blue-sky law that allows it, general solicitation and general advertising may be permitted. However, sales are allowed only to "accredited investors."

(2) **SEC Rule 505.** No registration is required if no more than $5 million of securities are sold within a 12-month period with the following:

    (a) No general public offering or advertising

    (b) No more than 35 unaccredited investors and an unlimited number of accredited investors

    (c) No required disclosures to accredited investors

    (d) Distribution of audited financial statements to nonaccredited investors

    (e) Restricted resale by the investor

(3) **SEC Rule 506.** No registration of securities is required for a private placement of an unlimited amount of securities as follows:

    (a) To any number of accredited investors

    (b) To up to 35 unaccredited but sophisticated investors experienced in financial matters and able to evaluate risks involved in the investment

    (c) With no general public offering or advertising

    (d) Restricted resale by the investor

    (e) Distribution of audited financial statements to nonaccredited investors

Exemptions Under Regulation D			
	Rule 504	**Rule 505**	**Rule 506**
Restrictions on Resale	None	Yes. Must hold for 2 years or more and not for resale.	See Rule 505
Number of Investors	Any number	Unlimited Accredited Investors:	Unlimited Accredited Investors
Type of Investors	Any type	o Banks o Insurance companies o Investment companies o Millionaires o Officer or director of issuer 35 or less Unaccredited Investors	35 or less Unaccredited Investors (but they must be **sophisticated**)
Maximum Dollar Limitation	$1 million (within 12 mos.)	$5 million (within 12 mos.)	Unlimited
General Advertising Allowed	No*	No	No
Disclosure Required	No disclosure required	Disclosure with audited financial statements required for unaccredited. If all accredited, no disclosure required.	See Rule 505
Companies Eligible	Unregistered companies only	Registered companies (SEC Reporting)	See Rule 505

*General solicitation and general advertising is permitted if registered exclusively under a state law that allows it. However, sales are allowed only to "accredited investors" as defined in Rule 501(a). See Rule 504(b).

  f. Sales by dealers of securities that have been registered and issued:

    (1) 90 days after offering to the public if the securities are the initial offering by the issuer or

    (2) 40 days after offering to the public.

4251.46 **Sale of unregistered securities.** If nonexempt securities are being offered and sold in interstate commerce without first being registered, the SEC can issue a stop order to prohibit further sales and the buyer can sue for any damages suffered.

  a. The sale of new unregistered securities is covered in Section 5 of the 1933 act. It is unlawful for any person to do either of the following:

    (1) Offer to sell a security unless a registration statement has been filed with the SEC.

    (2) Sell a security unless the registration statement is effective.

  b. When a preliminary prospectus has been filed with the SEC, securities can be offered to the public, but sales cannot occur until the prospectus is effective.

4251.47 False registration statements. If securities are offered and sold, and their registration statement including the prospectus, contains material misstatements and/or material omissions, the following are true about the purchaser:

a. Can sue if money was lost and the material misstatements and/or omissions are proved.

b. Is not required to show reliance on the misstatements or omissions.

c. Can sue the issuer. The issuer is absolutely liable for all misstatements. There is no defense that the issuer can use to avoid liability.

d. Can sue experts (CPAs, attorneys, engineers, appraisers), underwriters, officers, and directors who contribute to and sign the registration statement. These persons can avoid liability if they can show that they acted with the standard of care of an expert exercising due diligence. This is called the due diligence defense.

e. Can recover damages.

Or the SEC can issue a stop order to prohibit further transactions.

4251.48 Antifraud provisions. Fraudulent securities transactions are prohibited whether the securities are registered or are exempt from registration. There are no exemptions from the antifraud provisions of the act.

a. **Section 12.** Oral or written misstatements of material facts or omissions of material facts are prohibited where necessary to keep the statements from being misleading in the circumstances where they were made.

b. **Section 17.** It is illegal to use any type of fraud, any untrue statement of a material fact, or omission of a material fact involving the sale of securities in interstate commerce or through the mail.

4251.49 Sanctions. Both the SEC and private parties can seek sanctions.

a. **SEC actions.** The SEC can issue a stop order to prevent the illegal distribution of securities that do not have a registration statement or appear misleading. Section 24 provides for criminal liability for any person who willfully violates the 1933 act. Violators are subject to a $10,000 fine and up to five years' imprisonment.

b. **Section 12(1) and 12(2).** Purchasers of unregistered securities can sue the sellers (brokers, not the issuer) for rescission or damages. Privity of contract is required.

c. **Section 11.** Purchasers of securities can sue if the registration statement contains material misstatements or omissions.

(1) The purchaser of securities need not have relied on, or even have seen, the registration statement.

(2) The purchaser is not required to prove that the defendant either negligently or intentionally misstated or omitted a material fact.

(3) The purchaser must not know of the misstatement or omission. Actual knowledge by the purchaser is a defense that can be used by the defendant.

(4) Persons liable on registration statements that contain material misstatements or omissions who qualify as experts can avoid liability if they can show "due diligence." The auditors can use this "due diligence" defense, which involves proving that they were not negligent.

d. Reliance on an expert is a defense, except for the issuer. This reliance must include a reasonable investigation before reliance.

e. The following persons can be liable in a civil suit by the purchaser under Section 11:

      (1) Every person who signed the registration statement

      (2) Every corporate director or corporate officer or partner of a partnership that issues the securities

      (3) Every person who is about to become a director or partner of the issuer who consents to and is named in the registration statement

      (4) Every expert who assists in the preparation or certification of the registration statement (experts include the auditor, accountant, appraiser, and engineer)

      (5) Every underwriter who participates in the offering

      Disclaimers of liability and other types of warnings by these persons contained in the registration statement are not effective.

   f. Damages are the difference between the purchase price paid by the plaintiff and the value of the security at the time of filing the suit or at the time the plaintiff sold the security, whichever is first.

   g. The statute of limitations is one year for civil and criminal liability. The statute of limitations starts to run when the untrue statement or omission is discovered or when it should have been discovered, but it cannot be more than three years from issue.

   h. Where securities are issued with material misstatements or material omissions, the purchaser could recover for common law fraud in the inducement. The fraud action requires proof of material misstatement or omission, scienter, reliance, intent, privity, proximate cause, and damages. To recover under the 1933 act, only proof of material misstatement or omission and damages is needed.

Securities Exchange Act of 1934

4251.50 The purpose of the Securities Exchange Act of 1934 is to protect the unsophisticated investing public. This protection is accomplished by requiring companies that have their securities traded in secondary markets to register and report periodically; by requiring stock exchanges, security associations, brokers, and dealers to register; by supervising market activities, such as proxy solicitations, tender offers, insider trading, and short-swing profits; and by enforcing antifraud provisions.

4251.51 Who must register and report periodically:

   a. Companies whose securities are listed on the national and regional securities exchanges

      (1) Even if the securities were not registered under the 1933 act

      (2) From Section 12(b)

   b. Companies whose securities are traded over-the-counter if their total assets exceed $10 million, they have 500 or more shareholders, and if the securities are traded in interstate commerce

      (1) Even if the securities were not registered under the 1933 act

      (2) Companies that do not meet the asset and shareholder tests may decide to register and report voluntarily

      (3) From Section 12(g)

   c. National and regional stock exchanges

   d. Brokers and dealers who conduct securities business in interstate commerce

  e. Transfer agents

  f. Clearing agencies

  g. Brokers and dealers who sell municipal securities

  h. Securities information processors

  i. Companies whose securities are registered under the 1933 act

  j. Associations of stock dealers—NASD, for example

  Over 10,000 companies are now registered with the SEC, and most of them have securities traded over-the-counter (OTC).

4251.52   **Exempt securities.** The following securities need not be registered by the organization:

  a. Securities issued or guaranteed by the U.S. government

  b. Securities issued or guaranteed by a state government or political subdivisions

  c. Industrial development bonds

4251.53   **Reports** to file with the SEC:

  a. **8-K.** Current report for material events must be filed within 15 days of the material event. In the case of either the resignation of a director or the change of an auditor, notification must be made to the SEC within five days.

  b. **10-Q.** Quarterly report to the SEC must be filed for the first three fiscal quarters of the year.

  c. **10-K.** Annual report to the SEC must be filed at the end of the fiscal year. The annual report must have financial statements audited by a CPA.

4251.54   Companies having securities subject to the disclosure requirements of the 1934 act are subject to the other regulations under the 1934 act. These other regulations include proxy solicitation, tender offers, and short-swing profits.

4251.55   **Antifraud provisions.** When selling or buying securities, it is illegal to use any manipulative or deceptive device or contrivance to violate SEC rules.

  a. Use of the mails or interstate commerce must be involved.

  b. From Section 10(b) of the 1934 act. This section has been augmented by SEC Rule 10b-5.

4251.56   **Rule 10b-5.** Liability is imposed on any person who commits fraud (an intentional misrepresentation or omission of a material fact) in connection with the purchase or sale of any security.

  a. Scienter is required for liability. Negligence is not enough.

  b. Only actual purchasers or sellers of the security can recover. Those who failed to purchase cannot recover lost profits.

  c. To recover, the purchaser or seller must have relied upon the false statement and must not have known that the statement was false.

  d. Rule 10b-5 applies to officers, directors, majority shareholders, tippees, or anyone else who receives important nonpublic information that affects securities trading.

e. Examples of material facts could include the following:

    (1) Change in dividends

    (2) New product

    (3) New process

    (4) Change in company's financial condition

    (5) Discovery of mineral or petroleum reserves

f. The rule applies to any trading of securities:

    (1) through a stock exchange,

    (2) over-the-counter, or

    (3) by private sale between the buyer and seller.

g. The rule applies to all types of securities and could include the following:

    (1) Stocks

    (2) Bonds

    (3) Participation in a profit-sharing agreement

h. The securities can be registered under either the 1933 or 1934 acts, or unregistered.

i. The sale of the securities must involve interstate commerce. (Use of mail or national exchanges is considered interstate commerce even if the state line is not crossed.)

j. There are no securities and no transactions exempt from SEC Rule 10b-5.

k. It is not necessary that the buyer and seller of the securities deal directly with each other. There will be liability even if trading is done through the computerized system of a stock exchange.

l. The person who buys or sells securities in a transaction with the wrongdoer can recover damages. To recover damages, four factors must exist:

    (1) Existence of a material omission or misrepresentation made in connection with the sale of securities

    (2) Intent by the defendant, not mere negligence

    (3) Reliance and due diligence by the plaintiff

    (4) Damages

m. SEC Rule 10b-5 can apply to misstatements, mismanagement, and insider trading.

n. The rule imposes liability for misstatements. These misstatements could be from any company document, press release, report, or public statement by a company representative. Misstatements could include the following:

    (1) Misinformation about future prospects of the company

    (2) Overly optimistic statements by company representatives

    (3) Releasing unfounded pessimistic information

o. The rule imposes liability for mismanagement that reduces the value of securities held by investors. Mismanagement could include the following:

    (1) Unjustified merger

    (2) Transaction by a company in its own securities

(3) Abusing minority shareholder rights

(4) Any corporate management action that would reduce the value of securities of the corporation

4251.57 **Short-swing profits.** Inside information cannot be used to make short-term profits in the stock market.

    a. Insiders are directors, officers, and large shareholders.

    b. Directors, officers, and beneficial owners of 10% or more of the stock are required to file reports with the SEC disclosing stock ownership and changes in ownership.

    c. A beneficial owner of stock includes stock owned in the person's own name or in the name of a spouse, minor children, and relatives who live in the owner's home.

    d. Profits from the sale and purchase of stock within a period of less than six months by an insider can be recovered by the company. If the company does not act within 60 days of notification, the owner of any stock of the company can sue for the company.

    e. The statute of limitations is two years from the date of the sale.

    f. Intent need not be proven.

    g. Insiders cannot engage a short sale (sale of securities they do not own) or make a sale against the box (own the securities but not deliver them).

    h. Purchase and sale of securities for a loss in less than six months is permitted.

    i. From Section 16

4251.58 **Tender offers.** Any person seeking to acquire over 5% of a company's stock by purchase or tender offer and persons soliciting shareholders to accept or reject a tender offer must disclose important information to the SEC and shareholders.

    a. The requirement was established by the 1968 Williams Act, passed by Congress to regulate tender offers so shareholders may make an informed decision whether to tender their shares for purchase.

    b. If a person acquires 5% of a class of securities, they must report to the following:

        (1) Issuer

        (2) Stock exchange where the securities are traded

        (3) SEC

    c. The report must include the following:

        (1) The number of shares already owned

        (2) The purpose of acquiring control of 5% or more of stock

        (3) The changes planned in operation or structure of corporation

        (4) The identity of persons who are buying the stock

        (5) Tender offers planned for additional shares

4251.59 **Proxy solicitation.** Before solicitation of proxies, the persons seeking the proxies must disclose all material facts in a filing with the SEC. The SEC must approve the proxy statement by seeing that important information is disclosed. Full disclosure is required for any proxy contest between present management and dissident shareholders.

4251.60 **Margin trading.** The Board of Governors of the Federal Reserve System can set limitations on the amount of credit that can be extended for the purchase or carrying of securities. The SEC investigates and enforces the restriction.

    a. Applies to persons getting credit from brokers, dealers, and banks.

        (1) Does not apply to exempt securities.

        (2) Range of allowed credit is 50% to 100% of the sale price of the securities.

        (3) Margin means amount of credit.

4251.61 **Credit rules**

    a. Brokers, dealers, and exchange members can borrow money only from a bank that is a member of the Federal Reserve System or a bank that agrees to follow the rules of the Federal Reserve System.

    b. Brokers and dealers that have possession of the investor's securities cannot lend them unless they have written permission.

    c. Brokers and dealers cannot pledge (hypothecate) securities owned by a customer that are in the possession of the broker or dealer for the loans of the broker or dealer.

    d. An exchange member cannot trade in their own account, except for odd-lot dealers.

4251.62 **Sanctions.** The SEC can use these sanctions:

    a. **Injunction.** Used to stop violations of the act or the SEC rules.

    b. **Criminal prosecution.** The SEC can refer facts to the U.S. Department of Justice if fraud or willful violations are detected.

    c. **Administrative relief.** The SEC can suspend, expel, or revoke brokers and dealers, or prohibit individuals from employment with a registered firm.

Foreign Corrupt Practices Act of 1977

4251.63 The Foreign Corrupt Practices Act of 1977 is an amendment to the Securities Exchange Act of 1934.

4251.64 The Foreign Corrupt Practices Act of 1977 requires issuers of registered securities and issuers who are required to file reports with the SEC to keep records and have a system of internal controls. These requirements apply not only to foreign business transactions but also to domestic activities.

4251.65 Under the Foreign Corrupt Practices Act of 1977, it is unlawful for issuers or domestic businesses or their officers, directors, employees, agents, or shareholders to use interstate or foreign commerce (mail, phones, etc.) to offer or give anything of value (money) to a foreign official, foreign political party, or foreign political candidate for the purpose of influencing action or inducing those persons to use their influence in their official capacity to obtain or retain business for the organization.

4251.66 Under the Foreign Corrupt Practices Act of 1977, it is unlawful to transfer anything of value to an intermediary knowing that the end purpose is to use influence for business.

4251.67 The penalties for violation of the Foreign Corrupt Practices Act of 1977 are as follows:

    a. Up to $2 million for the company

    b. Up to $100,000 and/or up to five years' imprisonment for officers, directors, stockholders, employees, or agents (The organization may not pay the fine of an individual.)

4251.68 It is not a violation of the Foreign Corrupt Practices Act of 1977 to use facilitating or grease payments to low-level ministerial or clerical government officials. Examples are payments to do either of the following:

    a. Expedite a shipment of goods through customs.

    b. Get a permit or license.

Sarbanes-Oxley Act of 2002

4251.69 **Public Company Accounting Oversight Board**

    a. The Sarbanes-Oxley Act establishes the Public Company Accounting Oversight Board (PCAOB or Board), which is appointed and overseen by the Securities and Exchange Commission (SEC).

    b. The Board is composed of five members appointed for 5-year terms. Two of the members must be or must have been CPAs. The remaining three members must not be and cannot have been CPAs. The chair may be held by one of the CPAs provided he or she has not been engaged as a practicing CPA for five years.

    c. No member of the Board may currently "share in any of the profits of, or receive payments from, a public accounting firm," other than "fixed continuing payments" such as retirement payments.

    d. The duties of the Board include:

        (1) Registering public accounting firms

        (2) Establishing or adopting auditing, quality control, ethics, independence, and other standards relative to the preparation of audit reports for issuers

        (3) Conducting inspections of accounting firms

        (4) Conducting investigations and disciplinary proceedings

        (5) Imposing appropriate sanctions.

    e. The Board is required to issue standards or adopt standards issued by other groups or organizations. The Board has the authority to amend, modify, repeal, and reject any standards suggested by any other group. On an annual basis the Board must report on its standard setting activity to the SEC.

    f. The Board will conduct annual quality reviews of firms that audit more than 100 issuers. All other firms that are registered with the Board will be reviewed every three years. The SEC and/or Board may order a special inspection of any firm at any time.

    g. Foreign accounting firms that "prepare or furnish" an audit report involving U.S. registrants are subject to the authority of the Board. This includes a foreign firm that performs some audit work (i.e. auditing a foreign subsidiary of a US company). Also, if a U.S. accounting firm relies on the opinion of a foreign accounting firm, the audit workpapers of the foreign firm must be supplied upon request to the Board or the SEC.

h. A violation of the rules of the Board is treated as a violation of the Securities Exchange Act of 1934 and gives rise to the same penalties that may be imposed for violations of that Act.

4251.70 Sarbanes-Oxley Act Requirements for CPA Firms

a. CPA firms that participate in the preparation or issuance of any audit report with respect to a public company are required to register with the Board.

b. Registered accounting firms must prepare and maintain for a period of not less than seven years, audit work papers, and other information related to any audit report, in sufficient detail to support the conclusions reached in the report.

c. The Sarbanes-Oxley Act requires a second partner review and approval of all audit reports and their issuance.

d. The lead audit partner and audit review partner must rotate off of the audit every five years on public company engagements.

e. A registered accounting firm is prohibited from auditing any SEC registered client if the CEO, Controller, CFO, Chief Accounting Officer, or person in an equivalent position has been employed by the auditor during the 1-year period prior to the audit.

f. The accounting firm is required to report to the client's audit committee:

(1) All critical accounting policies and practices to be used

(2) All alternative treatments of financial information within GAAP that have been discussed with management

(3) The ramifications of the use of such alternative disclosures and treatments

(4) The treatment "preferred" by the firm

g. The Act makes it "unlawful" for a registered public accounting firm to provide certain nonaudit services to an issuer contemporaneously with the audit. These prohibited services include:

(1) Bookkeeping and related services

(2) Design and implementation of financial information systems

(3) Appraisal or valuation services, fairness opinions, or contribution-in-kind reports

(4) Actuarial services

(5) Internal auditor outsourcing services

(6) Management or human resource services

(7) Broker, dealer, investment adviser, or investment banking services

(8) Legal or expert services unrelated to the audit

(9) Any other services that the Board determines by regulation are impermissible

h. Firms may provide other services not listed above (i.e. tax services) provided the firm receives pre-approval by the audit committee. Pre-approval is not required provided:

(1) The aggregate amount of nonaudit services provided to the issuer constitutes less than 5% of the total amount of revenues paid by the issuer to its auditor,

(2) Such services were not recognized by the issuer at the time of the engagement to be nonaudit services, and

(3) Such services were promptly brought to the attention of the audit committee and approved prior to the completion of the audit.

4251.71 Sarbanes-Oxley Act Requirements for Corporations, Officers, and Board Members

a. Publicly traded companies subject to the Sarbanes-Oxley Act are those defined as an "issuer" under Section 3 of the Securities Exchange Act of 1934.

b. The Act requires the CEO and CFO of each issuer to certify the appropriateness of the financial statements and disclosures contained in the periodic report and that the financial statements and disclosures fairly present, in all material respects, the operations and financial condition of the issuer. Knowing and willful violations are subject to a fine of not more than $5 million and/or imprisonment of up to 20 years.

c. The Act provides that it is unlawful for any officer or director of an issuer to take any action to fraudulently influence, coerce, manipulate, or mislead any auditor engaged in the performance of an audit for the purpose of rendering financial statements materially misleading.

d. Under the Act, if an issuer is required to prepare a restatement due to "material noncompliance" with financial reporting requirements, the chief financial officer must reimburse the issuer for:

   (1) Any bonus or other incentive-based or equity-based compensation received during the 12-month period following the issuance or filing of the noncompliant document.

   (2) Any profits realized from the sale of securities of the user during that period.

e. The Act prohibits the purchase or sale of stock by officers and directors and other insiders during pension fund black-out periods.

f. The SEC is given the authority under the Act to:

   (1) Prohibit an individual from serving as an officer or director if it finds that their conduct violates securities laws and "demonstrates unfitness" to serve as an officer or director.

   (2) Freeze the payment of an extraordinary payment to any director, officer, partner, controlling person, agent, or employee of a company during an investigation of possible violations of securities laws.

g. The Act provides the following requirements regarding audit committees:

   (1) Each member of the audit committee shall be a member of the board of directors of the issuer, and shall otherwise be independent. The SEC "may make exceptions for certain individuals on a case-by-case basis."

   (2) "Independent" is defined as not receiving, other than for service on the board, any consulting, advisory, or other compensatory fee from the issuer, and as not being an affiliated person of the issuer, or any subsidiary thereof.

   (3) The audit committee shall be directly responsible for the appointment, compensation, and oversight of the work of any registered public accounting firm employed by that issuer.

   (4) The audit committee shall establish procedures for "receipt, retention, and treatment of complaints" that are received by the issuer regarding accounting, internal controls, and auditing.

   (5) The audit committee shall have authority to hire independent counsel or other advisors to carry out its duties.

Public Company Accounting Oversight Board (PCAOB) Rules

Selected PCAOB rules are discussed in this section. The rules should be consulted for more detailed explanation.

4251.72 Registration and Reporting (PCAOB)

    a. **Rule 2100. Registration Requirements for Public Accounting Firms.** Effective October 22, 2003 (or, for foreign public accounting firms, April 19, 2004), each public accounting firm that prepares or issues any audit report with respect to any issuer or plays a substantial role in the preparation or furnishing of an audit report with respect to any issuer must be registered with the Board.

    b. **Rule 2101. Application for Registration.** Any public accounting firm applying to the Board for registration pursuant to Rule 2100 must complete and file an application for registration on Form 1 by following the instructions to that form. Unless directed otherwise by the Board, the applicant must file such application and exhibits thereto electronically with the Board through the Board's web-based registration system. An applicant may withdraw its application for registration by written notice to the Board at any time before the approval or disapproval of the application.

    c. **Rule 2102. Date of Receipt.** Unless the Board directs otherwise, the date of receipt of an application for registration will be the later of (a) the date on which the registration fee has been paid, or (b) the date on which the application is submitted to the Board through its web-based registration system.

    d. **Rule 2103. Registration Fee.** Each applicant for registration must pay a registration fee. The Board will, from time to time, announce the current registration fee. No portion of the registration fee is refundable, regardless of whether the application for registration is approved, disapproved, or withdrawn.

    e. **Rule 2104. Signatures.** Each signatory to an application for registration (including, without limitation, each signatory to the consents required by such application) shall manually sign a signature page or other document authenticating, acknowledging or otherwise adopting his or her signature that appears in typed form within the electronic filing. Such document shall be executed before or at the time the electronic filing is made and shall be retained by the filer for a period of seven years. Upon request, an electronic filer shall furnish to the Board or its staff a copy of all documents retained pursuant to this Rule.

    f. **Rule 2105. Conflicting Non-U.S. Laws.** An applicant may withhold information from its application for registration when submission of such information would cause the applicant to violate a non-U.S. law if that information were submitted to the Board.

    g. **Rule 2106. Action on Applications for Registration.**

        (1) After reviewing the application for registration, any additional information provided by the applicant, and any other information obtained by the Board, the Board will determine whether approval of the application for registration is consistent with the Board's responsibilities under the Act to protect the interests of investors and to further the public interest in the preparation of informative, accurate, and independent audit reports for companies the securities of which are sold to, and held by and for, public investors.

        (2) Unless the applicant consents otherwise, the Board will take action on an application for registration not later than 45 days after the date of receipt of the application by the Board.

(3) If the Board requests more information from an applicant, and such applicant submits the requested information to the Board, the Board will treat the application, as supplemented by the requested information, as if it were a new application. The Board will take action on such supplemented applications as soon as practicable, and not later than 45 days after receipt of the supplemented application by the Board.

h. **Rule 2107. Withdrawal from Registration.** A registered public accounting firm's registration with the Board is deemed withdrawn if the firm requests leave to withdraw by filing a Form 1-WD and the Board grants leave to withdraw, or the Board does not, within 60 days of receipt of the request, order that withdrawal of the firm's registration be delayed.

(1) A completed Form 1-WD shall include, among other things, a statement signed by an authorized partner or officer of the firm certifying that the firm is not currently, and will not during the pendency of its request for leave to withdraw be, engaged in the preparation or issuance of or playing a substantial role in the preparation or furnishing of, an audit report, other than to issue a consent to the use of an audit report for a prior period.

(2) Beginning on the date of Board receipt of a completed Form 1-WD, the firm that filed the Form 1-WD shall not engage in the preparation or issuance of, or play a substantial role in the preparation or furnishing of, an audit report, other than to issue a consent to the use of an audit report for a prior period, unless it first withdraws its Form 1-WD.

(3) Within 60 days of Board receipt of a completed Form 1-WD, the Board may order that withdrawal of registration be delayed for period of up to eighteen months from the date of such receipt if the Board determines that such withdrawal would be inconsistent with the Board's responsibilities under the Act, including its responsibilities to conduct:

(a) inspections to assess the degree of compliance of each registered public accounting firm and associated persons of that firm with the Act, the rules of the Board, the rules of the Commission, or professional standards, in connection with its performance of audits, issuance of audit reports, and related matters involving issuers; and

(b) investigations or disciplinary proceedings with respect to any act or practice, or omission to act, by a registered public accounting firm, any associated person of such firm, or both, that may violate any provision of the Act, the rules of the Board, the provisions of the securities laws relating to the preparation and issuance of audit reports and the obligations and liabilities of accountants with respect thereto, including the rules of the Commission issued under the Act, or professional standards.

If, on the 60th day after the Board's receipt of a Form 1-WD or at the conclusion of any period for which the Board has ordered that withdrawal be delayed, there is pending any Board disciplinary proceeding against the firm that filed the Form 1-WD or against any associated person of that firm, or there is pending any Commission or court review of a Board sanction against such firm or person, the requested withdrawal from registration shall not take effect before the completion of all such disciplinary proceedings and reviews, unless the Board orders otherwise.

A registered public accounting firm that has submitted a Form 1-WD may withdraw the form at any time by filing with the Board a written notice of intent to withdraw the Form 1-WD along with any annual fee and annual report that the firm would have been required to submit during the period that the Form 1-WD was pending if not for the provisions of paragraph (c)(2).

If the Board determines, within three years after the date a firm's registration is deemed withdrawn, that there are reasonable grounds to believe that a firm that has withdrawn from registration filed with the Board a Form 1-WD that was materially incomplete or materially inaccurate on the date of filing, such firm's registration shall be reinstated, effective retroactively to the date the registration was deemed withdrawn.

i. **Rule 2300. Public Availability of Information Submitted to the Board; Confidential Treatment Requests.** An application for registration will be publicly available as soon as practicable after the Board approves or disapproves such application. A public accounting firm may request confidential treatment of any information submitted to the Board in connection with its application for registration, provided that the information as to which confidential treatment is requested:

(1) has not otherwise been publicly disclosed, and

(2) either (i) contains information reasonably identified by the public accounting firm as proprietary information, or (ii) is protected from public disclosure by applicable laws related to the confidentiality of proprietary, personal, or other information.

Pending a determination by the Board as to whether to grant the request for confidential treatment, the information for which confidential treatment has been requested will not be made available to the public.

4251.73 Professional Standards (PCAOB)

a. **Rule 3100. Compliance with Auditing and Related Professional Practice Standards.** A registered public accounting firm and its associated persons shall comply with all applicable auditing and related professional practice standards.

b. **Rule 3101. Certain Terms Used in Auditing and Related Professional Practice Standards.** The Board's auditing and related professional practice standards use certain terms set forth in this rule to describe the degree of responsibility that the standards impose on auditors.

(1) Unconditional Responsibility: The words "must," "shall," and "is required" indicate unconditional responsibilities. The auditor must fulfill responsibilities of this type in all cases in which the circumstances exist to which the requirement applies. Failure to discharge an unconditional responsibility is a violation of the relevant standard and Rule 3100.

(2) Presumptively Mandatory Responsibility: The word "should" indicates responsibilities that are presumptively mandatory. The auditor must comply with requirements of this type specified in the Board's standards unless the auditor demonstrates that alternative actions he or she followed in the circumstances were sufficient to achieve the objectives of the standard. Failure to discharge a presumptively mandatory responsibility is a violation of the relevant standard and Rule 3100 unless the auditor demonstrates that, in the circumstances, compliance with the specified responsibility was not necessary to achieve the objectives of the standard. In the rare circumstances in which the auditor believes the objectives of the standard can be met by alternative means, the auditor, as part of documenting the planning and performance of the work, must document the information that demonstrates that the objectives were achieved.

(3) Responsibility to Consider: The words "may," "might," "could," and other terms and phrases describe actions and procedures that auditors have a responsibility to consider. Matters described in this fashion require the auditor's attention and understanding. How and whether the auditor implements these matters in the audit will depend on the exercise of professional judgment in the circumstances consistent with the objectives of the standard. If a Board standard provides that the auditor

"should consider" an action or procedure, consideration of the action or procedure is presumptively mandatory, while the action or procedure is not.

c. **Rule 3200T. Interim Auditing Standards.** In connection with the preparation or issuance of any audit report, a registered public accounting firm, and its associated persons, shall comply with generally accepted auditing standards, as described in the AICPA Auditing Standards Board's Statement of Auditing Standards No. 95, as in existence on April 16, 2003 (Codification of Statements on Auditing Standards, AU 150 (AICPA 2002)).

d. **Rule 3300T. Interim Attestation Standards.** In connection with an engagement (i) described in the AICPA's Auditing Standards Board's Statement on Standards for Attestation Engagements No. 10 (Codification of Statements on Auditing Standards, AT Section 101.01 (AICPA 2002)) and (ii) related to the preparation or issuance of audit reports for issuers, a registered public accounting firm, and its associated persons, shall comply with the AICPA Auditing Standards Board's Statements on Standards for Attestation Engagements, and related interpretations and Statements of Position, as in existence on April 16, 2003.

e. **Rule 3400T. Interim Quality Control Standards.** A registered public accounting firm, and its associated persons, shall comply with quality control standards, as described in:

(1) the AICPA's Auditing Standards Board's Statements on Quality Control Standards, as in existence on April 16, 2003 (AICPA Professional Standards, QC Sections 20-40 (AICPA 2002)); and

(2) the AICPA SEC Practice Section's Requirements of Membership (d), (f) (first sentence), (l), (m), (n), (1), and (o), as in existence on April 16, 2003 (AICPA SEC Practice Section Manual Section 1000.08(d), (f), (j), (m), (n), (1), and (o)).

f. **Rule 3500T. Interim Ethics Standards.** In connection with the preparation or issuance of any audit report, a registered public accounting firm, and its associated persons, shall comply with ethics standards, as described in the AICPA's Code of Professional Conduct Rule 102, and interpretations and rulings thereunder, as in existence on April 16, 2003 (AICPA Professional Standards, ET Sections 102 and 191 (AICPA 2002)).

g. **Rule 3501. Definition of Terms.**

(1) Affiliate of the Accounting Firm. The term "affiliate of the accounting firm" (or "affiliate of the registered public accounting firm" or "affiliate of the firm") includes the accounting firm's parents; subsidiaries; pension, retirement, investment or similar plans; and any associated entities of the firm, as that term is used in Rule 2-01 of the Commission's Regulation S-X, 17 C.F.R. section 21 0.2-01 (f)(2).

(2) Affiliate of the Audit Client. The term "affiliate of the audit client" means:

(a) An entity that has control over the audit client, or over which the audit client has control, or which is under common control with the audit client, including the audit client's parents and subsidiaries;

(b) An entity over which the audit client has significant influence, unless the entity is not material to the audit client;

(c) An entity that has significant influence over the audit client, unless the audit client is not material to the entity; and

(d) Each entity in the investment company complex when the audit client is an entity that is part of an investment company complex.

(3) Audit and Professional Engagement Period. The term "audit and professional engagement period" includes both:

   (a) The period covered by any financial statements being audited or reviewed (the "audit period"); and

   (b) The period of the engagement to audit or review the audit client's financial statements or to prepare a report filed with the Commission (the "professional engagement period"):

   i. The professional engagement period begins when the registered public accounting firm either signs an initial engagement letter (or other agreement to review or audit a client's financial statements) or begins audit, review, or attest procedures, whichever is earlier; and

   ii. The professional engagement period ends when the audit client or the registered public accounting firm notifies the Commission that the client is no longer that firm's audit client.

   (c) For audits of the financial statements of foreign private issuers, the "audit and professional engagement period" does not include periods ended prior to the first day of the last fiscal year before the foreign private issuer first filed, or was required to file, a registration statement or report with the Commission, provided there has been full compliance with home country independence standards in all prior periods covered by any registration statement or report filed with the Commission.

(4) Audit Client. The term "audit client" means the entity whose financial statements or other information is being audited, reviewed, or attested and any affiliates of the audit client.

(5) Confidential Transaction. The term "confidential transaction" means:

   (a) In general. A confidential transaction is a transaction that is offered to a taxpayer under conditions of confidentiality and for which the taxpayer has paid an advisor a fee.

   (b) Conditions of confidentiality. A transaction is considered to be offered to a taxpayer under conditions of confidentiality if the advisor who is paid the fee places a limitation on disclosure by the taxpayer of the tax treatment or tax structure of the transaction and the limitation on disclosure protects the confidentiality of that advisor's tax strategies. A transaction is treated as confidential even if the conditions of confidentiality are not legally binding on the taxpayer. A claim that a transaction is proprietary or exclusive is not treated as a limitation on disclosure if the advisor confirms to the taxpayer that there is no limitation on disclosure of the tax treatment or tax structure of the transaction.

   (c) Determination of fee. For purposes of this definition, a fee includes all fees for a tax strategy or for services for advice (whether or not tax advice) or for the implementation of a transaction. These fees include consideration in whatever form paid, whether in cash or in kind, for services to analyze the transaction (whether or not related to the tax consequences of the transaction), for services to implement the transaction, for services to document the transaction, and for services to prepare tax returns to the extent that the fees exceed the fees customary for return preparation. For purposes of this definition, a taxpayer also is treated as paying fees to an advisor if the taxpayer knows or should know that the amount it pays will be paid indirectly to the advisor, such as through a referral fee or fee-sharing arrangement. A fee does not include amounts paid to a person, including an advisor, in that person's capacity as a party to the transaction. For example, a fee does not include reasonable charges for the use of capital or the sale or use of property.

(d) Related parties. For purposes of this definition, persons who bear a relationship to each other as described in section 267(b) or 707(b) of the Internal Revenue Code will be treated as the same person.

(6) Contingent Fee. The term "contingent fee" means:

(a) Except as stated below, any fee established for the sale of a product or the performance of any service pursuant to an arrangement in which no fee will be charged unless a specified finding or result is attained, or in which the amount of the fee is otherwise dependent upon the finding or result of such product or service.

(b) Solely for the purposes of this definition, a fee is not a "contingent fee" if the amount is fixed by courts or other public authorities and not dependent on a finding or result.

(7) Financial Reporting Oversight Role. The term "financial reporting oversight role" means a role in which a person is in a position to or does exercise influence over the contents of the financial statements or anyone who prepares them, such as when the person is a member of the board of directors or similar management or governing body, chief executive officer, president, chief financial officer, chief operating officer, general counsel, chief accounting officer, controller, director of internal audit, director of financial reporting, treasurer, or any equivalent position.

(8) Immediate Family Member. The term "immediate family member" means a person's spouse, spousal equivalent, and dependents.

(9) Investment Company Complex. The term "investment company complex" includes:

(a) An investment company and its investment adviser or sponsor. An investment adviser, for purposes of this definition, does not include a sub-adviser whose role is primarily portfolio management and is subcontracted with or overseen by another investment adviser. A sponsor, for purposes of this definition, is an entity that establishes a unit investment trust.

(b) Any entity controlled by or controlling an investment adviser or sponsor or any entity under common control with an investment adviser or sponsor if the entity is an investment adviser or sponsor, or is engaged in the business of providing administrative, custodian, underwriting, or transfer agent services to any investment company, investment adviser, or sponsor.

(c) Any investment company or entity that would be an investment company but for the exclusions provided by section 3(c) of the Investment Company Act of 1940 (15 U.S.C. section 80a-3(c)) that has an investment adviser or sponsor included in this definition by either (a) or (b) of this definition.

h. **Rule 3502. Responsibility Not to Knowingly or Recklessly Contribute to Violations.** A person associated with a registered public accounting firm shall not take or omit to take an action knowing, or recklessly not knowing, that the act or omission would directly and substantially contribute to a violation by that registered public accounting firm of the Act, the Rules of the Board, the provisions of the securities laws relating to the preparation and issuance of audit reports and the obligations and liabilities of accountants with respect thereto, including the rules of the Commission issued under the Act, or professional standards.

i. **Rule 3520. Auditor Independence.** A registered public accounting firm and its associated persons must be independent of the firm's audit client throughout the audit and professional engagement period. A registered public accounting firm or associated person's independence obligation with respect to an audit client that is an issuer encompasses not only an obligation to satisfy the independence criteria set out in the rules and standards of the PCAOB, but also an obligation to satisfy all other independence criteria applicable to the engagement, including the independence criteria set out in the rules and regulations of the Commission under the federal securities laws. This rule applies only to those associated persons of a registered public accounting firm required to be independent of the firm's audit client by standards, rules, or regulations of the Commission or other applicable independence criteria.

j. **Rule 3521. Contingent Fees.** A registered public accounting firm is not independent of its audit client if the firm, or any affiliate of the firm, during the audit and professional engagement period, provides any service or product to the audit client for a contingent fee or a commission, or receives from the audit client, directly or indirectly, a contingent fee or commission.

k. **Rule 3522. Tax Transactions.** A registered public accounting firm is not independent of its audit client if the firm, or any affiliate of the firm, during the audit and professional engagement period, provides any nonaudit service to the audit client related to marketing, planning, or opining in favor of the tax treatment of, a transaction:

   (1) Confidential Transactions - that is a confidential transaction; or

   (2) Aggressive Tax Position Transactions - that was initially recommended, directly or indirectly, by the registered public accounting firm and a significant purpose of which is tax avoidance, unless the proposed tax treatment is at least more likely than not to be allowable under applicable tax laws. With respect to transactions subject to the U.S. tax laws, this rule includes, but is not limited to, any transaction that is a listed transaction within the meaning of 26 C.F.R. section 1.6011-4(b)(2). A registered public accounting firm indirectly recommends a transaction when an affiliate of the firm or another tax advisor, with which the firm has a formal agreement or other arrangement related to the promotion of such transactions, recommends engaging in the transaction.

l. **Rule 3523. Tax Services for Persons in Financial Reporting Oversight Roles.** A registered public accounting firm is not independent of its audit client if the firm, or any affiliate of the firm, during the audit and professional engagement period provides any tax service to a person in a financial reporting oversight role at the audit client, or an immediate family member of such person, unless:

   (1) the person is in a financial reporting oversight role at the audit client only because he or she serves as a member of the board of directors or similar management or governing body of the audit client;

   (2) the person is in a financial reporting oversight role at the audit client only because of the person's relationship to an affiliate of the entity being audited:

      (a) whose financial statements are not material to the consolidated financial statements of the entity being audited; or

      (b) whose financial statements are audited by an auditor other than the firm or an associated person of the firm; or

   (3) the person was not in a financial reporting oversight role at the audit client before a hiring, promotion, or other change in employment event and the tax services are:

      (a) provided pursuant to an engagement in process before the hiring, promotion, or other change in employment event; and

      (b) completed on or before 180 days after the hiring or promotion event.

m. **Rule 3524. Audit Committee Pre-approval of Certain Tax Services.** In connection with seeking audit committee pre-approval to perform for an audit client any permissible tax service, a registered public accounting firm shall:

   (1) describe, in writing, to the audit committee of the issuer:

   (a) the scope of the service, the fee structure for the engagement, and any side letter or other amendment to the engagement letter, or any other agreement (whether oral, written, or otherwise) between the firm and the audit client, relating to the service; and

   (b) any compensation arrangement or other agreement, such as a referral agreement, a referral fee or fee-sharing arrangement, between the registered public accounting firm (or an affiliate of the firm) and any person (other than the audit client) with respect to the promoting, marketing, or recommending of a transaction covered by the service;

   (2) discuss with the audit committee of the issuer the potential effects of the services on the independence of the firm; and

   (3) document the substance of its discussion with the audit committee of the issuer.

n. **Rule 3525. Audit Committee Pre-approval of Nonaudit Services Related to Internal Control Over Financial Reporting.** In connection with seeking audit committee pre-approval to perform for an audit client any permissible nonaudit service related to internal control over financial reporting, a registered public accounting firm shall:

   (1) describe, in writing, to the audit committee of the issuer the scope of the service;

   (2) discuss with the audit committee of the issuer the potential effects of the service on the independence of the firm; and

   Note: Independence requirements provide that an auditor is not independent of his or her audit client if the auditor is not, or a reasonable investor with knowledge of all relevant facts and circumstances would conclude that the auditor is not, capable of exercising objective and impartial judgment on all issues encompassed within the accountant's engagement. Several principles guide the application of this general standard, including whether the auditor assumes a management role or audits his or her own work. Therefore, an auditor would not be independent if, for example, management had delegated its responsibility for internal control over financial reporting to the auditor or if the auditor had designed or implemented the audit client's internal control over financial reporting.

   (3) document the substance of its discussion with the audit committee of the issuer.

o. **Rule 3526. Communication with Audit Committees Concerning Independence.** A registered public accounting firm must:

   (1) prior to accepting an initial engagement pursuant to the standards of the PCAOB:

   (a) describe, in writing, to the audit committee of the issuer, all relationships between the registered public accounting firm or any affiliates of the firm and the potential audit client or persons in financial reporting oversight roles at the potential audit client that, as of the date of the communication, may reasonably be thought to bear on independence;

   (b) discuss with the audit committee of the issuer the potential effects of the relationships described in (1)(a) above on the independence of the registered public accounting firm, should it be appointed the issuer's auditor; and

   (c) document the substance of its discussion with the audit committee of the issuer.

(2) at least annually with respect to each of its issuer audit clients:

    (a) describe, in writing, to the audit committee of the issuer, all relationships between the registered public accounting firm or any affiliates of the firm and the audit client or persons in financial reporting oversight roles at the audit client that, as of the date of the communication, may reasonably be thought to bear on independence;

    (b) discuss with the audit committee of the issuer the potential effects of the relationships described in (2)(a) above on the independence of the registered public accounting firm;

    (c) affirm to the audit committee of the issuer, in writing, that, as of the date of the communication, the registered public accounting firm is independent in compliance with Rule 3520; and

    (d) document the substance of its discussion with the audit committee of the issuer.

p. **Rule 3600T. Interim Independence Standards.** In connection with the preparation or issuance of any audit report, a registered public accounting firm, and its associated persons, shall comply with independence standards:

    (1) as described in the AICPA's Code of Professional Conduct Rule 101, and interpretations and rulings thereunder, as in existence on April 16, 2003 (AICPA Professional Standards, ET Sections 101 and 191 (AICPA 2002)); and

    (2) Standards Nos. 1, 2, and 3, and Interpretations 99-1, 00-1, and 00-2, of the Independence Standards Board.

q. **Rule 3700. Advisory Groups.**

    (1) Formation: To assist it in carrying out its responsibility to establish auditing and related professional practice standards, the Board will convene one or more advisory groups, in accordance with Section 103(a)(4) of the Act.

    (2) Composition: Advisory groups, in combination or as sub-groups designated by the Board within one advisory group, will contain individuals with expertise in one or more of the following areas: accounting; auditing; corporate finance; corporate governance; investing in public companies; and other areas that the Board deems to be relevant to one or more auditing or related professional practice standards.

    (3) Selection of Members of Advisory Groups: Members of advisory groups will be selected by the Board, in its sole discretion, based upon nominations, including self-nominations, received from any person or organization.

    (4) Ad Hoc Task Forces: The Board may, in its discretion, establish ad hoc task forces. The membership of such task forces may include, but is not limited to, advisory group members.

4251.74 Inspections (PCAOB)

a. **Rule 4000. General.** Every registered public accounting firm shall be subject to all such regular and special inspections as the Board may from time-to-time conduct in order to assess the degree of compliance of each registered public accounting firm and associated persons of that firm with the Act, the Board's rules, the rules of the Commission, and professional standards, in connection with its performance of audits, issuance of audit reports, and related matters involving issuers.

b. **Rule 4001. Regular Inspections.** In performing a regular inspection, the staff of the Division of Registration and Inspections and any other person authorized by the Board to participate in the inspection shall take such steps, and perform such procedures, as the Board determines are necessary or appropriate.

c. **Rule 4002. Special Inspections.** In performing a special inspection, the staff of the Division of Registration and Inspections and any other person authorized by the Board to participate in the inspection shall take such steps, and perform such procedures, as are necessary or appropriate concerning the issue or issues specified by the Board in connection with its authorization of the special inspection. The Board may authorize a special inspection on its own initiative or at the request of the Commission.

d. **Rule 4003. Frequency of Inspections.** During each calendar year, beginning no later than the calendar year following the calendar year in which its application for registration with the Board is approved, a registered public accounting firm that, during the prior calendar year, issued audit reports with respect to more than 100 issuers shall be subject to a regular inspection.

   (1) At least once in every three calendar years, beginning with the 3-year period following the calendar year in which its application for registration with the Board is approved, a registered public accounting firm that, during any of the three prior calendar years, issued an audit report with respect to at least one, but no more than 100, issuers, or that played a substantial role in the preparation or furnishing of an audit report with respect to at least one issuer, shall be subject to a regular inspection.

   (2) With respect to a registered public accounting firm that has filed a completed Form 1-WD under Rule 2107, the Board shall have the discretion to forego any regular inspection that would otherwise commence during the period beginning on the fifth day following the filing of the completed Form 1-WD and continuing until the firm's registration is deemed withdrawn or the firm withdraws the Form 1-WD.

e. **Rule 4004. Procedure Regarding Possible Violations.** If the Board determines that information obtained by the Board's staff during any inspection indicates that the registered public accounting firm subject to such inspection, any associated person thereof, or any other person, may have engaged, or may be engaged, in any act, practice, or omission to act that is or may be in violation of the Act, the rules of the Board, any statute or rule administered by the Commission, the firm's own quality control policies, or any professional standard, the Board shall, if it determines appropriate:

   (1) report information concerning such act, practice, or omission to:

      (a) the Commission; and

      (b) each appropriate state regulatory authority; and

   (2) commence an investigation of such act, practice, or omission in accordance with Section 105(b) of the Act and the Board's rules thereunder or a disciplinary proceeding in accordance with Section 105(c) of the Act and the Board's rules thereunder.

   The Board may, as appropriate, make referrals or report information to regulatory and law enforcement agencies other than those specifically described in Rule 4004.

f. **Rule 4006. Duty to Cooperate with Inspectors.** Every registered public accounting firm, and every associated person of a registered public accounting firm, shall cooperate with the Board in the performance of any Board inspection. Cooperation shall include, but is not limited to, cooperating and complying with any request, made in furtherance of the Board's authority and responsibilities under the Act, to:

   (1) provide access to, and the ability to copy, any record in the possession, custody, or control of such firm or person, and

   (2) provide information by oral interviews, written responses, or otherwise.

g. **Rule 4007. Procedures Concerning Draft Inspection Reports.** The Director of the Division of Registration and Inspections shall make a draft inspection report available for review by the firm that is the subject of the report. The firm may, within the 30 days after the draft inspection report is first made available for the firm's review, or such longer period as the Board may order, submit to the Board a written response to the draft report.

  (1) In submitting a response pursuant to paragraph (a), the firm may indicate any portions of the response for which the firm requests confidential treatment under Section 104(f) of the Act, and may supply any supporting authority or other justification for according confidential treatment to the information.

  (2) The Board shall attach to, and make part of the inspection report, any response submitted pursuant to paragraph (a), but shall redact from the response attached to the inspection report any information for which the firm requested confidential treatment and which it is reasonable to characterize as confidential.

  (3) After receiving and reviewing any response letter, the Board may take such action with respect to the draft inspection report as it considers appropriate, including adopting the draft report as the final report, revising the draft report, or continuing or supplementing the inspection before issuing a final report. In the event that, prior to issuing a final report, the Board directs the staff to continue or supplement the inspection or revise the draft report, the Board may, in its discretion, afford the firm the opportunity to review any revised draft inspection report.

h. **Rule 4008. Procedures Concerning Final Inspection Reports.** Promptly following the Board's issuance of a final inspection report, the Board shall:

  (1) make the final report available for review by the firm that is the subject of the report;

  (2) transmit to the Commission the final report, any additional letter or comments by the Board or the Board's inspectors that the Board deems appropriate, and any response submitted by the firm to a draft inspection report; and

  (3) transmit to each appropriate state regulatory authority, in appropriate detail, the final report, any additional letter or comments by the Board or the Board's inspectors that the Board deems appropriate, and any response submitted by the firm to a draft inspection report.

i. **Rule 4009. Firm Response to Quality Control Defects.** With respect to any final inspection report that contains criticisms of, or potential defects in, the quality control systems of the firm under inspection, the firm may submit evidence or otherwise demonstrate to the Director of the Division of Registration and Inspections that it has improved such systems, and remedied such defects no later than 12 months after the issuance of the Board's final inspection report. After reviewing such evidence, the Director shall advise the firm whether he or she will recommend to the Board that the Board determine that the firm has satisfactorily addressed the criticisms or defects in the quality control system of the firm identified in the final inspection report and, if not, why not.

  (1) If the Board determines that the firm has satisfactorily addressed the criticisms or defects in the quality control system, the Board shall provide notice of that determination to the Commission and to any appropriate state regulatory authority to which the Board had supplied any portion of the final inspection report.

  (2) The Board shall notify the firm of its final determination concerning whether the firm has addressed the criticisms or defects in the quality control system of the firm identified in the final inspection report to the satisfaction of the Board.

(3) The portions of the Board's inspection report that deal with criticisms of or potential defects in quality control systems that the firm has not addressed to the satisfaction of the Board shall be made public by the Board:

    (a) upon the expiration of the 12-month period described above, if the firm fails to make any submission;

    (b) upon the expiration of the period in which the firm may seek Commission review of any board determination, if the firm does not seek Commission review of the Board determination; or

    (c) unless otherwise directed by Commission order or rule, 30 days after the firm formally requests Commission review.

j. **Rule 4010. Board Public Reports.** Notwithstanding any provision of Rules 4007, 4008, and 4009, the Board may, at any time, publish such summaries, compilations, or other general reports concerning the procedures, findings, and results of its various inspections as the Board deems appropriate. Such reports may include discussion of criticisms of, or potential defects in, quality control systems of any firm or firms that were the subject of a Board inspection, provided that no such published report shall Identify the firm or firms to which such criticisms relate, or at which such defects were found, unless that information has previously been made public in accordance with Rule 4009, by the firm or firms involved, or by other lawful means.

k. **Rule 4011. Statement by Foreign Registered Public Accounting Firms.** A foreign registered public accounting firm that seeks to have the Board rely, to the extent deemed appropriate by the Board, on a non-U.S. inspection when the Board conducts an inspection of such firm pursuant to Rule 4000 shall submit a written statement signed by an authorized partner or officer of the firm to the Board certifying that the firm seeks such reliance for all Board inspections.

l. **Rule 4012. Inspections of Foreign Registered Public Accounting Firms.** If a foreign registered public accounting firm has submitted a statement pursuant to Rule 4011, the Board will, at an appropriate time before each inspection of such firm, determine the degree, if any, to which the Board may rely on the non-U.S. inspection. To the extent consistent with the Board's responsibilities under the Act, the Board will conduct its inspection under Rule 4000 in a manner that relies to that degree on the non-U.S. inspection. In making that determination, the Board will evaluate:

(1) information concerning the level of the non-U.S. system's independence and rigor, including the adequacy and integrity of the system, the independence of the system's operation from the auditing profession, the nature of the system's source of funding, the transparency of the system, and the system's historical performance; and

(2) discussions with the appropriate entity or entities within the system concerning an inspection work program.

(3) The Board's evaluation may include, but not be limited to, consideration of:

    (a) the adequacy and integrity of the system;

    (b) the independence of the system from the auditing profession;

    (c) the source of funding for the system, including whether the system has an appropriate source of funding that is not subject to change, approval or influence by any person affiliated or otherwise connected with a public accounting firm or an association of such persons or firms;

    (d) the transparency of the system, including whether the system's rulemaking procedures and periodic reporting to the public are openly visible and accessible; and

(e) the system's historical performance, including whether there is a record of disciplinary proceedings and appropriate sanctions, but only for those systems that have existed for a reasonable period of time.

4251.75   Investigations and Adjudications (PCAOB)

Rules 5000–5501 provide detailed rules regarding investigations and adjudications. These rules should be consulted for more detailed information.

a. Under the rules, the Board and its staff may conduct investigations concerning any acts or practices, or omissions of acts, by registered public accounting firms and persons associated with such firms.

b. The rules require registered public accounting firms and their associated persons to cooperate with Board investigations, including producing documents and providing testimony.

c. The rules also permit the board to seek information from other persons, including clients of registered firms.

d. If violations are detected, the Board will provide an opportunity for a hearing, and in appropriate cases, impose sanctions.

e. Sanctions can include revoking a firm's registration or barring a person from participating in audits of public companies. Also, monetary penalties and requirements for remedial measures, such as training, new quality control procedures, and the appointment of an independent monitor can be imposed.

f. The Board may also hold hearings on registration applications.

  (1) If the Board is unable to determine that a public accounting firm has met the standard for approval of its application, the Board may provide the firm with a notice of hearing.

  (2) The firm may elect to treat this as a written notice of disapproval for purposes of making an appeal to the Commission.

  (3) The firm may instead choose to request a hearing before the Board. The Board would then, in appropriate circumstances, afford the firm a hearing pursuant to the rules.

4251.76   International (PCAOB)

a. **Rule 6001. Assisting Non-U.S. Authorities in Inspections.** The Board may provide assistance in an inspection of a registered public accounting firm organized and operated under the laws of the United States conducted pursuant to the laws and/or regulations of a non-U.S. jurisdiction. The independence and rigor of the non-U.S. system may be considered in determining the extent of the Board's assistance.

b. **Rule 6002. Assisting Non-U.S. Authorities in Investigations.** The Board may provide assistance in an investigation of a registered public accounting firm organized and operated under the laws of the U.S. conducted pursuant to the laws and/or regulations of a non-U.S. jurisdiction. The independence and rigor of the non-U.S. system may be considered in determining the extent of the Board's assistance.

4251.77   Funding (PCAOB)

a. **Rule 7100. Accounting Support Fee.** The Board shall calculate an accounting support fee each year. The accounting support fee shall equal the budget of the Board, as approved by the Commission, less the sum of all registration fees and annual fees received during the preceding calendar year from public accounting firms.

b. **Rule 7101. Allocation of Accounting Support Fee.** For purposes of allocating the accounting support fee, those entities that are issuers as of the date the accounting support fee is calculated under Rule 7100 shall be divided into four classes:

   (1) Equity Issuers: All issuers whose average, monthly issuer market capitalization during the preceding calendar year is greater than $25 million and whose share price on a monthly, or more frequent, basis is publicly available.

   (2) Investment Company Issuers: All issuers (i) who, as of the date the accounting support fee is calculated under Rule 7100, are registered under Section 8 of the Investment Company Act or have elected to be regulated as business development companies pursuant to Section 54 of the Investment Company Act, other than those described in paragraph (a)(3), (ii) whose average, monthly issuer market capitalization during the preceding calendar year is greater than $250 million, and (iii) whose share price (or net asset value) on a monthly, or more frequent, basis is publicly available.

   (3) Issuers Permitted Not to File Audited Financial Statements and Bankrupt Issuers that File Modified Reports: All issuers that, as of the date the accounting support fee is calculated under Rule 7100, (i) have a basis, under a Commission rule or pursuant to other action of the Commission or its staff, not to file audited financial statements, (ii) are employee stock purchase, savings and similar plans, interests in which constitute securities registered under the Securities Act, or (iii) are subject to the jurisdiction of a bankruptcy court and satisfy the modified reporting requirements of Commission Staff Legal Bulletin No. 2.

   (4) All Other Public Company Issuers: All issuers other than those described above.

   Entities described in categories (1) and (2) above are required to pay an accounting support fee based on a formula in the Rule. Those in categories (3) and (4) are not required to pay any portion of the fee.

c. **Rule 7102. Assessment of Accounting Support Fee.** Each issuer is required to pay its share of the accounting support fee, as allocated under Rule 7101, rounded to the nearest hundred. Any issuer who disagrees with the class in which it has been placed, or with the calculation by which its share of the accounting support fee was determined, may petition the Board for a correction of the share of the accounting support fee it was allocated.

d. **Rule 7103. Collection of Accounting Support Fee.** Unless the Board directs otherwise, payment shall be due on the 30th day after the notice is sent. Beginning on the 31st day, payment shall be deemed past due and interest shall accrue at a rate of 6% per annum. Generally, no registered public accounting firm shall sign an unqualified audit opinion with respect to an issuer's financial statements, or issue a consent to include an audit opinion issued previously, unless the registered public accounting firm has ascertained that the issuer has outstanding no past-due share of the accounting support fee or has a petition pending.

e. **Rule 7104. Services Designated Collection Agent.** If the Board is designated to serve as collection agent for an accounting support fee of a standard-setting body designated by the Commission pursuant to Section 19(b) of the Securities Act, the assessment and collection of the accounting support fee shall be governed by Rules 7102 and 7103 as if the accounting support fee of the standard-setting body were the accounting support fee of the Board.

Securities and Exchange Commission (SEC)

4251.78 The SEC was created by the Securities Exchange Act of 1934.

4251.79 The SEC has five commissioners appointed for a term of five years by the president with the advice and consent of the Senate. Not more than three of the commissioners can be from a particular political party. The appointments are staggered so that one appointment expires on June 5 of each year. The chairman is designated by the president.

4251.80 The SEC is an independent, bipartisan administrative agency created to administer laws that protect investors and the general public in securities transactions.

4251.81 Some of the federal laws administered by the SEC include the following:

   a. Securities Act of 1933

   b. Securities Exchange Act of 1934

   c. Public Utility Holding Company Act of 1935

   d. Trust Indenture Act of 1939

   e. Investment Company Act of 1940

   An investment company is an organization that invests and trades in securities. Open-ended investment companies are better known as mutual funds. Mutual funds must register with and are regulated by the SEC. Excluded from coverage are banks, insurance companies, savings and loan associations, finance companies, oil and gas drilling firms, charitable foundations, tax-exempt pension funds, and closely held companies.

   f. Investment Advisers Act of 1940

   g. Securities Investor Protection Act of 1970

   h. Foreign Corrupt Practices Act of 1977

4251.82 The following are some of the activities of the SEC:

   a. **Registration of securities.** Before securities can be offered to the public, the issuer must file a registration statement with the SEC. The SEC examines the registration statement for content and allows correcting amendments. After a lapse of 20 days, the securities may be sold, but each investor must file a registration application with the SEC. After initial registration, the companies must file annual, quarterly, and other reports with the SEC.

   b. **Corporate reporting.** All companies that have their securities listed on a securities exchange must file a registration application with the SEC. Larger companies that have their securities traded over-the-counter must also file a registration application with the SEC. After initial registration, the companies must file annual, quarterly, and other reports with the SEC.

   c. **Proxy solicitation.** Before making a proxy solicitation for registered securities, persons must file with the SEC documents that are reviewed for content.

   d. **Tender offer solicitation.** Any person who makes a tender offer for more than 5% of a registered security must file with the SEC documents that show disclosure of important information.

   e. **Margin trading.** After establishment by the Board of Governors of the Federal Reserve System, the SEC investigates and enforces margin trading regulations for the purchase and carrying of securities.

f. **Market surveillance.** The SEC monitors securities exchanges and over-the-counter trading of securities. They look for undesirable market practices, such as the following:

   (1) Fraud

   (2) Market manipulation

   (3) Misrepresentation

   (4) Stabilization—underwriters bid for securities to stabilize their price during issue.

g. **Registration** of national and regional stock exchanges, brokers and dealers who sell securities in interstate commerce, transfer agents, clearing agencies, municipal brokers and dealers, and securities information processors. All of these persons and organizations must file registration applications with the SEC. (There are about 13 national and regional stock exchanges.)

h. **Investigation.** The SEC investigates possible violation of the securities laws.

i. **Enforcement.** The SEC enforces the securities laws by the following:

   (1) **Civil injunction.** By going to the U.S. District Court, the SEC can get an injunction to stop activities that violate the securities laws.

   (2) **Criminal prosecution.** The SEC can refer cases of fraud or willful violations to the U.S. Justice Department.

   (3) **Administrative remedies.** The SEC can issue orders to suspend or expel members from an exchange or dealer association; denying, suspending, or revoking registration of brokers and dealers; censuring individuals for misconduct; and temporarily or permanently banning individuals from employment with a registered firm.

j. **Dealer or broker revocations.** The SEC can revoke the license to operate as a dealer or broker in securities transactions.

k. **Registration and supervision** of the activities of the mutual funds.

l. **Making of rules.** The SEC makes rules to implement the acts it administers. The best known rule is Rule 10b-5.

Final SEC Rule: Strengthening the Commission's Requirements Regarding Auditor Independence

4251.83 In early 2003, the SEC adopted rules which strengthen the auditor independence requirements consistent with the provisions of the Sarbanes-Oxley Act.

4251.84 The SEC rules reiterate many of the provisions found in Sarbanes-Oxley regarding nonaudit services.

4251.85 The SEC rules provide that an accounting firm can provide tax services to an audit client without impairing independence.

   a. The audit committee however, must pre-approve these services.

   b. Companies must also disclose the amount paid for tax services in this situation.

   c. The rules state that certain tax services could in certain circumstances impair independence. The rules state that audit committees should carefully review use of their audit firm for a transaction recommended by the accountant which may have tax avoidance as its sole purpose and whose tax treatment may not be supported by the Internal Revenue Code.

4251.86 The SEC rules also require the lead audit partner and audit review partner to rotate off the audit every five years. The rules also state that there is a 5-year "time-out" period for these partners before they can return to that audit client. Also, audit partners with significant involvement on the audit must rotate off after seven years and are subject to a 2-year "time-out" period before they can return.

Other SEC Rules

4251.87 **SEC Rule 144.** This rule allows the purchaser of restricted securities to resell those securities without registration if the following are true:

    a. The seller has held them for two years.

    b. The seller sells through a broker.

    c. The total sales of the security for the prior three months are 1% or less of the average weekly sales during the prior four weeks.

4251.88 **SEC Rule 145.** The issue of securities from a corporate reorganization, like a merger or consolidation, is subject to registration unless the securities qualify for an exemption under the 1933 act.

4251.89 **SEC Rule 242** exempts security issues of less than $2 million within any 6-month period if sold to accredited persons. Accredited persons are institutional investors, buyers of $100,000 or more in securities, and the issuer's officers and directors. The issuer can sell to up to 35 nonaccredited investors but must furnish a simplified prospectus to all purchasers, even if they are accredited persons.

SEC Forms

4251.90 Many forms are utilized by the SEC in regulating and administering the securities laws.

4251.91 For the Securities Act of 1933, these are some of the more important forms:

    a. **Form S-1.** To register a security for issue in the primary market.

    b. **Form S-18.** To register a security issue of under $5 million, of which $1.5 million can be sold to persons other than the issuer.

4251.92 For the Securities Exchange Act of 1934, there are at least 21 forms. These are some of the more important forms listed in approximate order of importance:

    a. **Form 10-K.** Annual report of a company. Must be filed within 90 days after the close of the fiscal year.

    b. **Form 10-Q.** Quarterly report of a company.

    c. **Form 8-K.** Current report that must be filed within 15 days of a "material" event. The deadline is five days for reporting the resignation of a director or for a change in auditors.

    d. **Form 10.** For registration of a class of securities to be listed on a national securities exchange or sold over-the-counter.

    e. **Form BD.** For registration of brokers and dealers.

4252 Other Federal Laws and Regulations (Antitrust, Copyright, Patents, Money-Laundering, Labor, Employment, and ERISA)

Social Security (FICA)

4252.01 Social Security is a federal law administered by the Social Security Administration under the Department of Health and Human Services (DHHS). It is also called FICA (Federal Insurance Contributions Act).

4252.02 **Historical development of Social Security (FICA)**

1935—Law passed. Covered only retired workers in industry and commerce.

1939—Paid survivors when worker died.

1950—Coverage extended to self-employed persons, state and local government employees, household and farm workers, members of the armed forces, and members of the clergy.

1954—Disability insurance added to cover a worker who was totally disabled.

1965—Medicare added. Hospital and medical insurance to persons aged 65 and older.

1972—Benefits go up automatically as cost of living goes up.

1973—Medicare coverage expanded to cover people under the age of 65 who are disabled for two years and people with permanent kidney failure who need dialysis or kidney transplants.

1983—Medicare coverage expanded to federal employees.

1984—Employers paid more than employees for one year only. Coverage extended to all newly hired federal employees plus all current and future members of Congress, the president and vice president, all sitting federal judges, magistrates, bankruptcy judges and referees in bankruptcy, and all executive level and senior executive service political appointees. Other current federal employees at the time could elect coverage under Social Security.

1990—Self-employed persons paid the same combined amount as an employee and employer.

1991—Social Security (OASDI—Old Age, Survivors, and Disability Insurance) and Medicare (HI—Hospital Insurance) separated and became subject to different maximums.

1994—Maximum income limit removed from the Medicare portion of the payment.

2000—Retirement age for those born after 1937 is gradually extended, eventually to the age of 67.

4252.03 **Major programs of Social Security (FICA)** (under which payments are received)

a. **Retirement**

(1) At age 62 with reduced payments

(2) At age 65 with regular payments

b. **Disability before age 65**

(1) The individual must have a physical or mental condition that keeps the person from working, which is expected to last 12 months or result in death.

(2) Payments start for sixth full month of the disability.

c. **Survivors of deceased worker**

   Those who may receive payments include the following:

   (1) Unmarried child under the age of 18

   (2) Unmarried child under the age of 19 if a full-time student in primary or high school, but *not* college

   (3) Surviving spouse aged 60 or older

   (4) Surviving spouse or divorced parent who takes care of the deceased's children under 16 years of age

   (5) Dependent parents aged 62 or older

   (6) Divorced spouse if marriage lasted 10 years

d. **Retired or disabled workers**

   Those who may receive payments include the following:

   (1) Unmarried child under the age of 18

   (2) Unmarried child under the age of 22 if a full-time student

   (3) Surviving spouse aged 62 or older

   (4) Wife under the age of 62 if taking care of child(ren) under the age of 18

e. **Medicare**

   (1) Hospital insurance and medical insurance for the following:

      (a) Individuals aged 65 and older

      (b) Disabled individuals under the age of 65 who are entitled to Social Security disability benefits

      (c) Workers and dependents who need dialysis treatment or a kidney transplant because of permanent kidney failure

   (2) Hospital insurance covers cost of inpatient hospital care.

      (a) No cost to the individual

      (b) Covered automatically

   (3) Medical insurance covers cost of physicians, outpatient hospital care, and other medical expenses.

      (a) Medical insurance requires a monthly premium.

      (b) The premium covers about 30% of the actual cost. The remainder comes from general revenues of the federal government.

f. **Supplemental Security Income (SSI)**

   (1) Additional income to help the aged, blind, and disabled person

   (2) Financed from general revenues (not a special trust fund)

   (3) Monthly payments are received by the eligible individuals.

   (4) The individual must have little or no regular cash income and no substantial assets that can be sold for cash (excludes house and household goods).

   (5) An individual can get both Social Security and SSI if eligible for both.

4252.04 Contribution rates and amounts

    a. Starting in 1991, the Old Age, Survivors, and Disability Insurance (OASDI) (Social Security) and Medicare Hospital Insurance (HI) (Medicare) components were separated and different maximum wage bases were applied.

    b. The following table shows the rates and the amounts since the inception in 1937:

Year(s)		Employee Percentage	Maximum Income	Paid by Employee	Employer Percentage	Paid by Employer
1937-50		1.00	$ 3,000	$ 30.00	1.00	$ 30.00
1951-54		1.00	3,600	36.00	1.00	36.00
1955-58		2.00	4,200	84.00	2.00	84.00
1959-65		2.00	4,800	96.00	2.00	96.00
1966-67		2.00	6,600	132.00	2.00	132.00
1968-71		5.20	7,800	405.60	5.20	405.60
1972		5.20	9,000	468.00	5.20	468.00
1973		5.85	10,800	631.80	5.85	631.80
1974		5.85	13,200	772.20	5.85	772.20
1975		5.85	14,100	824.85	5.85	824.85
1976		5.85	15,300	895.05	5.85	895.05
1977		5.85	16,500	965.25	5.85	965.25
1978		6.05	17,700	1,070.85	6.05	1,070.85
1979		6.13	22,900	1,403.77	6.13	1,403.77
1980		6.13	25,900	1,587.67	6.13	1,587.67
1981		6.65	29,700	1,975.05	6.65	1,975.05
1982		6.70	32,400	2,170.80	6.70	2,170.80
1983		6.70	35,700	2,391.90	6.70	2,391.90
1984		6.70	37,800	2,532.60	7.00	2,646.00
1985		7.05	39,600	2,791.80	7.05	2,791.80
1986		7.15	42,000	3,003.00	7.15	3,003.00
1987		7.15	43,800	3,131.70	7.15	3,131.70
1988		7.51	45,000	3,379.50	7.51	3,379.50
1989		7.51	48,000	3,604.80	7.51	3,604.80
1990		7.65	51,300	3,924.45	7.65	3,924.45
1991	OASDI	6.20	53,400	3,310.80	6.20	3,310.80
1991	HI	1.45	125,000	1,812.50	1.45	1,812.50
1992	OASDI	6.20	55,500	3,441.00	6.20	3,441.00
1992	HI	1.45	130,200	1,887.00	1.45	1,887.00
1993	OASDI	6.20	57,600	3,571.20	6.20	3,571.20
1993	HI	1.45	135,000	1,957.50	1.45	1,957.50
1994	OASDI	6.20	60,600	3,757.20	6.20	3,757.20
1994	HI*	1.45	No Limit	Unlimited	1.45	Unlimited
1995	OASDI	6.20	61,200	3,794.40	6.20	3,794.40
1996	OASDI	6.20	62,700	3,887.40	6.20	3,887.40
1997	OASDI	6.20	65,400	4,054.80	6.20	4,054.80
1998	OASDI	6.20	68,400	4,240.80	6.20	4,240.80
1999	OASDI	6.20	72,600	4,501.20	6.20	4,501.20
2000	OASDI	6.20	76,200	4,724.40	6.20	4,724.40
2001	OASDI	6.20	80,400	4,984.80	6.20	4,984.80
2002	OASDI	6.20	84,900	5,263.80	6.20	5,263.80
2003	OASDI	6.20	87,000	5,394.00	6.20	5,394.00
2004	OASDI	6.20	87,900	5,449.80	6.20	5,449.80
2005	OASDI	6.20	90,000	5,580.00	6.20	5,580.00
2006	OASDI	6.20	94,200	5,840.40	6.20	5,840.40

Table continued on next page

Table continued from previous page

Year(s)		Employee Percentage	Maximum Income	Paid by Employee	Employer Percentage	Paid by Employer
2007	OASDI	6.20	97,500	6,045.00	6.20	6,045.00
2008	OASDI	6.20	102,000	6,324.00	6.20	6,324.00
2009	OASDI	6.20	106,800	6,621.60	6.20	6,621.60
2010	OASDI	6.20	106,800	6,621.60	6.20	6,621.60

* Since 1994, limits on the Hospitalization Insurance (HI) have been removed and all earned income is taxed at 1.45%.

    c. For the past few years the rate and the amount for the self-employed were as follows:

Year		Percentage	Maximum Income
1990		15.3	51,300
1991	OASDI	12.4	53,400
1991	HI	2.9	125,000
1992	OASDI	12.4	55,500
1992	HI	2.9	130,200
1993	OASDI	12.4	57,600
1993	HI	2.9	135,000
1994	OASDI	12.4	60,600
1994	HI*	2.9	No Limit
1995	OASDI	12.4	61,200
1996	OASDI	12.4	62,700
1997	OASDI	12.4	65,400
1998	OASDI	12.4	68,400
1999	OASDI	12.4	72,600
2000	OASDI	12.4	76,200
2001	OASDI	12.4	80,400
2002	OASDI	12.4	84,900
2003	OASDI	12.4	87,000
2004	OASDI	12.4	87,900
2005	OASDI	12.4	90,000
2006	OASDI	12.4	94,200
2007	OASDI	12.4	97,500
2008	OASDI	12.4	102,000
2009	OASDI	12.4	106,800
2010	OASDI	12.4	106,800

* Since 1994, limits on the Hospitalization Insurance (HI) have been removed and all self-employment income is taxed at 2.9%.

    d. Until 1984, the employer and the employee paid the same amount. In 1984, the employer's percentage was increased to 7.0%, while the employee's percentage remained at 6.7%. In 1985 and years thereafter, the equality between employer and employee was reinstated.

    e. If an individual works for two employers, each is required to withhold up to the maximum. If the employee's combined income exceeds the maximum income amount, the FICA tax withheld will exceed the maximum employee tax for the year. If this occurs, the excess FICA tax paid is claimed as a credit on the individual's income tax return.

    f. The maximum amount of salary and wages that is taxable automatically increases based on a formula that uses national average wage index ratios.

    g. The employer portion of the FICA tax is deductible as an ordinary and necessary business expense by the employer.

4252.05 Social Security (FICA) Compensation:
  a. Includes earnings from wages and salary.
  b. Includes vacation pay and dismissal pay.
  c. Includes bonuses, commissions, and prizes.
  d. Does not include expenses reimbursed.
  e. Does not include fringe benefits paid by employer (like hospitalization, group life insurance, and pension payments).

4252.06 Employees subject to the withholding:
  a. Includes corporate officers.
  b. Includes domestic workers (maids and babysitters) making at least $50 per quarter.
  c. Need not include spouse and minor children of the employer.
  d. Does not include independent contractors (they pay as self-employed persons).

4252.07 Federal employees hired after 1983 are covered by Social Security.

4252.08 State employees
  a. State employees as a group can elect to be covered by Social Security.
  b. Some states have recently decided to get out of Social Security.

4252.09 Social Security benefits have been taxable in certain cases since 1984 based on the amount of the individual's modified adjusted gross income.

4252.10 Social Security Trust Fund:
  a. Is the accumulation of receipts less benefits.
  b. Currently has a surplus that will continue to grow, then gradually decrease as post-World War II baby boom persons reach retirement age and start receiving their Social Security benefits.
  c. Can be used to pay other government bills but will likely be dedicated only to Social Security benefits.

4252.11 Retirement age for full benefits:
  a. Beginning with the year 2000 (workers and spouses born 1938 or later, widow(er)s born 1940 or later), the retirement age increases gradually from age 65 until it reaches age 67 in the year 2022.

b. The following chart contains the full retirement age for workers and spouses born after 1937:

If the birth date is...	Then full retirement age is...
1/2/38-1/1/39	65 years and 2 months
1/2/39-1/1/40	65 years and 4 months
1/2/40-1/1/41	65 years and 6 months
1/2/41-1/1/42	65 years and 8 months
1/2/42-1/1/43	65 years and 10 months
1/2/43-1/1/55	66 years
1/2/55-1/1/56	66 years and 2 months
1/2/56-1/1/57	66 years and 4 months
1/2/57-1/1/58	66 years and 6 months
1/2/58-1/1/59	66 years and 8 months
1/2/59-1/1/60	66 years and 10 months
1/2/60 and later	67 years

Legal Liability for Payroll and Social Security Taxes

4252.12 Along with the Social Security tax, an employer is generally required to withhold income tax on each payment of wages made to an employee.

4252.13 An employer who is subject to either social security taxes or income tax withholding, or both, is required to fill a quarterly return on Form 941. This quarterly form combines the reporting of FICA and income taxes withheld from employees' wages.

4252.14 Generally, an employer is required to deposit the FICA taxes and income taxes withheld at an authorized commercial bank depository.

4252.15 Generally, an employer is classified as either a monthly or semiweekly depositor. The status for a particular calendar year is decided annually, based on the employment tax reporting history for a 12-month lookback period ending on June 30 of the prior year. The IRS notifies employers by November of each year as to their classification for the next calendar year. The classification is based on the aggregate amount of employment taxes reported during the lookback period.

4252.16 In spite of the above rule, an employer with $100,000 or more of accumulated liability during a monthly or semi-weekly period are required to deposit the taxes by the first banking day after the $100,000 amount is reached.

4252.17 Employers that have less than $2,500 of liability during the quarter are not required to deposit the taxes. Instead, they send the full payment for the quarter with their quarterly Form 941.

4252.18 Employers that fail to deposit the full amount of taxes due are not subject to penalty if the shortfall does not exceed the greater of $100 or 2% of the amount of employment taxes due. This is true provided the shortfall is deposited on or before a prescribed makeup date.

4252.19 An employer also will not be subject to a penalty if they can show that the failure to deposit was due to reasonable cause (IRC Section 6656).

4252.20 A multi-tier penalty structure generally applies to situations where the employer fails to make timely deposits of employment taxes. The penalty is as follows:

a. 2% of the amount of the underpayment if the failure is for no more than five days.

b. 5% of the amount of the underpayment if the failure is for more than five days but for no more than 15 days.

  c. 10% of the amount of the underpayment if the failure is for more than 15 days.

  d. 15% of the amount of the underpayment if a required tax deposit is not made on or before the day that is 10 days after the date of the first delinquency notice to the employer.

4252.21 Under IRC Section 6672 any responsible person (usually a corporate officer or employee) who willfully fails to withhold, account for, or pay over withholding tax is liable for a penalty equal to 100% of such tax. Generally, the IRS only assesses this penalty in situations where the employment taxes cannot be collected from the employer.

Federal Unemployment Tax Act (FUTA)

4252.22 The Federal Unemployment Tax Act (FUTA) is also known as unemployment compensation tax.

4252.23 FUTA's purpose is to provide economic security for temporarily unemployed workers.

4252.24 An employer is obligated to pay FUTA taxes if the employer either:

  a. paid wages of $1,500 or more in any calendar quarter or

  b. had one or more employees for any 20 calendar weeks during the year.

  These requirements allow very few employers to escape payment of the FUTA tax. The FUTA tax is deductible as an ordinary and necessary business expense of the employer.

4252.25 Funds for the unemployment insurance system come from taxes paid by employers. Unlike FICA, only employers pay the tax.

4252.26 Employers cannot charge employees for the cost of the federal unemployment insurance tax.

4252.27 The FUTA tax rate is 6.2% through June 30, 2011, (a permanent tax of 6% plus an extended benefit tax of 0.2%) on the first $7,000 paid to an individual employee during the calendar year. The extended benefit tax of 0.2% expires as of June 30, 2011. Therefore, the FUTA tax rate for July 2011 and after is 6%.

4252.28 **Credit on the FUTA tax for payments to a state unemployment insurance fund.** For years 1985 and thereafter, there is a credit of 5.4% on the first $7,000 paid to an individual employee. Thus, under normal circumstances the effective federal tax rate would be 0.8% through June 30, 2011, (6.2% – 5.4%) and 0.6% starting in July 2011 (6.0% – 5.4%). The 5.4% credit is reduced if the state where the employer is domiciled has borrowed money from the federal government for unemployment benefits and has not repaid the loan. Some states now pay an effective rate of 1.6% rather than the normal 0.8%.

  Example: An employee is paid $12,600 for 2010. The employer's FUTA tax for this employee is $434 (0.062 × $7,000). If the state where the employer is located has a state unemployment insurance tax (all states do), it is probably set at a rate of 5.4% of the first $7,000 of wages. The employer would pay $378 to the state. This payment would be a credit to the FUTA tax. The amount actually paid to the federal government would then be $56 ($434 – $378).

4252.29 Administration and enforcement of FUTA are under the jurisdiction of the Social Security Administration. The federal taxes are paid to the United States Treasury.

4252.30 The FUTA tax return is filed annually. Payments are due quarterly if $100 or more is owed.

4252.31 **Sanctions.** Willful failure to pay, file returns, or keep records is a misdemeanor and subject to a fine of up to $10,000, or imprisonment of not more than one year, or both. There are civil penalties of an additional tax for late filing and liability for double the tax amount.

Workers' Compensation

4252.32 Workers' compensation used to be called workmen's compensation. Coverage under these statutes varies from state to state.

4252.33 **Problems with the common law tort liability system before workers' compensation**

    a. Time. Possibly years in the court system before the injured worker could collect.

    b. Attorney's contingent fees (often 20%–50%) reduced the dollar amount the injured worker actually received.

    c. Defenses available to the defendant employer include the following:

        (1) Employee plaintiff assumed a known risk in accepting the job.

        (2) Employee plaintiff was contributorily negligent. In some states, a plaintiff cannot collect unless totally fault free. Other states with a comparative negligence allow a percentage recovery based on the comparative fault of the two parties.

        (3) Fellow servant rule. If the injury was caused by a fellow employee, the employer is not liable. The negligence of the employee is not imputed to the employer as is the usual case with the doctrine of *respondeat superior.* The injured employee can only sue the fellow employee for the negligence.

4252.34 **Purpose of workers' compensation law enacted by the states**

    a. To protect employees and their families from the risks of financial loss as a result of accidental injury, death, disease, or disability resulting from employment

    b. To correct the problems of the common law tort liability system

    c. To provide an employee's exclusive remedy against the employer for covered injuries

4252.35 Employers are strictly liable without fault for injury, death, disability, or disease resulting from employment.

4252.36 **Typical statutory exclusions from workers' compensation coverage:**

    a. Domestic employees (e.g., maids)

    b. Agricultural employees

    c. Employers having less than some minimum number of employees

4252.37 **Two types of workers' compensation statutes:**

    1. **Compulsory law**

        (a) Employer has no choice—must be covered by workers' compensation law.

        (b) Majority of states have a compulsory law.

    2. **Noncompulsory law**

        (a) Employer liable for injury or death resulting from and proximately caused by employer's negligence if employer does not elect coverage.

        (b) No statutory limit on the amount of damages that can be recovered.

(c) Employer may elect to be covered by the workers' compensation law that provides statutory limits.

(d) If employer does not elect the workers' compensation coverage, the employer loses the usual common law defenses.

4252.38 **Ways of providing coverage:**

a. **Self-insurance**

(1) Employer pays all claims directly.

(2) Employer must demonstrate capability. Usually only large corporations can do this.

b. **Insurance with a private company**

(1) Some insurance companies specialize in this type of insurance.

(2) Rate is determined by claim experience and number of employees.

c. **Insurance with the state fund**

(1) Usually the most expensive way.

(2) Rate is based on claim experience and number of employees.

4252.39 **Workers' compensation**

a. Employer must pay the entire cost. It cannot be deducted from the employee's wages.

b. Was the first form of social insurance in the United States.

c. Was the first "liability without fault" system in the United States.

d. Today all 50 states have workers' compensation systems.

4252.40 **New trends**

a. Covers diseases as well as injuries as long as they are work related.

b. Covers psychological injuries as well as physical injuries.

Example: High-pressure job causing an air traffic controller to have a mental breakdown

c. Established by the 1972 report by the 15 members of the presidentially appointed commission on state workmen's compensation laws. Their recommendations were as follows:

(1) Require all states to conform to specific standards as to coverage and benefits.

(2) Cover all employees.

(3) No time or money limits on type, extent, or expense of medical care.

(4) Weekly death or total benefits of at least two-thirds of the average weekly wage.

(5) Offer rehabilitation services to reduce disability and restore physical, psychological, social, and vocational functioning of injured employees.

(6) Spouse gets death benefits for life or until remarriage.

(7) Children get death benefits until the age of 18, or 25 if a full-time student.

(8) Adjust compensation benefits to reflect increases in wage levels.

4252.41 Employers' reaction to the workers' compensation law has been to reduce the frequency and severity of job-related disabilities to minimize the premium and other expenses.

    a. Inspect physical facilities for the following:

        (1) Gas

        (2) Vapor

        (3) Fumes

        (4) Dust

        (5) Heat

        (6) Noise

        (7) Lighting

        (8) Radiation

        (9) Ventilation

        (10) Any other dangerous conditions

    b. Education programs for loss control include the following:

        (1) Accident investigation

        (2) Safety rules (e.g., wearing hard hats when there is overhead danger)

        (3) Feedback information

4252.42 **Admiralty law.** Under the Jones Act of 1920, injured seamen are entitled to a trial by jury with no limit on awards for occupational injuries. Injured seamen may elect to be covered by the liberal federal law and avoid the state workers' compensation laws. Commercial fishing is also subject to U.S. admiralty law and the Jones Act.

4252.43 Various federal statutes cover other employees, such as railroad workers, longshoremen, and harbor workers, for job-related injuries.

The Occupational Safety and Health Act

4252.44 The Occupational Safety and Health Act is a federal statute administered by the Occupational Safety and Health Administration (OSHA) of the Department of Labor. OSHA has the power to promulgate standards, conduct inspections, and enforce the provisions of the act.

4252.45 Generally, the Occupational Safety and Health Act requires that employers provide a workplace that is free from recognized hazards that are likely to cause death or serious harm.

4252.46 Employers engaged in a business affecting interstate commerce are covered by the Occupational Safety and Health Act. Exempted from the act are the following:

    a. The U.S. government

    b. States and their political subdivisions

    c. Certain industries covered by other federal safety statutes

4252.47 Both employers and employees are required by OSHA to comply with safety rules and regulations promulgated under the act.

4252.48 The act provides that employers cannot discharge or discriminate against an employee for filing a complaint with OSHA or for refusing to work in a high-risk area.

4252.49 Enforcement of the act occurs through OSHA inspections and the issuance of citations requiring employers to correct violations. Employers can require OSHA to obtain a warrant before conducting an inspection.

4252.50 OSHA may impose civil penalties as well as criminal penalties for certain willful violations. These penalties can run as high as $1,000 per violation per day.

4252.51 Among the duties of employers under the act are the following:
   a. To maintain records of workplace deaths, injuries, and illnesses
   b. To file reports with OSHA regarding workplace deaths, injuries, and illnesses
   c. To maintain records of employee exposure to harmful substances
   d. To provide notification to employees regarding various items such as immediate notice regarding employee exposure to harmful substances

4252.52 The act allows states to regulate workplace safety within certain minimal acceptable standards provided OSHA approves the plan.

Title VII of the Civil Rights Act of 1964

4252.53 Title VII of the Civil Rights Act of 1964 prohibits discrimination in employment on the basis of race, color, national origin, religion, or sex. Most employment decisions such as hiring, firing, compensation, and employee training are covered.

4252.54 All employers who employ 15 or more employees and are engaged in a business affecting interstate commerce fall within Title VII of the Civil Rights Act of 1964.

4252.55 The Equal Employment Opportunity Commission (EEOC) is responsible for enforcement of Title VII.
   a. The plaintiff must first file a complaint with the EEOC, which investigates the case.
   b. If the complaint is found to be valid, the EEOC will attempt to obtain a voluntary settlement between the plaintiff and employer.
   c. If no settlement is reached, the EEOC can sue the employer under Title VII.
   d. If the EEOC does not file suit, it issues a "right to sue letter," which allows the plaintiff to file suit.

4252.56 Disparate treatment discrimination

These types of cases under Title VII generally involve an individual plaintiff.
   a. First, the plaintiff must prove a *prima facie* case of discrimination that requires the employer to present a defense.
   b. The employer is then required to present legitimate nondiscriminatory reasons for its treatment of the plaintiff. If the employer fails, the employer loses the case.
   c. If the employer presents satisfactory reasons for the treatment, the employer will win the case unless the plaintiff can show that the reasons are only a pretext for a decision made for a discriminatory purpose.

4252.57 Disparate impact discrimination

These types of cases under Title VII generally involve several plaintiffs who file a class action against the employer.

   a. First, the plaintiff must identify the discriminatory employment practice.

   b. Next, the plaintiff must prove that the discriminatory practice had a substantial adverse impact on a class protected by Title VII.

   c. The employer is then required to show that the practice is required by business necessity and is job-related.

   d. If the employer proves that the practice is job-related, the plaintiff can still prevail if it can be shown that there is a less discriminatory practice that can meet the employer's business necessity.

4252.58 Defenses

If the plaintiff proves a Title VII violation, the employer can still win if they can make use of one of the following defenses:

   a. **Seniority.** If the employer treats employees differently based on a bona fide seniority system, there is no Title VII violation. The seniority system must also not be the result of any intentional discrimination.

   b. **Merit system.** If the employer selects or promotes employees under a system based on job-related merit, there is no Title VII violation.

   c. **Bona fide occupational qualifications (BFOQ).** Discrimination based on sex, religion, or national origin is allowable under Title VII if it is a BFOQ that is reasonably related to the business involved. Race or color discrimination is never justified as a BFOQ.

4252.59 Remedies

Various remedies are available under Title VII, including the following:

   a. Back pay for up to two years prior to the filing of a charge

   b. Reasonable attorney fees

   c. Equitable remedies such as reinstatement, awarding retroactive seniority, and injunctions to compel hiring or promotion

   d. Compensatory and possibly punitive damages within specified limits

4252.60 Section 1981

   a. Standards are much like Title VII, to prevent discrimination in employment (in such areas as hiring and promotion), harassment, and on-the-job discrimination.

   b. Title VII has been applied to discrimination based on race, racially characterized national origin, and alienage.

   c. Title VII's methods of proof and defenses are generally used in these cases by the courts.

Executive Order 112

4252.61 Executive Order 112 prohibits discrimination based on race, color, sex, religion, or national origin by contractors who enter contracts with the federal government.

4252.62 Under Executive Order 112, federal contractors also are required to take affirmative action in recruiting employees and generally must have a written affirmative action plan to be in compliance.

4252.63 Executive Order 112 is enforced by the Office of Federal Contract Compliance Programs (OFCCP).

Age Discrimination in Employment Act (ADEA)

4252.64 The Age Discrimination in Employment Act (ADEA) prohibits discrimination in employment against employees who are 40 years of age and older.

4252.65 ADEA applies to private employers who employ at least 20 persons and whose business affects interstate commerce and governmental units.

4252.66 For a suit to be brought under ADEA, the procedures are similar to those under Title VII, where a charge must first be filed with the EEOC.

4252.67 Proof of the case is similar to Title VII in that disparate treatment and disparate impact theories are used.

4252.68 Defenses for employers include a bona fide seniority system and bona fide occupational qualifications (BFOQ) like under Title VII.

4252.69 Remedies

Remedies available under ADEA include the following:

a. Back pay and other benefits

b. An additional award of liquidated damages equal to the back pay award for willful violations by the employer

c. Reasonable attorney fees

d. Equitable remedies such as reinstatement and promotions

Americans with Disabilities Act (ADA)

4252.70 The Americans with Disabilities Act (ADA) prohibits discrimination in employment in such areas as hiring, firing, promotion, and pay against qualified persons with a disability.

4252.71 The Americans with Disabilities Act (ADA) applies to private employers with 25 or more employees as of July 26, 1992. It applies as of July 26, 1994, to employers with 15 or more employees.

4252.72 Disability is defined as:

a. a physical or mental impairment that substantially limits one or more of an individual's major life activities,

b. a record of such impairment, or

c. one who is regarded as having such an impairment.

4252.73 Current illegal drug use, homosexuality, transvestism, and other sex-related traits are not considered disabilities under the ADA (Americans with Disabilities Act).

4252.74 Under the ADA (Americans with Disabilities Act), protected qualified individuals with a disability are those who can perform the essential functions of the job either with or without reasonable accommodation by the employer.

4252.75 Under the ADA (Americans with Disabilities Act), employers are required to make reasonable accommodations, such as installing ramps or restructuring jobs, as long as doing so does not cause undue hardship to the employer.

4252.76 Undue hardship is defined as significant difficulty or expense to the employer. Factors to be considered include the following:

    a. The cost of the accommodation

    b. The employer's financial resources

    c. The accommodation's effect on the employer's activities

4252.77 The procedures to be followed and the remedies available under the ADA (Americans with Disabilities Act) are generally the same as under Title VII.

Fair Labor Standards Act (FLSA)

4252.78 The Fair Labor Standards Act (FLSA) is also known as the Wage-Hour Law and covers employers engaged in interstate commerce.

4252.79 Certain employees are exempt from the FLSA. These include executive, administrative, professional, and outside sales personnel.

4252.80 Covered employees are entitled to a specified minimum wage, the amount of which is changed periodically by Congress.

4252.81 Covered employees are generally entitled to be paid time and a half for hours worked in excess of 40 hours per week.

4252.82 The FLSA also prohibits oppressive child labor. These provisions include the following:

    a. Prohibiting employment of children under the age of 14 in nonfarm work, except for newspaper delivery and acting

    b. Regulating the employment of 14- and 15-year-olds in certain nonhazardous occupations

    c. Prohibiting employment of 16- and 17-year-olds in certain hazardous jobs such as mining

4252.83 Both employees and the Labor Department can sue employers for violations of the FLSA. Available remedies include recovery of unpaid minimum wages or overtime and recovery of liquidated damages.

4252.84 Employers who violate the FLSA can be held liable for civil penalties as well as criminal penalties for willful violations.

Equal Pay Act (EPA)

4252.85 The Equal Pay Act (EPA) is an amendment to the FLSA that prohibits discrimination in pay based on sex.

4252.86 Most EPA cases involve claims by women that they have received lower pay than male employees who perform substantially equal work.

4252.87 As a defense, the employer can show that any pay disparity is based on any of the following:

    a. Seniority

    b. Merit

    c. Quality or quantity of production

    d. Some factor other than gender

4252.88 Under the EPA, employees may recover back pay lost due to discrimination as well as an equal amount as liquidated damages for willful violations.

4252.89 The EPA is enforced by the EEOC rather than the Labor Department.

4252.90 Employees are not required to file a charge with the EEOC before bringing a private suit as they are with most other discrimination statutes.

Employee Retirement Income Security Act (ERISA)

4252.91 The Employee Retirement Income Security Act (ERISA) is a federal act dealing with pension plans. Pension plans may be contributory, meaning the employee contributes funds to the plan. Pension plans may also be noncontributory, meaning the employee does not contribute to the plan and all of the funds are contributed by the employer.

4252.92 ERISA does not require that employers set up pension funds for employees. Rather, it establishes complex rules for the management of private pension funds.

4252.93 The act generally requires that pension plan managers diversify plan investments in order to minimize risk of loss.

4252.94 ERISA requires that plan participants receive annual reports and also specifies what information must be included in the reports.

4252.95 ERISA contains funding and plan termination insurance requirements and also established the Pension Benefit Guaranty Corporation (an insurance agency).

4252.96 Key provisions of ERISA deal with vesting requirements that determine when an employee's right to receive benefits under the plan becomes nonforfeitable.

4252.97 Complex rules also deal with the ability of an employer to delay an employee's right to participate in any pension plan.

4252.98 ERISA gives both plan participants and beneficiaries the right to sue to enforce their rights under the plan.

4252.99 ERISA also provides for criminal penalties for any willful violations of the act.

Consolidated Omnibus Budget Reconciliation Act (COBRA)

4252.100 COBRA requires employers that sponsor a group health plan to allow "qualified beneficiaries" (covered employees and their spouses and dependent children) to elect to continue coverage if they lose coverage after occurrence of a "qualifying event."

4252.101 "Qualifying events" that affect covered employees are the following:

    a. Voluntary or involuntary termination of employment for reasons other than gross misconduct

    b. Reduction in the number of hours of employment

4252.102 Qualifying events affecting spouses include those affecting covered employees plus the following:

    a. Death of the covered employee

    b. Divorce or legal separation of the covered employee

    c. Entitlement to Medicare for the covered employee

4252.103 Qualifying events affecting dependent children include those affecting both covered employees and spouses plus the loss of dependent child status under the plan.

4252.104 COBRA rules apply to the health plans of all employers, except the following:

    a. Churches (but not other tax-exempt organizations)

    b. Small employers (defined as an employer who had fewer than 20 employees on at least 50% of its working days during the preceding calendar year)

    c. The federal government

4252.105 COBRA applies to "group health plans," which include (but are not limited to) HMOs; insured and self-insured plans providing medical benefits; vision, hearing, and dental plans; prescription drug plans; and mental health plans.

Life insurance and traditional disability plans do not fall under COBRA.

4252.106 The qualified beneficiary must elect COBRA coverage within 60 days of the later of either of the following:

    a. The date coverage is lost

    b. The date that notice to the qualified beneficiary is sent

4252.107 Continuation coverage provided under COBRA must be identical to that provided under the employer's plan to similar beneficiaries who have not experienced a qualifying event. The COBRA coverage may not be conditioned on evidence of insurability.

4252.108 COBRA generally provides a maximum continuation period of 18, 29, or 36 months, depending on the type of qualifying event.

    a. For termination (other than for gross misconduct) or reduction of hours all qualified beneficiaries are entitled to 18 months of continuation coverage.

    b. If a qualified beneficiary is disabled at the time of termination or reduction in hours, the continuation period is 29 months.

    c. Qualified beneficiaries are entitled to 36 months of continuation coverage due to any of the following:

        (1) Death of the covered employee

        (2) Divorce or legal separation of the covered employee

(3) Entitlement to Medicare of the covered employee

(4) Loss of dependent child status under the plan

4252.109 Under COBRA, qualified beneficiaries may be required to pay 102% of the cost of coverage for similar individuals still covered under the plan.

Norris-LaGuardia Act

4252.110 The Norris-LaGuardia Act, passed in 1932, protects the right of employees to engage in peaceful strikes, picketing, and boycotts. The Act restricts federal courts' power to issue injunctions against unions engaged in these activities.

National Labor Relations Act (NLRA or the Wagner Act)

4252.111 The National Labor Relations Act (NLRA), passed in 1935, gave employees the right to organize by forming, joining, and assisting labor organizations. It also established the right of employees to engage in collective bargaining and to strike.

4252.112 The NLRA also prohibits certain unfair labor practices by employers. Among these are:

   a. interfering with employees' rights to form, join, or assist labor organizations or to engage in concerted activities for their mutual aid or protection.

   b. dominating or interfering with a labor union, or giving a union financial or other support.

   c. discriminating against employees based on union affiliation in hiring, tenure, or term of employment.

   d. discriminating against employees because they have filed charges or given testimony under the Act.

   e. refusing to bargain collectively with the duly designated employee representative.

4252.113 The NLRA also established the National Labor Relations Board (NLRB).

4252.114 The NLRB has two major functions:

   a. Overseeing union elections

   b. Determining whether challenged employer or union activity constitutes an unfair labor practice

Labor Management Relations Act (LMRA or the Taft-Hartley Act)

4252.115 The Labor Management Relations Act (LMRA), passed in 1947, amended the National Labor Relations Act (NLRA).

4252.116 The LMRA established certain acts by labor unions as unfair labor practices. Among those are the following:

   a. Restraining or coercing employees in the exercise of their bargaining rights (i.e., forcing employees to join the union).

   b. Causing an employer to discriminate against an employee who is not a union member.

   c. Failing to bargain collectively with an employer.

   d. Striking or boycotting against a third party in order to coerce them not to deal with the employer.

      e. Requiring the payment of excessive or discriminatory initiation fees or dues by employees covered by union-shop contracts.

      f. Forcing an employer to pay for work not actually performed (featherbedding).

4252.117 The LMRA creates an 80-day "cooling-off" period for strikes that the president believes will endanger national safety or health.

4252.118 The LMRA created a Federal Mediation and Conciliation Service. The purpose of this service is to assist unions and employers in the settlement of labor disputes.

Labor Management Reporting and Disclosure Act (LMRDA or the Landrum-Griffin Act)

4252.119 The Labor Management Reporting and Disclosure Act (LMRDA), passed in 1959, created a "bill of rights" for union members and established reporting requirements for union activities.

4252.120 Under the LMRDA, union members have the right to attend and participate in union meetings, to nominate officers, and to vote in most union decisions. The Act also requires that unions have regularly scheduled elections of officers and that secret ballots be used in these elections.

The Sherman Act

4252.121 The Sherman Act was passed in 1890 by Congress in order to make it unlawful for businesses to engage in certain anti-competitive practices. The Act addresses agreements in restraint of trade, monopolization, and attempted monopolization.

4252.122 Section 1 of the Sherman Act provides that contracts, combinations in the form of trust or otherwise, or conspiracies, in restraint of trade are illegal.

4252.123 The Supreme Court has developed two different approaches in analyzing potential violations under Section 1 of the Sherman Act.

      a. Some types of actions are considered to always have an anticompetitive effect that is never justified. These are actions classified as per se unlawful.

      b. Other actions (not per se violations) are judged under a rule of reason. Here the courts compare the actual anticompetitive effect of the action with any justification advanced by the defendant in determining whether the action violates the Act.

4252.124 Among the actions considered to be per se violations of Section 1 of the Sherman Act are the following:

      a. Horizontal Price-Fixing. This would occur where competitors agree on a price at which they will sell or buy goods or services, or the quantity of goods they will produce, sell, or buy.

      b. Vertical Price-Fixing. This action, also called resale price maintenance, occurs where there is concerted action (such as a manufacturer-dealer agreement) to control the resale price of the product.

      c. Horizontal Divisions of Markets. This action occurs where competitors agree to divide up the available market by establishing exclusive territories or customers.

      d. Group Boycotts and Concerted Refusals to Deal. This occurs where competitors agree to refuse to deal with particular third parties, to deal with others only on certain terms, or coerce suppliers or customers not to deal with one of their competitors.

4252.125 Section 2 of the Sherman Act provides that "every person who shall monopolize or attempt to monopolize, or combine or conspire with any other person to monopolize any part of trade or commerce among the several state or with foreign nations, shall be deemed guilty of a felony."

4252.126 Under Section 2 of the Sherman Act, a single business can be found in violation by monopolizing or attempting to monopolize. Joint action however, is required when two or more businesses are charged with a conspiracy to monopolize.

4252.127 Monopoly power is generally defined as the power to fix prices or exclude competitors in a given relevant market. The two elements of a relevant market determination are the relevant product market and the relevant geographic market.

4252.128 To find a violation of Section 2 of the Sherman Act, more than simply showing that a monopoly exists is required. It must be shown that the defendant had an intent to monopolize. It must be shown that there was an intent to acquire monopoly power or an attempt to maintain a monopoly after it is acquired.

4252.129 Violations of the Sherman Act can result in both criminal and civil cases being filed by the Department of Justice. Also, private parties who have been harmed can bring civil actions under the Act.

4252.130 Individuals who criminally violate the Sherman Act can be fined up to $350,000 per violation and receive a prison term of up to three years. Corporations that violate the Act may be fined up to $10 million per violation.

4252.131 Courts may order broad injunctive relief in civil violation cases under the Sherman Act. This can include refraining from certain conduct in the future, cancellation of existing contracts, or requiring defendants to divest themselves of stock or assets of acquired companies.

4252.132 Private parties also may bring civil actions when they are injured due to violations of the Sherman Act. Under Section 4 of the Clayton Act (discussed below), a plaintiff injured by a violation of the Sherman Act or the Clayton Act may recover treble (triple) damages as well as court costs and attorney fees.

The Clayton Act

4252.133 The Clayton Act was passed by Congress in 1914. There are no criminal penalties for violation of the Act. However, private parties may bring civil actions for treble damages or for injunctive relief.

4252.134 Section 3 of the Clayton Act makes it unlawful for anyone engaged in interstate commerce to lease or sell commodities, or to fix a price for commodities, on the condition, agreement, or understanding that the lessee or buyer of the commodities will not use or deal in the commodities of the lessor's or seller's competitors, if the effect of doing so may be to substantially lessen competition or tend to create a monopoly in any line of commerce.

4252.135 The purpose of Section 3 of the Clayton Act is to attack tying agreements and exclusive dealing agreements. The Act applies, however, only to these types of agreements that deal with commodities. If a tying agreement or an exclusive dealing agreement deals with something else, such as services, the Clayton Act does not apply. In that case, the anticompetitive practice must be attacked under the Sherman Act.

4252.136 A tying agreement is an agreement that requires a buyer to purchase a particular product (the tied product) in order to be able to purchase another product (the tying product) from the seller. A tying agreement will violate the Clayton Act if it may *"substantially lessen competition or tend to create a monopoly."*

4252.137 An exclusive dealing agreement is one in which a buyer agrees to sell one seller's product exclusively or to purchase all of their requirements of a particular commodity from one seller. Again, these types of agreements violate the Clayton Act only if they may *"substantially lessen competition or tend to create a monopoly."*

4252.138 Section 7 of the Clayton Act prohibits anyone engaged in commerce or in an activity affecting commerce from acquiring the stock or assets of another party if the effect, in any line of commerce or any activity affecting commerce in any section of the country, may be to substantially lessen competition or tend to create a monopoly.

4252.139 Section 7 of the Clayton Act differs from the monopoly provision under the Sherman Act in that it does not require that the defendant have already obtained monopoly power in order to be in violation.

4252.140 Section 8 of the Clayton Act initially prohibited any person from serving as a director of two or more corporations if either had *"capital, surplus, and undivided profits aggregating more than $1 million"* and the corporations were or had been, competitors *"so that elimination of competition between them would violate anti-trust laws."*

4252.141 The Antitrust Amendments Act of 1990 changed the language of Section 8 of the Clayton Act in two major ways:

    a. First, the dollar amount necessary to fall under this provision was increased from $1 million to $10 million. This amount is adjusted annually by an amount equal to the percentage increase or decrease in the gross national product.

    b. Secondly, the amendment provides that Section 8 applies to not only individuals serving as directors but also as senior officers (officers chosen by the board of directors).

The Robinson-Patman Act

4252.142 The Robinson-Patman Act was passed by Congress in 1936 to broaden the scope of Section 2 of the Clayton Act which prohibits local and territorial price discrimination by sellers (selling low in an area where there is competition and at higher prices in an area where there is no competition).

4252.143 Section 2(a) of the Robinson-Patman Act prohibits sellers from discriminating in price between different purchasers of commodities of like grade or quality where the effect is to:

    a. Substantially lessen competition or tend to create a monopoly in any line of commerce, or

    b. Injure, destroy, or prevent competition with any person who either grants or knowingly receives the benefit of such discrimination, or with customers of either of them.

4252.144 The Robinson-Patman Act provides three major defenses to liability under Section 2(a). This section is not violated if:

    a. The price differential is due to an appropriate allowance for differences in the cost of manufacture, sale, or delivery resulting from the differing methods or quantities in which the goods are sold or delivered to buyers,

    b. The price difference simply reflects changing conditions in the market or for the marketability of the goods, or

c. The lower price sale was made in good faith in order to meet an equally low price of a competitor.

4252.145 The Robinson-Patman Act addresses indirect price discrimination in the following provisions:

   a. Section 2(c) prevents sellers from providing, and buyers from receiving any commission, brokerage, or other compensation, or any allowance or discount in lieu thereof, except in the case of actual services rendered in connection with the sale or purchase of goods.

   b. Section 2(d) prohibits sellers from making discriminatory payments to competing customers for customer services (i.e., advertising or promotional activities) or for customer provided facilities (i.e., shelf space).

   c. Section 2(e) prohibits sellers from discriminating in the services that they provide to competing customers.

4252.146 Section 2(f) provides that it is a violation of the Robinson-Patman Act for a buyer to knowingly induce or receive a discriminatory price in violation of Section 2(a). A key element is that it must be shown that the buyer knew that the discriminatory price that they received was not justified based on differences in the seller's costs, changing market conditions, or the attempt of the seller to meet the price of a competitor.

Comprehensive Environmental Response, Compensation, and Liability Act (CERCLA)

4252.147 The most important statute in the area of environmental regulation is the Comprehensive Environmental Response, Compensation, and Liability Act (CERCLA)—commonly referred to as Superfund.

4252.148 CERCLA provides for the creation of a fund to clean up hazardous waste sites and is administered by the Environmental Protection Agency (EPA).

4252.149 CERCLA requires the EPA to identify U.S. sites where hazardous waste has been disposed of, stored, abandoned, or spilled and to rank the sites regarding the severity of risk.

4252.150 The EPA can order a responsible party to clean up a site. Responsible party is defined as any of the following:

   a. The generator who deposited the waste

   b. The transporter of the waste to the site

   c. The owner of the site at the time of disposal

   d. The current owner and operator of the site

4252.151 The liability of the responsible party under CERCLA is joint and several. This means that one party can be held responsible for all cleanup costs, regardless of their degree of responsibility relative to other responsible parties.

4252.152 A party held responsible under CERCLA can seek recovery of costs or a contribution from other responsible parties.

4252.153 Under CERCLA, the only defenses available to a responsible party in order to avoid liability are that the occurrence was the result of any of the following:

   a. An act of God

   b. An act of war

   c. An act or omission of a third party (third-party defense)

4252.154 To make use of the third-party defense, the responsible party under CERCLA must show that the following are true:

    a. The third party was solely responsible for the hazardous condition.

    b. The third party was not their employee.

    c. No contractual relationship exists with the third party.

4252.155 Under CERCLA, if the property was acquired from the third party, the transfer documents will create a contractual relationship unless:

    a. the purchaser acquired the property after the hazardous waste was disposed of, or

    b. the purchaser had no actual knowledge or reason to know that hazardous waste was disposed of on the property.

To meet this requirement, it must generally be shown that the purchaser engaged in a "due diligence" investigation prior to the purchase of the property.

The Clean Air Act

4252.156 The Clean Air Act (as amended by the Clean Air Act of 1990) establishes air quality goals.

4252.157 The Clean Air Act requires the EPA to establish national ambient air quality standards. These standards are maximum levels of air pollutants. Standards have been set for the following:

    a. Particulate matter

    b. Sulfur dioxide

    c. Ozone

    d. Nitrogen dioxide

    e. Carbon monoxide

    f. Lead

4252.158 The Clean Air Act requires that air quality not fall in those areas that currently meet national ambient air quality standards.

4252.159 The preservation of natural visibility within major national parks and wilderness areas is also required under the Clean Air Act.

4252.160 The Clean Air Act requires the EPA to establish emission standards to protect public health, within certain margins of safety.

4252.161 Under the Clean Air Act, national ambient air quality standards are to be achieved by the following:

    a. State implementation plans approved by the EPA

    b. Technological controls, which include new source performance standards established by the EPA

    c. Mobile source controls established by the EPA

4252.162 Performance standards for new sources are set by the EPA based on the best control technology available for that type of source.

4252.163 For new sources of emissions in areas that have achieved national ambient air quality goals, the best available control technology (BACT) is required. This is the emission limitation that achieves the maximum reduction of pollutants, considering energy, environmental, and economic factors.

4252.164 For new sources of emissions in nonattainment areas, the lowest achievable emission rate (LAER) is required.

4252.165 The 1990 amendment to the Clean Air Act requires the federal government to impose penalties on nonattainment areas that fail to develop plans to attain national standards. These penalties include imposing bans on the construction of new sources of pollution, limits on federal highway funds, and withholding of federal air pollution funds.

4252.166 The 1990 amendment to the Clean Air Act, among other things, requires reductions in vehicle tailpipe emissions, use of reformulated gasolines, and phases out methylchloroform and chlorofluorocarbons.

The Clean Water Act

4252.167 The Clean Water Act is the common name given to the Federal Water Pollution Control Act of 1972 as amended by the Clean Water Act of 1977 and the Water Quality Act of 1987.

4252.168 The purpose of the Clean Water Act is to eliminate discharge of pollutants into navigable waters of the United States.

4252.169 The Clean Water Act defines navigable waters as all waters of the United States that are used in interstate commerce. The definition also includes all freshwater wetlands that are adjacent to all covered waterways.

4252.170 The National Pollutant Discharge Elimination System (NPDES) is the major program set up under the Clean Water Act. This program requires permits in order to discharge pollutants from any "point source" into navigable waters.

4252.171 EPA regulations under the Clean Water Act establish national effluent limitations on pollutant discharges.

4252.172 New sources are subject to more stringent standards based on "national standards of performance."

4252.173 The NPDES is administered primarily by federally approved state programs.

Resource Conservation and Recovery Act (RCRA)

4252.174 RCRA is the common name given to the Solid Waste Disposal Act as amended by the Resource Conservation and Recovery Act of 1976 and the Hazardous and Solid Waste Amendments of 1984.

4252.175 RCRA empowers the EPA to do the following:

a. Identify and list hazardous wastes.

b. Develop standards for management of hazardous waste by those who either generate or transport them.

c. Establish standards for the construction and operation of hazardous waste treatment, storage, and disposal facilities.

4252.176 RCRA imposes "cradle to grave" responsibility on those who generate the hazardous waste.

4252.177 The generators of the waste must obtain an identification number from the EPA. They are also required to use a transportation manifest when they transport the waste for treatment, disposal, or to an approved storage facility.

4252.178 Under RCRA, operators of hazardous waste facilities must obtain permits and meet stringent requirements.

Check Clearing for the 21st Century Act (Check 21)

4252.179 Check 21 was signed into law on October 28, 2003, and became effective on October 28, 2004. The law is designed to enable banks to handle more checks electronically, which should make check processing faster and more efficient.

4252.180 The Check 21 authorizes the use of a new negotiable instrument called a substitute check. A substitute check is a paper reproduction of the original check created during the collection process from an electronic image of the original check.

4252.181 The substitute check must:

   a. Contain an image of the front and back of the original check.

   b. Bear a MICR line containing all of the information appearing on the MICR line of the original check.

   c. Conform, in paper stock, dimension, and otherwise, with generally applicable industry standards for substitute checks.

   d. Be suitable for automated processing in the same manner as the original check.

4252.182 The substitute check must:

   a. Accurately represents all the information on the front and back of the original check at the time the original was truncated, and

   b. Bears a legend that states "This is a legal copy of your check. You can use it the same way you would use the original check."

4252.183 Check 21 requires financial institutions to accept a substitute check from a presenting institution and grant it equivalent status as the original check.

4252.184 Instead of physically moving paper checks from one bank to another, Check 21 allows banks to process more checks electronically. If a receiving bank or its customer needs a paper check, the bank can use the electronic picture and payment information to create a substitute check.

4252.185 Substitute checks are subject to all of the consumer protections granted under existing check law:

   a. U.C.C. Articles 3 and 4. A bank may only charge a properly payable check to a customer's account, and must resolve claims in a timely fashion in order to limit liability.

   b. The Federal Reserve Board's Regulation CC.

4252.186 Check 21 also provides additional warranties and indemnity protection. A bank that transfers, presents, or returns a substitute check:

    a. warrants that the substitute check meets legal equivalence requirements.

    b. warrants that payment will not be requested based on a check that has already been presented (no double debit).

    c. indemnifies substitute check recipients for a loss that is due to the receipt of a substitute check instead of the original check.

4252.187 The indemnity applies to any loss (up to the amount of the substitute check, interest and expenses) incurred by any recipient of a substitute check if that loss occurred due to the receipt of a substitute check instead of the original check. If the loss is due to a warranty breach, the indemnity could also include proximate caused damages.

4252.188 The bank is only liable for losses up to when the original or copy is provided, and the bank is entitled to a return of any funds in excess of that amount.

4252.189 The indemnifying bank can recover from other parties. The indemnified party must comply with all reasonable requests for assistance from an indemnifying bank. The comparative negligence provision reduces the indemnity in proportion to the amount of negligence or bad faith.

4252.190 Check 21 also includes expedited recredit provisions for consumers who suffer a loss because of a substitute check. A consumer may file a claim for expedited recredit within 40 days of receipt of the relevant statement or substitute check if certain conditions apply.

Patents

4252.191 A patent granted by the U.S. Patent and Trademark Office can be obtained for an invention, discovery, process, or design that is genuine, novel, useful, and not obvious based on the current technology.

4252.192 Generally, a patent gives the holder exclusive rights to the invention for a 20-year period from the filing date of the patent application. Design patents are valid for a 14-year period.

4252.193 After a patent expires, the invention or design becomes part of the public domain. At this point, anyone can use the patent without having to compensate the prior patent holder.

4252.194 In the United States, the first to invent rule applies (not the first to file rule). This means that the first person to invent a process or item gets the patent as opposed to the one who first files a patent application.

4252.195 To receive a patent, the subject matter must be patentable. Patentable subject matter includes:

    a. machines,

    b. processes,

    c. compositions of matter,

    d. improvements to already existing machines, processes, or composition of matter,

    e. designs for articles of manufacture,

    f. asexually produced plants, and

    g. living material invented by an individual.

4252.196 A holder of a patent is given the exclusive right to use that patent.

4252.197 Patent infringement is the use of another's patent without permission. In a patent infringement suit, the plaintiff can recover:

   a. monetary damages equal to a reasonable royalty rate for the sale of the infringed articles,

   b. an order to destroy the infringing articles,

   c. an injunction to prevent infringement by the defendant in the future, and

   d. other damages resulting from the infringement.

   A court in its discretion can award up to treble damages if the patent infringement was intentional.

4252.198 Computer hardware inventions are patentable provided all of the requirements are met for obtaining the patent.

4252.199 A patent may also be obtained for a process that incorporates a computer program as long as the process itself is patentable.

Copyrights

4252.200 The federal Copyright Revision Act of 1976 governs copyright law.

4252.201 Only tangible writings can be protected under the federal copyright law. The term "writing" is broadly defined and includes books, musical compositions, articles, maps, works of art, movies, and photographs.

4252.202 A copyright comes into existence when the author produces their work, as long as it is an original work.

4252.203 Registration of a work with the U.S. Copyright Office is voluntary and can be done at any time during the copyright term.

4252.204 Under the Sony Bono Copyright Term Extension Act of 1998, individuals are granted copyright protection for their life plus 70 years. A copyright owned by a business entity is protected for 95 years from the year of first publication or 120 years from the year of creation, whichever is shorter.

4252.205 Once a copyright period expires, the work enters the public domain. It can then be published without permission of the prior copyright holder.

4252.206 The law allows certain limited use of copyrighted material based on the fair use doctrine. Under this doctrine, the following are protected uses:

   a. Quotation of the copyrighted work for review or criticism in a scholarly or technical work

   b. Use in a parody or satire

   c. Brief quotation in a news report

   d. Reproduction of a small part of the work for teaching purposes

   e. Incidental reproduction of the work in a broadcast of an event being reported

   f. Reproduction of the work in a legislative or judicial proceeding

4252.207 Copyright infringement is the copying of a substantial and material part of the copyrighted work without consent.

4252.208 In a suit for copyright infringement, a plaintiff can recover:

    a. the profit made by the person infringing the copyright,

    b. damages suffered by the plaintiff,

    c. an order for the destruction of the infringing works, and

    d. an injunction preventing the infringer from infringing in the future.

4252.209 In its discretion, the court may award statutory damages of up to $150,000, in lieu of actual damages, for willful infringement.

4252.210 The Computer Software Copyright Act of 1980 amended the Copyright Act of 1976 to extend federal copyright protection to computer software.

4252.211 Under the Computer Software Copyright Act, a computer program is defined as a set of statements or instructions to be used directly or indirectly in a computer in order to bring about a certain result.

4252.212 Court cases have held that both the source code and the binary language object code of a computer program are copyrightable. Also, copyright protection may be obtained for the structure and organization of a computer program.

4252.213 However, courts that have dealt with the issue have generally held that the "look and feel" aspects of a computer program (menus, windows, and other screen displays) are not copyrightable.

Money Laundering

4252.214 Money laundering is when money made from illegal activities is run through a "legitimate" business in order to create the impression that the funds were earned legally. The federal Money Laundering Control Act (18 USC Section 1957) covers this issue.

4252.215 Under the Money Laundering Control Act, it is a crime to engage in a monetary transaction through a financial institution involving property, obtained from an illegal activity, worth more than $10,000. This includes making deposits, making withdrawals, or obtaining money orders or cashier's checks from a financial institution. Also illegal under the Act is knowingly engaging in a financial transaction involving illegal proceeds. This would include any purchase of property with proceeds obtained from an illegal activity.

4252.216 Anyone convicted of money laundering can be fined up to $500,000 or twice the value of the property involved, whichever is greater. Also, any property traceable back to the illegal funds is forfeited to the government. In addition, anyone convicted can be sentenced up to 20 years in federal prison.

4260 Business Structure (Selection of a Business Entity)
4261 Advantages, Disadvantages, Implications, and Constraints

Partnerships

4261.01 Partnerships

a. A *partnership* is a voluntary legal relationship created by two or more persons to carry on as co-owners of a business for profit. If the profit motive is lacking, it is an unincorporated association.

b. Partnerships are governed by the Uniform Partnership Act (UPA) or the Revised Uniform Partnership Act (RUPA). Generally, if the partners do not specifically address particular matters in the partnership agreement, the applicable Act provision will apply.

c. **Trading** (or commercial): Buying and selling or leasing property. A partner in a trading partnership has a great deal of implied authority to act for the partnership.

d. **Nontrading:** Rendering a service; practicing a profession (e.g., CPA, physician, or lawyer). A partner in a nontrading partnership has less implied authority than a partner in a trading partnership.

e. A partnership is not a legal entity (legal existence separate from the persons associated together to create it) for the purpose of insulating the partners from personal liability.

f. It is a legal entity for the purpose of owning property or employing persons to transact business on the partnership's behalf.

4261.02 Limited Partnerships: Limited partnerships are governed by the Uniform Limited Partnership Act (ULPA) and the Revised Uniform Limited Partnership Act (RULPA). These have been adopted by almost all states.

a. The limited partnership must have one or more general partners and one or more limited partners.

b. The limited partnership must file a certificate with the state that lists the following:

   (1) Name of the limited partnership

   (2) Type of business and its location

   (3) General and limited partners

   (4) Contribution of each limited partner (this can be cash or other property)

   (5) Other rights, including rights of limited partners to profits

c. The name of the partnership cannot use the last name of a limited partner unless a general partner has the same last name.

d. A limited partner can be given the right to substitute an assignee in their place with no partnership dissolution if the partnership agreement so provides.

e. One limited partner may obtain priority over other limited partners in distributing profits.

f. A limited partner who allows the use of his name in the partnership name or who participates in management is liable as a general partner to the creditors of the partnership.

g. A new general or limited partner cannot be added unless all general and limited partners agree or it is provided for in the partnership agreement.

- **h.** Order of distribution of assets on dissolution is as follows:
  - (1) To creditors
  - (2) To limited partners for profit
  - (3) To limited partners for return of capital contribution
  - (4) To general partners for loans to partnership
  - (5) To general partners for profits
  - (6) To general partners for return of capital contribution
- **i.** Sale of a limited partnership interest may be regulated by the federal securities laws.

4261.03 Joint Ventures

- **a.** Joint ventures are similar to general partnerships in that they involve the co-ownership of a business for profit.
- **b.** Typically, joint ventures are established for conducting a single enterprise or transaction and usually continue for a shorter duration than most general partnerships. Since general partnerships can have the same limitations, however, it is often difficult to distinguish the two types of entities.
- **c.** Most courts hold that joint ventures are governed by partnership law.
  - (1) Joint venturers, therefore, owe each other fiduciary duties.
  - (2) Joint venturers generally have the same unlimited liability as general partners.
  - (3) Joint venturers have equal rights to manage the business; however, they may agree to delegate this power to one participant or employ a third-party manager.
  - (4) The duration of a joint venture can be specified in the agreement of the parties, terminable at will by any participant, or related to the completion of a specific project such as the purchase and development of a tract of land.
  - (5) Members of a joint venture do not generally have the same broad implied or apparent authority that a general partner may possess due to the usual limited purpose of a joint venture.
  - (6) The death of a joint venturer, however, does not automatically dissolve the joint venture.

4261.04 Limited Liability Company (LLC)

- **a.** An LLC is generally created under state law by filing articles of organization with the secretary of state's office. The articles must include such information as the following:
  - (1) The name of the LLC
  - (2) The duration of its existence
  - (3) The name and address of the LLC's registered agent (for such purposes as service of process)
- **b.** The LLC's name must generally include the words "limited liability company" or similar words that indicate to third parties that the owners of the entity have limited liability.
- **c.** Owners of the interests in an LLC are referred to as members. Most statutes require an LLC to have two or more members; however, some states do allow single member LLCs. Generally, members of an LLC can be individuals, partnerships, corporations, or other LLCs.

d. An LLC is treated as a separate legal entity. Members have no personal liability for any of the LLC's debts simply by reason of being a member.

e. The members of an LLC have a right to manage that which is proportionate to their capital contributions. Members who actually engage in management owe fiduciary duties to the LLC.

f. If the actual authority of a member is not restricted, a member generally may have implied and apparent authority to bind the LLC on contracts entered in the ordinary course of the LLC's business.

g. State LLC statutes generally allow an LLC interest to be transferred as provided in the member's operating agreement.

h. If an LLC interest is transferred, the transferee generally has no right to become a member unless the other LLC members consent. A transferee who does not become a member is still entitled to receive either the return of their capital contribution or the fair market value of their LLC interest.

i. An LLC will generally dissolve upon the death, retirement, bankruptcy, or dissolution of a member. Liquidation of an LLC, however, can generally be avoided by unanimous consent of the remaining members to continue the LLC's business.

4261.05 Limited Liability Partnership (LLP)

a. An LLP is generally created by filing the required forms with the secretary of state's office.

b. State LLP statutes also generally require that the LLP maintain some specified level of professional liability insurance and pay an annual fee to the state (usually on a per-partner basis).

c. The unique feature of an LLP is that a partner's liability for a fellow partner's professional malpractice is limited to the partnership's assets. In other words, a partner does not have unlimited personal liability for another partner's malpractice.

d. However, partners in an LLP do retain unlimited personal liability for their own malpractice as well as for any other partnership obligations.

4261.06 Sole Proprietorship

a. A sole proprietorship is a form of business that is simply an extension of the sole, individual owner.

b. No formalities are required for the formation of a sole proprietorship. They are formed very easily and inexpensively. If the individual fails to choose another form in which to operate the business, the business is a sole proprietorship by default.

c. A sole proprietorship is not recognized as a legal entity. Plaintiffs must sue the individual owner, not the sole proprietorship. Also, the sole proprietor must individually sue anyone that causes harm to the business.

d. For federal income tax purposes, the sole proprietorship is not a taxable entity. All of the income and expenses of the business are reported on the sole proprietor's individual federal income tax return.

Corporations

4261.07 Classifications of Corporations

a. **De jure.** A corporation that has generally complied with all the statutory regulations for incorporation except for an insignificant deviation from the statute that causes no harm to the public interest. Corporate existence can generally not be challenged.

b. **De facto.** A corporation that has failed to comply with some provision of the incorporation law. There must be a valid statute under which the corporation could be formed, a good faith attempt to organize under the statute, and an actual use of corporate power. If so, a de facto corporation has the same rights and powers of a de jure corporation insofar as any person or entity, other than the state, is concerned. This recognition prevents harsh rules making the individual owners liable.

c. **Corporation by estoppel.** An organization representing itself to be a corporation or a person contracting with an organization as if it were a corporation is estopped from later denying the corporate existence.

d. **Private.** Organized for private purposes by private parties.

e. **Public (or governmental).** Created by the state to fulfill governmental purposes.

Example: Federal Deposit Insurance Corporation (FDIC)

f. **Quasi-public.** A private corporation furnishing service upon which the public is dependent, such as a public service corporation or utility. It is usually given a special franchise and power.

g. **Profit.** Organized primarily to make a profit for the owners.

h. **Nonprofit.** Formed for religious, charitable, social, educational, or mutual-benefit purposes. They are called eleemosynary (related to, or supported by charity). Examples are athletic clubs, fraternities, hospitals, and private universities. They may be carried on at a profit if the profit is incidental to the main purpose. They must be nonstock.

i. **Domestic.** A corporation is referred to as being a domestic corporation in the state in which it is incorporated.

j. **Foreign.** A corporation is referred to as foreign in a state other than the one in which it is incorporated.

k. **Alien.** Incorporated in a foreign country.

l. **Closely held, closed, close.** A corporation with one or only a few shareholders whose shares are not generally available to the public.

m. **Publicly held.** A corporation whose shares are publicly traded and are generally held by a large number of shareholders.

n. **Professional corporation.** A corporation organized to carry on a profession. Most often these are physicians, CPAs, lawyers, etc.

o. **Stock.** Ownership is evidenced by shares of stock.

p. **Nonstock.** Stock is not issued by the corporation—done only for social or charitable corporations.

4261.08 Constitutional Rights of a Corporation

    a. A corporation has the following constitutional rights:

        (1) To be secure from unreasonable searches and seizures

        (2) Not to be deprived of life, liberty, or property without due process of law

        (3) Not to be tried twice for the same criminal offense (called double jeopardy)

        (4) Not to be denied equal protection of the laws

        (5) First Amendment right of freedom of speech

    b. A corporation does not have the constitutional right against self-incrimination. This right applies only to real persons.

4261.09 Powers of a Corporation

    a. A corporation has only the powers expressly given in the law adopted by the legislature (such as the MBCA). Individuals, on the other hand, have any power not denied to them by the Constitution.

    b. Corporations derive their power from three sources, as follows:

        (1) **Statutory:** From the state's corporation laws. Examples of this power include the following:

            (a) Having a corporate name

            (b) Purchasing and holding property for corporate purposes

            (c) Making bylaws

            (d) Borrowing money

            (e) Making contracts

        (2) **Express:** From the articles of incorporation and the corporate bylaws; cannot conflict with statutory powers.

        (3) **Implied:** Activities needed to carry out the statutory and express powers; these activities fill the gaps that exist in the statutory and express powers.

    c. Corporate liability for wrongful conduct:

        (1) A corporation is liable under the doctrine of *respondeat superior* for the torts of its employees committed within the course of employment. This fact is true even if the activity is beyond the powers of the corporation.

        (2) A corporation can be punished by fine for the criminal conduct of its employees.

        (3) An *ultra vires* act is one beyond the scope of the powers of the corporation. An *ultra vires* act is not necessarily an illegal act, but an illegal act is always an *ultra vires* act.

    d. *Ultra vires* can be used only as a defense in limited cases.

        (1) It cannot be used by the corporation to avoid a contract unless it is totally executory.

        (2) It can be used by the following:

            (a) A shareholder against a corporation to prohibit the corporation from performing a totally executory contract

            (b) The corporation, or shareholders acting for the corporation, against former or present officers or directors to recover damages

(c) The state attorney general against the corporation to stop performance of an *ultra vires* contract or to dissolve the corporation

4261.10 **S Corporation**

 a. If certain requirements are met, a corporation and its shareholders can elect to be taxed under Subchapter S of the Internal Revenue Code.

 b. For a discussion of the details regarding S corporations, see section **4640**.

4261.11 Detailed Comparison of Business Entities

Comparison of Business Entity Table

Characteristics	C Corporation	S Corporation	General Partnership	Limited Partnership	Limited Liability Company	Limited Liability Partnership	Sole Proprietorship
Available in all states	Yes	Yes, but state taxation varies	Yes	Yes	Yes	Yes	Yes
Ease of formation	Simple	Simple	Simple to complex	Simple to complex	Simple to complex	More complex	Simple
Governing documents	Articles and bylaws	Articles and bylaws plus "S" elections	Partnership agreement	Partnership agreement	Operating agreement	Partnership agreement	None
Cost of formation	Minimal	Minimal	Moderate to expensive	Moderate to expensive	Moderate to expensive	Moderate to expensive	None
Formal acts required	Yes	Yes	No	Yes; generally must be filed by secretary of state	Yes; generally must be filed by secretary of state	Yes; generally must be filed by secretary of state	No
Existence of uniform act	Yes; Model Business Corporation Act	Not applicable; status as an S corporation is a federal income tax concept	Yes; Uniform Partnership Act (UPA) and the Revised Uniform Partnership Act (RUPA)	Yes; Uniform Limited Partnership Act (ULPA) and the Revised Uniform Limited Partnership Act (RULPA)	Yes; Uniform Limited Liability Company Act (ULLCA)	No	Not applicable
Limited liability of owners	All shareholders	All shareholders	None	None for general partners; limited partners have limited liability unless they significantly participate in the business	All members unless otherwise provided for by statutes	Generally only for debt and obligations arising from action of another partner	None
Number of owners	No limitations	Limited to 100	Minimum of two; no upper limit	Minimum of two; no upper limit	No upper limit; some states permit single-member LLCs	Minimum of two; no upper limit	One

Characteristics	C Corporation	S Corporation	General Partnership	Limited Partnership	Limited Liability Company	Limited Liability Partnership	Sole Proprietorship
Type of owner permitted	No limitations	Basically limited to individual citizens and resident aliens; some corporate and trust ownership permitted	None	No limitations	No limitations	No limitations, except that for professional partnerships each partner may have to be certified or licensed in the profession	No limitations
Multiple classes of ownership	No restrictions	Only one class of stock allowed, but differences in voting rights permitted	No restrictions	No restrictions	No restrictions	No restrictions	No
Permissible businesses	No limitations, except that some states may not allow professional services to be performed through a corporation	No limitations, except that some states may not allow professional services to be performed through a corporation	No limitations	No limitations	No limitations, except that some states may not allow professional services to be performed through an LLC	Most states limit this type of entity to certain professional services	No limitations
Participation in management	No restrictions	No restrictions	No restrictions	Generally restricted to general partners only	No restrictions	No restrictions if formed as a general partnership under state law	No restrictions
Legal title to property	Corporate name	Corporate name	Generally in the partnership name	Partnership name	LLC or member name	Partnership name	Proprietor's name
Transferability of interests	Generally freely transferable	Generally freely transferable, except for limitations as to number and type of shareholders	Transfer generally requires consent of other partners	Transfer generally requires consent of other partners	Follows corporation or partnership, depending on how it is taxed	Transfer generally requires consent of other partners	Freely transferable

Tax Comparison of Business Entity Table

Characteristics	C Corporation	S Corporation	General Partnership	Limited Partnership	Limited Liability Company	Limited Liability Partnership	Sole Proprietorship
Identity of the taxpayer	Corporation	Shareholder, except for built-in gains or passive income	Partners	Partners	Follows corporation or partnership, depending on how it is taxed	Partners	Individual proprietor
Applicable tax rates	Generally, a graduated rate scale from 15% to 35%; but 15% (starting in 2003) on taxable personal holding company income and accumulated taxable income; graduated rates not available to personal service corporations	Individual shareholder tax rates; highest corporate rates on built-in gains or excess passive income	Individual, fiduciary, or corporate tax rates depending on the type of partner	Individual, fiduciary, or corporate tax rates depending on the type of partner	Follows corporation or partnership, depending on how it is taxed	Individual, fiduciary, or corporate tax rates depending on the type of partner	Individual income tax rates
Double taxation	Yes	Generally no	No	No	Follows corporation or partnership, depending on how it is taxed	No	No
Election required	No	Form 2553	No	No	Use Form 8832 if prefer to file as a corporation	No	No
Tax year	Any	Calendar year unless §444 election	The same tax year as a majority of its partners; otherwise calendar unless §444 election	Follows partnership or corporate rules, depending on how it is taxed	Follows partnership or corporate rules, depending on how it is taxed	The same tax year as a majority of its partners; otherwise calendar unless §444 election	Calendar year

Characteristics	C Corporation	S Corporation	General Partnership	Limited Partnership	Limited Liability Company	Limited Liability Partnership	Sole Proprietorship
Contributions of property in exchange for interests in the entity	Generally tax-free under §351	Generally tax-free under §351	Generally tax-free under §721	Generally tax-free under §721	Generally tax-free under §721	Generally tax-free under §721	Not applicable
Contributions of services in exchange for interests in the entity	Taxable unless subject to substantial risk of forfeiture	Taxable unless subject to substantial risk of forfeiture	Generally taxable if made in exchange for capital interest; generally not taxable if made in exchange for profits interest	Generally taxable if made in exchange for capital interest; generally not taxable if made in exchange for profits interest	Follows rules of partnership or corporation, depending on how it is taxed	Generally taxable if made in exchange for capital interest; generally not taxable if made in exchange for profits interest	Not applicable
Method of accounting	Cash method may be permitted except for inventory	Cash method permitted except for inventory	Cash method permitted except for inventory	Cash method generally permitted except for inventory	Generally follows rules for limited partnership unless taxed as a corporation	Generally follows rules for limited partnerships	Cash method permitted except for inventory
Special allocation of tax attributes	Not available	Not available	Very flexible if substantial economic effect	Very flexible if substantial economic effect	Follows corporation or partnership, depending on how it is taxed	Very flexible if substantial economic effect	Not applicable
Retroactive modification to agreement	No	No	Yes	Yes	Follows corporation or partnership, depending on how it is taxed	Yes	Not applicable
Timing of income recognition by owners	When distributed	In year in which S corporation's year ends, whether or not distributed	In year in which partnership's year ends, whether or not distributed	In year in which partnership's year ends, whether or not distributed	Follows corporation or partnership, depending on how it is taxed	In year in which partnership's year ends, whether or not distributed	Based on owner's tax year
Deductibility of losses	Deducted at corporate level	Deduction by shareholders limited to basis in stock plus loans to company	Deduction by partners limited to basis in partnership interest	Deduction by partners limited to basis in partnership interest	Follows corporation or partnership, depending on how it is taxed	Deduction by partners limited to basis in partnership interest	Limited to amount at risk

Characteristics	C Corporation	S Corporation	General Partnership	Limited Partnership	Limited Liability Company	Limited Liability Partnership	Sole Proprietorship
Subject to at-risk provisions	Only if more than 50% of the stock is owned by five or fewer shareholders	Rules applied at shareholder level	Rules applied at partner level	Rules applied at partner level	Follows corporation or partnership, depending on how it is taxed	Rules applied at partner level	Yes
Subject to passive activity rules	Generally no, but exceptions for closely held corporations	Rules applied at shareholder level	Rules applied at partner level	Rules applied at partner level	Follows corporation or partnership, depending on how it is taxed	Rules applied at partner level	Generally no limitations
Treatment of capital losses	Must be used to offset capital gains	Passed through to shareholders	Passed through to partners	Passed through to partners	Follows corporation or partnership, depending on how it is taxed	Passed through to partners	Net $3,000 annual loss allowed after offset of capital gains
Income accumulations within the entity	Reasonable needs of the business	No restrictions	No restrictions	No restrictions	Follows corporation or partnership, depending on how it is taxed	No restrictions	No restrictions
Fringe benefits	No limitations	Owners of more than 2% of the shares cannot receive tax-deductible fringe benefits	Partners are generally not eligible to receive tax-deductible fringe benefits	Partners are generally not eligible to receive tax-deductible fringe benefits	Follows corporation or partnership, depending on how it is taxed	Partners are generally not eligible to receive tax-deductible fringe benefits	Owner is generally not eligible to receive tax-deductible fringe benefits
IRS filing requirements	Files Form 1120	Files Form 1120S and distributes K-1s to shareholders	Files Form 1065 and distributes K-1s to shareholders	Files Form 1065 and distributes K-1s to shareholders	Follows corporation or partnership, depending on how it is taxed	Files Form 1065 and distributes K-1s to shareholders	Proprietor files Schedule C to Form 1040

Characteristics	C Corporation	S Corporation	General Partnership	Limited Partnership	Limited Liability Company	Limited Liability Partnership	Sole Proprietorship
Effect of transfer of interest on the entity	Transfer of more than 50% ownership over a 3-year testing period may limit corporation's use of net operating loss carryovers and other tax attributes	Transfer to an ineligible shareholder may cause termination of "S" election	Transfer of more than 50% of capital and profit interests within 12-month period results in technical termination of the partnership	Transfer of more than 50% of capital and profit interests within 12-month period results in technical termination of the partnership	Follows corporation or partnership, depending on how it is taxed	Transfer of more than 50% of capital and profit interests within 12-month period results in technical termination of the partnership	Not applicable
Character of gain or loss on sale of interest in the entity	Capital	Capital	Capital, except to the extent of partner's allocable share of partnership's ordinary income assets	Capital, except to the extent of partner's allocable share of partnership's ordinary income assets	Follows corporation or partnership, depending on how it is taxed	Capital, except to the extent of partner's allocable share of partnership's ordinary income assets	Not applicable

4262 Formation, Operation, and Termination

Partnerships

4262.01 Creation of a Partnership

    a. No formalities are required; it is a voluntary contractual relationship. A partnership can be created by express agreement or through an implied agreement. A partnership can also generally be created either orally or in writing.

    b. Intent governs. It can be by express words (oral or written) or implied by the actions of the parties.

    c. Tests of Existence:

        (1) The sharing of net profits and losses creates a rebuttable presumption that a partnership exists. This presumption can be overcome by showing that profits are being shared for another reason. The following are examples:

            (a) Repayment of a debt owed to the other party by way of the transfer of a portion of the profits

            (b) Wages or rent owed to another party being paid as a portion of the profits

            (c) Annuity to a deceased partner's spouse (Thus the spouse is *not* a partner simply because the spouse is receiving an annuity payment based on profits.)

            (d) Interest on a loan owed to another party being paid as a portion of the profits

            (e) Consideration for the sale of goods being paid from the profits

(2) Co-ownership of property—this does not of itself establish that a partnership exists but is a factor courts look at in determining if the relationship between the parties is a partnership.

(3) Joint control and management is another factor considered. Courts often view delegating management responsibilities or giving up control as an exercise of joint control.

4262.02 **Partnership by estoppel.** This doctrine is used to hold a person liable as a partner to a third party when they either hold themselves out as a partner or consent to the holding out of themselves as a partner. Partnership by estoppel does not actually make a person a partner, but it creates the same legal effect of being a partner. A partnership can only be created by the voluntary agreement between the persons. Therefore a partner by estoppel receives no rights of a true partner (i.e., right to manage, right to profits).

4262.03 **Types of Partners**

a. **General.** Has a right to manage the partnership business. Has unlimited personal liability to the creditors of the partnership for partnership debts.

b. **Limited.** Merely an investor in a partnership whose liability is limited to the possible loss of their capital contribution. This limited liability rests upon the fact that the partner does not participate in management of the partnership.

c. **Nominal (ostensible)/partner by estoppel:** A person who is not in fact a partner but holds himself out as a partner or allows others to hold him out as a partner. In some instances, he may be liable as a partner to third persons who rely on this holding out.

Example: Brian tells Erin that Kevin is his partner during contract negotiations. Kevin is present at the time and does nothing to indicate that this is untrue. Kevin also tells Erin, "We will be sure to do a first-rate job if you enter this contract." If Erin enters the agreement with Brian, Kevin is liable on the agreement as a partner by estoppel.

4262.04 **Partnership Agreement**

a. A partnership agreement is also sometimes referred to as *articles of partnership* and *articles of co-partnerships.*

b. A formal written agreement creating the partnership relationship is not required, but it is a good idea to prevent disputes between or among the partners.

c. Generally, a partnership agreement can be oral. If any part of the partnership agreement falls under the statute of frauds, however, a writing is needed as a practical matter to make the agreement enforceable.

Example: Caitlin and Jennifer enter a partnership agreement and specify that the duration of the partnership will last for a period of more than one year (i.e., for two years). For the agreement to be enforceable, a writing is required under the statute of frauds.

d. The UPA fills in the rules regarding the relationship between or among the partners unless the agreement specifies a different rule. Thus, the UPA operates as a gap filler.

4262.05 **Ordinary Business Matters**

a. In deciding ordinary business matters, a majority vote of the partners prevails as long as it does not violate any special provisions in the partnership agreement.

b. A tie vote leaves the matter as it was, since this is viewed as a deadlock.

4262.06 Extraordinary Matters

Unanimous agreement of all partners is necessary to make a change involving an extraordinary matter. A majority vote is not sufficient. The decision to go out of business or to change the nature of the partnership business would be examples of extraordinary matters requiring unanimous agreement of all the partners.

4262.07 Ending a Partnership

a. **Dissolution.** This is the point in time when the object of all or any of the partners changes from continuing the organization in its current form to discontinuing it.

b. **Winding up.** Settling partnership affairs after dissolution. No new business can be carried on during the winding-up period. This is the span of time between dissolution and termination.

c. **Termination.** End of the winding-up period.

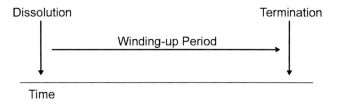

4262.08 Causes of Dissolution

a. **Without violation of the partnership agreement**

(1) The agreed time limit of the partnership ends.

(2) The agreed partnership purpose has been completed.

(3) A partner quits a partnership that has no stated duration. This type of partnership is called a partnership at will. The withdrawing partner has no liability to the other partners since they may withdraw at any time.

(4) A mutual agreement of all partners may terminate the partnership.

b. **In violation of agreement.** Any partner may dissolve a partnership at any time, but that partner may be liable for damages. The partner has the power, but may not have the right, to dissolve the partnership.

Example: Caitlin and Erin form a partnership and agree that the partnership will have a duration of five years. After one year a dispute arises and Caitlin withdraws, causing a dissolution of the partnership. Caitlin had the power to dissolve the partnership, but not the legal right; therefore, she could be held liable for damages by Erin.

c. **By operation of law** (done without agreement of the partners)

(1) The business becomes illegal. This automatically terminates the partnership.

(2) Bankruptcy of the partnership or an individual partner. Must be by adjudication and not merely insolvency.

(3) Death of one or more of the partners

(4) Court decree. A court decree can be obtained based on the following:

(a) If just and equitable to terminate the partnership

(b) Serious misconduct of a partner—such as habitual drunkenness

(c) Incapacity of a partner; cannot perform duties—such as insanity

(d) Business is impractical

(e) Other partner habitually or purposely commits breach of the partnership contract

4262.09 Priority of Payments on Dissolution

    a. Creditors of the partnership are paid first.

    b. Loans made to partnership by partners are next repaid to the extent capital remains.

    c. Return of capital contributions made by the partners is next in line of priority.

    d. Profits or losses are then divided among the partners as follows:

        (1) As agreed upon in the partnership agreement

        (2) Equally if there is no partnership agreement to the contrary

        (3) Losses are divided the same as profits if there is no partnership agreement to the contrary.

4262.10 Marshaling of Assets

    a. Partnership creditors get first rights on the partnership assets, and individual creditors get first rights on individual partners' assets.

    b. Partnership creditors must be completely paid before creditors of individual partners have any rights in partnership assets.

    c. Creditors of individual partners must be completely paid before partnership creditors have any rights in the personal assets of the individual partner.

Corporations

4262.11 Entity

    a. A corporation is an organization formed under state law or federal law that is legally separate and distinct from those persons who own the corporation. This means the shareholders are not liable for corporate obligations except to the extent of their investment in the corporation.

    b. Due to its separate legal existence, the corporation is also generally not liable for the personal obligations of its shareholders, directors, officers, or employees.

    c. The corporate entity is recognized as being separate except when it is used to defeat public convenience, perpetrate fraud, evade the law, or commit a crime.

    d. Ignoring the corporate entity is referred to as "piercing the corporate veil." When this is done, the shareholders can be held liable by the creditors of the corporation for corporate obligations.

    e. For courts to ignore the corporate entity and *"pierce the corporate veil,"* two elements must generally be present:

        (1) **Domination by a shareholder or group of shareholders.** The idea here is that the shareholder or shareholders control the corporation for their own benefit in an attempt to insulate themselves from liability for wrongdoing.

        (2) **Improper use of the corporation.** Various types of improper use by the dominating shareholder can cause the corporation to be disregarded as a separate entity. For example:

            (a) Using the corporation to perpetrate a fraud

(b) Thin capitalization of the corporation; here the corporation is formed as a "dummy" entity with insufficient capital to meet reasonably expected business obligations.

(c) Shareholders looting the corporation to the detriment of the corporation's creditors, such as having the corporation sell assets to a shareholder for a price far below fair market value

f. The corporation can hold property in the corporation's name.

g. The corporation can sue and be sued in the corporation's name.

h. Contracts can be entered in the corporation's name with the corporation as a party to the contract.

4262.12 State Incorporation Laws

a. When states first allowed corporations to be formed, it was necessary for the incorporators to appear before the state legislature to ask it to be allowed to form the corporation.

b. If the legislature decided to allow the formation of the corporation, it granted a corporate charter. Legally, this was permission to operate as a corporation in the state.

c. The individual appearances of the incorporators before the legislature became very time-consuming, so the legislatures drafted a general incorporation law and delegated the administrative responsibility to a state official. Most states designate the secretary of state.

d. **Model Business Corporation Act (MBCA)**

(1) The act is the model that most states use as the basis for their incorporation laws.

(2) The MBCA was first drafted in 1946 and has been amended many times. It was completely revised in 1984 and has been amended since then.

(3) The majority of states have adopted the revised MBCA, in whole or in part.

(4) The revised MBCA is used on the CPA Examination to cover the topic of corporation law.

(5) Individual state corporation law may differ somewhat from the revised MBCA. Questions on the CPA Examination, however, should be answered using the rules of the revised MBCA.

e. **Foreign corporations**

(1) All of the states allow foreign corporations to do business in the state.

(2) Foreign corporations doing business in intrastate commerce must qualify to do business in the state and obtain a certificate of authority from the state. Failure to obtain a certificate results in the denial of access to the courts by the corporation as a plaintiff, a statutory penalty, and personal liability of the officers and directors.

(3) A foreign corporation engaged wholly in interstate commerce need not qualify or obtain a certificate of authority.

(4) Only the state of incorporation can regulate the internal affairs of a corporation.

(5) Foreign corporations are treated the same as domestic corporations for regulation purposes. If a state treated foreign and domestic corporations differently, it would be a burden on interstate commerce and, therefore, a violation of the Commerce Clause (unconstitutional).

(6) A foreign corporation, registered or unregistered, can always defend itself as a defendant. A state cannot take away this right, because it would be a denial of due process.

(7) The following is a diagram of a foreign corporation applying to do business in the state:

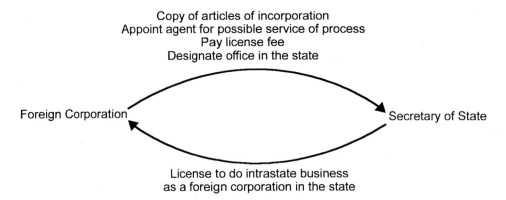

4262.13 Formation of a Corporation

a. A corporation is formed by applying to the state. The following diagram shows the activities that occur when a corporation is formed. Note that the incorporators do the paperwork with the state, while the promoters sell the stock.

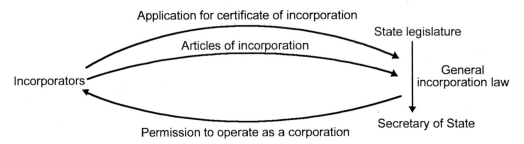

Charter: Old name
Certificate of incorporation: New name

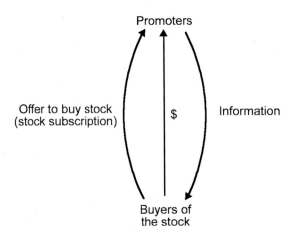

        b. **Start of corporate existence.** Issuance of a certificate of incorporation by the secretary of state is considered the start of corporate existence.

        c. **Domicile.** A corporation may have only one domicile—its state of incorporation. However, it can qualify to do business in any other state.

4262.14 **Incorporators**

        a. Incorporators are the individuals who apply to the state for incorporation.

        b. Incorporators need not have any interest in the corporation. Sometimes the secretaries in the lawyer's office are made the incorporators.

        c. Incorporators owe a fiduciary duty to the corporation being formed.

4262.15 **Promoters**

        a. Promoters are the motivating force in creating the corporation. They do such things as employing services of attorneys and accountants, borrowing funds, and purchasing property for use by the nascent (to be formed) corporation.

        b. Promoters owe a fiduciary duty to the corporation being formed.

        c. Promoters are liable on preincorporation contracts to third parties unless the following are true:

            (1) The corporation adopts the contract.

            (2) The contract expressly says the promoter is not liable on the contract.

            (3) The contract indicates that neither party is obligated unless the corporation is formed.

        d. Promoters are liable on preincorporation contracts if they contract in their own name or in the name of the not-yet-formed corporation, and the corporation is not formed or does not adopt the contract.

        e. Promoters cannot make secret profits in forming the corporation.

4262.16 **Corporation Citizenship**

        a. Citizenship must be determined to see if a federal court has jurisdiction of a case involving the corporation based on diversity of citizenship.

        b. The federal courts have jurisdiction only if the parties (plaintiff and defendant) are citizens of different states and the amount in controversy exceeds $50,000.

        c. For this purpose, a corporation is a citizen of both the state of incorporation and the state where its principal place of business is located.

4262.17 **Articles of Incorporation**

        a. The articles of incorporation are like a constitution—they outline the organization of the corporation.

        b. Corporate existence starts when the articles of incorporation are filed or when the certificate of incorporation is issued. There is a split of authority. It depends on which view the state selects.

        c. The articles are prepared by the promoters or incorporators.

        d. The articles of incorporation include the following:

            (1) Name of the corporation

            (2) Period of time for the corporation's existence—usually is perpetual

(3) Purpose—usually stated as any legal purpose

(4) Share structure, including the number of authorized shares and whether or not there is a preemptive right

(5) Address of registered office

(6) Structure of the board of directors and names and addresses of persons serving as directors until the first annual meeting

(7) Name and address of each incorporator

e. Amending the articles of incorporation:

(1) All corporations allow for changing, deleting, or adding to their articles of incorporation.

(2) To amend the articles of incorporation, the following must be done:

(a) The board of directors adopts a resolution and submits it to the vote of the shareholders.

(b) Shareholders must be given written notice.

(c) A majority of shares entitled to vote is generally necessary for approval.

4262.18 Bylaws

a. **Bylaws:** Rules adopted by the corporation's board of directors for regulation and management of the affairs of the corporation

(1) Bylaws are subordinate to the articles of incorporation and the state of incorporation's corporation laws.

(2) Bylaws may not conflict with the articles of incorporation or with the state's corporation laws.

b. Initial bylaws are adopted by the board of directors.

c. Bylaws can be changed by the board of directors unless reserved to the shareholders in the articles of incorporation.

4262.19 Suing a Corporation

a. Due process requires that anyone being sued, even a corporation, must be given notice.

b. When a corporation incorporates (for a domestic corporation) or applies to do business in another state (for a foreign corporation), it must designate a registered agent to receive service of process if the corporation is sued.

c. The secretary of state maintains a listing of the registered agents for all corporations in the state.

4262.20 Permitted Actions of a Corporation

a. **Owning own shares.** A corporation may buy and sell its own shares if cash and retained earnings permit. If insolvent or if the purchase would cause insolvency, the corporation cannot acquire the shares. Shares repurchased by the corporation are called treasury shares.

b. **Indemnification of officers, directors, employees, and agents**

(1) A corporation may indemnify an officer, director, employee, or agent of the corporation for any legal action (civil or criminal) done in good faith for the corporation. Generally, indemnification cannot be made if there was negligence or misconduct on the part of the officer, director, employee, or agent.

(2) Indemnification is often done through insurance.

c. **Loans to officers and directors**

(1) A corporation may make loans to officers and directors. Generally, either the shareholders must approve the loan, or the directors must approve it after finding that approval of the loan will benefit the corporation.

(2) The loans can even be without interest.

d. **Employment incentives.** A corporation may offer incentives to officers and key employees. These incentives may include the following:

(1) Stock purchase option

(2) Bonus

(3) Liberal expense account

(4) Country club membership

4262.21 Prohibited Actions of a Corporation

The state incorporation law and the corporation's articles of incorporation and bylaws often contain items that cannot be done. These items may include the following:

a. Paying a dividend that would impair stated capital

b. Taking advantage of a minority shareholder

4262.22 Major Changes in Corporate Structure

a. Some major changes in a corporation are permitted only if approved by a majority vote of the shareholders. These changes include the following:

(1) **Merger.** One or more corporations are acquired by another existing corporation, thereby losing their separate corporate existence.

(2) **Consolidation.** Two or more corporations join together as a new corporation, thereby losing their separate corporate existence.

(3) **Sale** of substantially all the assets of a corporation not in the ordinary course of business.

b. **Merger or consolidation**

(1) Two or more corporations can merge or consolidate. To do so, the following must occur:

(a) The board of directors approves a plan and submits it for shareholder approval.

(b) Written notice of an annual or special meeting must be given to shareholders at least 20 days prior to the meeting.

(c) A majority of shares entitled to vote is necessary for approval.

(2) Creditors of the existing corporation are still creditors of the new or surviving corporation.

c. **Merger of subsidiary corporation.** If a corporation owns at least 90% of a subsidiary corporation, it may merge without vote of the shareholders of either corporation.

d. **Sale of substantially all the assets of a corporation**

(1) A sale of assets in the usual course of business can be done by the board of directors alone, without shareholder approval.

(2) A sale of assets not in the usual course of business must be done by resolution of the board of directors, notice to shareholders, and approval by a majority of shareholders.

4262.23 Termination of the Corporation

a. Articles of dissolution are filed with the secretary of state after a corporation has been dissolved.

b. Dissolution of a corporation requires the corporation to wind up its business affairs and liquidate its assets.

c. If the corporation has not yet done business or issued shares, it can be dissolved by majority vote of the incorporators or initial directors.

d. A corporation that is doing business can be dissolved by a resolution of the directors approved by shareholder vote.

e. The secretary of state has the power to force a corporation to dissolve involuntarily through administrative or judicial proceedings for such conduct as the following:

(1) Failing to file annual reports

(2) Failing to pay taxes

(3) Failing to appoint a registered agent in the state

(4) Obtaining the articles of incorporation by fraud

f. A shareholder may obtain judicial dissolution of a corporation if any of the following occur:

(1) The directors are deadlocked, and irreparable injury to the corporation is threatened.

(2) The directors or those in control of the corporation are acting in a manner which is illegal, oppressive, or fraudulent.

(3) Shareholders are deadlocked and cannot elect directors for two years.

(4) Corporate assets are being misapplied or wasted.

g. Creditors may obtain a judicial dissolution if the corporation is insolvent.

h. Termination of the corporation occurs when the assets are liquidated and the proceeds distributed to creditors and shareholders.

4263 Financial Structure, Capitalization, Profit and Loss Allocation, and Distributions

Partnerships

4263.01 Partnership Property

a. **Partnership capital.** Money and property contributed by partners for permanent use by the partnership is called partnership capital.

b. **Tenancy in partnership.** Tenancy in partnership is the term given to the ownership by partners of the partnership's property. All partners have equal rights to use partnership property for partnership purposes.

A partner has no transferable rights in specific partnership property.

c. **Partnership property.** Partnership capital plus retained profits constitute partnership property.

d. **Real property.** A partnership may acquire real property in the name of the partnership. The partnership is a legal entity for this purpose.

Profits and Losses

4263.02 **General Partnership**

   a. Unless the partners agree otherwise, each partner has the right to an equal share in the partnership's profits and losses.

   b. If the partnership agreement states how profits are to be shared among the partners, but is silent as to how losses are shared, then losses are allocated in the same manner as the profits.

   c. If the partnership agreement states how losses are allocated, but is silent as to how profits are shared, profits are shared equally.

   d. In many cases, a partnership agreement will specify that partnership profits are to be shared in the same ratio as the partner's capital contribution.

4263.03 **Limited Partnership**

   a. Unless the partners agree otherwise, the profits and losses of a limited partnership are shared in the same ratio as the capital contributions of each partner.

   b. A limited partner, however, can generally not be held liable for the amount of any losses that exceed their capital contribution.

Corporations

4263.04 **Initial Issue of Shares**

   a. After a corporation is formed and the board of directors meets for the first time, one of the first tasks is to accept the offers to buy stock. The board of directors can accept or reject these offers to buy shares.

   b. **Preincorporation share subscription**

      (1) **Share subscription:** Offer to buy shares of the corporation not yet formed.

      (2) Irrevocable for six months unless some other provision exists.

      (3) These subscriptions are solicited by the promoters while incorporation is in progress.

   c. **Payment for shares**

      (1) Payment may be in money, property, or services already performed.

      (2) Payment cannot generally be a promise to pay money in the future (promissory note) or a promise to do services in the future.

      (3) The money value assigned by the board of directors or shareholders for property or services shall be conclusive as long as the following are true:

         (a) They acted as prudent directors would act.

         (b) There is a reasonable basis for the valuation (appraisal, etc.).

         (c) They acted in the corporation's best interest.

   d. **Shares issued but not fully paid**

      (1) Corporation or corporation creditors can collect the unpaid portion from the original purchaser even if the original purchaser has sold the shares.

(2) Buyer of not fully paid shares is not liable if shares were purchased in good faith and without knowledge from the first person to whom the shares were originally issued by the corporation.

e. Shareholders are liable to the corporation for the difference in value if they purchase shares from the corporation at a discount. At a minimum, the shareholder should pay as follows:

(1) **Par value shares:** Not less than the par value in dollars for the original issue

(2) **No-par shares:** Not less than the dollar amount fixed by the board of directors for the original issue (stated value)

(3) **Treasury shares:** Any dollar amount fixed by the board of directors (this amount can be less than the par value of the shares as originally issued as long as they are sold for FMV)

4263.05 Types of Shares

a. **Authorized:** The maximum number of shares a corporation can issue. The limit is stated in the articles of incorporation.

b. **Issued:** The number of shares actually distributed by the corporation.

(1) Each issue must be approved by the board of directors.

(2) Each issue must be equal to or less than the authorized shares.

c. **Outstanding:** The number of shares owned by shareholders of the corporation. Outstanding shares must be equal to or less than the issued shares.

d. **Treasury:** The number of shares of the corporation owned by the corporation itself.

(1) These shares are reacquired shares.

(2) They are considered to be authorized and issued but no longer outstanding since they were purchased on the open market by the corporation.

(3) Treasury shares are often held to give stock options to key officers and employees.

(4) Formula: Issued – Outstanding = Treasury

(5) The number of treasury shares must be equal to or less than the number of outstanding shares of the corporation.

4263.06 Issue of Shares

a. Shares may be issued for any of the following:

(1) Money

(2) Property

(3) Services already performed, but not for services to be performed

b. If money is exchanged for shares:

(1) It cannot be less than the par value or the stated value.

(2) The initial shareholder receiving the shares is liable to the corporation and creditors of the corporation if the money is less than par or stated value.

c. If property or services performed is exchanged for shares, the value assigned by the board of directors is conclusive as long as the following are true:

(1) They acted as prudent directors would act.

(2) There is a reasonable basis for the valuation (appraisal, etc.).

(3) They acted in the corporation's best interest.

4263.07 Accounting Versus Legal Terminology

a. The difference between accounting and legal terminology in the owner's equity section of the balance sheet is shown in the following table:

Accounting Terminology	Corporate Law Terminology
Retained Earnings	Earned Surplus
Additional Paid-in Capital	Capital Surplus
Capital in Excess of Stated Value	Capital Surplus
Par Value of Shares	Stated Capital
Stated Value of Shares	Stated Capital

b. Most of the corporate laws are written using the corporate law terminology rather than the more commonly used accounting terminology.

4263.08 Amount of Stated Capital

a. **For par shares.** Par value is the stated capital. Any excess received for the shares would be capital surplus.

b. **For no-par shares.** The entire amount received is stated capital, unless the board of directors allocates between stated capital and capital surplus within 60 days.

4264 Rights, Duties, Legal Obligations, and Authority of Owners and Management

Partnerships

4264.01 Who Can and Cannot Be a Partner

a. **Minor.** May become a partner, but can disaffirm the partnership contract. Partnership creditors have a preference on partnership assets before a minor gets their capital contribution returned. Partnership creditors may not get personal assets of a minor partner if the minor partner disaffirms.

b. **Insane person.** A judicially declared insane person cannot make a contract—any effort is void. If a person becomes insane after making a contract, the other partner may get dissolution due to the insanity by way of a court order.

c. **Corporation.** The UPA allows a corporation to become a partner, but the general corporation laws of some of the states do not allow a corporation to become a partner.

4264.02 Authority of a Partner

a. Authority of a partner is merely an extension of agency law.

b. Agency law applies to partnerships in the following manner:

(1) Each partner is an agent for the partnership. The partnership is the principal.

(2) A partnership is liable for the actions of a partner if the partner either:

(a) has actual authority or

(b) is acting within the apparent scope of the partnership activity and the third party does not know the actual authority of the party.

(3) If the partnership is not liable on a contract, then the individual partner making the contract is liable.

(4) A partner is personally liable for the torts the partner commits.

(5) A partnership is liable for the torts of a partner if the partner was acting within the scope of the partnership business when the tort occurred.

(6) A partner is personally responsible for their crimes.

(7) A partnership is not liable for a partner's crimes unless the other partners actually participated in the crimes.

(8) If a partner enters a contract without authority, the partnership may recover damages from the wrongdoing partner if the partnership is held liable to a third party.

4264.03 **Types of authority**

a. **Actual**

(1) Also called *real authority*.

(2) May be expressed or implied authority.

b. **Apparent**

(1) Sometimes called *ostensible* or *customary authority*.

(2) When a partnership restricts a partner's actual authority, the partner may still have apparent authority to act. This occurs because a third party can reasonably believe that the partner, who is an agent for the partnership, can perform acts necessary to carry out the partnership business.

Example: Erin, Brian, Kevin, and Caitlin are partners and agree that only Kevin can enter contracts to purchase inventory for the partnership. If third parties are not notified of this restriction, Erin, Brian, and Caitlin will have apparent authority to purchase inventory.

(3) Different types of firms have different authority.

(a) **Trading partnership:** Much customary authority

(b) **Nontrading partnership:** Little customary authority (A nontrading partnership does not normally engage in activities such as borrowing money. There is, therefore, no apparent or customary authority to borrow money. A trading partnership would regularly do this to finance inventory, etc.)

(4) Typical customary or apparent authority examples include the following:

(a) Entering into usual contracts for that type of business

(b) Sales in the ordinary course of business

(c) Purchasing goods in the scope of business

(d) Loans for a trading partnership

(e) Insuring property of the partnership

(f) Employing persons for the partnership

c. Certain actions are completely unauthorized and no partner can bind the partnership by these acts. They require the unanimous consent of all partners. Examples include the following:

(1) A decision to go out of business

(2) Suretyship (guaranty)—cannot promise to pay somebody else's debts or obligations

(3) A decision to arbitrate a dispute between the partnership and a third party

(4) Confess judgment—this is equivalent to pleading guilty in advance

(5) Assignment for the benefit of creditors

(6) Make a personal obligation for the partnership to pay

4264.04 Partner's Individual Liability

a. Every partner is the agent of the partnership for the purpose of its business. The partnership is bound by all transactions negotiated by a partner if such transactions are within the usual course of partnership business.

b. **Tort.** If the wrongful act is committed within the scope of and in the course of partnership business, the partners and the partnership will be jointly and severally liable. *Severally* means individually.

c. **Crimes.** Only the partner who commits a crime is liable unless the other partners participate.

d. **Contracts.** Partners are jointly (all together at the same time) liable for contracts made by a partner within the scope of the real or apparent authority of a partnership. If the contract is made in the partner's personal name, the other partners are liable as undisclosed principals.

4264.05 Withdrawal of a Partner

a. Existing creditors are entitled to actual notice of a partner withdrawing. If there is no notice, the withdrawing partner could still be liable to a creditor of the partnership for partnership debts that happened after the withdrawal.

b. Creditors who have not dealt with the partnership previously are entitled only to constructive notice (i.e., in a newspaper).

4264.06 Admission of a New Partner

a. New partners are liable for all partnership obligations that arise after they are admitted.

b. New partners are liable for all partnership obligations that arose before admission, but only to the extent of their share of the partnerships' assets. The new partner's individual assets are not available to satisfy these claims.

4264.07 Rights of Partners

a. **Right to share in profits.** Partners share equally in profit regardless of the amount of capital contributions or the amount of time spent in the partnership business. The partnership agreement may specify that profits are shared differently.

b. **Right to return of capital.** When a partnership is being dissolved, each partner has the right to obtain the return of their capital contribution before the partnership profit or loss is calculated. This occurs after partnership creditors are paid.

c. **Right to participate in management.** There is equal right to participation in management among partners unless they agree otherwise. This is true regardless of the amount of capital contributed or the amount of services rendered to the partnership.

d. **Right to information and inspection of the books.** Any partner has the right to demand to see the books and accounts of record at any point in time.

e. **Right to an accounting.** This is the right of a partner to come into court to force other partners to give an accounting of the partnership activities.

- **f. Rights in specific partnership property.** Individual partners do not own any part of any specific partnership property. Unless agreed otherwise, the UPA states that each partner has an equal right to possess partnership property for partnership purposes. The right to possess and control partnership property cannot be transferred to a third party.

- **g. Right to compensation.** Unless agreed otherwise, a partner is not entitled to any salary for services provided to the partnership. After a partnership is dissolved, however, a partner who is in charge of winding up the affairs of the partnership is entitled to reasonable compensation for those services.

- **h. Right to reimbursement.** A partner that incurs reasonable expenses in carrying out partnership business has a right to reimbursement from the partnership.

    Example: Dave, a partner, attempts to deliver goods to Brian on behalf of the partnership. Brian breaches the contract by refusing to accept the goods. Dave pays storage expenses for the goods and incurs costs to ship them to another buyer. If Dave pays these expenses, he can generally get reimbursed by the partnership.

4264.08 Duties of Partners

- **a. Fiduciary.** This means trust and confidence, loyalty and good faith to the firm, obedience to the partnership agreement, exercise of reasonable care in doing partnership business, providing needed information to the partnership, and providing an accounting of partnership matters.

- **b. Duty to share in losses.** Division of losses is done in the same percentage as sharing of the profits unless agreed otherwise in the partnership agreement.

4264.09 Assignment or Transfer of Partnership Interest

- **a.** A partner may assign or transfer all or part of her interest in the partnership to someone else.

    (1) This does not dissolve the partnership. The assignor is still a partner.

    (2) Consent of the other partners is not required for a valid assignment or transfer.

    (3) The assignee does not automatically become a partner nor does the assignee have any of the rights of a partner. If the other partners agree, the assignee could become a partner.

    (4) The assignee obtains only the right to the assignor's share of partnership profits and what the assignor would receive if the partnership is dissolved.

- **b.** As long as the assigning partner performs their required duties, the other partners are not adversely affected by the assignment.

Corporations

4264.10 Board of directors

- **a.** Exercises corporate powers and manages the business. They are in a fiduciary relationship with the corporation.

- **b.** Directors need not be residents of the state of incorporation.

- **c.** Directors need not be shareholders.

- **d.** They have authority to fix their own compensation unless the articles of incorporation or bylaws say they are prohibited from doing so.

- e. The board can be one or more persons as fixed by the articles of incorporation or bylaws. Traditionally, state statutes required at least three directors. Today most statutes permit fewer than three directors for corporations that have fewer than three shareholders.
- f. The board holds office until the next annual meeting or until replaced.
- g. It can be divided into classes, with staggered election dates, if there are nine or more directors.
- h. It can fill vacancies for the unexpired time by a majority vote of the remaining directors.
- i. Directors can be removed by the shareholders' vote with or without cause. Directors serve at the pleasure of the shareholders.
- j. The board has a quorum when a majority of the number of directors is present.
- k. It can make an act effective if it is passed by the majority of the directors present at a meeting when a quorum exists.
- l. The board of directors can divide itself into committees and delegate power to them. Examples are the executive committee and the audit committee.
- m. The board can meet anywhere. It need not be in the state of incorporation.

4264.11 Notification to directors of regular or special meetings of the board of directors is specified by the bylaws.

4264.12 Meetings of the board of directors can be conducted via a conference call. They merely have to be able to hear each other at the same time.

4264.13 The board of directors may act without a meeting if all directors consent in writing.

4264.14 Loans to directors. Loans to directors are allowed only if authorized by the shareholders.

4264.15 Liability of directors. A director is individually liable if the director engages in illegal conduct or conduct that is a breach of fiduciary duty to the corporation. For example, if the director votes:

- a. for an illegal dividend, such as a dividend that would make the corporation insolvent,
- b. to illegally buy shares of the corporation, or
- c. to pay off shareholders before creditors,

then the director would be individually liable.

4264.16 Business judgment rule. This rule protects the directors from shareholder lawsuits alleging a lack of due care on the part of the directors in carrying out the corporation's business. This rule will apply as follows:

- a. When the board makes an informed decision
- b. When there is no conflict of interest
- c. When there is a rational basis for the board's decision

4264.17 Dividends

- a. Dividends are declared by the board of directors.
- b. They may be paid in cash, property, or shares of the corporation.
- c. They cannot be declared if the dividend would make the corporation insolvent.

d. Cash and property dividends are paid out of unreserved and unrestricted earned surplus (retained earnings). Some states allow payment out of net earnings of the current year and the previous year taken together, even if there is a negative earned surplus.

4264.18 **Officers of the Corporation**

a. The *officers* are appointed by the board of directors.

b. They are the president, vice president(s), secretary, and treasurer.

c. One person can hold multiple offices, but the president and secretary generally cannot be the same person. Exceptions to this rule exist in some states where "one person corporations" are allowed.

d. The officers can be removed by the board of directors for any reason, but firing an officer may be a breach of an employment contract for which the corporation may be liable.

e. Officers of a corporation owe a fiduciary duty to the corporation.

4264.19 **Managers of the Corporation**

a. The *managers* are hired by the officers.

b. The managers serve at the pleasure of the *officers,* unless they have negotiated an employment contract.

c. The managers owe a fiduciary duty to the corporation.

4264.20 **Shareholders**

a. Shareholders are the owners of the corporation.

b. Shareholders do not generally owe fiduciary duties to the corporation. Controlling shareholders may be deemed to owe fiduciary duties that prevent them from exercising control to further their own interests to the detriment of the corporation and minority shareholders.

c. Shareholders elect the board of directors.

4264.21 **Shareholder voting**

a. A *quorum* for a meeting is a majority of shares outstanding, unless the articles of incorporation specify otherwise.

b. A majority of the quorum prevails on votes, unless articles of incorporation specify otherwise.

c. Treasury shares get no votes. Treasury shares are those owned by the corporation.

d. A vote can be in person or by proxy. A proxy is a signed document authorizing another person to vote the shareholders' shares of stock. Proxy must be written and is valid for a maximum of 11 months.

e. **Cumulative voting**

(1) Applies only for electing the board of directors.

(2) The number of votes a shareholder gets is determined as follows: Number of shares owned × number of directors being elected.

(3) A shareholder can distribute votes in any way desired. All the votes can be put on one nominee.

(4) Cumulative voting increases the chance of minority representation on the board of directors.

(5) Most states permit cumulative voting if the articles provide for it.

f. **Straight voting:** One vote for each share for each directorship to be filled.

4264.22 **Voting by proxy**

    a. A shareholder may vote by proxy.

    b. A director is not permitted to vote by proxy.

4264.23 **Shareholder meetings**

    a. Annual meeting details are fixed by the bylaws.

    b. Shareholders are entitled to notice of place, day, and hour of meetings 10 to 50 days before the meeting.

    c. The purpose must also be given for holding special (not annual) shareholder meetings. The meeting is then limited to these stated purposes.

    d. **Notice:** Mailing details by U.S. mail to shareholders of record.

4264.24 **Preemptive right**

    a. Preemptive right is the right of a shareholder to buy a pro rata share of newly issued stock.

    b. The purpose is to allow the current shareholders to maintain their proportionate interest in the corporation.

    c. In most states, a shareholder has no preemptive right unless the right is given in the articles of incorporation.

    d. In some states, a shareholder has a preemptive right unless it is denied in the articles of incorporation.

4264.25 **Dissenting shareholders**

    a. Dissenter's rights exist for shareholders who disagree with certain corporate actions. Shareholders can dissent from the following actions:

       (1) Merger

       (2) Consolidation

       (3) Sale of substantially all the assets of the corporation, not in the usual course of business

    b. To dissent, the shareholder must file a written objection with the corporation, vote against the proposal, and make written demand for payment of the fair value of the shareholders' stock within 10 days of the vote.

    c. Fair value is the stock value on the day before the proposal was voted on by the shareholders.

4264.26 **Shareholders' lawsuits**

    a. If a group of shareholders has been injured, a shareholder may be able to file a *class action suit* on behalf of the class.

    b. Most of these suits arise from violations of federal securities laws and have the following requirements:

       (1) The number in the class is so large it is impractical for all to sue.

       (2) The shareholder suing has substantially the same interest as others in the class.

(3) The shareholder can fairly and adequately protect and present the interests of the class.

c. A shareholder may also be able to file a *derivative suit* on behalf of the corporation when the corporation has been injured.

d. Most of these suits are brought against directors, officers, or someone closely related to them. These suits require that the shareholder is either of the following:

(1) Currently a shareholder at the time the derivative suit is filed

(2) Was a shareholder when the wrongful act was committed against the corporation

e. Generally, a derivative suit can be brought only after the shareholder demands that the board of directors file suit. This demand requirement is excused if it would be futile (e.g., all of the directors have committed fraud against the corporation).

4264.27 Inspection of records

a. At common law, shareholders have certain rights to inspect the books and records of the corporation. Generally, the shareholder right to inspect is found in state corporation statutes.

b. The MBCA requires that a shareholder must have a proper purpose for an inspection. Also, the right of inspection may be limited to shareholders who own at least 5% of the corporation's stock *or* have owned their stock for at least six months.

c. The Revised Model Business Corporation Act (RMBCA) gives all shareholders an absolute right to inspect the following:

(1) Shareholder lists

(2) Articles of incorporation

(3) Bylaws

(4) Minutes of shareholder meetings held during the past three years

d. The RMBCA requires that the shareholder have a proper purpose for inspection of other records such as accounting and tax records, minutes of board of directors' meetings, and minutes of shareholder meetings held more than three years in the past.

e. Officers or agents of the corporation who improperly deny a shareholder's inspection request can be held liable for damages. Under the RMBCA, the shareholder can recover an amount that equals up to 10% of the value of the shares owned in the corporation.

f. The shareholder can appoint an agent, such as an attorney or accountant, to inspect the books and records of the corporation on their behalf.

Section 4300
Federal Tax Process, Procedures, Accounting, and Planning

4310 Federal Tax Legislative Process

4320 Federal Tax Procedures
    4321 Due Dates and Related Extensions of Time
    4322 Internal Revenue Service (IRS) Audit and Appeals Process
    4323 Judicial Process
    4324 Required Disclosure of Tax Return Positions
    4325 Substantiation Requirements
    4326 Penalties
    4327 Statute of Limitations

4330 Accounting Periods

4340 Accounting Methods
    4341 Recognition of Revenues and Expenses Under Cash, Accrual, or Other Permitted Methods
    4342 Inventory Valuation Methods, Including Uniform Capitalization Rules
    4343 Accounting for Long-Term Contracts
    4344 Installment Sales

4350 Tax Return Elections, Including Federal Status Elections, Alternative Treatment Elections, or Other Types of Elections Applicable to an Individual or Entity's Tax Return

4360 Tax Planning
    4361 Alternative Treatments
    4362 Projections of Tax Consequences
    4363 Implications of Different Business Entities
    4364 Impact of Proposed Tax Audit Adjustments
    4365 Impact of Estimated Tax Payment Rules on Planning
    4366 Role of Taxes in Decision-Making

4370 Impact of Multijurisdictional Tax Issues on Federal Taxation (Including Consideration of Local, State, and Multinational Tax Issues)

4380 Tax Research and Communication
    4381 Authoritative Hierarchy
    4382 Communications with or on Behalf of Clients

4310 Federal Tax Legislative Process

4310.01 House of Representatives

a. Federal tax legislation generally originates in the House of Representatives.

b. The House Ways and Means Committee is the starting point for federal tax bills. If the Ways and Means Committee passes a tax bill, it is then sent to the full House for approval or rejection.

c. If the House passes the tax bill, the bill is then sent to the Senate.

4310.02 Senate

a. Once the Senate receives a tax bill from the House, it is sent to the Senate Finance Committee for consideration.

b. The Senate Finance Committee generally will make changes to the bill that it has received from the House Ways and Means Committee. This means that, in most cases, the Finance Committee will vote to approve or disapprove a tax bill that is different than the tax bill approved by the full House.

c. If the tax bill is approved by the Senate Finance Committee, it goes to the full Senate for a vote. Amendments can also be made to the bill on the Senate floor.

d. If the Senate approves the tax bill, the bill (which generally is not the same as the bill passed by the House) is sent to a Joint Conference Committee.

4310.03 Joint Conference Committee

a. The job of the Joint Conference Committee is to produce a compromise bill from the bills passed by the House and the Senate.

b. The Joint Conference Committee is made up of members from both the House Ways and Means Committee and the Senate Finance Committee.

c. If the Joint Conference Committee creates a compromise bill, it is sent to the full House and full Senate for approval.

d. If the House and Senate pass the bill, it goes to the President for their signature. If the President signs the bill, it becomes law based on the effective date provisions in the bill.

e. If the President vetoes the bill, it does not become law unless the veto is overridden by the vote of both the House and the Senate.

4320 Federal Tax Procedures

4321 Due Dates and Related Extensions of Time

4321.01 Due Dates for Returns

a. Income tax returns of individuals are due by the 15th day of the fourth month after the close of the tax year. For individuals with a calendar tax year, the return is due by April 15.

b. The due date for the income tax return of a corporation is the 15th day of the third month following the close of the tax year.

c. The tax return of a partnership is due on the 15th day of the fourth month following the close of the tax year.

- **d.** A gift tax return must be filed by April 15 of the year following the year of the gift. If a taxpayer dies during the year, the gift tax return for the year of death must be filed by the due date of the estate tax return.
- **e.** An estate tax return is due nine months after the date of the death of the decedent.
- **f.** If the due date, or the last date of an authorized extension, to file a return falls on a Saturday, Sunday, or legal holiday, the return is due on the next date that is not a Saturday, Sunday, or legal holiday. No matter where the filing occurs, the term **legal holiday** means a legal holiday in the District of Columbia.

4321.02 Extensions to File Returns

- **a.** Internal Revenue Code (IRC) Section 6081 gives the Secretary of the Treasury the power to grant reasonable extensions of time for filing returns and documents.
- **b.** An extension of time to file a return does not generally extend the time for payment of any tax which is due.
- **c.** An individual can obtain an automatic six-month extension to file by filing an IRS Form 4868 on or before the due date of the return.
- **d.** Some taxpayers can receive an automatic extension for filing their income tax returns and for paying any tax due. This automatic extension extends the due date to the 15th day of the sixth month after the close of the taxpayer's tax year. U.S. citizens or residents in military service on duty outside the United States or Puerto Rico on the due date for filing the return qualify for this automatic extension.
- **e.** Corporations can receive an automatic six-month extension to file their income tax returns by filing an IRS Form 7004. The extension must be filed before the due date of the corporation's tax return and the corporation must pay the full amount of the tentative unpaid tax liability estimated on the Form 7004.
- **f.** Partnerships also obtain an automatic extension to file an income tax return by filing Form 7004. The form must be filed by the due date of the partnership return and the extension runs for six months from the original due date.
- **g.** An estate can obtain an automatic six-month extension to file an estate tax return if a Form 4768 is filed on or before the due date for filing the estate tax return.
- **h.** The IRS has discretionary authority to allow extensions for income, estate, gift, and certain other returns. This generally is not done until any available automatic extension has been allowed. A discretionary extension may be allowed for longer than six months for taxpayers that are abroad.

4321.03 Due Dates for Payment of Tax

- **a.** Generally, the tax shown on an income, estate, or gift tax return is to be paid at the time for filing the return.
- **b.** The requirement to pay exists without any assessment of the tax or any notice or demand for payment by the IRS.
- **c.** If a taxpayer receives an extension to file a return, this does not also give the taxpayer an extension to pay the tax due.

4321.04 Extension of Time to Pay Tax

- **a.** The IRS can generally extend the time for paying tax for a reasonable time, not to exceed six months.
- **b.** For a taxpayer who is abroad, the extension can exceed the six-month period.

  c. To be granted an extension to pay income or gift taxes, the taxpayer is required to show that payment by the due date will cause undue hardship.

  d. An extension of time to pay estate tax may be granted for up to 12 months by the IRS. This extension must be based on a showing of reasonable cause by the taxpayer.

  e. Reasonable cause will exist where the estate does not have sufficient funds and liquid assets to pay the estate tax, pay claims against the estate, and provide the decedent's spouse and dependent children a reasonable allowance during estate administration without borrowing funds at interest rates higher than prevailing rates.

  f. Also, if the estate contains substantial assets that can only be collected through litigation, reasonable cause for an extension will be deemed to exist.

  g. Based on reasonable cause, the IRS can extend for up to 10 years the time for payment of estate tax. This is done on a year-to-year basis with an annual review as to whether reasonable cause still exists.

4322 Internal Revenue Service (IRS) Audit and Appeals Process

4322.01 Preliminary Review

  a. The IRS Service Center where the return is filed conducts a routine review of the return for obvious errors such as:

    (1) a failure to sign the return,

    (2) a failure to report an item from an information return on the tax return, or

    (3) a mathematical error or clerical error, such as the use of an incorrect table.

  b. The taxpayer is then mailed a corrected tax calculation and, if there is a deficiency, a request to pay the additional amount.

  c. If the taxpayer fails to respond, the IRS generally conducts either a correspondence or an office audit.

  d. This review process is not considered a formal examination of the return. Therefore, the taxpayer is not entitled to the administrative remedies available for formal examinations.

4322.02 Selection of Returns for Audit

  a. The IRS uses a method called the **Discriminant Function System (DIF),** which uses mathematical formulas in order to select returns that are most likely to contain errors and to generate the most additional revenue on audit. The formulas used are developed from information gained in regular audits and audits of randomly selected returns. The randomly selected returns are chosen under the National Research Program (NRP).

  b. Specific factors used by the IRS in determining which returns are selected for audit are not disclosed by the IRS.

  c. In addition to the computerized selection process, returns can be selected for audit under a number of other methods. For example, returns can be selected for audit:

    (1) due to information obtained as a result of information exchange programs with state or foreign agencies,

    (2) due to information obtained from an informant,

    (3) because the return is linked in some way to another return already being audited, or

    (4) because the taxpayer's taxable income, total assets, gross receipts, or deductions exceed certain thresholds established by the IRS.

4322.03 Types of Examinations: Correspondence Examinations

a. If only a few items are in question on the taxpayer's return, an examination may be conducted through correspondence with the taxpayer.

b. The examiner will contact the taxpayer by letter and ask that the questionable items on the return be verified by appropriate documentation.

c. A taxpayer involved in a correspondence examination has the same appeal rights as a taxpayer involved in an office or field examination.

d. If the issues cannot be resolved, the case will be referred for handling as either an office or field examination.

4322.04 Types of Examinations: Office Examinations

a. For more complex issues, the examination will be conducted as an office examination at the appropriate IRS District Office by a tax auditor.

b. The taxpayer will be asked to bring particular records to support items claimed on the return.

c. Generally, the scope of the office examination is limited to the issues stated in the notification letter sent to the taxpayer.

4322.05 Types of Examinations: Field Examinations

a. If the tax issues are more complex, the IRS generally conducts a field examination.

b. In this situation, the IRS examiner, a revenue agent, goes to the taxpayer's place of residence or business to examine the taxpayer's records. The revenue agent is also authorized to take related testimony and to administer oaths.

c. A field examination is open-ended. The revenue agent may investigate any questionable items on the taxpayer's return (not only those previously identified) or any questionable items in the taxpayer's records.

4322.06 Audit Process

a. Before the start of an examination, the IRS is required to provide the taxpayer with an explanation of the audit process and the rights available to the taxpayer. The taxpayer must also be informed that they can suspend the interview at any time to consult with a representative.

b. A taxpayer may represent themselves or they may be represented by a CPA, an attorney, an enrolled agent, or the preparer of the return who signed the return as the preparer.

c. The taxpayer must give a representative written authority to represent them. This is generally done by use of IRS Form 2848 (*Power of Attorney and Declaration of Representative*).

d. At the conclusion of the exam, the tax auditor or revenue agent provides the taxpayer any proposed adjustments of tax liability and any tax balance due.

e. If the taxpayer agrees with the adjustments, they will sign a Form 870 (*Waiver of Restrictions on Assessment and Collection of Deficiency in Tax*). By signing this form, the taxpayer waives the right to receive a statutory notice of deficiency (90-day letter) needed to petition the Tax Court and also gives up the right to go to the IRS Appeals Division.

  f. If the taxpayer does not agree with the adjustments, the taxpayer will receive a 30-day letter notifying them of the right to appeal the proposed adjustment to the IRS Appeals Office within a 30-day period. If an appeal is not requested, the taxpayer is issued a Notice of Deficiency (90-day letter), which gives them 90 days in which to file a Tax Court petition.

4322.07 Appeals Process

  a. An oral request for an Appeals conference can be made in the case of an office examination or a correspondence examination.

  b. In the case of a field examination, a written request is necessary in order to have the case sent to the IRS Appeals Office.

  c. If the proposed adjustment in tax for a particular period is $25,000 or less, the taxpayer only has to file a small case request indicating the adjustments they disagree with and stating the reasons for disagreement.

  d. If the total amount of proposed adjustment in tax for a particular period is over $25,000, a formal written protest is required.

  e. The written protest must include:

    (1) a list of the proposed changes that the taxpayer does not agree with and the reason for disagreement,

    (2) the tax periods involved,

    (3) a statement of facts supporting the taxpayer's position, and

    (4) a statement of the law or other authorities that the taxpayer relies upon.

  f. The Appeals Division will settle disputes based on the hazards of litigating the issues in court.

  g. If a taxpayer agrees to settle the case with the Appeals Division, they will sign an IRS Form 870-AD (*Offer of Waiver of Restrictions on Assessment and Collection of Deficiency*). Acceptance of this form means that the case will not be reopened unless there has been fraud, misrepresentation of a material fact, a significant error in a mathematical calculation, or other administrative wrongdoing.

  h. If a settlement is not reached with the Appeals Division, a statutory notice of deficiency (90-day letter) is sent to the taxpayer. This gives the taxpayer the opportunity to file a petition, within 90 days, with the Tax Court.

4323 Judicial Process

4323.01 Judicial Process (in General)

  a. After a taxpayer has exhausted their administrative remedies with the IRS, the taxpayer may generally litigate the case in court.

  b. All cases must start at the trial court level. For a federal tax dispute, there are three trial courts in which the case may be heard:

    (1) Tax Court

    (2) U.S. District Court

    (3) U.S. Court of Federal Claims

c. As discussed in elsewhere in section **4323**, if either the government or the taxpayer does not agree with the trial court's decision, the case may be appealed to either the appropriate U.S. Court of Appeals or the U.S. Court of Appeals for the Federal Circuit.

4323.02 **Trial Court: U.S. Tax Court**

a. The U.S. Tax Court hears only federal tax disputes. The Tax Court is officially located in Washington, D.C., but judges travel to various cities across the United States to hear cases.

b. Generally, the case is heard by one judge. There are no juries in the Tax Court.

c. The Tax Court is a "deficiency court" in that the taxpayer can have the Tax Court hear their tax dispute without first paying the tax deficiency.

d. The Tax Court also has a Small Tax Division where procedures are informal and cases are heard by magistrates. To have a case heard by the Small Tax Division, the amount of tax in dispute cannot exceed $50,000. Also, there is no appeal from a Small Tax Division decision.

e. Appeals from the Tax Court go to the U.S. Court of Federal Appeals that covers the geographic area in which the taxpayer resides.

4323.03 **Trial Court: U.S. District Court**

a. A taxpayer can also have their tax dispute heard by the U.S. District Court for the federal district in which they reside. The United States is divided into 11 regional Court of Appeal circuits. Each Circuit is then subdivided into Districts.

b. To have the case heard by the U.S. District Court, the taxpayer must first pay the tax and then sue the government in the District Court for a refund.

c. In District Court, one judge hears the case and the taxpayer may also request a jury trial.

d. The District Court hears both tax and nontax cases.

e. Appeals from the U.S. District Court go to the U.S. Court of Federal Appeals for the geographic area in which the taxpayer resides.

4323.04 **Trial Court: U.S. Court of Federal Claims**

a. The U.S. Court of Federal Claims generally hears cases in Washington, D.C. There is one judge and no jury.

b. This trial court hears cases involving claims (tax and nontax) against the federal government. Therefore, the taxpayer must first pay the tax and sue for a refund in this court.

c. Appeals from the U.S. Court of Federal Claims are heard by the U.S. Court of Appeals for the Federal Circuit, which sits in Washington, D.C.

4323.05 **Trial Court: U.S. Federal Court of Appeals**

a. An appeal can be filed with the appropriate U.S. Federal Court of Appeals as a matter of right by either the taxpayer or the government if they disagree with the trial court decision. This means the appeals court must hear the appeal as long as proper procedures are followed in filing the appeal.

b. Normally the appeal is heard by a three-judge panel. In certain cases, all of the judges of the Circuit may hear the case and take part in the decision.

c. The trial courts whose decisions are appealable to a particular Court of Appeals are bound to follow the prior decision of the appellate court on the same issue.

    d. One Court of Appeals, though, is not bound to follow a decision of another Court of Appeals on the same issue.

    e. The Court of Appeals hears appeals of both tax and nontax cases from the trial courts.

    f. Decisions of the U.S. Federal Courts of Appeals are appealable to the U.S. Supreme Court.

4323.06 **U.S. Supreme Court**

    a. Either the taxpayer or the government can request that the U.S. Supreme Court review a decision in a tax case which has been rendered by the U.S. Court of Appeals. There is no appeal as a matter of right to the U.S. Supreme Court in a federal tax case.

    b. To file an appeal, the taxpayer or the government must file a writ of certiorari requesting that the Supreme Court hear the case.

    c. The Supreme Court generally does not hear appeals of tax cases. The situations in which the Court grants the writ of certiorari and hears the appeal in a tax case will usually involve either a situation in which the Courts of Appeals have issued opinions that are in conflict, the tax issue in the case impacts a large number of taxpayers, or the tax issue involves a large amount of tax revenue.

    d. If the Supreme Court grants the appeal and renders a decision in the case, this is generally the final word on the issue (unless Congress acts legislatively). This is due to the fact that all of the lower courts, trial and appellate, must follow the decision in future cases.

4324 Required Disclosure of Tax Return Positions

4324.01 **Required Disclosure of Tax Return Positions (in General)**

    a. In IRS Schedule UTP, certain companies are required to disclose specific information regarding uncertain tax positions taken on their tax return.

    b. Schedule UTP requires the reporting of each U.S. federal income tax position taken by an applicable corporation on its U.S. federal income tax return if the following two conditions are met:

        (1) The corporation has taken a tax position on its federal income tax return for the current tax year or a prior tax year.

        (2) Either the corporation or a related party has recorded a reserve with respect to that tax position for U.S. federal income tax in audited financial statements, or the corporation or related party did not record a reserve for that tax position because the corporation expects to litigate the position.

    c. A tax position meeting one of the two above criteria must be reported regardless of whether the audited financial statements are prepared based on U.S. generally accepted accounting principles (GAAP), International Financial Reporting Standards (IFRS), or other country-specific accounting standards, including a modified version of any of the above.

    d. A tax position taken on a tax return is a tax position that would result in an adjustment to a line item on that return if the position is not sustained. If multiple tax positions affect a single line item, each tax position must be reported separately on the Schedule UTP.

    e. Analysis of whether a reserve has been recorded for the purpose of completing Schedule UTP is determined by reference to the reserve decisions made by the corporation or related party for audited financial statement purposes.

f. A corporation is not require to report on Schedule UTP, a tax position taken in a tax year beginning before January 1, 2010, even if a reserve is recorded with respect to that tax position in audited financial statements issued in 2010 or later.

4324.02 Who Must File

a. A corporation must file Schedule UTP with its income tax return if:

(1) the corporation files IRS Forms 1120, 1120-L, or 1120-PC,

(2) the corporation has assets that equal or exceed $100 million,

(3) the corporation or a related party issued audited financial statements reporting all or a portion of the corporation's operations for all or a portion of the corporation's tax year, and

(4) the corporation has one or more tax positions that must be reported on Schedule UTP.

b. The Schedule UTP should not be filed separately, but should be attached to the corporation's income tax return.

4324.03 Policy of Restraint

a. The IRS has announced that it will use a policy of restraint and forgo seeking certain documents that relate to uncertain tax positions and the workpapers that document the completion of IRS Schedule UTP.

b. If a document is otherwise privileged under the attorney-client privilege, the tax advice privilege in IRC Section 7525, or the work product doctrine and the document was provided to an independent auditor as part of an audit of the taxpayer's financial statements, the IRS will not assert during an examination that privilege has been waived by such disclosure.

c. The above will not apply if:

(1) the taxpayer has engaged in any activity or taken any action, other than those described in that paragraph, that would waive the attorney-client privilege, the tax advice privilege in IRC Section 7525, or the work product doctrine; or

(2) a request for tax accrual workpapers is made because unusual circumstances exist or the taxpayer has claimed the benefits of one or more listed transactions.

d. Under current procedures, examiners request tax reconciliation workpapers as a matter of course. The taxpayer may redact the following information from any copies of tax reconciliation workpapers relating to the preparation of Schedule UTP it is asked to produce during an examination:

(1) Working drafts, revisions, or comments concerning the concise description of tax positions reported on Schedule UTP

(2) The amount of any reserve related to a tax position reported on Schedule UTP

(3) Computations determining the ranking of tax positions to be reported on Schedule UTP or the designation of a tax position as a Major Tax Position

e. Other than requiring the disclosure of the information on the schedule, the requirement to file Schedule UTP does not affect the policy of restraint.

4325 Substantiation Requirements

4325.01 Substantiation Requirements (in General)

a. A taxpayer must generally be able to substantiate any item on their tax return if an issue is raised regarding the item by the IRS.

b. In addition to the general requirement that all items must be able to be substantiated, the Internal Revenue Code, regulations, and other tax pronouncements contain numerous rules regarding the specific substantiation requirements for certain types of deductions or credits taken on a taxpayer's return.

c. While including all of the specific situations where specific substantiation requirements are laid out in the tax rules is beyond the scope of this outline, two examples follow (sections **4325.02** and **4325.03**).

4325.02 Substantiation of Business Expenses

a. The following business expenses can only be deducted if they are substantiated by adequate records:

   (1) Travel away from home (including meals and lodging while in travel status)

   (2) Entertainment expenses

   (3) Business gifts

   (4) Expenses in connection with the use of "listed property" (cars, computers, etc.)

b. To substantiate these business expenses, the records should contain information regarding:

   (1) the amount of the expense,

   (2) the time and place of the travel or entertainment or the day of the gift,

   (3) the business purpose of the expense, and

   (4) for entertainment or gifts, the business relationship of the person being entertained or the person who received the gift.

c. An employee's substantiation of reimbursed expenses for purposes of the accountable plan requirements are met if the employee provides the employer with adequate records of the expense. This would generally require the submission of an account book, expense log, or similar record recorded at or near the time of the expense.

d. Documentary evidence (a receipt or paid bill) is generally not required for expenses of less than $75. However, documentary evidence is required for lodging expense.

e. For substantiating the amount of expenses for meals, lodging, and incidental expenses while traveling away from home, a per diem allowance or reimbursement procedure can be used.

f. The amount of the expense is deemed substantiated if it is equal to or lower than the federal per diem rate for the area of travel.

g. The per diem rate only substantiates the amount of the expense. The taxpayer must still substantiate the place, time, and business purpose of the expense.

4325.03 Substantiation of Charitable Contributions

a. For cash contributions, a deduction is only allowed if the taxpayer has written receipts such as a canceled check or a written statement from the charity that show:

   (1) the name of the charity and

   (2) the date and amount of the contribution.

b. A written statement must provide an estimate of the value of any goods or services received by the donor if:

   (1) a payment is made to the charity for more than $75 and

   (2) the payment is partly a charitable contribution and partly a payment for goods and services.

c. For gifts of property other than money, the taxpayer must have a receipt from the charity. If the property is clothing or other household items, the property must in "good used condition or better."

d. To deduct a single cash or noncash property contribution of $250 or more, the taxpayer must receive a written acknowledgment from the charity. The acknowledgment must include:

   (1) the amount of cash received or a description of the noncash property contributed,

   (2) whether or not the charity provided the donor any goods or services for the contribution, and

   (3) a description and estimate of the value of any goods or services that were provided.

e. If the taxpayer donates noncash gifts valued at more than $500, additional substantiation must be provided with the taxpayer's return. This includes:

   (1) how the property was acquired and

   (2) the taxpayer's basis in the property.

f. If a taxpayer makes a noncash contribution that exceeds $5,000 in value, a qualified appraisal regarding the value of the property may also be required.

g. If a taxpayer donates a used car to a charity, they must obtain a statement from the charity stating the sales price of the car in cases where the car is sold by the charity. The amount that the charity receives from selling the car generally is the amount that the taxpayer can deduct for contributing the car to the charity.

4326 Penalties

4326.01 Failure to File and Failure to Pay

a. If a taxpayer fails to file a tax return by the due date, including any extension, a penalty of 5% per month (up to a maximum of 25%) is imposed on the amount of tax shown as being due on the return. The minimum penalty amount is $135.

b. If the failure to file is due to fraud, the penalty is 15% per month (up to a maximum of 75%).

c. If a taxpayer fails to pay the tax shown as due on the return, a penalty of 0.5% per month (up to a maximum of 25%) is imposed on the tax due. The penalty amount is doubled if the taxpayer fails to pay the tax once a deficiency assessment has been made.

d. During any month in which both the failure to file and failure to pay penalties are applicable, the failure to file penalty is reduced by the amount of the failure to pay penalty.

e. These penalties do not apply if the taxpayer can show that either the failure to file or failure to pay was due to reasonable cause, not willful neglect.

4326.02 Failure to Pay Estimated Tax

a. A penalty can be imposed on a taxpayer who fails to pay a sufficient amount of estimated income taxes. The amount of the penalty is based on the interest rate in effect at the time for deficiency assessments.

b. The penalty is not applied if the tax due for the year after withholding and credits is less than $500 for corporations or $1,000 for all other taxpayers.

c. For an individual, the underpayment of estimated tax is the difference between the estimated tax paid and the lowest of:

  (1) 90% of the current year's tax,

  (2) 100% of the prior year's tax, or

  (3) 90% of the tax that would be due on an annualized income computation for the period that runs through the end of the quarter.

  If the prior-year AGI of the taxpayer exceeds $150,000, the 100% above becomes 110%.

d. A corporation's underpayment of estimated tax is generally the difference between the estimated taxes paid and the lowest of:

  (1) the current-year tax,

  (2) the prior-year tax, or

  (3) the tax on an annualized income computation using of one of three computation methods allowed by the Internal Revenue Code.

4326.03 Accuracy-Related Penalties

a. The accuracy-related penalty combines several related penalties so that multiple penalties will not apply to a single understatement of tax.

b. Each of the accuracy-related penalties is 20% of the portion of the tax underpayment attributable to:

  (1) negligence or disregard of rules and regulations,

  (2) substantial understatement of tax liability,

  (3) substantial valuation overstatement, or

  (4) substantial valuation understatement.

c. The penalty will not apply if the taxpayer can show a reasonable basis for the position that was taken on the return.

d. Interest on the accuracy-related penalty runs from the due date of the return, including extensions, until the penalty is paid.

e. The negligence penalty will apply to an underpayment that is attributable to a failure to make a reasonable attempt to comply with the tax law. A taxpayer is automatically considered negligent if they fail to report income that is covered by an information return (Form 1099) filed by the payor with the IRS.

f. A substantial understatement of tax liability occurs if the understatement exceeds the larger of 10% of the tax due or $5,000:

    (1) For a C corporation, a substantial understatement is the lesser of 10% of the tax due (at least $10,000) or $10 million.

    (2) In all cases, the understatement to which the penalty applies is the difference between the amount of tax shown on the return and the amount of tax that should have been shown.

    (3) The penalty can be avoided if:

        (a) the taxpayer has substantial authority for the position taken or

        (b) there is adequate disclosure of the position taken on the by attachment of Form 8275 to the return.

g. Substantial valuation overstatement:

    (1) The penalty is 20% of the additional tax that should have been paid if the correct value of the property had been used.

    (2) The penalty applies only if the valuation used is 150% or more of the correct valuation. The penalty is doubled if the taxpayer makes a gross overvaluation (200% or more).

    (3) The penalty only applies when the income tax underpayment that results from the overvaluation exceeds $5,000 ($10,000 for a C corporation).

h. Substantial valuation understatement:

    (1) An accuracy penalty can be imposed for an estate or gift tax valuation understatement.

    (2) The penalty is 20% of the additional estate or gift tax that would be due if the correct valuation had been used.

    (3) The penalty is imposed only if the value of the property claimed on the return is 65% or less than the correct valuation.

    (4) The penalty is doubled if the taxpayer makes a gross undervaluation (the reported value is 40% or less than the correct value).

    (5) The penalty only applies if the additional estate or gift tax liability exceeds $5,000.

4326.04 Civil Fraud Penalty

a. A 75% civil penalty is applied to any underpayment of tax resulting from fraud by the taxpayer.

b. If the fraud penalty is applicable, then the accuracy-related penalty is not applied to the same portion of the underpayment of tax.

4326.05 Penalty on Erroneous Refund Claims

a. If a taxpayer files a claim for refund that is greater than the amount actually allowable, a penalty equal to 20% of the improperly claimed amount applies.

b. The penalty does not apply if the taxpayer can show that they had a reasonable basis for the excessive refund claim.

4326.06 False Information: Withholding

a. A civil penalty of $500 applies if a taxpayer claims withholding allowances that are based on false information.

b. A criminal penalty can also apply to a willful failure to supply information or for willfully supplying false or fraudulent information regarding withholding. The penalty is an additional fine of up to $1,000 and/or up to one year in prison.

4326.07 Failure to Deposit Taxes

a. A penalty can be applied if there is a failure by the taxpayer to deposit amounts withheld from employee wages for FICA and income tax.

b. A penalty of up to 15% of any under-deposited amount can be imposed unless the employer can show that the failure was due to reasonable cause and not due to willful neglect.

c. If the action of the employer is willful, a 100% penalty can be imposed on any "responsible person" of the business. While there may be several persons who meet the definition of a "responsible person," the IRS may not collect more than the total amount due.

4326.08 Criminal Penalties: The criminal tax penalties in the Internal Revenue Code include the following:

a. Willful attempt to evade or defeat tax: The maximum penalty is a $100,000 fine and/or five years in prison. For a corporation, there is no imprisonment, but the maximum fine is $500,000.

b. Willful failure to collect or account for and pay overtax: The maximum penalty is $10,000 fine and/or five years in prison.

c. Willful failure to pay a tax or an estimated tax, to file a required return, to keep required records, or to provide required information: The maximum penalty is a $25,000 fine and/or one year in prison. For a corporation, there is no imprisonment, but the maximum fine is $100,000.

d. Willfully furnishing an employee with a false statement regarding tax withholding on wages: The maximum penalty is a $1,000 fine and/or one year in prison.

e. Making a knowingly false declaration under penalty of perjury, preparing or assisting in preparation of a fraudulent return or other documents, or concealing goods or property in respect of any tax: The maximum penalty is a fine of $100,000 and/or three years in prison.

4327 Statute of Limitations

4327.01 Assessment

a. Generally, the time period in which tax must be assessed against the taxpayer is three years from the date the return is filed or the date the return is due, whichever is later.

b. If the taxpayer fails to file a return or files a fraudulent return, an assessment can be made at any time. In effect, there is an unlimited statute of limitation in these cases.

c. If a taxpayer makes a substantial omission of income on the return, the statute of limitation on assessment is extended to six years rather than three. A substantial omission of income occurs in the case where a taxpayer omits gross income from the return in an amount which is greater than 25% of the gross income actually shown on the returns.

- d. The statute of limitation can be extended for a set period of time if the IRS and taxpayer both consent. This is done by signing IRS Form 872 (*Consent to Extend the Time to Assess Tax*). This is often requested by the IRS during an audit when the period for assessment is about to expire.
- e. The statute of limitation on assessment is suspended if a notice of deficiency (90-day letter) is sent to the taxpayer. If the taxpayer files a petition with the Tax Court, the suspension continues until 60 days after the Tax Court's decision in the case becomes final.

4327.02 Collection

- a. Once a proper assessment has been made, the IRS has 10 years from the date of the assessment of tax to collect the tax that is due by either levying against the taxpayer's property or by filing a court action.
- b. The limitation period for collection may be extended by written agreement of both the taxpayer and the IRS.

4327.03 Refund Claims

- a. To receive a refund for an overpayment of tax, a taxpayer must file a timely refund claim. Individuals use IRS Form 1040X, corporations use Form 1120X, and other taxpayers use Form 843.
- b. The claim for refund must be filed within three years from the date on which the tax return that relates to the refund was filed, or within two years of actual payment of the tax if that date is later.
- c. If no return has been filed, the refund claim must be filed within two years of the date the tax was paid.

4330 Accounting Periods

4330.01 Accounting Periods

- a. If a taxpayer keeps adequate books and records, they are generally permitted to use a fiscal tax year (a 12-month period ending on the last day of a month other than December). If adequate books and records are not kept, the taxpayer generally must use a calendar tax year.
- b. Generally, most individuals use a calendar tax year and most corporations use fiscal tax years.
- c. Certain taxpayers may elect to use a 52/53-week tax year.
  - (1) In this case, the tax accounting period varies from 52 to 53 weeks.
  - (2) Under this method, the taxpayer's tax year ends on the same day of the week (e.g., the last Sunday in November) each year.
- d. A taxpayer makes the election to use either a calendar or fiscal year at the time of filing their initial tax return.
- e. For all subsequent tax years, the taxpayer is required to use the tax year initially selected unless they obtain approval to change their tax year from the IRS.
- f. The request to change the taxpayer's tax year must be filed on IRS Form 1128 (*Application for Change in Accounting Period*).
- g. The IRS generally will not grant permission to change the taxpayer's accounting period unless there is a substantial nontax business reason for the change.

      h. If the IRS allows the taxpayer to change their accounting period, the taxpayer must generally comply with certain conditions set out by the IRS.

4330.02 Partnerships and S Corporations

      a. To prevent a deferral of income due to a difference between the tax year of the entity and its members, both partnership and S corporations are generally limited in the choice of their tax years.

      b. A partnership must generally adopt a tax year under the majority partner rule. Under this rule, the partnership must use the same tax year as that which is used by any partner or partners who hold a more than 50% interest in the partnership capital and profits.

      c. If the majority partner rule does not apply, the partnership must use the same tax year as all of its principal partners. A principal partner is a partner who holds a 5% or more interest in partnership capital or profits. For this rule to apply, all of the principal partners must have the same tax year.

      d. If the principal partner rule does not apply, the partnership must use the tax year that results in the least aggregate deferral of income. Under the least aggregate deferral rule, the different tax years of the principal partners are tested to see which of those tax years results in the least aggregate deferral overall for the partnership. This year is then the required partnership tax year.

      e. Generally, an S corporation is required to use a calendar tax year.

      f. Partnerships and S corporations can generally elect to use a tax year other than their required tax year if:

          (1) a business purpose for the tax year can be shown or

          (2) the tax year selected results in a deferral of income of not more than three months from the required tax year and the entity agrees to make required tax deposits (a Section 444 election).

      g. A business purpose will be considered to exist if the entity can show that the requested tax year conforms to the natural business year of the entity.

      h. In the case where the partnership or S corporation makes a Section 444 election, the deposit due is computed by multiplying the income deferred under the elective tax year by the highest individual tax rate plus 1%. The amount to be deposited is reduced by the amount already on deposit from the prior tax year.

4330.03 Personal Service Corporations

      a. A personal service corporation (PSC) is a corporation in which shareholder-employees provide personal services in the area of health, law, accounting, actuarial science, consulting, engineering, architecture, or performing arts.

      b. Generally, a personal service corporation is required to use a calendar year.

      c. A personal service corporation can generally elect a fiscal year if:

          (1) a business purpose exists for the fiscal tax year or

          (2) the following occurs:

              (a) the fiscal tax year of the personal service corporation results in a deferral of no more than three months of income,

              (b) the personal service corporation pays the shareholder-employee's salary during the part of the calendar year after the close of its fiscal tax year, and

(c) the salary for that period is proportionate to the shareholder-employee's salary for the previous fiscal tax year.

If the salary tests above are not satisfied, the personal service corporation can still retain its fiscal year. However, the corporation's deduction for the salary paid to the shareholder-employee for the fiscal year will be limited.

4340 Accounting Methods

4341 Recognition of Revenues and Expenses Under Cash, Accrual, or Other Permitted Methods

4341.01 Recognition of Revenues and Expenses (in General)

a. Internal Revenue Code (IRC) Section 446 states that a taxpayer must compute their taxable income using the accounting method regularly used to keep their books and records.

b. If the method of accounting used by the taxpayer does not clearly reflect income, the Internal Revenue Service (IRS) can specify the accounting method that the taxpayer must use so that their income is clearly reflected.

c. A taxpayer may compute their taxable income under any of the following methods of accounting:

(1) The cash receipts and disbursements methods

(2) The accrual method

(3) Any other method permitted by the IRC (i.e., the installment method)

(4) Any combination of permissible methods

d. A taxpayer who is engaged in more than one trade or business can use a different method of accounting for each trade or business.

e. The accrual method must generally be used for sales and cost of goods sold if inventories are an income-producing factor in the taxpayer's business.

f. Generally, a taxpayer must get IRS consent in order to change their method of accounting.

4341.02 Cash Method

a. Under the cash method, a taxpayer generally reports income when it is actually received. Income can be received in the form of cash, a cash equivalent (a check), or in the form of property or services (e.g., fair market value of the property or services received).

b. A taxpayer using the cash method is required to report income if it is constructively received. For constructive receipt to exist:

(1) the amount must be made available to the taxpayer and

(2) actual receipt of the income by the taxpayer is not subject to any substantial limitations or restrictions.

c. The constructive receipt doctrine prevents a cash method taxpayer from being able to turn their back on income in order to defer recognition to a future tax year.

d. Generally, a cash method taxpayer deducts expenses in the year they are actually paid.

  e. However, if a cash method taxpayer prepays expenses that cover a period substantially beyond the end of the tax year, the expenses must be capitalized and amortized over the period to which they relate.

  f. Taxpayers, though, may generally currently deduct prepaid expenses if the period covered by the prepaid expenses expires by the end of the tax year following the year of payment.

  g. The one-year rule does not apply to the deduction of prepaid interest. Prepaid interest expense can only be deducted over the period to which the interest relates.

4341.03 Accrual Method

  a. Under the accrual method, a taxpayer includes an item in income when:

    (1) all events have occurred that create the taxpayer's right to receive the income (generally, the goods or services have been provided to the other party) and

    (2) the amount of income to be received can be determined with reasonable certainty.

  b. An accrual method taxpayer can generally deduct an expense only when:

    (1) all of the events have occurred that create the taxpayer's liability,

    (2) the amount of the liability can be determined with reasonable accuracy, and

    (3) the taxpayer has received economic performance from the other party.

  c. The economic performance requirement is when the services or property that give rise to the taxpayer's liability are actually received by the taxpayer.

  d. An exception to the economic performance requirement allows the deduction of recurring items before economic performance has been received, provided:

    (1) the item is recurring in nature and is treated consistently from year to year by the taxpayer,

    (2) the item accrued is either not material or accruing before economic performance results in a better matching of income and expenses, and

    (3) economic performance is received within a reasonable time that is no later than 8-1/2 months after the close of the tax year.

  Under this exception to economic performance, all of the events must still have occurred to create the taxpayer's liability and the amount of the liability must be known with reasonable certainty.

4341.04 Hybrid Method

  a. The taxpayer may use a hybrid method that combines more than one method, provided the use of the hybrid method clearly reflects income.

  b. The most common example of a hybrid method is when a taxpayer uses the accrual method for sales and cost of goods sold, but uses the cash method to report other income and expenses.

4341.05 Restriction on Use of the Cash Method

  a. Certain taxpayers generally are prevented from using the cash method and are required to use the accrual method. The accrual method generally must be used by:

    (1) a C corporation,

    (2) a partnership that has a C corporation as a partner, and

    (3) a tax shelter.

b. However, the cash method may still be used provided the entity is not a tax shelter and:

  (1) the entity is engaged in a farming or tree-raising business, or

  (2) the entity is a qualified personal service corporation (a corporation performing services in health, law, engineering, architecture, accounting, actuarial science, performing arts, or consulting), or

  (3) the entity has average annual gross receipts for the more recent three tax years of $5 million or less.

c. The IRS also generally allows most taxpayers whose average annual gross receipts do not exceed $1 million to use the cash method. (IRS Revenue Procedure 2001-10)

d. Also, the cash method may be used by some select taxpayers whose average annual gross receipts do not exceed $10 million. (IRS Revenue Procedure 2002-28)

4342 Inventory Valuation Methods, Including Uniform Capitalization Rules

4342.01 Inventory Valuation Methods, Including Uniform Capitalization Rules (in General)

a. Generally, the tax accounting and financial accounting rules for inventories are very similar.

b. This is due to the fact that Internal Revenue Code (IRC) Section 471 states that inventories shall be taken on such basis as conforms to the best accounting practice in the trade or business and as most clearly reflecting of income.

c. All items included in inventory should be valued at either:

  (1) cost or

  (2) lower of cost or market.

4342.02 Uniform Capitalization (UNICAP) Rules

a. Under Internal Revenue Code (IRC) Section 263A, taxpayers subject to the UNICAP rules are required to capitalize all direct costs and an allocable share of most indirect costs associated with production or resale activities.

b. The UNICAP rules apply to:

  (1) real or tangible personal property produced by the taxpayer for use in a trade or business or in an activity engaged in for profit,

  (2) real or tangible personal property produced by the taxpayer for sale to customers, and

  (3) real or personal property (tangible and intangible) acquired for resale by the taxpayer.

  The UNICAP rules do not apply to personal property acquired by the taxpayer for resale if the taxpayer's average annual gross receipts for the most recent three tax years do not exceed $10 million.

c. Among the type of property excluded from the UNICAP rules are:

  (1) property produced by the taxpayer for their own use other than in a trade or business or production of income activity,

  (2) research and experimental expenditures,

(3) property produced by the taxpayer under a long-term contract, and

(4) costs incurred in raising, growing, or harvesting certain types of trees (generally, trees other than trees bearing fruit, nuts, or other crops, or ornamental trees).

    d. To value inventory under the UNICAP rules, a producer is required to:

(1) categorize all costs as production, general administrative expenses, or mixed services,

(2) allocate the mixed services costs between production and general administrative expenses, and

(3) finally, allocate the production costs between the cost of goods sold and ending inventory.

    e. Mixed services costs must be allocated to production on some rational basis. Rather than allocating each mixed services cost, a taxpayer may elect a simplified method to allocate the total mixed services costs to production.

    f. Under the simplified method, the mixed services costs allocated to production are as follows:

$$\frac{\text{Total production costs (other than mixed services and interest)}}{\text{Total costs (other than mixed services, interest, and state, local, or foreign income taxes)}} \times \text{Total mixed services costs}$$

    g. Regular cost accounting techniques are then used to allocate the costs between the costs of goods sold and ending inventory.

    h. For a taxpayer who is a reseller, many of the costs are included in the price paid for the property. However, a reseller must capitalize the following costs:

(1) Storage costs for wholesalers

(2) Offsite storage costs for retailers

(3) Purchasing costs

(4) Handling, processing, assembly, and repackaging costs

(5) The portion of mixed services costs allocated to the above functions

    i. Under the UNICAP rules, some costs may end up being capitalized for tax purposes that are not capitalized for financial reporting purposes.

4342.03 Inventory Valuation Methods

    a. Unless a taxpayer uses the LIFO method, inventories may be valued at the lower of cost or market.

    b. A taxpayer using the LIFO method is generally required to value inventory at cost.

    c. In determining cost, a taxpayer may generally use specific identification, FIFO, or LIFO (specific goods or dollar-value LIFO) as long as the method selected is applied consistently from tax year to tax year.

4342.04 Election of Method

    a. A taxpayer does not have to request IRS approval to change to the LIFO method. However, once the election is made, it cannot be revoked by the taxpayer.

    b. If a taxpayer wishes to change from the LIFO method to any other method, IRS approval must be obtained.

c. If the taxpayer elects to use the LIFO method for tax purposes, the taxpayer's financial reports must also be prepared using the LIFO method.

4343 Accounting for Long-Term Contracts

4343.01 Accounting for Long-Term Contracts (in General)

a. A long-term contract is a contract for the manufacture, building, installation, or construction of property if the contract is not completed within the taxable year in which the contract is entered.

b. However, a manufacturing contract is not a long-term contract unless it involves the manufacture of:

(1) any unique item of a type that is not normally included in the finished goods inventory of the taxpayer or

(2) any item that normally requires more than 12 calendar months to complete (without regard to the period of the contract).

c. A taxpayer is generally required to accumulate all of the direct and indirect costs involved with a particular contract and allocate them to that contract.

d. Costs that benefit the contract as well as general operations of the business (mixed services costs) must be allocated in part to each contract. The taxpayer must use some reasonable basis to do this cost allocation.

e. Costs are then deducted when the contract revenue is recognized by the taxpayer.

f. The two methods used to decide when revenue from a contract is recognized are:

(1) the completed contract method and

(2) the percentage of completion method.

4343.02 Completed Contract Method

a. The completed contract method can be used for:

(1) home construction contracts in which at least 80% of the estimated costs are for dwelling units in buildings which have four or fewer units, and

(2) other real estate construction contracts, provided:

(a) the contract is expected to be completed within the two-year period beginning on the start date of the contract, and

(b) the contract is performed by a taxpayer whose average annual gross receipts for the most recent three taxable years before the year the contract is entered do not exceed $10 million.

b. No revenue is recognized under the completed contract method until the contract is completed and accepted as satisfactory.

c. If a dispute exists regarding the contract and the dispute is substantial, no income or loss is recognized on the contract until the dispute is resolved.

d. If the dispute is not substantial, income or loss, reduced by the amount in dispute, is recognized currently.

4343.03 Percentage of Completion Method

a. If the taxpayer does not qualify to use the completed contract method under the two cases discussed in section **4343.02**, the percentage of completion method must be used to account for long-term contracts.

b. Under the percentage of completion method, a portion of the gross contract price is taken into income during each period as work is carried out under the contract.

c. The revenue accrued each period is determined by the following formula:

$$\frac{\text{Contract costs during the period}}{\text{Estimated total contract costs}} \times \text{Contract price}$$

d. Costs that are allocated to the contract during the period are deducted during that period and thus reduce that period's revenue.

e. In the final period, the taxpayer reports any unreported revenue under the contract.

f. Under a de minimus rule, the taxpayer can delay recognition of income under a specific contract if less than 10% of the estimated contract costs have been incurred by the end of the tax period.

g. If this de minimus rule applies, the taxpayer can elect to defer recognition of income (and related costs) until the tax year in which the cumulative contract costs are at least 10% of the estimated contract costs.

h. Under a lookback rule, the taxpayer is required to recalculate the annual profit reported on the contract. If taxes were actually overpaid, the taxpayer is entitled to interest from the government on the overpayment. If taxes were actually underpaid, the taxpayer is required to pay interest to the government for the period of the underpayment.

4344 Installment Sales

4344.01 Installment Sales (in General)

a. Generally, a taxpayer is required to recognize the gain or loss from the sale or exchange of property at the time of the sale or exchange.

b. Under the installment sales method, a taxpayer is allowed to report the gain from an installment sale over the period during which payments are received. The installment sale rule does not apply to the reporting of losses.

c. The installment method generally applies to sales in which the taxpayer has a gain if at least one payment will be received after the tax year in which the sale occurs.

d. The installment sale reporting method may not be used:

   (1) to report gains on property held for sale in the ordinary course of business (inventory),

   (2) for gain that must be recaptured as ordinary income under IRC Section 1245 or 1250, or

   (3) for any gain on stocks or securities that are traded on an established securities market.

e. However, the installment method can be used to report gain on the sale of:

   (1) time-share units,

   (2) residential real estate lots if the seller has made no improvements to the lots, and

   (3) property used or produced in farming.

    f. If the installment method applies to a sale, the taxpayer generally must use that method unless they elect out.

4344.02 Computation of Gain

    a. The gain recognized under the installment method is computed using the following formula:

$$\frac{\text{Total gain}}{\text{Contract price}} \times \text{Payments received during the tax year} = \text{Gain recognized}$$

    b. **Total gain** is the selling price of the property reduced by the adjusted basis of the property and any selling expenses.

    c. The **contract price** is the selling price of the property reduced by any of the seller's liabilities that are assumed by the buyer as part of the sale.

4344.03 Installment Sales: Other Issues

    a. Generally, if a taxpayer disposes of the installment obligation, the remainder of the gain under the installment sale is accelerated and must be recognized in the year of the disposition of the obligation.

    b. A taxpayer can make an election not to use the installment reporting method. This election is made by reporting all of the recognized gain from the installment sale in the tax year of the sale.

    c. A taxpayer must receive IRS permission to revoke an election not to use the installment sales reporting method.

4350 Tax Return Elections, Including Federal Status Elections, Alternative Treatment Elections, or Other Types of Elections Applicable to an Individual or Entity's Tax Return

4350.01 Tax Return Elections (in General)

The Internal Revenue Code provides for numerous tax elections that can be made by a taxpayer and impact the taxpayer's tax return. The following material highlights some of the tax elections available to a taxpayer.

4350.02 Check the Box

    a. Under the "check the box" regulations under Internal Revenue Code (IRC) Section 7701, certain entities can make an election as to how they wish to be treated for federal tax purposes. This eliminates the need for taxpayers to artificially shape business organizations to produce the desired entity classification.

    b. In order to fall under the check-the-box regulations, the entity must meet three requirements:

        (1) First, it must be separate from its owners or members.

        (2) Second, the entity must be a business entity and not classified as a trust or otherwise subject to special treatment under the Internal Revenue Code.

        (3) Finally, the entity must be an eligible entity. An eligible entity is one not organized under either a state or federal incorporation statute.

  c. Generally, a domestic entity with at least two members will be classified as a partnership, unless the entity elects to be taxed as a corporation for federal tax purposes.

  d. A single member entity will be treated as not separate from the owner (i.e., if the member is an individual, it will be treated as a sole proprietorship), unless there is an affirmative election to be treated as a corporation.

  e. An entity that wishes to elect out of its default classification, or change its classification, can do so by filing IRS Form 8832 (*Entity Classification Election*).

  f. An entity can file its initial election at any time. However, an entity is generally prohibited from filing more than one election to change the entity's classification during any 60-month period.

  g. If there is a more than 50% change in ownership of the entity, the IRS may waive the 60-month wait period for a new election.

4350.03 Depreciation Elections

  a. In depreciating property for federal tax purposes, a number of elections are available to a taxpayer.

  b. For personal property, a taxpayer may elect to use the modified accelerated cost recovery system (MACRS). Under this method, the cost recovery is computed using a declining-balance method in the early years, switching to straight-line for the later years.

  c. Another option for personal property that can be selected by the taxpayer is using a straight-line method of cost recovery over the applicable class life (3-, 5-, 7-, 10-, 15-, or 20-year class period).

  d. A final option for personal property is to elect to recover the cost using the alternative depreciation system (ADS) method. The ADS method recovers the cost of the property using a straight-line method, but the recovery period is generally longer than under the straight-line method.

  e. For personal property, the taxpayer must elect one of the above cost recovery methods and use that method for all of the assets in a particular class (3, 5, 7, 10, 15, or 20 years) put in service during the tax year.

  f. For real property placed in service during the year, the taxpayer generally has two cost recovery potions. One is to use the MACRS method. Under ACRS, cost recovery is done using a straight-line method over a period of 27.5 years for residential rental real estate or 39 years for nonresidential real estate.

  g. The other option that may be selected for real estate is the ADS method of cost recovery. Under ADS, the cost of the real estate (residential and nonresidential) is recovered using a straight-line method over 40 years.

  h. The election of cost recovery method for real estate is done on a per-property basis.

4350.04 Section 179 Election

  a. Internal Revenue Code (IRC) Section 179 provides a taxpayer with the election to immediately expense the cost of an asset (within certain limits discussed below) rather than recovering the cost over the property's recovery period.

  b. Property that qualifies for the Section 179 expensing election generally must be tangible personal property that is used in a trade or business. (For 2010 and 2011, certain real property can be expensed under Section 179 at reduced limits from those discussed below.)

  c. For 2010 and 2011, the maximum dollar amount that can be expensed is $500,000.

    d. To the extent that the total cost of qualifying property placed in service during the year exceeds a threshold amount ($2 million for 2010 and 2011). The maximum dollar amount that can be expensed is reduced dollar for dollar.

    Example: For 2011, the taxpayer placed into service property that qualifies for Section 179 expensing that cost $2,050,000. This exceeds the threshold of $2,000,000 for 2011 by $50,000. Therefore, the maximum amount that the taxpayer can expense for 2011 is $450,000 ($500,000 - $50,000).

    e. Finally, a third limit also exists on how much a taxpayer can expense for the year under Section 179. The amount expensed for the tax year cannot exceed the total amount of taxable income which the taxpayer has from all trade or business activities during the year.

4350.05 Joint Versus Separate Returns

    a. At the time of filing their tax return, a husband and wife can elect to file as married filling joint or married filing separate.

    b. A husband and wife may elect to file a joint return even though one spouse has no income, deductions, or credits.

    c. A husband and wife can change their election to file separate returns to file a joint return. Generally, this is done by filing an IRS Form 1040X within three years from the due date for filing the separate returns.

4350.06 S Corporation Election

Certain corporations can elect S corporation status. In order to elect S corporation status, the corporation must be a small business corporation. This means that:

    a. the entity must be a domestic corporation organized under the laws of a state or a U.S. territory or an unincorporated entity that has elected to be taxed as a corporation under the check-the-box rules,

    b. the corporation must have only individuals, estates, certain trusts, banks, and certain exempt organizations as shareholders,

    c. the shareholders must be citizens or residents of the United States, and

    d. the corporation can have only one class of stock.

4360 Tax Planning

4361 Alternative Treatments

4361.01 When engaging in tax planning, the tax practitioner researches the tax consequences of various potential causes of action.

4361.02 In certain situations, conflicting sources of tax authority may be found. If this is the case, there should be a thorough analysis of the alternative tax treatments that could result.

4361.03 Alternative tax outcomes should be communicated to the taxpayer so that they can make a fully informed decision as to the course of action they wish to take.

4362 Projections of Tax Consequences

4362.01 Part of the tax planning process is developing alternative courses of action for the taxpayer.

4362.02 As potential courses of action are developed, the tax planner also develops projections of the tax consequences that will result from each option.

4362.03 As a result, the taxpayer can make an informed decision as to the option that will provide them with the optimal after-tax result.

4363 Implications of Different Business Entities

4363.01 One of the major issues in tax planning is often determining the best form in which to operate a business.

4363.02 When making this determination, tax factors play a significant part in the final decision. However, nontax factors such as limiting legal liability and the ability to raise capital in the future are also major factors in deciding which type of entity is ultimately chosen.

4363.03 Detailed information as to the tax and nontax characteristics of different business entities that factor into the choice of entity are found in sections **4260** and **4600**.

4364 Impact of Proposed Tax Audit Adjustments

4364.01 It is important to factor the impact of proposed tax audit adjustments into the tax planning process.

4364.02 If a taxpayer follows a particular course of action, is audited, and audit adjustments result, this will generally result in additional costs to the taxpayer. Not only will the taxpayer be liable for the back taxes due, but they also will be liable for interest on the tax deficiency. Additionally, the taxpayer may be liable for penalties.

4364.03 A major part of tax planning is to be sure that any course of action taken by the taxpayer can be justified if the taxpayer is audited and adjustments are proposed.

4364.04 Planning for any potential IRS challenges to the position taken by the taxpayer will minimize the impact of any potential tax audit adjustments.

4365 Impact of Estimated Tax Payment Rules on Planning

4365.01 Part of the tax planning process is determining the tax liability that will result for the taxpayer from various courses of action. This is especially important for the particular course of action that is actually chosen by the taxpayer.

4365.02 By properly projecting the tax liability that will be due, the appropriate estimated tax payments that will be due throughout the tax year can be calculated. This will allow the taxpayer to plan ahead to be sure that the resources are available to make the required estimated tax payments that are required. This in turn will allow the taxpayer to avoid the imposition of any penalties that could result from the failure to pay the correct amount of estimated tax as the payments come due throughout the year.

4366 Role of Taxes in Decision Making

4366.01 In the decision-making process, the role of taxes should play a significant part. Whether the decision is being made in a personal or business context, one of the goals of tax planning should be to minimize the taxpayer's tax liability as much as possible. However, the ultimate goal should be to optimize the taxpayer's after-tax result. This may not in all cases result in the lowest tax liability for the taxpayer.

4366.02 In making decisions, taxes should be a factor, but not the only factor. In certain cases, nontax considerations may be as important, or more important, than the tax considerations. Therefore, in decision-making, all factors, tax and nontax, should be considered. Generally, no decision should be made based on the tax considerations alone if the personal or business considerations involved would point to not making the same decision.

4370 Impact of Multijurisdictional Tax Issues on Federal Taxation (Including Consideration of Local, State, and Multinational Tax Issues)

4370.01 While taxpayers often focus on the impact of federal taxation, taxes imposed by state and local jurisdictions and, in some cases, foreign jurisdictions can create a significant tax burden on the taxpayer.

4370.02 **State and Local Taxes**

a. Local jurisdictions in all 50 states impose real estate taxes on the real property located within the boundaries of the jurisdiction. This tax is generally imposed on an annual basis, based on the real estate tax year, and is computed based on the value of the property.

b. Most of the states also allow local jurisdictions to impose a local tax on personal property. These personal property taxes vary significantly from state to state as to the rate of taxation as well as to the type of personal property subject to the tax. Typical types of property that may be subject to a personal property tax include:

(1) automobiles,

(2) stocks and bonds, and

(3) tangible business property such as inventory, machinery, or equipment.

c. State governments generally impose a statewide general sales tax on the sale of personal property and, in some cases, certain types of services. This tax is usually based on a percentage of the retail sales price of the goods or services.

d. States that impose a general sales tax also impose a use tax. The state use tax applies when a taxpayer purchases goods outside the state and therefore did not pay the home state's sales tax. Generally, a taxpayer may receive a credit against the use tax for the amount of sales tax paid out of state.

e. Most states also impose some type of personal income tax on individuals. The rates of these taxes vary greatly and the manner in which the state income tax is computed varies from state to state. Many states also allow local jurisdictions to impose a personal income tax.

f. Corporate income tax is also imposed by most states. The tax is generally imposed on the corporation's income that is attributable to that particular state. State corporate income tax rates vary greatly, with most states having a flat rate structure.

4370.03 Foreign Taxes

a. If a taxpayer conducts business internationally, they will be subject to numerous taxes imposed by various foreign jurisdictions.

b. These taxes can range from foreign income taxes, real and personal property taxes, and sales tax. These taxes vary widely from jurisdiction to jurisdiction as to the types of tax imposed and the rate of tax.

c. Often a treaty that has been entered between the United States and the foreign country will have an impact on the rate of tax or type of tax imposed.

d. Often a taxpayer will encounter some type of value added tax (VAT) in the foreign jurisdiction. This type of tax is computed based on the incremental value that has been added to the goods.

4380 Tax Research and Communication

4381 Authoritative Hierarchy

4381.01 Assessing Tax Sources

a. When conducting tax research, the first step is locating sources of tax authority that have a bearing on the tax issue being researched.

b. Once the sources are located, it is important to assess the sources and determine the authoritative hierarchy of the sources that have been found.

4381.02 Legislative Sources

a. The Internal Revenue Code (IRC) is the ultimate authoritative source since it is the tax law enacted by Congress. All other tax sources are simply interpreting what Congress intended by the language that was used in the statute.

b. If the Code provides the answer to the researcher's question, no other tax sources are necessary. However, in most cases, the researcher must consult other tax sources in order to determine the scope of the applicable Code section.

c. The legislative history behind the Code section is also a valuable source since it often answers questions regarding the intent of Congress in enacting the Code section and the scope of the Code section itself.

d. The legislative history is found in the:

(1) House Ways and Means Committee Report,

(2) Senate Finance Committee Report, and

(3) Joint Conference Committee Report (if one exists).

4381.03 Administrative Sources

a. The Treasury Regulations are the official interpretation of the Internal Revenue Code by the Department of the Treasury. The regulations are the administrative source of tax authority that carry the most weight.

b. Regulations are given great deference by the courts if the taxpayer ends up litigating their tax dispute with the government. This is because the regulations are the interpretation of the Code by the government department responsible for administering the tax law.

- c. A court will generally only invalidate a regulation if the taxpayer can convince the court that the regulation does not clearly reflect the intent of Congress in enacting the Code section.

- d. The second most important source of administrative tax authority is revenue rulings.

- e. Revenue rulings carry far less weight than regulations. This is because a Revenue Ruling is issued by the Internal Revenue Service and is therefore viewed as the position of the IRS on a particular tax issue.

- f. Revenue rulings are therefore easier to challenge in court. As a result, finding a revenue ruling that conflicts with the position of the taxpayer may not be fatal. It does, however, show the IRS position on the issue.

- g. Other administrative tax sources generally carry less weight than regulations and revenue rulings. However, in a given situation, one of these other sources may be very valuable to the taxpayer position in question. These other administrative sources include the following:

    (1) Revenue Procedures

    (2) Letter Rulings (these technically cannot be cited as authority by any taxpayer other than the taxpayer requesting the ruling)

    (3) Treasury Decisions

    (4) Determination Letters

    (5) Technical Advice Memoranda

4381.04 Judicial Sources

- a. Generally, the higher the level of the court that rendered a decision, the greater the weight the decision should be given.

- b. A decision rendered by the U.S. Supreme Court is the definitive answer on a tax issue. The only way that the rule laid down by a Supreme Court decision can be impacted is if Congress disagrees with the Supreme Court's interpretation and changes the tax law by amending the Internal Revenue Code.

- c. A decision rendered by a court of appeals (e.g., the Sixth Circuit Court of Appeals) should generally be given more weight than a decision rendered by a trial court (e.g., a U.S. Federal District Court).

- d. Regarding the Tax Court, a reviewed decision of the Tax Court (in which all the Tax Court judges participate) should generally carry greater weight than a normal Tax Court decision (decided by a single Tax Court judge).

- e. The geographic location of the court rendering the decision should also be factored into the weight given to the case. More weight should be given to an opinion from a court in which the taxpayer could possibly have his case heard. For example, a taxpayer located in Florida should put more weight on an opinion from the Eleventh Circuit Court of Appeals than one from the Sixth Circuit Court of Appeals, since Florida is located in the Eleventh Circuit.

- f. Finally, if a court opinion is consistent with decisions rendered by other courts, that opinion should be given more weight than an opinion not supported by other decisions.

4382 Communications with or on Behalf of Clients

4382.01 Once tax research has been completed, the results will generally have to be communicated to the client and also possibly to a third party, such as the IRS.

4382.02 How much detail should be included in the communication and how technical the communication should be will be determined by the audience. Communication addressed to a taxpayer with little tax knowledge should obviously be much less detailed and technical than a communication directed toward an IRS agent or a superior within the researcher's accounting firm.

4382.03 Generally, a communication should include the following elements:

a. A brief statement of the essential facts necessary to answer the tax question(s)

b. The identification of the tax issue(s). If there are multiple tax issues to be researched, each issue should be separately laid out for clarity.

c. A clear identification of the conclusion(s) reached by the researcher. A separate conclusion should be stated for each tax issue. Also, if more than one conclusion may exist due to a conflict in the tax authorities, this should be clearly communicated.

d. A clear statement of the tax sources on which the conclusion was based and the reasoning that supports the conclusion

Section 4400
Federal Taxation of Property Transactions

4410 Types of Assets

4420 Basis and Holding Period of Assets

4430 Cost Recovery (Depreciation, Depletion, and Amortization)

4440 Taxable and Nontaxable Sales and Exchanges

4450 Amount and Character of Gains and Losses, and Netting Process

4460 Related Party Transactions

4470 Estate and Gift Taxation
    4471 Transfers Subject to the Gift Tax
    4472 Annual Exclusion and Gift Tax Deductions
    4473 Determination of Taxable Estate
    4474 Marital Deduction
    4475 Unified Credit

4410 Types of Assets

4410.01 For federal tax purposes, all property is either classified as ordinary income property or as a capital asset.

Tax Treatment of Gains and Losses

4410.02 When a taxpayer has determined that the taxpayer has a gain or a loss to be recognized, the next step is to establish whether it is to be treated as a capital gain or loss or as an ordinary income or loss item.

4410.03 A capital gain or loss is that gain or loss arising from the sale or exchange of a capital asset.

4410.04 **Capital assets** are defined as all property, *except* for the following:

    a. Property held for resale (inventory)

    b. Real or depreciable property used in a trade or business

    c. Accounts or notes receivable acquired in normal business operations

    d. A copyright or a literary, artistic, or musical composition in the hands of the creator or anyone who assumes the creator's basis (property received through gift)

    e. U.S. government publications received from the government other than by purchase at the price that it is offered for sale to the public

    f. Certain commodities derivative instruments held by a commodities derivatives dealer.

- g. Any hedging transaction that is clearly identified as such before the close of the day on which it is acquired, originated, or entered into.
- h. Supplies of a type regularly used or consumed by the taxpayer in the ordinary course of a trade or business of the taxpayer.

4410.05 Taxpayers may elect to treat the sale or exchange of self-created musical compositions or copyrights as the sale or exchange of a capital asset. This special treatment is effective for sales or exchanges in tax years beginning after May 17, 2006 and ending December 31, 2010.

4410.06 **Real property subdivided for sale:**

- a. Individuals and S corporations subdividing real estate for sale may qualify for capital gain treatment if the following conditions apply:
    - (1) Subdivider must not be a real estate dealer or a C corporation.
    - (2) No substantial improvements may be made to the lots sold.
    - (3) Lots sold must be held at least five years (unless inherited).
- b. All gain is capital gain until the year the sixth lot is sold. Contiguous lots sold to one buyer are treated as one lot.
    - (1) When the sixth lot is sold, 5% of the revenue from all lots sold that year is potential ordinary income.
    - (2) This potential ordinary income is offset by any selling expenses to determine the net amount taxed as ordinary income. Any gain not taxed as ordinary income is capital gain.

Section 1231 Assets

4410.07 Section 1231 of the Internal Revenue Code provides long-term capital gain treatment for certain transactions involving noncapital assets (generally, land, buildings, and equipment used in business).

4410.08 Section 1231 transactions include the following:

- a. Sale or exchange of real or depreciable/MACRS (ACRS) recovery business property
- b. Involuntary conversion of real or depreciable/MACRS (ACRS) recovery business property
- c. Involuntary conversion of certain capital assets
- d. Certain farming transactions involving crops and livestock
- e. Certain transactions involving timber, iron ore, and coal

4410.09 To qualify as Section 1231 property, the property items listed must be held long enough to meet the long-term capital gain and loss holding period requirement.

4410.10 **Section 1231 benefits:**

- a. Gains and losses from Section 1231 transactions must be grouped and compared.
    - (1) If Section 1231 gains exceed Section 1231 losses, the net gain will be treated as ordinary income to the extent of net Section 1231 losses claimed by the taxpayer in the previous five years. Any remaining gain will receive long-term capital gain treatment.

(2) If Section 1231 losses exceed Section 1231 gains, the net loss will receive *ordinary loss* treatment.

Example: The taxpayer has a net Section 1231 gain of $21,000 for the current year. This is the taxpayer's first net Section 1231 gain in over six years. Looking back, the taxpayer was able to deduct $9,000 of net Section 1231 losses during the last five years. The gain is taxed as follows—$9,000 is taxed as ordinary income and the remaining gain of $12,000 is taxed as long-term capital gain.

    b. A special rule applies to casualty and theft losses on business or income-producing property held long enough to meet the long-term gain and loss holding period requirement.

        (1) Gains and losses from these involuntary conversions must be separately grouped and compared.

        (2) If casualty gains exceed casualty losses, these gains and losses are then grouped with Section 1231 items to compute the net Section 1231 gain or loss.

        (3) If casualty losses exceed casualty gains, the resulting net loss is treated as an ordinary loss. In this situation, these casualty gains and losses are not grouped with the Section 1231 items.

4420 Basis and Holding Period of Assets

4420.01 In determining the taxpayer's investment (adjusted basis) in an asset, several cost factors must be considered.

```
    Original basis
  + Capital additions
  - Capital recoveries
  = Adjusted basis
```

    a. The basis of property must be adjusted by the cost of any improvements made since its acquisition. Real property taxes and mortgage interest on unimproved and unproductive real property may be capitalized at the election of the taxpayer.

    b. The basis of property must be reduced for depreciation and depletion (see section **4430**) along with other recoveries such as casualty losses.

4420.02 Establishing the basis of property acquisitions depends primarily on the method by which the property was acquired.

    a. **Standard purchase**—basis is cost.

    b. **Group purchase**—the cost is allocated to the individual assets in proportion to their fair market values.

    c. **Bargain purchase**—basis is the cost plus the bargain (fair market value at the date of the bargain purchase).

    d. **Inherited property**—basis is usually the fair market value at date of death.

        (1) Fair market value six months after death is an alternative for an estate tax return if this produces a lower value for the gross estate and a lower estate tax liability. The FMV at six months after death can only be used for basis if an estate tax return is filed using that FMV.

        (2) If the alternative value is chosen and property is disposed of before the 6-month period has expired, that property shall be valued at the fair market value at the date of disposition, the sale price.

e. **Gift property acquired since January 1, 1921:**

   (1) **Basis to compute gain**—donor's basis.

   (a) On gifts made before 1977, any gift taxes paid by the donor could be added to the donor's basis as long as the addition of the taxes did not cause the basis of the property in the donee's hands to exceed the fair market value of the property at the date of the gift.

   (b) On gifts made after 1976, the basis of the property is increased by the gift tax attributable to the net appreciation in the value of the gift property, but the donee's basis cannot be increased beyond the fair market value of the property at the date of the gift.

   (2) **Basis to compute loss**—lower of:

   (a) donor's basis plus the gift tax adjustment or

   (b) fair market value at date of gift.

   In certain situations, neither a gain nor a loss can be computed on the sale of property received by gift. In such a situation, the selling price is less than the basis for gain and more than the basis for loss.

   (3) **Basis for calculating depreciation**—use the gain basis.

   (4) **Basis of gifts made prior to 1921**—fair market value at date of gift.

f. **Personal property converted to income production:**

   (1) **Basis for gain**—adjusted basis of the asset at conversion minus allowable depreciation after conversion.

   (2) **Basis for loss**—lower of:

   (a) the adjusted basis of the asset at conversion minus allowable depreciation or

   (b) fair market value at conversion minus allowable depreciation thereafter.

   (3) **Basis for calculating depreciation**—lower of:

   (a) the adjusted basis of the asset at conversion or

   (b) fair market value at conversion.

g. **Property received as compensation for services:** basis is the fair market value of the property when received.

h. **Property transferred to a controlled corporation:**

   (1) The basis of stock received for property transferred to a controlled corporation is equal to the basis of the property exchanged plus any recognized gain on the exchange minus any cash and/or other property received.

   (2) The basis of property acquired by the corporation is the same as it was in the possession of the transferor plus any gain recognized by the transferor on the exchange.

   (3) To qualify as a controlled corporation, persons transferring property to a corporation for its stock or securities must own 80% of the voting stock plus 80% of all other stock of the corporation immediately after the exchange.

i. **Taxable exchange**—basis is the fair market value of the property received.

j. **Acquisitions before March 1, 1913:**

   (1) **Basis for gain**—the higher of:

      (a) adjusted basis at March 1, 1913, or

      (b) the fair market value at March 1, 1913.

   (2) **Basis for loss**—the adjusted basis at March 1, 1913.

   (3) **Basis for calculating depreciation**—use the gain basis.

k. The calculation of basis for the following property acquisitions is covered in section **4440**.

   (1) Tax-free exchange

   (2) Involuntary conversion

   (3) Sale of personal residence

   (4) Wash sale

4420.03 Capital gains and losses, once determined, must be classified as either short term or long term depending on the holding period of the asset given up.

   a. Holding period requirements:

      (1) One year or less—short term

      (2) More than 12 months—long term

   b. The holding period for long-term capital gains and losses is measured as follows:

      (1) As a minimum, property must be held to that day of the 12th month following the month of acquisition that is numerically one day later than the date acquired.

      (2) If property is purchased on the last day of the month, it must be held to at least the first day of the 13th month.

   c. The holding period normally begins on the day that the basis originated.

   d. In transactions in which some portion of the basis of an asset carries forward, the holding period begins at the time the carryover basis originated.

   Example: If the donor's basis is used to establish the basis of gift property, the holding period for the donee begins at the time the donor's basis originated.

   If the fair market value is used as the basis of gift property (a loss situation), the holding period begins at the date of the gift.

   e. The statute provides that inherited property disposed of within one year shall be considered to have been held for more than one year.

4430 Cost Recovery (Depreciation, Depletion, and Amortization)

Depreciation

4430.01 A deduction is allowed for wear, tear, exhaustion, and normal obsolescence of property held for the production of income or for property used in a trade or business.

   a. This cost recovery process can take the form of depreciation, cost recovery, amortization, or depletion.

b. While depletion relates to natural resources, no depreciation, cost recovery, or amortization is available for the following:

(1) Personal property not used in a trade or business

(2) Inventory

(3) Land

4430.02 For assets acquired after 1986, depreciation is computed using the modified accelerated cost recovery system (MACRS). Under this system, the full cost of the property (including salvage value) is written off over a prescribed recovery period:

a. MACRS depreciation cannot be used for intangible property and property not depreciated in terms of years (units-of-production method).

b. Real estate:

(1) Under MACRS, real estate acquired after 1986 is depreciated using the straight-line method over the following periods:

Residential real estate	27.5 years
Nonresidential real estate placed in service before May 13, 1993	31.5 years
Nonresidential real estate placed in service after May 12, 1993	39.0 years

(2) Real property acquisitions are subject to the *mid-month convention.* One-half month's cost recovery is allowed in both the month of acquisition and the month of disposition.

c. Personal property:

(1) There are six recovery periods for personal property—3, 5, 7, 10, 15, and 20 years.

(a) Under MACRS, the 200% declining-balance method is used for the 3-, 5-, 7-, and 10-year properties. The 150% declining-balance method applies to the 15- and 20-year properties. Both methods switch to straight-line depreciation when that method produces a larger deduction.

(b) The 5- and 7-year properties are most common.

i. The 5-year class includes automobiles, general-purpose light trucks, computers, and office machinery (typewriters, calculators, copiers, etc.).

ii. The 7-year class includes heavy, special-purpose trucks and office furniture and fixtures (desks, filing cabinets, etc.).

(2) Generally, a half-year's recovery deduction is taken in the first year of use regardless of the month the property was placed in service (half-year convention).

(3) Basically, the recovery deduction is determined by applying a prescribed statutory percentage to the unadjusted basis of the property. The government provides tables listing the applicable percentages.

(4) A mid-quarter convention will apply to property acquired after 1986 if more than 40% of the value of the property acquired during a tax year is placed in service during the last quarter of the year.

(a) If the mid-quarter convention applies, property acquisitions must be grouped by the quarter they were acquired.

(b) A cost recovery deduction for each of these groups is computed as follows:

Acquisitions	Depreciation Allowable
1st quarter	10.5 months
2nd quarter	7.5 months
3rd quarter	4.5 months
4th quarter	1.5 months

(5) Disposal of personal property generally results in a cost recovery deduction in the year of disposal.

   (a) In most cases, a half-year of cost recovery is allowed in the year of disposition or retirement.

   (b) If the mid-quarter convention applies, the cost recovery will range from 1.5 months to 10.5 months of depreciation depending on which quarter the disposal of the property takes place.

(6) The taxpayer may elect to use the straight-line method of depreciation for personal property. This election is available on a class-by-class basis for each tax year.

(7) Bonus depreciation of 50% is allowed on qualifying property acquired in 2010 (or 2011 for certain long-lived property and transportation property).

(8) Under Section 179 of the Internal Revenue Code for 2010 and 2011, the taxpayer may elect to expense up to $500,000 of tangible personal property placed in service during the year. Both new and used property qualify. Property qualifying for Section 179 expensing also includes certain real property (qualified leasehold improvement property, qualified restaurant property, and qualified retail improvement property). The maximum deductible expensing amount with respect to qualifying real property is $250,000 for tax years beginning in 2010 and 2011.

   (a) The basis of the asset(s) must be reduced by the amount so expensed.

   (b) Two limits apply:

      1. The amount "expensed" cannot exceed the taxpayer's aggregate taxable income from trade or business activities. Amounts in excess of trade or business income that would otherwise be deductible are carried forward indefinitely.

      2. The ceiling amount of $500,000 is reduced dollar-for-dollar for personal property acquisitions in excess of $2,000,000 (i.e., if more than $2,500,000 of property is placed in service during a tax year, no Section 179 deduction is allowed).

   (c) The property must be purchased from an unrelated party.

d. Alternative depreciation system:

   (1) After 1986, an alternative depreciation system (ADS) must be used in certain computations.

      (a) To compute that portion of depreciation treated as a tax preference item for purposes of the alternative minimum tax

      (b) To calculate depreciation for property:

         i. Used predominantly outside the United States

         ii. Leased or used by a tax-exempt entity

         iii. Financed with the proceeds from tax-exempt bonds

         iv. Imported from countries engaged in discriminatory practices

      (c) To compute depreciation for earnings and profits purposes

   (2) Generally, depreciation under this method is calculated using the straight-line method without regard to salvage value.

   (3) Depreciation of personal property for the alternative minimum tax is calculated by using 150% declining-balance depreciation, switching to the straight-line method when appropriate to maximize deductions.

(4) The recovery period for the ADS is generally the ADR midpoint life of the asset.

(5) Taxpayers may elect to use ADS in lieu of MACRS.

e. The government publishes tables that automatically provide for each of the special conventions that a taxpayer may use in the year of acquisition for both real estate and personal property.

f. **Listed property:**

(1) Special rules apply to property suitable for both business and personal use (e.g., automobiles, computers).

(a) If business usage of such property is not more than 50%, the property does not qualify for regular (accelerated) MACRS or the Section 179 first-year expense. It must be depreciated under ADS using the straight-line method.

(b) If business usage exceeds 50%, the property is available for regular MACRS and Section 179 depreciation. If future business usage drops below 50%, a permanent switch to the straight-line method is required. In addition, previous cost recoveries in excess of straight-line depreciation must be recaptured as additional income.

(2) An additional limitation is placed on luxury automobiles. A dollar limit for depreciation is mandated for each year the car is in use. These dollar limits change on an annual basis.

(a) These limits must be reduced proportionately if business usage is less than 100%.

(b) Trucks, SUVs, and vans weighing over 6,000 pounds are not subject to the luxury automobile limits. Likewise, ambulances, hearses, taxis, and limousines are not subject to these limits.

Recovering the Cost of Leasehold Improvements and Intangible Assets

4430.03 Improvements made by the lessee that are made in lieu of rent are deductible as rent.

4430.04 Improvements made by the lessee that are *not* made in lieu of rent must be capitalized and written off using MACRS.

4430.05 Taxpayers generally amortize the cost of intangibles acquired after August 10, 1993, over a 15-year period on a straight-line basis, beginning with the month acquired.

a. Section 197 intangibles are a qualifying asset acquired and held in connection with the conduct of a trade or business. This includes goodwill, going-concern value, trademarks, and franchises.

b. Copyrights, patents, and covenants not to compete are included when acquired with the purchase of a business.

c. Intangibles not required to be written off over 15 years are amortized over their useful lives. Such assets include copyrights and patents acquired separately, not acquired with the purchase of a business.

d. Instruments, interests in land, financial interests, contracts, and leases of tangible personal property are excluded from the definition of Section 197 intangibles.

e. A loss cannot be recognized on the disposition of Section 197 intangibles if the taxpayer retains other Section 197 intangibles acquired in the same transaction.

Depletion

4430.06 **Depletion** is the process whereby owners of an economic interest in natural resources may recover the cost of their investment (e.g., oil, timber, gas, minerals).

4430.07 Two methods are available for computing depletion. Annually, the taxpayer must choose the method that gives the *greatest* depletion deduction for that year.

  a. **Cost depletion method:**

  (1) Divide the estimated number of units in a resource deposit into the cost or other adjusted basis of the property to obtain the cost depletion per unit.

  (2) Multiply this quotient by the number of extracted units that were sold for that year to obtain the cost depletion deduction.

  (3) Cost depletion is no longer applicable when the adjusted basis of the resource is reduced to $0.

  b. **Percentage depletion method:**

  (1) Percentage depletion is the *lesser* of the following two figures:

   (a) A flat percentage of gross receipts from the property. The percentage is specified by the government and varies according to the type of resource or

   (b) 50% of taxable income from the property before taking a depletion deduction.

  (2) Percentage depletion is not restricted to the cost basis of the resource. Consequently, taxpayers can recover through depletion deductions far more than they have invested in the resource.

  c. The cost basis of the resource must be reduced each year by the amount claimed as depletion, whether determined by the cost or the percentage method. The basis will not be reduced below $0, however.

4430.08 Timber is not available for percentage depletion; the cost method must be used.

4430.09 Percentage depletion is generally not available for oil and gas wells. Exceptions include certain domestic gas wells and small independent producers and royalty owners. Special rules apply to these interests.

Depreciation and Recovery Allowance Recapture

4430.10 Whereas IRC Section 1231 provides long-term capital gain treatment for certain noncapital assets, IRC Sections 1245 and 1250 deny this special treatment, where the gain represents a recovery of some or all of the depreciation or accelerated cost recovery system (ACRS) allowances previously deducted. IRC Sections 1245 and 1250 take precedence over IRC Section 1231.

4430.11 **IRC Section 1245 recapture:**

  a. IRC Section 1245 requires that any gain on IRC Section 1245 property will be treated as ordinary income to the extent of *all* depreciation or ACRS deductions taken.

  b. Any gain on IRC Section 1245 property which is not recaptured as ordinary income becomes IRC Section 1231 gain.

  c. IRC Section 1245 property refers primarily to equipment used in a trade or business. It also includes most buildings acquired during the ACRS recovery period (1981–1986).

d Depreciation/ACRS recapture rules do not apply when property is disposed of by gift or by transfer at death.

e. Gift property retains its ordinary income potential in the hands of the donee.

f. The charitable contribution deduction for Section 1245 property must be reduced by the amount that would have been recognized as ordinary income if the item had been sold at its fair market value.

g. In tax-free exchanges and involuntary conversions of Section 1245 property, depreciation or ACRS recapture is considered only to the extent that a gain is recognized on the exchange or conversion.

h. After June 6, 1984, any depreciation recapture resulting from an installment sale is to be recognized in the year of sale even if no proceeds are received.

4430.12 **IRC Section 1250 Property Rules:**

    a. IRC Section 1250 applies to real property—buildings and their structural components.

    b. IRC Section 1250 requires that excess depreciation (actual depreciation in excess of straight-line depreciation) be recaptured as ordinary income. However, this provision no longer applies since straight-line depreciation has been required on buildings acquired after 1986. Thus, there is no excess depreciation, and all of the depreciation is "unrecaptured."

    c. The unrecaptured gain on the sale of a building becomes IRC Section 1231 gain. If Section 1231 gains exceed Section 1231 losses for the current and past five years, the remaining gain receives long-term capital gain treatment. However, unrecaptured Section 1250 gain may be taxed at a special rate of 25%.

        (1) Unrecaptured Section 1250 gain is equal to the lesser of the gain or the total depreciation taken on the property.

        (2) Any gain not treated as unrecaptured Section 1250 gain is taxed at the regular 15% (0%) long-term capital gain rate.

        Example: A commercial building acquired at a cost of $2,028,000 was sold for $3 million after deducting straight-line depreciation of $650,000 over the years. Assuming that no other Section 1231 events affect this transaction, the taxation of the $1,622,000 gain is illustrated as follows.

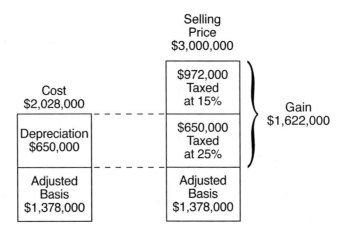

Because straight-line depreciation was used, no depreciation is recaptured as ordinary income. Consequently, there is unrecaptured Section 1250 gain of $650,000. This portion of the gain is taxed at 25%. The remaining gain of $972,000 is taxed at 15%.

d. The unrecaptured Section 1250 gain rules apply to individuals, not corporations.

e. Special rule for corporations (IRC Section 291):

(1) A corporation's ordinary income of the sale of IRC Section 1250 real property will be increased by 20% of the lesser of: (1) depreciation taken, or (2) the recognized gain.

Example: Over the years, $30,000 of straight-line depreciation was taken on a building costing $100,000. If this property is sold for $110,000, a gain of $40,000 results ($110,000-($100,000-$30,000)). The corporation must recognize $6,000 ($30,000 x 20%) of this gain as ordinary income under IRC Section 291.

(2) This provision does not affect Subchapter S corporations.

4440 Taxable and Nontaxable Sales and Exchanges

4440.01 Once the amount of gain or loss has been calculated, the amount of the gain or loss to be recognized for tax purposes must be computed.

a. Generally, gains on property transactions are recognized, but the recognized gain never exceeds the realized gain.

b. Losses on the sale, exchange, or condemnation of personal use assets are *not* recognized.

c. Losses on the sale of income-producing property to certain related parties are *not* recognized. However, the disallowed loss may be used by the related purchasing party to offset any gain on a later disposition of this property.

d. Gains are generally recognized in the year of the sale.

(1) Taxpayers using the installment method of reporting sales recognize and report their gain as the payments are received.

(2) The gain reported each year is determined by multiplying the gross profit percentage on the sale by the payments received that year.

(3) The installment method cannot be used to report losses.

e. In certain transactions, some or all of the gain or loss may be postponed.

(1) Postponement is possible in these transactions *only if replacement property is acquired.*

(2) Postponement is accomplished by modifying the basis of the new property according to the following guidelines:

(a) Postponed gains: *Decrease* the basis (FMV) of the new asset by the amount of the unrecognized gain.

(b) Postponed losses: *Increase* the basis (FMV) of the new asset by the amount of the unrecognized loss.

4440.02 Property transactions in which the gain or loss may be postponed by adjusting the basis of the replacement property include the following:

a. Tax-free exchange

b. Involuntary conversions (condemnation, casualty, theft)

c. Sale or exchange of a personal residence

d. Wash sale

4440.03 **Tax-free exchange:**

    a. To postpone a gain or loss, property held for productive use in a trade or business, or for investment, must be exchanged for property of like kind to be held for business or investment purposes.

        (1) Generally, this means that real estate must be traded for real estate and personalty for personalty. The trade must be U.S. property for U.S. property, and foreign property for foreign property.

        (2) There are restrictions on certain classes of tangible personal property. The following items may only be exchanged for similar items:

            (a) Office furniture, fixtures, and equipment

            (b) Computers and peripheral equipment

            (c) Airplanes

            (d) Automobiles and taxis

            (e) Buses

            (f) Light general-purpose trucks

            (g) Heavy general-purpose trucks

    b. Treatment of gains and losses:

        (1) If a gain is realized on the exchange of properties, the gain is recognized to the extent of the lesser of the gain realized or the FMV of the boot received. Any unrecognized gain is postponed.

        (2) A loss incurred in a tax-free exchange is generally not recognized. The unrecognized loss is postponed.

        (3) If boot is given in the exchange, gain or loss on the boot is recognized to the extent that the boot has appreciated or depreciated in value.

    c. The following property items are not tax-free exchange items:

        (1) Property held primarily for sale

        (2) Securities

    d. The following items do *not* qualify as like-kind items:

        (1) Real property for personal property

        (2) Livestock of different sexes

        (3) Interests in a partnership

    e. Tax-free exchanges *do* include the following special items:

        (1) Exchanges of the same type of stock in the same corporation

        (2) Transfer of property to a controlled corporation (80% owned)

            (a) No gain or loss is recognized if property is exchanged solely for stock or securities.

            (b) If cash or other property is received in addition to the securities, gain is recognized to the extent of the lesser of the gain realized or the cash or FMV of the other property received.

        (3) Certain types of corporate reorganizations, including the following:

            (a) A statutory merger or consolidation (Type A)

(b) An exchange of stock for voting stock (Type B)

(c) An exchange of assets for voting stock (Type C)

(d) A divisive reorganization—spin-offs, split-offs, split-ups (Type D)

f. The basis of property acquired in a tax-free exchange is equal to the adjusted basis of the property surrendered, *or*:

(1) the amount derived when the unrecognized gain is subtracted from the FMV of the new asset or

(2) the amount derived when the unrecognized loss is added to the FMV of the new asset.

4440.04 **Involuntary conversions** (condemnation, casualty, theft):

a. Gains:

(1) Taxpayer may elect to recognize the gain.

(2) Taxpayer may elect postponement.

(3) Taxpayer must recognize gains to the extent that there are proceeds left over after replacement of the asset.

b. Losses:

(1) If income-producing property, the loss is recognized.

(2) If nonincome-producing property, the loss is recognized only to the extent that the casualty or theft (but not a condemnation) exceeds $100 for each event.

(a) The deduction for casualty and theft losses on nonbusiness property is further limited to the excess of the loss over 10% of the adjusted gross income (AGI).

(b) Taxpayers experiencing several losses during the year may deduct the amount by which the combined losses (each reduced by $100) exceed 10% of AGI.

(3) In calculating the loss:

(a) The loss is limited to the decline in the fair market value immediately before and immediately after the event *or* the adjusted basis of the property, whichever is smaller.

(b) If business or income-producing property is completely destroyed, the adjusted basis may be deducted if it is greater than the fair market value immediately preceding the casualty.

(c) Insurance and/or other compensation received acts to reduce the loss.

c. If a taxpayer has both recognized gains and recognized losses from casualties and thefts involving nonbusiness assets, the gains and losses must be netted.

(1) If the recognized gains exceed the recognized losses, *all* gains and losses are treated as capital gains and losses.

(2) If the recognized losses exceed the recognized gains, *all* gains and losses are treated as ordinary. The net loss is deductible from AGI as an itemized deduction. Losses in excess of gains are subject to the 10% AGI limitation.

d. Taxpayers must also net gains and losses when there are both recognized gains and recognized losses from the involuntary conversion of trade or business property held for more than one year.

(1) If the gains exceed the losses, *all* casualty and theft gains and losses are combined with the other Section 1231 transactions (see section **4410.07–.10**).

(2) If the losses exceed the gains, the net loss is deductible as an ordinary loss.

e. The basis of the replacement property is equal to the cost of the property reduced by any unrecognized gain.

f. Replacement must take place within a period that begins on the date of destruction, condemnation, etc. or the date when the property was first threatened with condemnation, whichever is earlier.

(1) The period ends two years after the close of the tax year in which some part of the gain is realized.

(2) On the condemnation (as opposed to casualty and theft) of business and investment real property, the replacement period ends three years after the close of the tax year in which some part of the gain is realized.

(3) The replacement period for the involuntary conversion of a personal residence in a declared federal disaster area is extended to four years beyond the year of gain.

4440.05 **Sale or exchange of a personal residence:**

a. Individuals may exclude $250,000 ($500,000 on a joint return) of gain on the sale or exchange of a personal residence. Gains in excess of the excludible amount will be taxed. These excess gains may not be postponed by adjusting the basis of a replacement residence.

(1) The residence must have been owned and occupied by the taxpayer for an aggregate of at least two of the five years before the sale or exchange.

(2) The exclusion may be used only once every two years.

(3) The $500,000 exclusion is available to married taxpayers filing jointly if (a) *either* spouse satisfies the ownership test, (b) *both* spouses meet the occupancy test, and (c) neither spouse has used the exclusion within the last two years.

(a) When the spouse has used the exclusion within the past two years, an eligible taxpayer may still exclude $250,000 on either a joint return or a separate return.

(b) When a husband and wife each sell a principal residence, they are each eligible to exclude $250,000 on the sale of their residences. They may claim their exclusions on either a joint return or separate returns.

(c) A surviving spouse can exclude up to $500,000 from the sale of a principal residence if the sale is within two years of the date of death and the other requirements were met on the date of death.

(4) If the ownership and occupancy tests are not met, a prorated exclusion is available if the sale or exchange is the result of (a) change of place of employment, (b) health, or (c) unforeseen circumstances.

b. Losses are not recognized; neither are they postponed.

c. The basis of any new residence is its cost. There is no basis adjustment for unrecognized gains and losses.

4440.06 Wash sale:

   a. A wash sale takes place when securities are sold at a loss and replaced with substantially identical securities within 30 days *before* or *after* the sale.

   b. Such losses are not recognized—they are postponed. The disallowed loss increases the basis of the stock or securities acquired.

   c. This law does not apply to dealers.

4450 Amount and Character of Gains and Losses, and Netting Process

4450.01 The following summarizes the tax treatment of gains and losses.

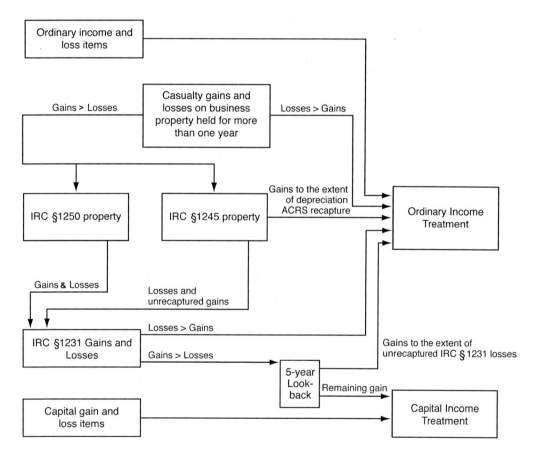

4450.02 The gain or loss on the disposal of property is computed by comparing the value of the assets received with the investment in the property given up.

```
   Amount realized
-  Adjusted basis
=  Gain or loss
```

4450.03 The amount realized on the disposition of property is equal to the net proceeds received for that property.

	Gross selling price
-	Selling expenses
=	Amount realized

  a. The gross selling price includes everything received for the property given up, including the following:

   (1) Cash

   (2) Fair market value of property and services received

   (3) Amount of mortgage on mortgaged property given up

  b. Selling expenses include advertising, legal fees, commissions, and any other costs required to effect the transfer of property.

4450.04 All items receiving capital gain or loss treatment should be classified as short term or long term and summarized as follows:

```
LTCG  ┐
(LTCL)─┴─ NLTCG (L) ┐
                    ├─ Net
STCG  ┐             │  Gain (Loss)
(STCL)─┴─ NSTCG (L) ┘
```

The result is either a net gain or a net loss.

4450.05 Net gains for individuals, estates, and trusts:

  a. Any of the net gain arising from short-term sales and exchanges receives ordinary income treatment.

  b. Any of the net gain arising from long-term sales or exchanges will be taxed at a maximum rate of 15% (0% for people in the 15% or 10% tax bracket). These are the same rates that apply to dividends. Note the following exceptions:

   (1) Unrecaptured Section 1250 gain (section **4430.12**) will be taxed at a maximum rate of 25%.

   (2) Taxable gains arising from the sale of collectibles (e.g., art, coins, antiques) and Section 1202 stock (section **4512.39**) will be taxed at a maximum rate of 28%.

  Note: The current 15% and 0% tax rates on long-term capital gains are currently set to expire after December 31, 2010. Starting in 2011, the long-term capital gains rates are set to go back to 20% and 10% for lower income taxpayers. At the time of publication, there is a possibility that the 15% and 0% tax rates may be retained.

4450.06 Net losses for individuals, estates, and trusts:

  a. If the taxpayer has a net loss, up to $3,000 may be deducted in the current year as a deduction toward adjusted gross income (reported on Schedule D).

  b. Short-term losses are used before long-term losses.

  c. Both short-term and long-term losses are deductible dollar-for-dollar.

  d. Any remaining capital loss will be carried forward indefinitely.

  e. The carryover will be treated as STCL or LTCL depending on its origin.

4450.07 Special netting procedures:

    a. Long-term capital gain and loss items are netted in the following manner. Separately list 28% gains (losses), 25% gains, 15/0% gains (losses), then:

        (1) Offset any 28% losses against 25% gains, then against 15/0% gains. If a loss still exists, offset it against any available net short-term gain. Any remaining loss is eligible for the $3,000 deduction. A loss in excess of $3,000 carries forward indefinitely.

        (2) Offset any 15/0% losses against 28% gains, then 25% gains. Offset any remaining loss against available net short-term gain. If a loss remains, it is eligible for the $3,000 deduction. A loss in excess of $3,000 carries forward indefinitely.

        (3) While losses can result from the sale of 28% and 15/0% items, the 25% situation involves only gains (by definition).

    Summary of the netting process for long-term capital gains and losses:

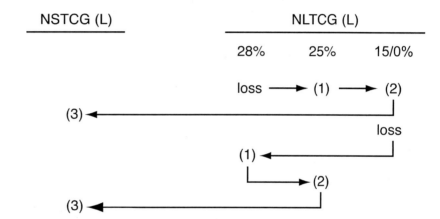

When the netting process produces a net long-term capital gain, the gain is used to absorb any net short-term capital loss. Any remaining 28%, 25%, or 15/0% gains will be taxed at those rates (see short-term netting process in part b, following).

Example: Taxpayer with $250,000 of taxable income (33% tax bracket) has no short-term gains and losses, but does have the following long-term capital gains and losses:

    (a) 28% gain from the sale of stamp collection—$4,000

    (b) 25% gain from unrecaptured depreciation on sale of a commercial building—$105,000

    (c) 15% loss from sale of stock held as investment—$65,000

In this situation, taxpayer first offsets the $65,000 loss against the $4,000 gain. The remaining loss of $61,000 then offsets the 25% gain of $105,000. The remaining NLTCG of $44,000 is taxed at 25%.

    b. Short-term capital gains and losses are netted to produce a net short-term gain or loss.

        (1) If the result is a gain, the gain is used to absorb any net long-term capital loss. Any remaining short-term capital gain is taxed as ordinary income.

        (2) If the netting process results in a net short-term capital loss, the loss will offset available net long-term capital gain in the following order: 28% gains, 25% gains, and 15/0% gains. If a loss remains, up to $3,000 may be deducted as a deduction for AGI. Any additional loss is carried forward indefinitely.

> **Example:** If the taxpayer in the preceding example also had a net short-term capital loss of $15,000, the loss would offset the NLTCG of $44,000. The remaining $29,000 gain would be taxed at 25%.

(3) Capital losses of individuals carry forward as either long-term or short-term depending on their origin. However, short-term losses are used first in calculating the $3,000 deduction.

4450.08 **Net capital gains for corporations:**

a. Corporate capital gains are taxed as ordinary income.

b. Before 1987, corporate capital gains received favorable tax treatment through an alternative tax.

4450.09 **Net capital losses for corporations:**

a. Corporations are not allowed to deduct capital losses in excess of capital gains from ordinary income.

b. Capital losses of a corporation can only be used to offset capital gains.

c. All net capital losses carry back three years and forward five years as *short-term* capital losses.

4460 Related Party Transactions

4460.01 IRC Section 267 places certain restrictions on related party transactions. One of these restrictions is that there is a disallowance of the recognition of any losses from the sale or exchange of property, directly or indirectly, between related parties. If the property, on which loss is derived in a related party transaction, is later sold to an unrelated party, any gain on that sale is reduced by the previously disallowed loss.

> **Example:** Father sells property to Son (a related party) at a loss of $10,000, which is not recognized due to the related party rules. If Son later sells the property to an unrelated party at a gain of $14,000, Son only has to recognize a $4,000 gain (realized gain of $14,000 - $10,000 related party disallowed loss).

4460.02 IRC Section 267 also contains a special rule dealing with expenses that are unpaid to a related party at the end of the tax year.

a. This rule only applies in a transaction between related parties where the related party that will have the deduction is on the accrual basis and the related party that will receive the income is on the cash basis.

b. This rule states that the accrual-basis related party can only deduct the expense to the cash-basis related party, when the cash-basis related party includes the payment in income (generally when it is actually received).

c. This effectively means that the related accrual basis payor is on the cash basis as to deduction of this payment.

4460.03 For purposes of IRC Section 267, related parties are:

a. brothers and sisters, spouses, ancestors, and lineal descendents,

b. a corporation and a shareholder, if the shareholder owns (directly or indirectly) more than 50% by value of the outstanding stock of the corporation,

c. two corporations that are members of a controlled group, and

d. a series of other relationships between trusts, corporations, and individuals.

4460.04 Constructive ownership rules apply in determining if two taxpayers are related. Under these rules, a taxpayer is considered to own stock owned by:

a. a family member (brother or sister, spouse, ancestor, or lineal descendent),

b. a proportionate share of any stock owned by an entity (partnership, corporation, estate, or trust) of which the taxpayer is a member, and

c. partners of the taxpayer (if the taxpayer is a partner in a partnership).

4470 Estate and Gift Taxation

4470.01 Updates to estate and gift tax rules may be found in IRS Publication 950.

4470.02 As a result of the Tax Reform Act of 1976, the estate tax and the gift tax are computed under a unified rate schedule.

4471 Transfers Subject to the Gift Tax

4471.01 The gift tax is levied against the donor on the fair market value of all taxable gifts made in each calendar year. The gift tax is an excise tax levied on the transfer of property where less than adequate and full consideration was received.

4471.02 A gift tax return is required by each donor who makes gifts of a present interest in property, where the total value of such gifts to any one donee exceeds $13,000 during the year.

a. Any gift of a future interest in property must be reported on a gift tax return.

b. The gift tax return (Form 709) is filed on a calendar-year basis, and the due date for filing the return and paying the tax is April 15.

c. Gifts in excess of $13,000 to a qualified charity do not require a gift tax return if the donor's entire interest in the property was transferred.

4471.03 The gift tax formula is as follows:

```
    Gross gifts for the current period
  − Deductions
  = Taxable gifts for the current period
  + Taxable gifts from prior periods
  = Total taxable gifts by the donor
  × Unified tax rate
  = Gift tax on total gifts
  − Gift tax computed on prior gifts using the unified tax rate
  = Tentative tax on current gifts
  − Applicable credit ($345,800)
  = Tax due on gifts of the current period
```

4472 Annual Exclusion and Gift Tax Deductions

4472.01 Gross gifts:

a. Gross gifts include only the fair market value of gifts made to a donee in excess of $13,000 during the year due to the annual exclusion.

b. Exclusions:

(1) Although the first $13,000 of gifts made to each donee in each calendar year is excluded in determining the amount of gross gifts for the year, gifts of future interest are not available for the $13,000 exclusion and must be included in gross gifts in their entirety.

(2) The following payments are not subject to the federal gift tax:

(a) Tuition payments made to an educational organization on another's behalf

(b) Medical care payments for the health care of another person; payments must be made directly to the care provider

(c) Transfers to political organizations

4472.02 Gift splitting:

a. Gift splitting may be used by married taxpayers to reduce the amount of property subject to the gift tax. This technique reduces the total amount of gift taxes payable.

b. The donor's spouse may elect to treat the donor's gift as though the gift was made one-half by each.

c. Each spouse will then apply the $13,000 annual exclusion to the gifts made to each donee.

d. Each spouse will also apply the gift tax applicable credit, or that portion of it that still remains available, against the gift tax liability.

e. Since each taxpayer must compute the gift tax individually (a joint return for gift taxes is not permissible), the half of the gift reported by each spouse will be taxed in a lower tax bracket than would be the case if the entire gift were credited to one

4472.03 Deductions from gross gifts:

a. **Charitable deduction:** An unlimited deduction is available for charitable contributions where the value of such contributions has been included in gross gifts.

b. **Marital deduction:** An unlimited deduction is available for all property given to a spouse. No deduction is allowed, however, where the interest given to the spouse is terminable.

4473 Determination of Taxable Estate

4473.01 The estate tax is imposed on the estate of the decedent rather than on the beneficiaries. Consequently, the executor of the decedent's estate is generally responsible for the payment of the tax.

4473.02 Generally, the estate tax return (Form 706) must be filed and the tax paid within nine months after the death of the decedent, if a tax return is required. As of November 1, 2010, there is no U.S. estate tax in effect for citizens or residents dying in the year 2010. Under current law, the estate tax will be restored in the year 2011.

4473.03 The estate tax formula is as follows (when the estate tax is restored in 2011):

```
    Gross estate
  − Deductions:
      Funeral expenses
      Administration expenses
      Debts of the decedent
      Casualty losses
      Charitable bequests (unlimited)
      Marital deduction (unlimited)
  = Taxable estate
  + Post-1976 taxable gifts
  = Total post-1976 transfers
  × Unified tax rate
  = Unified tax on total post-1976 transfers
  − Unified tax previously paid on post-1976 gifts
  = Tentative estate tax
  − Applicable credit ($345,800)
  − Other credits
  = Estate tax
```

4473.04 Gross estate:

    a. The gross estate includes all property, regardless of location, in which the decedent had an interest at the time of death. The taxable estate of nonresident aliens is limited to property situated within the United States.

    b. The value of property included in the decedent's gross estate is generally the fair market value of such property at the date of decedent's death.

        (1) The executor of the estate may elect an alternate valuation date that is six months after the date of the decedent's death if this election reduces both the gross estate and the federal estate tax liability.

        (2) If the alternate valuation date is elected and the property is distributed during this 6-month period, the property is valued at its fair market value at the date of distribution.

    c. Examples of properties included in the gross estate:

        (1) Joint ownerships:

            (a) Husbands/wives: A spouse's estate should include the following:

                i. One-half of community property

                ii. One-half of property held by spouses in joint tenancy or tenancy by the entirety

            (b) Tenants in common: Include only decedent's share of property.

            (c) Joint tenants (other than spouses): Include only that portion of the property that reflects the decedent's contribution to the total cost of the property.

        (2) Lifetime transfers of property by the decedent where certain privileges were retained:

            (a) Transfers with a retained life estate

            (b) Transfers with the power to alter, amend, revoke, or terminate the transfer

        (3) Properties in which the decedent possessed a general power of appointment—special powers of appointment are not included

        (4) Life insurance proceeds payable to the estate and proceeds from policies in which the decedent possessed any of the incidents of ownership: power to change beneficiaries, revoke an assignment, cancel the policy, or pledge the policy for a loan

(5) Income earned by the decedent at the time of death

(6) Gift taxes paid on gifts made within three years of death

4473.05 **Deductions from the gross estate:**

a. The following items may be deducted from the gross estate:

(1) Funeral expenses

(2) Expenses incurred in the administration of the decedent's estate

(3) Debts of the decedent

(4) Casualty and theft losses occurring during the period of administration

(5) Charitable bequests (these *must* have been specified by the decedent)

(6) The value of all property left outright to the surviving spouse (marital deduction) but not property with a terminable interest

b. The resulting taxable estate is then subject to taxation under the unified gift and estate tax rate schedule.

4473.06 **Estate tax structure:**

a. The taxable estate must be combined with taxable gifts made after 1976 to determine total life and death transfers made after 1976.

b. The unified transfer tax is computed on the total of these transfers.

c. This unified transfer tax is then reduced by any taxes previously paid on post-1976 gifts.

d. The applicable tax credit is used to offset the remaining tax.

e. Other tax credits may also be available.

4473.07 **Estate tax credits:**

a. **Tax on prior transfers:** Where property included in the decedent's estate was recently taxed in a prior estate, all or part of the estate tax paid by the prior estate will be allowed as a credit to the decedent's estate.

b. **Foreign death taxes:** A limited credit is available to U.S. citizens and residents for death taxes paid to foreign countries.

c. **Gift taxes:** A limited credit is allowed for gift taxes that have been paid on any property that is included in the donor-decedent's gross estate.

4474 Marital Deduction

4474.01 In computing the gift tax, an unlimited marital deduction is available for gifts made to the donor's spouse. Therefore, a donor can generally transfer an unlimited amount of gifts to a spouse free of the gift tax.

4474.02 For the gift tax marital deduction to apply, the spouse must be a U.S. citizen at the time of the gift.

4474.03 A gift tax marital deduction does not apply to a transfer of a terminable interest in property. A terminable interest is one that will terminate on a lapse of time or on the occurrence, or failure to occur of a contingency.

4474.04 An unlimited marital deduction is also allowed against the estate tax. For this deduction to apply:

- **a.** the decedent must be married and survived by their spouse,
- **b.** the spouse must be a U.S. citizen,
- **c.** the property must be included in the decedent's gross estate and pass to the surviving spouse, and
- **d.** the spouse's interest in the property must not be a terminable interest.

4475 Unified Credit

4475.01 The unified credit is a credit that allows donors and decedents to transfer a limited amount of property without being subject to the gift or estate tax.

4475.02 For 2011 (as of publication date), the exemption amount for both the gift and estate tax is $1,000,000. This is the amount of property that a taxpayer may transfer free of either the gift or estate tax. This results in an applicable credit for estate tax of $345,800 in 2011 (no estate tax in 2010). The gift tax remains in effect for 2010. Taxable gifts given during the taxpayer's lifetime reduce the applicable credit against the estate tax.

4475.03 For 2011 (as of publication date), the unified credit amount is $345,800 (no estate tax in 2010). This credit offsets the tax due on the first $1,000,000 transferred by gift or through the estate.

This page intentionally left blank.

Section 4500
Federal Taxation of Individuals

4510 Gross Income
  4511 Inclusions and Exclusions
  4512 Characterization of Income

4520 Reporting of Items from Pass-Through Entities

4530 Adjustments and Deductions to Arrive at Taxable Income

4540 Passive Activity Losses

4550 Loss Limitations

4560 Taxation of Retirement Plan Benefits

4570 Filing Status and Exemptions

4580 Tax Computations and Credits

4590 Alternative Minimum Tax

4510 Gross Income

4511 Inclusions and Exclusions

4511.01 **Gross income** is all income from whatever source, except for those items that are specifically excluded by the Internal Revenue Code.

  a. Gains are included in gross income in the year in which the gain is realized as determined by the taxpayer's accounting method (cash or accrual basis).

   (1) Cash-basis taxpayers report income when they actually or constructively receive cash or property.

   (2) Taxpayers using the accrual method of accounting report income in the year when the right to the income becomes fixed and the amount can be determined with reasonable accuracy.

      (a) If reported income is properly accrued on the basis of a reasonable estimate and, in a subsequent year, the exact amount is higher than estimated, the difference is reported as income in the year that such a determination is made.

      (b) An amended return is not required.

  b. Income received in advance is generally taxed in the year in which it is received, even though the accrual basis is used.

  c. Mere appreciation in the value of property is not considered income. The property must be converted into cash or other property before a gain is realized.

4511.02 In computing gross income, the taxpayer faces two problems:

    a. Recognizing potential income items

    b. Identifying those income items specifically excluded by law

4512 Characterization of Income

4512.01 A complete list of potential income items and exclusions is impossible. Many items can only be identified as includible or excludible after the facts of the individual case have been examined. This portion of the tax review lists selected items that are frequently encountered.

4512.02 **Alimony and separate maintenance payments:**

    a. Excluding the portion that is designated for child support, qualified payments are included in the gross income of the recipient and deductible from gross income by the payor if the payments are made after:

        (1) decree of divorce or separate maintenance,

        (2) written separation agreement, or

        (3) decree for support (this applies to periods pending finality of divorce or legal separation).

    b. Qualified payments are required to meet the following guidelines:

        (1) Payments must be in cash.

        (2) Payments must terminate at the death of the recipient.

        (3) Payments cannot be made to a payee who lives in the same household as the payor.

        (4) Payments cannot be specified as something other than alimony.

    c. Special rules apply if alimony payments in the second or third year decrease by more than $15,000 from the payments made in the previous year.

        (1) If the change in payments exceeds statutory limits, recapture of excessive alimony payments will result.

        (2) All of the recapture will take place in the third year.

             (a) The payor must include the excess amounts in gross income.

             (b) The payee is allowed to deduct the excess payments from gross income to arrive at adjusted gross income.

    d. Any amount that can be identified as *child support* cannot be treated as alimony.

        (1) Child support payments are not deductible by the payor nor are they income to the recipient.

        (2) If both child support and alimony are provided for in the agreement, any amounts paid are first considered to be child support until that obligation is met.

    e. The transfer of property between divorcing spouses in exchange for release from marital obligations is nontaxable after July 18, 1984. The basis of the transferred property to the transferee will be the same as it was to the transferor.

4512.03 Annuity proceeds:

    a. The taxpayer may exclude from income that portion of any annuity proceeds which represents the recovery of the taxpayer's previously taxed investment. Excess proceeds are included in gross income.

    b. To determine the portion of annuity proceeds that is excluded from gross income, an exclusion ratio is applied against the amount received:

$$\frac{\text{Taxpayer's investment in contract}}{\text{Total expected return on contract}} \times \text{Amount received}$$

        (1) Life expectancy tables (annuity tables) are used to compute the expected return on the contract.

        (2) The exclusion ratio, once computed, does not change. It is used each year until the taxpayer's total investment in the annuity is recovered. Additional receipts are fully taxed.

    c. For qualified retirement plan annuities starting after November 18, 1996, a different procedure applies:

$$\frac{\text{Taxpayer's investment in contract}}{\text{Number of anticipated monthly payments}} = \text{Amount excluded}$$

        (1) The number of anticipated monthly payments is determined from the following table:

Age of Annuitant on Annuity Starting Date	Number of Anticipated Monthly Payments
55 and under	360
56-60	310
61-65	260
66-70	210
71 and over	160

        (2) The number of payments requires adjustment when the annuity payments are not made on a monthly basis. For example, if the number of payments is fixed, the number of payments becomes the denominator.

    d. In "b" and "c" above, the "taxpayer's investment" includes only non-deductible (fully taxed) amounts invested.

    e. If the annuitant dies before the total investment is recovered, the remaining investment is deductible as an itemized deduction on the decedent's final return.

4512.04 Bargain purchase:

    a. Property purchased at a cost less than market value by an employee or shareholder is a bargain purchase.

    b. The difference between fair market value and cost is income at the time of purchase.

    c. The taxpayer's basis for the purchased property is market value.

    d. Generally, property purchased by an employee under an employee discount policy does not constitute a bargain purchase. However, certain employee discounts may create income under the bargain purchase provisions.

        (1) If the discount is for merchandise, the excludible amount cannot exceed the selling price of the item to the public multiplied by the employer's gross profit percentage.

        (2) If the discount is for services, the discount exclusion is limited to 20% of the price at which it is offered to the public.

4512.05 **Bequests:**

    a. The value of property received by bequest, devise, or inheritance is excluded from gross income.

    b. Income produced by such property is taxable.

4512.06 **Canceled debt:**

    a. Generally, a canceled debt is income to the debtor when the cancellation is not intended to be a gift.

    b. The presence or absence of consideration is a vital factor in determining whether or not a gift was intended.

    c. Where a seller cancels a buyer's indebtedness, the buyer can generally avoid income recognition by electing to reduce the basis of the property by the amount of the debt discharged.

    d. Discharge of indebtedness due to debtor insolvency or federal bankruptcy law is generally not included in gross income but is used instead to reduce the basis of assets or other items carrying favorable tax attributes, such as loss or credit carryovers.

    e. A shareholder's cancellation of a corporation's indebtedness is treated as a contribution of capital.

    f. Some *states* make loans to students under an agreement that the loan will be canceled if the student works in a certain profession within the state after graduation.

        (1) The canceled debt is excluded from gross income.

        (2) This exclusion also applies to loans from tax-exempt charitable organizations. However, the debt cancellation cannot relate to services performed for the lender organization.

4512.07 **Child support:**

    a. Amounts received as child support are not included in the income of the recipient.

    b. Child support cannot be deducted by the payor but may be used to measure support for a possible dependency exemption under pre-1985 agreements.

4512.08 **Childcare facilities:**

    a. The value of child and dependent care services provided by the employer are excludible up to $5,000 per year ($2,500 for married persons filing separately).

    b. The exclusion cannot exceed the taxpayer's earned income or, if married, the earned income of the spouse with the lesser amount of earned income.

4512.09 **Damages collected:**

    a. Compensatory damages received under a suit for physical injury or sickness are excluded from income.

    b. Punitive damages and damages for loss of profits are income.

4512.10 **Dividends of cash or property:**

    a. Generally, dividends are taxable when received.

    b. A special dividend tax rate of 15% applies (0% for taxpayers in the 15% or 10% tax brackets).

- c. If the taxpayer has a choice of stock or cash:
  - (1) Any cash received is income.
  - (2) Any stock received is income to the extent of the fair market value of the stock.
    - (a) The basis of the new stock is also the fair market value of the stock.
    - (b) The holding period for the new stock begins on the date the dividend is received.
- d. Stock dividends that do not result in a disproportionate distribution are not considered income. Likewise, stock splits do not produce income for the shareholders.
  - (1) The basis of original shares must be allocated between the new and the original shares.
  - (2) The holding period of the acquired stock is the same as that of the old stock.
- e. Any distribution of stock or stock rights made to preferred shareholders is taxable as a dividend.
  - (1) The fair market value of the property received constitutes income and establishes the basis of that property.
  - (2) The holding period for this property begins at the date of receipt.
- f. Property received as a dividend is income.
  - (1) The fair market value of the property on the date of distribution constitutes income.
  - (2) The basis of the property is also equal to the fair market value.
  - (3) The holding period of the property acquired begins on the date the property is received.
- g. Amounts received in a partial or complete liquidation are treated as follows:
  - (1) A return of capital *until* the taxpayer's investment is recovered
  - (2) A capital gain after the taxpayer's investment is recovered

4512.11 Employee death benefit:

- a. Employer payments to the employee's survivors will be taxed unless the payment qualifies as a gift.

4512.12 Farming income:

- a. The cash-basis farmer includes in gross income all cash receipts and the value of all property received from the sale of livestock and produce raised or bought for resale. Income received from any other source is also included.
  - (1) Insurance proceeds may be included in the next year's income if the taxpayer can prove that the destroyed crop's income would have been included in next year's income.
  - (2) Tangible personal property must be depreciated under the MACRS 150% declining-balance method.
  - (3) The income from a sale of a crop should be included in the year the crop is sold. The farmer may have pledged his crop to secure a Commodity Credit Corporation loan; the farmer may then report the loan proceeds in the year received rather than when the crop was sold.

    b. Schedule F (Form 1040, Farm Income and Expenses) is the schedule that all farmers should file. Schedule SE is also needed for the computation of self-employment tax earnings.

    c. The accrual-basis farmer computes gross income from farming as follows:

          Ending inventory of produce and livestock raised or bought for sale
      + All farming receipts for the year
      − Beginning inventory of the products and livestock held for resale
      − <u>Cost of inventory items bought during the year</u>
      = <u>Gross income from farming</u>

    d. Farming income is essentially the same as income from any other business.

4512.13 **Gambling winnings and losses:**

    a. All gambling winnings are included in gross income.

    b. Losses are deductible as an itemized deduction, but only to the extent of winnings.

4512.14 **Gifts:**

    a. The value of gifts received is excluded from income.

    b. Income generated by property received as a gift is taxable.

4512.15 **Group-term life insurance:**

    a. Where the employer pays the premiums on nondiscriminatory group-term life insurance for its employees, the cost of insurance coverage in excess of $50,000 is considered as income to the employee.

    b. *Any* amount paid by the employee for the group-term life insurance can be used to reduce this income.

4512.16 **Employer contributions to a health savings account:**

    a. Within limits, employer contributions to an employee's health savings account (HSA) are excluded from the employee's income.

    b. Both employer and employee contributions are combined to determine the maximum allowable contribution.

    c. Contributions to an HSA are limited:

        (1) Individuals may deduct (for AGI) contributions to an HSA equal to 65% of the insurance deductible. The percentage is 75% for family coverage.

        (2) Employer contributions to an employee's HSA are excluded from income. However, both employer and employee contributions are combined to determine the maximum allowable contribution.

        (3) After 2007, no new contributions may be made to HSAs except by or on behalf of those people who already have an HSA or those employees who work for a participating employer.

4512.17 **Illness or injury benefits:**

    a. Benefits received for physical injury and sickness are excluded if received:

        (1) under the Workers' Compensation Act,

        (2) as compensatory damages from a suit or settlement, or

        (3) under self-purchased accident and health insurance.

- **b.** Benefits received under an employer-financed accident and health plan may be exempt from taxation.
    - (1) Contributions by the employer to accident and health plans for personal injury or sickness are excludible.
    - (2) Payments received under the plan for medical care and permanent injury are excludible.
    - (3) Health and accident benefits other than those listed are income to the extent they are attributable to the employer's contribution.

4512.18 Improvements made by lessee:
- **a.** Generally, the value of improvements made by the lessee is not income to the lessor, and the basis of such improvements to the lessor is $0.
- **b.** If the improvements are made in lieu of rent, improvements are income to the lessor.
    - (1) The income is recognized in the year improvements are completed.
    - (2) The market value of the improvements is the amount recognized as income.
    - (3) The landlord's basis in such improvements is the market value.

4512.19 Income from illegal acts:
- **a.** Income from illegal activities is included in gross income.
- **b.** Legitimate business expenses incurred to produce such income are deductible as a business expense.
- **c.** In the case of illegal drug trafficking, only the cost of goods sold is deductible. No other expenses can be deducted.

4512.20 Interest:
- **a.** Generally, all interest received (or accrued if using the accrual method) or available for withdrawal is taxable.
- **b.** Interest on state and municipal obligations is excluded from gross income.
- **c.** Interest on U.S. savings bonds may be reported in the year accrued or postponed until the year of surrender by a cash-basis taxpayer.
- **d.** Amortization of premiums on taxable bonds is treated as an offset to interest income on bonds acquired after 1987.
- **e.** Imputed interest:
    - (1) Certain lenders may be required to recognize imputed interest income on loans made below the market rate of interest. The interest rate is published by the IRS and reflects the rate paid by the government on new borrowing. The interest is compounded semi-annually.
    - (2) Imputed interest applies to the following types of below-market loans:
        - (a) Loans made out of love, affection, or generosity (gift loans)
        - (b) Loans to employees
        - (c) Loans to shareholders
        - (d) Tax avoidance loans

(3) Imputed interest will affect the lender and borrower in the following manner:

    (a) The lender must recognize interest income, and the borrower will have interest expense.

    (b) The amount of the imputed interest will be considered as a payment from the lender to the borrower. In most situations, this payment will be treated as a gift, as compensation, or as a dividend between the two parties.

(4) Exceptions:

    (a) No interest is imputed on gift loans of $10,000 or less between individuals, unless the loan proceeds are used to purchase income-producing property. Employee and shareholder loans of $10,000 or less are also exempt unless tax avoidance is the principal purpose of the loan.

    (b) Imputed interest cannot exceed the borrower's net investment income on loans of $100,000 or less between individuals.

    (c) No interest will be imputed if the borrower's net investment income is $1,000 or less and the loan is not more than $100,000, unless the purpose of the loan is tax avoidance.

4512.21 Life insurance proceeds:

a. Life insurance proceeds paid by reason of death are not taxed as income (except for a policy received in a transfer for a valuable consideration).

    (1) A lump-sum payment of the principal sum is fully excluded from gross income.

    (2) The interest portion of any installment payments is taxable.

b. Dividends received on unmatured policies are not taxed unless the amount received exceeds the consideration (premiums) paid.

    (1) Dividends received before maturity of the policy are considered as a return of premium.

    (2) Dividends collected after maturity of the policy are fully taxable.

c. Qualified individuals may generally "cash-out" their life insurance policy before death and receive tax-free treatment for the amount received.

    (1) **Qualifications:** Insured person must be terminally or chronically ill.

    (2) For chronically ill persons, the exclusion is limited to their unreimbursed long-term care costs paid by the amount received. Terminally ill taxpayers may use the proceeds for any purpose.

    (3) Generally, the proceeds from the assignment or sale of a life insurance policy will also qualify for this tax-free treatment.

4512.22 Meals and lodging:

a. If meals are served on the premises of the employer and are for the convenience of the employer, the value of such meals is not income.

b. To exclude lodging from income, lodging on the premises must also be a condition of employment.

c. The rental value of housing provided for a minister is tax exempt as is a housing allowance used to pay for housing.

4512.23 Pensions:

    a. Pensions paid to retirees are generally taxable.

    b. Payments made under the Railroad Retirement Act or the Social Security Act are generally nontaxable.

        (1) A portion of the taxpayer's Social Security and Railroad Retirement benefits may be included in gross income.

        (2) Basically, the amount includible is the lesser of:

            (a) one-half of the benefits received or

            (b) one-half of the excess of:

                1. AGI (with modifications) plus one-half of the benefits received *over*

                2. the base amount.

                    i. The base amount is $25,000 for singles, $32,000 for married persons filing jointly, and $0 for married persons filing separately.

                    ii. For this calculation, AGI must be modified to include excludible income earned outside of the United States and tax-exempt interest.

        (3) Additionally, when the taxpayer's provisional income (modified AGI plus one-half of the benefits received) exceeds $34,000 (singles) or $44,000 (married persons filing jointly), the following rules apply:

            (a) If provisional income exceeds $34,000 ($44,000 for married persons filing jointly), the amount of the benefits subject to tax is the lesser of:

                1. 85% of the benefits received or

                2. the sum of:

                    i. 85% of the excess of provisional income over $34,000 ($44,000) plus

                    ii. the lesser of:

                        1) the amount included under the basic rules listed previously or

                        2) $4,500 ($6,000 for married persons filing jointly).

            (b) Married persons filing separately will include in income the lesser of:

                1. 85% of the benefits received or

                2. 85% of the provisional income.

4512.24 Prizes and awards:

    a. Prizes and awards are generally taxable.

    b. Awards given in recognition of achievement in religious, charitable, scientific, educational, artistic, literary, or civic areas are generally taxable. These types of awards may be excluded from gross income if:

        (1) the taxpayer is selected through no action on their part,

        (2) the taxpayer need not perform any substantial future services for the award, and

        (3) the award is transferred to a government unit or charitable organization before the taxpayer receives any benefit from it.

    c. Awards given in recognition of safety achievement or length of service are not taxable if the award is tangible personal property valued at not more than $400.

4512.25 Rents and royalties:

    a. Royalties are included in gross income.

    b. Rent is taxable when received if the taxpayer uses the cash basis; when accrued, if on the accrual basis.

    c. Prepaid rental income is recognized in the year received whether the taxpayer is on the accrual or the cash basis.

    d. Personal residence:

        (1) When a personal residence is rented out for less than 15 days, no rental income is recognized and expenses are not required to be prorated between personal use and rental use.

        (2) When a personal residence is rented out for more than 14 days, the rental income is recognized and the expenses must be allocated between personal use and rental use. A portion of mortgage interest and real estate taxes must be allocated to reduce the rental income. Taxpayers cannot deduct a loss from renting a personal residence.

4512.26 Recoveries (tax benefit rule):

    a. If an income tax benefit was obtained by deducting an item on a previous tax return, any amount recovered must be included in current gross income.

    b. If no tax benefit was received in prior years as a result of the item, no income is recognized on current recoveries.

4512.27 Scholarships and fellowships:

    a. A degree candidate may exclude scholarships and fellowships to the extent the amount received is used for tuition, course fees, books, and supplies. Amounts used for room and board are taxable.

    b. Amounts received are taxable if specific services, such as teaching, are required to receive the scholarship or fellowship.

    c. Any amount paid to a nondegree candidate is taxable.

4512.28 Educational assistance:

    a. Amounts paid by the employer for educational expenses (tuition, fees, books, and supplies) are excludible from gross income. The annual exclusion is limited to $5,250.

    b. The exclusion applies to both undergraduate- and graduate-level courses.

4512.29 Stock options:

    a. An employee receiving a qualified incentive stock option will not realize income when it is granted or exercised.

    b. A sale of the stock will produce long-term capital gain if the sale occurs more than one year after exercise and two years after grant.

    c. However, when computing the alternative minimum tax, the taxpayer generally must include the excess of the fair market value of the incentive stock options exercised during the year over the option price.

4512.30 Stock rights:

a. Generally, the distribution of stock rights does not constitute income. Exceptions include the following:

(1) The option to receive cash or other property in lieu of money

(2) A distribution of stock rights made on preferred stock

b. Nontaxable stock rights:

(1) No income is recognized when rights are received.

(2) The basis of the rights received is generally $0.

(a) The taxpayer may elect to allocate a portion of the basis of the underlying stock to the rights according to the relative fair market values of each at the time of distribution.

(b) If the fair market value of the rights at the date of distribution is 15% or more of the fair market value of the stock on which they are issued, the basis of the stock *must* be allocated between the stock and the rights according to the relative fair market values of each.

(3) The holding period for stock acquired through the exercise of the rights begins at the date of exercise.

c. Taxable stock rights:

(1) Gross income is realized to the extent of the fair market value of the rights at the time of distribution.

(2) The basis of the rights received is equal to the fair market value of the rights.

(3) The holding period for stock acquired through exercise of the rights begins at the date of exercise.

d. The basis of the stock acquired through the exercise of the rights is equal to the subscription price plus the basis of the rights.

4512.31 Unemployment compensation:

a. All unemployment compensation benefits are includible in income.

b. Company-financed supplemental benefits are taxed.

c. Guaranteed annual wage payments are taxed.

d. For 2009, the first $2,400 was excluded from taxable income. This deduction has not been extended to 2010, although Congress could take action later in 2010. (**Note:** As of the publication date, the deduction had not been extended to 2010.)

4512.32 Foreign income exclusion:

a. Certain taxpayers may elect to exclude foreign earned income of up to a maximum of $91,500 per year for 2010. Exclusion must be calculated on a daily (per diem) basis.

b. Taxpayers may also elect to exclude those housing costs incurred that exceed 16% of the foreign earned income exclusion amount. The amount of housing costs excluded is also subject to a maximum of 30% of the foreign earned income exclusion amount. The amount of housing costs excluded reduces the foreign earned income exclusion available. The foreign earned income and housing cost exclusions may be elected separately or together.

c. To qualify for these exclusions, the taxpayer must be a bona fide resident of a foreign country for an entire taxable year *or* must be physically present in a foreign country for 330 full days out of 12 consecutive months.

4512.33 **Income in respect of a decedent:**

a. Only amounts properly includible as income at the time of death under the decedent's method of accounting are included as income on the decedent's final tax returns.

b. Income in respect of a decedent is the income that the decedent had a right to receive at the time of death that was not included on the final return. This income is taxed to the decedent's estate or to the person who receives it as a result of the decedent's death.

4512.34 **Educational savings bonds:**

a. Interest on Series EE and Series I U.S. savings bonds may be excluded from gross income if the redemption proceeds are used for qualified higher education expenses.

b. Requirements include the following:

(1) The bonds must be issued after December 31, 1989.

(2) The bonds must be issued to a person at least 24 years old.

(3) A joint return is required, if married.

c. Qualified higher education expenses mean tuition and fees required to enroll the taxpayer, spouse, or dependent in an eligible educational institution. These expenses do not include room and board.

d. Qualified expenses must be reduced by scholarships and similar benefits not included in gross income.

e. When the redemption proceeds (including interest) exceed the education expenses, only a portion of the interest is excluded from income:

$$\frac{\text{Education expenses}}{\text{Redemption proceeds (including interest)}} \times \text{Interest} = \text{Interest exclusion}$$

f. In addition, the exclusion is phased out when AGI (with modifications) exceeds a threshold amount. For 2010, the phaseout begins at $70,100 ($105,100 for joint returns).

4512.35 **Adoption assistance programs:**

a. Qualified adoption expenses paid or incurred by an employer for an employee's adoption of a child are excluded from the employee's income.

b. Payments must be pursuant to a written, nondiscriminatory adoption assistance program.

c. The exclusion is limited to $12,150 per child.

d. The allowable exclusion is phased out ratably as the employee's AGI rises from $182,180 or more and is completely phased out if the employee has MAGI of $222,180 or more.

4512.36 **Coverdell Education Savings Account:**

a. Distributions from a Coverdell Education Savings Account are excluded from the income of the student (beneficiary of the account) if the funds are used to pay qualified education expenses.

(1) The student must be under age 30.

(2) Qualified expenses include the following postsecondary education expenses: tuition, fees, books, supplies, equipment, and room and board. For room and board to

qualify, the student must attend school on at least a half-time basis in a program leading to a recognized education credential.

- (3) Qualified expenses also include elementary and secondary school tuition and expenses. Tuition to both public and private schools is allowed.

- (4) The Hope and Lifetime Learning tax credits (see section **4580.19**) may be claimed in the same year as a distribution from a Coverdell Education Savings Account as long as the proceeds from the distribution are not used for qualified expenditures toward these education credits.

b. When distributions exceed qualified educational expenses, some of the distributed earnings are taxed and some are excluded from income.

- (1) $$\frac{\text{Qualified educational expenses}}{\text{Total distributions}} \times \text{Earnings} = \text{Excluded earnings}$$

- (2) Earnings − Excluded earnings = Taxable earnings

- (3) Distributions are treated as a pro rata distribution of contributions and earnings. Thus, if 25% of the account balance is earnings, 25% of the distribution is earnings.

c. Setting up a Coverdell Education Savings Account:

- (1) Taxpayers may contribute up to $2,000 per child (beneficiary) per year to a Coverdell Education Savings Account. The amount is nondeductible.

- (2) Contributions must be for a child of the taxpayer or any other child under the age of 18.

- (3) Contribution limits:

    - (a) The annual $2,000 contribution limit is phased out proportionately between the following AGI levels:
        - i. Singles: $95,000–$110,000
        - ii. Joint filers: $190,000–$220,000
        - iii. Corporations and other entities making contributions to Coverdell Education Savings Accounts are not subject to the phase-out rules.

    - (b) The maximum annual contribution to anyone's Coverdell account is $2,000.

    - (c) The deadline for making contributions is April 15 of the following year.

d. Unused balance:

- (1) When the beneficiary reaches age 30, any unused amount in the savings account must be distributed to the beneficiary.

- (2) Any earnings included in the distribution will be added to the beneficiary's gross income and taxed.

- (3) An additional 10% penalty tax on the earnings will also apply to the beneficiary.

- (4) Unused amounts may be rolled over tax- and penalty-free into a Coverdell Education Savings Account of a child or a sibling or spouse of the beneficiary (if the person is under age 30).

4512.37 **Parking and transportation provided by employer:**

    a. Up to $230 per month in 2010 can be excluded for parking provided by the employer.

        (1) Employees can have a choice between cash and employer-provided parking.

        (2) If cash is selected, it is included in gross income.

    b. Up to $120 per month can be excluded for employer-provided transit passes and transportation in a commuter highway vehicle between home and work. Starting in February 2009 the amount is raised to $230 per month and remains in effect in 2010.

    c. Up to $20 per month can be excluded for qualified bicycle commuting reimbursement. This benefit can be paid for any month that the employee uses the bicycle regularly to commute to work.

4512.38 **Qualified state tuition programs:**

    a. Some states and private institutions make it possible for parents to prepay their children's college tuition and lock in current tuition rates.

    b. If the child does not go to college, the payments, plus interest, are refunded to the parents. The interest is included in the parent's gross income.

    c. When the accumulated funds are used to pay qualified higher education expenses, the entire distribution, including earnings, is tax-free.

    d. Qualified higher education costs include tuition, fees, books, supplies, room and board, and equipment needed to complete course requirements.

4512.39 **Section 1202 small business stock:**

    a. Noncorporate taxpayers may exclude 50% of the gain on the sale or exchange of qualified small business stock held for more than five years. For qualified stock purchased in 2010, the excludable is 75%.

        (1) Eligible gain cannot exceed the greater of $10 million or 10 times the taxpayer's basis in the stock.

        (2) The stock must be C corporation stock acquired as original issue stock.

        (3) Corporate assets cannot exceed $50 million at the date of issuance.

        (4) At least 80% of the assets must be used in the active conduct of a trade or business.

        (5) Service-based corporations do not qualify (e.g., law, insurance, engineering, architecture).

    b. Any gain not excluded under this provision is capital gain.

4512.40 **Employee contributions to retirement plans:**

    a. Employees who participate in their company's retirement plan may exclude (defer) from the current year's income amounts they contribute to the plan within the following guidelines for 2010.

        (1) Participants in 401(k) plans, 403(b) annuities, and SEP programs may elect to contribute and defer taxes on a maximum of $16,500. Taxpayers age 50 and above may make an additional "catch-up" contribution of $5,000.

        (2) Employees participating in a SIMPLE plan may contribute and defer taxes on $11,500. Taxpayers age 50 and above may make an additional "catch-up" contribution of $2,500.

  b. Contributions and their subsequent earnings are taxed when withdrawn from the plan.

  c. Qualified employer contributions to the program and related earnings are also taxed when withdrawn from the plan.

4520 Reporting of Items from Pass-Through Entities

4520.01 Certain domestic corporations may elect not to be taxed. Instead, the income is passed through to the stockholders, who are taxed on their share of the corporation's earnings. Stockholders are taxed on their share of the earnings even though the earnings are not distributed.

4520.02 Each shareholder must include on their personal tax return their share of the corporation's income or loss and special items from the corporate tax year that has ended with or within the personal tax year. Thus, income is recognized on a basis similar to that of partnerships.

  a. Where ownership has changed during the year, each owner must recognize a pro rata share of the income or loss allocated on a daily basis.

  b. Loss pass-throughs in excess of the taxpayer's basis in the corporation may be carried forward indefinitely and deducted when the taxpayer's basis has increased sufficiently to absorb the loss.

4520.03 Distributions of cash and property are basically given the same treatment. Shareholders must recognize as a distribution the amount of cash and the fair market value of any property distributed.

  a. The taxability of a distribution is determined by its source.

  b. Distributions come from the following sources in the order listed:

    (1) Distributions are first considered to come from an "accumulated adjustments account" (AAA).

     (a) The AAA represents income earned after 1982 adjusted by any additions and subtractions that shareholders were required to make to the basis of their stock for this period. However, no adjustment is made for the following:

      i. Tax-exempt income

      ii. Corporate expenses not deductible in computing taxable income and not chargeable to a capital account

     (b) Distributions from the AAA are nontaxable.

    (2) Distributions are then considered as dividends to the extent of any accumulated earnings and profits (E&P).

    (3) Beyond accumulated E&P, distributions represent a return of capital and then a capital gain.

  c. If an S corporation distributes appreciated property to its shareholders, the transfer is treated as if the property had been sold to the shareholders at fair market value.

    (1) A gain is recognized at the corporate level.

    (2) The gain is subsequently passed through to the shareholders.

4520.04 Partnerships are not taxable entities. They are reporting entities. Partnerships function as a conduit for income tax purposes and are therefore passed through to the individual.

    a. Ordinary income and losses along with special gain and loss items channel through the partnership down to the individual partners, who report these items on their personal tax returns.

    b. The partnership must report each partner's distributive share of the ordinary gain or loss as well as any specially treated items that the partner might use on an individual return.

    c. Self-employment taxes apply to all ordinary income passing to the owners.

4530 Adjustments and Deductions to Arrive at Taxable Income

4530.01 In computing the tax of individuals, special attention must be given to three different income concepts: gross income, adjusted gross income, and taxable income.

4530.02 **Gross income** includes all income from whatever source derived minus certain exclusions that are specifically provided for by law.

    a. It is the gross income figure that is used to determine whether or not a person must file a tax return.

    b. Gross income is also one of the standards used to determine whether a person may be claimed as the dependent of another taxpayer.

4530.03 **Adjusted gross income** (AGI) is determined by subtracting business expenses and other deductions allowed by the Internal Revenue Code from gross income.

    a. Deductible from gross income are the following:

        (1) Expenses of producing business income (Schedule C)

        (2) The net capital loss deduction (Schedule D)

        (3) Expenses of producing rent and royalty income (Schedule E)

        (4) Educator's expenses (teacher's supplies): expired December 31, 2009, but Congress may extend (**Note:** As of the publication date, the deduction had not been extended to 2010.)

        (5) Certain expenses for reservists, performing artists, and fee-basis government officials

        (6) Contributions to a Health Savings Account (Form 8889)

        (7) Job-related moving expenses (Form 3903)

        (8) 50% of self-employment tax (Schedule SE)

        (9) Contributions to retirement plans, including IRAs

        (10) 100% of self-employed health insurance premiums

        (11) Penalty on early withdrawal of savings

        (12) Alimony payments

        (13) Qualified student loan interest up to $2,500

        (14) Qualified higher education expenses (tuition and fees; Form 8917): expired December 31, 2009, but Congress may extend (**Note:** As of the publication date, the deduction had not been extended to 2010.)

(15) Domestic production activities deduction (Form 8903)

 b. AGI is used as a standard for limiting the amount recognized for such items as medical expenses, casualty losses, charitable contributions, and the dependent care credit.

4530.04 **Taxable income** is adjusted gross income minus the larger of itemized deductions or the standard deduction, and minus exemptions.

 a. Itemized deductions include nonbusiness casualty and theft losses and qualified personal expenditures incurred for such items as the following:

  (1) Medical and dental care in excess of 7.5% of AGI

  (2) State and local taxes

  (3) Mortgage interest expense, limited to two residences

  (4) Charitable contributions

  (5) Casualty losses that exceed 10% of AGI

  (6) Investment expenses, including investment interest

  (7) Unreimbursed employee expenses

  (8) Tax preparation fees

  (9) Other miscellaneous deductions

 b. The standard deduction is an alternative to itemizing deductions. The standard deduction is used when it exceeds total itemized deductions.

  (1) The amount of the basic standard deduction is as follows.

	2010
Single	$ 5,700
Married, filing jointly	11,400
Surviving spouse	11,400
Head of household	8,400
Married, filing separately	5,700

  (2) The basic standard deduction may be increased by an additional standard deduction for age 65 or over and/or blind.

   (a) An additional standard deduction is allowed in each of the following situations:

    i. Taxpayer and/or spouse is 65 on or before January 1st of the following taxable year.

    ii. Taxpayer and/or spouse is blind on December 31st of the current taxable year.

   (b) The amount of each additional standard deduction is as follows:

	2010
Single	$1,400
Married, filing jointly	1,100
Surviving spouse	1,100
Head of household	1,400
Married, filing separately	1,100

   (c) In 2010, the maximum additional standard deduction is $2,800 for an unmarried person (if the individual meets both the age and blindness requirements) and $4,400 for married persons filing jointly (if both spouses meet both the age and blindness requirements).

(3) For **2008 and 2009**, the basic standard deduction may be increased (using Schedule L) by an additional standard deduction for non-itemizers for state and local real estate taxes and net disaster losses attributed to federally declared disasters. These deductions are **not available for 2010**.

    (a) State and local real estate taxes that would otherwise qualify as itemized deductions can be deducted at the lesser of the amount paid or $500 ($1,000 for married filing jointly). This standard deduction item is not available for 2010; it could be extended by Congress. (**Note:** As of the publication date, the deduction had not been extended to 2010.)

    (b) Net disaster losses attributable to federally declared disasters are calculated on Form 4684 (Casualties and Thefts).

    (c) If a taxpayer paid any state or local sales or excise taxes for the purchase of an automobile after February 16, 2009, the amount paid may be added to the standard deduction. To take this deduction, a taxpayer's AGI reported must be less than $135,000 (single) or $260,000 (joint). The allowable deduction is limited to the tax on a purchase price of $49,500 for each new vehicle. This standard deduction item is not available for 2010; it could be extended by Congress. (**Note:** As of the publication date, the deduction had not been extended to 2010.)

(4) A special limitation applies to persons who may be claimed as dependents.

    (a) A dependent's standard deduction is limited to the greater of $950 or the dependent's earned income plus $300. These amounts are increased by any additional standard deduction to which the dependent is entitled (earned income).

    (b) The deduction cannot exceed the normal standard deduction allowed by law for single taxpayers.

(5) The following taxpayers are not eligible to use the standard deduction, so they must itemize:

    (a) A married taxpayer filing separately where the other spouse itemizes deductions

    (b) A nonresident alien

    (c) A taxpayer filing for a period of less than 12 months

c. **Exemptions**

(1) An exemption of $3,650 is allowed in 2010 to the taxpayer for each of the following:

    (a) Taxpayer, if not eligible to be claimed as a dependent of another taxpayer

    (b) Taxpayer's spouse, if:

        i. a joint return is filed or

        ii. separate returns are filed and the spouse has no income and is not the dependent of another taxpayer

    (c) Qualified dependents—persons who qualify in one of the following three groups:

        1. **Qualifying Relative:** A qualifying relative is anyone who meets the following five tests but does not meet the definition of a qualifying child (defined below).

            i. **Gross income test:** The dependent must have less than $3,650 of gross income.

ii. **Support test:** The taxpayer must furnish more than half of the support of the dependent. (Exception—multiple support agreements)

iii. **Relationship test:** The dependent must be a closer relative than a cousin **or,** if not related must live in taxpayer's household for the entire tax year.

iv. **Joint return test:** The dependent must not have filed a joint return in a situation where a tax return was required.

v. **Citizenship test:** The dependent must be a U.S. citizen or resident of the United States, or a resident of Canada or Mexico.

2. **Qualifying Nonrelative:** A qualifying nonrelative must meet all of the following tests that apply to relatives.

    i. **Gross income test.**

    ii. **Support test.**

    iii. **Joint return test.**

    iv. **Citizenship test.**

    v. In addition, an unrelated person must live with the taxpayer for the entire year.

3. **Qualifying Child:** A qualifying child must meet all the following conditions.

    i. **Relationship:** The child must be the taxpayer's son, daughter, stepson, stepdaughter, eligible foster child or descendant of such a child, **or** the taxpayer's brother, sister, stepbrother, stepsister, half-brother, half-sister, or descendants of such relatives.

    ii. **Age:** The child must be under the age of 19, or under the age of 24 and a full-time student for at least part of five calendar months.

    iii. **Citizenship:** The child must be a citizen or resident of the United States, or a resident of Canada or Mexico.

    iv. **Principal residence:** The child must have the same principal residence as the taxpayer for more than half of the year.

    v. **Not self-supporting:** The child must not have provided more than 50% of their own support during the tax year.

    vi. **Joint return:** The child must not have filed a joint return in a situation where a tax return was required.

    vii. **Note:** A qualifying child is not subject to the "gross income test" and the "over half support test" that apply to qualifying relatives.

(d) A multiple support agreement may give the taxpayer the exemption if no one person contributed more than half the support, and:

1. more than half of the support was provided by two or more persons otherwise entitled to the exemption,

2. the taxpayer provided more than 10% of the support, and

3. all other persons who provided more than 10% of the support declare they will not claim the exemption in the current year.

(e) The exemption for children of divorced or legally separated parents will go to the parent who has custody of the child for the greater period of time unless there is a written agreement to the contrary.

(2) For 2010, there are no phaseout limits for exemptions, so all taxpayers can subtract the full amount of the exemption from taxable income. No additional exemption is available in 2010.

4530.05 **The tax table** is used by individuals to find their tax if taxable income is less than $100,000. Taxable income is computed by figuring AGI and subtracting deductions and exemptions. The table is broken down by single, married filing jointly, married filing separately, and head of household. If a person's taxable income is $100,000 or more, the tax rate schedules must be used to compute the tax.

A portion of the 2010 tax table for individuals follows:

If taxable income is...		And you are...			
At least:	But less than:	Single	Married filing jointly	Married filing separately	Head of household
$5,000	$5,050	$503	$503	$503	$503
5,050	5,100	508	508	508	508
5,100	5,150	513	513	513	513
5,150	5,200	518	518	518	518

4530.06 **Tax rate schedules** are available according to the filing status of the taxpayer.

a. There are six brackets (10%, 15%, 25%, 28%, 33%, and 35%) applicable to each filing status. To compute the tax, the taxpayer must choose from one of the following schedules, which are ranked in the order of desirability. (The tax table is organized on a similar basis.)

(1) Married (couples) filing joint return and surviving spouse

(2) Unmarried head of household

(3) Single individual

(4) Married individual filing separate return

b. A separate rate schedule applies to estates and trusts.

c. Special rates also apply to long-term capital gains and dividends.

(1) The maximum rate is generally 15%.

(2) However, the rate is 0% for taxpayers in the 15% and 10% tax brackets.

d. **Surviving spouses** may use the joint return rate schedule for the two tax years following the year in which the death of the husband or wife occurred if the following conditions are met:

(1) Spouse must be unmarried.

(2) Spouse must maintain a home as the household of a dependent son or daughter for the entire year.

(3) Spouse must have been entitled to file a joint return in the deceased's final tax year.

e. **Head of household** is available to the taxpayer who meets the following requirements:

(1) Unmarried individual, other than a nonresident alien or one who qualifies as a surviving spouse.

(2) Maintains his or her home as the principal place of abode for one or more of the persons described as follows:

  (a) A "qualifying child" (see section **4530.04.c**)

   i. However, a "qualifying child" who is married must meet the dependency tests of a relative.

   ii. Other children who do not meet the definition of a "qualifying child" (e.g., a child age 25) must also meet the dependency tests of a relative.

  (b) A relative who qualifies as a dependent other than through a multiple support agreement

   Exception: Dependent parents need not live with the taxpayer as long as the taxpayer maintains their household.

 (3) The taxpayer's household must be a qualified person's abode for "more than half" of the taxable year.

f. A portion of the 2010 tax rate schedule for single individuals follows:

Over:	But not over:	The tax is:	Of the amount over:
$ 0	$ 8,375	10%	$ 0
8,375	34,000	$ 837.50 + 15%	8,375
34,000	82,400	4,681.25 + 25%	34,000
82,400	171,850	16,781.25 + 28%	82,400
171,850	373,650	41,827.25 + 33%	171,850
373,650	---	108,421.25 + 35%	373,650

4530.07 **Unearned income** of minor children may be taxed at their parents' highest tax rate. This provision applies if:

a. one of three age requirements are met:

 (1) the child is under age 18 at year-end,

 (2) the child is age 18 at year-end and did not have earned income that was more than half of the child's support, or

 (3) the child is over age 18 and under age 24 at year-end and a full-time student and did not have earned income that was more than half of the child's support;

b. the child has at least one living parent;

c. the child has net unearned income of more than $1,900; and

d. the child does not file a joint return for the year.

4530.08 **Child's interest and dividends:** Parents may elect to report a child's interest and dividends on their tax return. Under this election, the child does not have to file a tax return.

a. This election is available only if the child meets all of the following criteria:

 (1) Under age 19 or under age 24 if a full-time student at year-end

 (2) Has income only from interest and dividends

 (3) Has gross income of more than $950 but less than $9,500

 (4) Has made no estimated tax payments for the year

 (5) Does not have a tax overpayment from the preceding year applied to the current year

 (6) Has not had tax withheld from the current year's income

 (7) Does not file a joint return for the year

b. To qualify for this election, the taxpayer (parent) must meet one of the following requirements:

(1) Parents file a joint return

(2) Parents file separate returns, but taxpayer has higher taxable income than spouse

(3) Taxpayer is the custodial parent

4530.09 **Income averaging for farmers:** Individual taxpayers may elect to compute their current-year tax liability by using a special 3-year averaging method for income attributable to the trade or business of farming.

4540 Passive Activity Losses

4540.01 **Losses and credits from passive activities:**

a. Generally, losses from passive activities may only be used to offset income from passive activities.

(1) Passive losses cannot be used to offset the following:

(a) Active income: wages, salaries

(b) Portfolio income: dividends, interest, royalties, annuities

(2) Unused passive losses carry forward to offset passive income in future years. In the year in which the taxpayer's entire interest in a passive activity is terminated, any remaining unused loss on that activity may be deducted in full.

b. Any tax credits related to passive activities can only be used to offset taxes attributable to passive income.

(1) Excess credits carry forward to offset future taxes on passive income.

(2) Carryover credits on a terminated activity may be lost forever if they cannot be fully utilized in the year of disposition.

c. Passive activities include the following:

(1) Trade or business in which the taxpayer does not materially participate

(2) Rental activities

(3) Limited partnership activity

d. Rental real estate exceptions:

(1) Certain taxpayers may deduct real estate rental losses from active and portfolio income. This treatment applies to taxpayers who materially participate in a real property trade or business. Both individuals and closely held C corporations may qualify.

(a) Individuals must meet these tests:

i. More than 50% of their personal services must be rendered to a trade or business involving real estate.

ii. At least 750 hours must be spent in such services during the year.

iii. A married couple meets these requirements only if one spouse separately satisfied both tests.

(b) A closely held C corporation meets the test if more than 50% of its gross receipts is from a real property trade or business.

(2) Other taxpayers who qualify as active participants in a rental real estate activity may also deduct losses from such activities against active and portfolio income.

    (a) Generally, up to $25,000 of losses from such activities may be deducted against active income and portfolio income.

    (b) This $25,000 deduction limit is reduced by 50% of the taxpayer's AGI in excess of $100,000.

    (c) To qualify for the $25,000 deduction, the taxpayer must:

        i. actively participate in the rental activity (e.g., be involved in decision making) and

        ii. own at least 10% of the activity.

4550 Loss Limitations

Calculation of Gain or Loss

4550.01 The gain or loss on the disposal of property is computed by comparing the value of the assets received with the investment in the property given up.

    Amount realized (section **4550.02**)
  − Adjusted basis (section **4420**)
  = Gain or loss

4550.02 The amount realized on the disposition of property is equal to the net proceeds received for that property.

    Gross selling price
  − Selling expenses
  = Amount realized

    a. The gross selling price includes everything received for the property given up, including the following:

        (1) Cash

        (2) Fair market value of property and services received

        (3) Amount of mortgage on mortgaged property given up

    b. Selling expenses include advertising, legal fees, commissions, and any other costs required to effect the transfer of property.

Recognition of Gain or Loss

4550.03 Once the amount of gain or loss has been calculated, the amount of the gain or loss to be recognized for tax purposes must be computed.

    a. Generally, gains on property transactions are recognized, but the recognized gain never exceeds the realized gain.

    b. Losses on the sale, exchange, or condemnation of personal use assets are *not* recognized.

    c. Losses on the sale of income-producing property to certain related parties are *not* recognized. However, the disallowed loss may be used by the related purchasing party to offset any gain on a later disposition of this property.

  d. Gains are generally recognized in the year of the sale.

    (1) Taxpayers using the installment method of reporting sales recognize and report their gain as the payments are received.

    (2) The gain reported each year is determined by multiplying the gross profit percentage on the sale by the payments received that year.

    (3) The installment method cannot be used to report losses.

  e. In certain transactions, some or all of the gain or loss may be postponed.

    (1) Postponement is possible in these transactions *only if replacement property is acquired.*

    (2) Postponement is accomplished by modifying the basis of the new property according to the following guidelines:

      (a) Postponed gains: *Decrease* the basis (FMV) of the new asset by the amount of the unrecognized gain.

      (b) Postponed losses: *Increase* the basis (FMV) of the new asset by the amount of the unrecognized loss.

4550.04 Property transactions in which the gain or loss may be postponed by adjusting the basis of the replacement property include the following:

  a. Tax-free exchange:

    (1) To postpone a gain or loss, property held for productive use in a trade or business, or for investment, must be exchanged for property of like kind to be held for business or investment purposes.

      (a) Generally, this means that real estate must be traded for real estate and personalty for personalty. The trade must be U.S. property for U.S. property, and foreign property for foreign property.

      (b) There are restrictions on certain classes of tangible personal property. The following items may only be exchanged for similar items:

        i. Office furniture, fixtures, and equipment

        ii. Computers and peripheral equipment

        iii. Airplanes

        iv. Automobiles and taxis

        v. Buses

        vi. Light general-purpose trucks

        vii. Heavy general-purpose trucks

    (2) Treatment of gains and losses:

      (a) If a gain is realized on the exchange of properties, the gain is recognized to the extent of the lesser of the gain realized or the FMV of the boot received. Any unrecognized gain is postponed.

      (b) A loss incurred in a tax-free exchange is generally not recognized. The unrecognized loss is postponed.

      (c) If boot is given in the exchange, gain or loss on the boot is recognized to the extent that the boot has appreciated or depreciated in value.

(3) The following property items are not tax-free exchange items:

    (a) Property held primarily for sale

    (b) Securities

(4) The following items do *not* qualify as like-kind items:

    (a) Real property for personal property

    (b) Livestock of different sexes

    (c) Interests in a partnership

(5) Tax-free exchanges *do* include the following special items:

    (a) Exchanges of the same type of stock in the same corporation

    (b) Transfer of property to a controlled corporation (80% owned)

        i. No gain or loss is recognized if property is exchanged solely for stock or securities.

        ii. If cash or other property is received in addition to the securities, gain is recognized to the extent of the lesser of the gain realized or the cash or FMV of the other property received.

    (c) Certain types of corporate reorganizations, including the following:

        i. A statutory merger or consolidation (Type A)

        ii. An exchange of stock for voting stock (Type B)

        iii. An exchange of assets for voting stock (Type C)

        iv. A divisive reorganization—spin-offs, split-offs, split-ups (Type D)

(6) The basis of property acquired in a tax-free exchange is equal to the adjusted basis of the property surrendered, *or*:

    (a) the amount derived when the unrecognized gain is subtracted from the FMV of the new asset or

    (b) the amount derived when the unrecognized loss is added to the FMV of the new asset.

b. Involuntary conversions (condemnation, casualty, theft):

(1) Gains:

    (a) Taxpayer may elect to recognize the gain.

    (b) Taxpayer may elect postponement.

    (c) Taxpayer must recognize gains to the extent that there are proceeds left over after replacement of the asset.

(2) Losses:

    (a) If income-producing property, the loss is recognized.

    (b) If nonincome-producing property, the loss is recognized only to the extent that the casualty or theft (but not a condemnation) exceeds $100 for each event (in 2010).

        i. The deduction for casualty and theft losses on nonbusiness property is further limited to the excess of the loss over 10% of the adjusted gross income (AGI).

ii. Taxpayers experiencing several losses during the year may deduct the amount by which the combined losses (each reduced by $100 in 2010) exceed 10% of AGI.

(c) In calculating the loss:

i. The loss is limited to the decline in the fair market value immediately before and immediately after the event *or* the adjusted basis of the property, whichever is smaller.

ii. If business or income-producing property is completely destroyed, the adjusted basis may be deducted if it is greater than the fair market value immediately preceding the casualty.

iii. Insurance and/or other compensation received acts to reduce the loss.

(3) If a taxpayer has both recognized gains and recognized losses from casualties and thefts involving nonbusiness assets, the gains and losses must be netted.

(a) If the recognized gains exceed the recognized losses, *all* gains and losses are treated as capital gains and losses.

(b) If the recognized losses exceed the recognized gains, *all* gains and losses are treated as ordinary. The net loss is deductible from AGI as an itemized deduction. Losses in excess of gains are subject to the 10% AGI limitation.

(4) Taxpayers must also net gains and losses when there are both recognized gains and recognized losses from the involuntary conversion of trade or business property held for more than one year.

(a) If the gains exceed the losses, *all* casualty and theft gains and losses are combined with the other Section 1231 transactions (see section **4410.07–.10**).

(b) If the losses exceed the gains, the net loss is deductible as an ordinary loss.

(5) The basis of the replacement property is equal to the cost of the property reduced by any unrecognized gain.

(6) Replacement must take place within a period that begins on the date of destruction, condemnation, etc. or the date when the property was first threatened with condemnation, whichever is earlier.

(a) The period ends two years after the close of the tax year in which some part of the gain is realized.

(b) On the condemnation (as opposed to casualty and theft) of business and investment real property, the replacement period ends three years after the close of the tax year in which some part of the gain is realized.

(c) The replacement period for the involuntary conversion of a personal residence in a declared federal disaster area is extended to four years beyond the year of gain.

c. **Sale or exchange of a personal residence:**

(1) Individuals may exclude $250,000 ($500,000 on a joint return) of gain on the sale or exchange of a personal residence. Gains in excess of the excludible amount will be taxed. These excess gains may not be postponed by adjusting the basis of a replacement residence.

(a) The residence must have been owned and occupied by the taxpayer for an aggregate of at least two of the five years before the sale or exchange.

(b) The exclusion may be used only once every two years.

(c) The $500,000 exclusion is available to married taxpayers filing jointly if (1) *either* spouse satisfies the ownership test, (2) *both* spouses meet the occupancy test, and (3) neither spouse has used the exclusion within the last two years.

   i. When the spouse has used the exclusion within the past two years, an eligible taxpayer may still exclude $250,000 on either a joint return or a separate return.

   ii. When a husband and wife each sell a principal residence, they are each eligible to exclude $250,000 on the sale of their residences. They may claim their exclusions on either a joint return or separate returns.

   iii. A surviving spouse can exclude up to $500,000 from the sale of a principal residence if the sale is within two years of the date of death and the other requirements were met on the date of death.

(d) If the ownership and occupancy tests are not met, a prorated exclusion is available if the sale or exchange is the result of (1) change of place of employment, (2) health, or (3) unforeseen circumstances.

(2) Losses are not recognized; neither are they postponed.

(3) The basis of any new residence is its cost. There is no basis adjustment for unrecognized gains and losses.

d. **Wash sale:**

(1) A wash sale takes place when securities are sold at a loss and replaced with substantially identical securities within 30 days *before* or *after* the sale.

(2) Such losses are not recognized—they are postponed. The disallowed loss increases the basis of the stock or securities acquired.

(3) This law does not apply to dealers.

Tax Treatment of Gains and Losses

4550.05 When a taxpayer has determined that the taxpayer has a gain or a loss to be recognized, the next step is to establish whether it is to be treated as a capital gain or loss or as an ordinary income or loss item.

4550.06 A capital gain or loss is that gain or loss arising from the sale or exchange of a capital asset.

4550.07 **Capital assets** are defined as all property, *except* for the following:

a. Property held for resale (inventory)

b. Real or depreciable property used in a trade or business

c. Accounts or notes receivable acquired in normal business operations

d. A copyright or a literary, artistic, or musical composition in the hands of the creator or anyone who assumes the creator's basis (property received through gift)

e. U.S. government publications received from the government other than by purchase at the price that it is offered for sale to the public

f. Certain commodities derivative instruments held by a commodities derivatives dealer.

g. Any hedging transaction that is clearly identified as such before the close of the day on which it is acquired, originated, or entered into.

h. Supplies of a type regularly used or consumed by the taxpayer in the ordinary course of a trade or business of the taxpayer.

4550.08 Taxpayers may elect to treat the sale or exchange of self-created musical compositions or copyrights as the sale or exchange of a capital asset. This special treatment is effective for sales or exchanges in tax years beginning after May 17, 2006, and ends on December 31, 2010.

4550.09 Real property subdivided for sale:

    a. Individuals and S corporations subdividing real estate for sale may qualify for capital gain treatment if the following conditions apply:

        (1) Subdivider must not be a real estate dealer or a C corporation.

        (2) No substantial improvements may be made to the lots sold.

        (3) Lots sold must be held at least five years (unless inherited).

    b. All gain is capital gain until the year the sixth lot is sold. Contiguous lots sold to one buyer are treated as one lot.

        (1) When the sixth lot is sold, 5% of the revenue from all lots sold that year is potential ordinary income.

        (2) This potential ordinary income is offset by any selling expenses to determine the net amount taxed as ordinary income. Any gain not taxed as ordinary income is capital gain.

4550.10 Capital gains and losses, once determined, must be classified as either short term or long term depending on the holding period of the asset given up.

    a. Holding period requirements:

        (1) One year or less—short term

        (2) More than 12 months—long term

    b. The holding period for long-term capital gains and losses is measured as follows:

        (1) As a minimum, property must be held to that day of the 12th month following the month of acquisition that is numerically one day later than the date acquired.

        (2) If property is purchased on the last day of the month, it must be held to at least the first day of the 13th month.

    c. The holding period normally begins on the day that the basis originated.

    d. In transactions in which some portion of the basis of an asset carries forward, the holding period begins at the time the carryover basis originated.

    Example: If the donor's basis is used to establish the basis of gift property, the holding period for the donee begins at the time the donor's basis originated.

    If the fair market value is used as the basis of gift property (a loss situation), the holding period begins at the date of the gift.

    e. The statute provides that inherited property disposed of within one year shall be considered to have been held for more than one year.

4550.11 All items receiving capital gain or loss treatment should be classified as short term or long term and summarized as follows:

```
LTCG  ┐
(LTCL)┴── NLTCG (L) ┐
STCG  ┐             ├── Net Gain (Loss)
(STCL)┴── NSTCG (L) ┘
```

The result is either a net gain or a net loss.

4550.12 **Net gains for individuals, estates, and trusts:**

  a. Any of the net gain arising from short-term sales and exchanges receives ordinary income treatment.

  b. Any of the net gain arising from long-term sales or exchanges will be taxed at a maximum rate of 15% (0% for people in the 15% or 10% tax bracket). These are the same rates that apply to dividends. Note the following exceptions:

  (1) Unrecaptured Section 1250 gain (section **4430.12**) will be taxed at a maximum rate of 25%.

  (2) Taxable gains arising from the sale of collectibles (e.g., art, coins, antiques) and Section 1202 stock (section **4512.39**) will be taxed at a maximum rate of 28%.

4550.13 **Net losses for individuals, estates, and trusts:**

  a. If the taxpayer has a net loss, up to $3,000 may be deducted in the current year as a deduction toward adjusted gross income (reported on Schedule D).

  b. Short-term losses are used before long-term losses.

  c. Both short-term and long-term losses are deductible dollar-for-dollar.

  d. Any remaining capital loss will be carried forward indefinitely.

  e. The carryover will be treated as STCL or LTCL depending on its origin.

4550.14 **Special netting procedures:**

  a. Long-term capital gain and loss items are netted in the following manner. Separately list 28% gains (losses), 25% gains, 15/0% gains (losses), then:

  (1) Offset any 28% losses against 25% gains, then against 15/0% gains. If a loss still exists, offset it against any available net short-term gain. Any remaining loss is eligible for the $3,000 deduction. A loss in excess of $3,000 carries forward indefinitely.

  (2) Offset any 15/0% losses against 28% gains, then 25% gains. Offset any remaining loss against available net short-term gain. If a loss remains, it is eligible for the $3,000 deduction. A loss in excess of $3,000 carries forward indefinitely.

  (3) While losses can result from the sale of 28% and 15/0% items, the 25% situation involves only gains (by definition).

Summary of the netting process for long-term capital gains and losses:

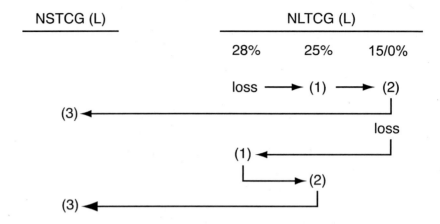

When the netting process produces a net long-term capital gain, the gain is used to absorb any net short-term capital loss. Any remaining 28%, 25%, or 15/0% gains will be taxed at those rates (see short-term netting process in part b, following).

Example: Taxpayer with $250,000 of taxable income (33% tax bracket) has no short-term gains and losses, but does have the following long-term capital gains and losses:

(a) 28% gain from the sale of stamp collection—$4,000

(b) 25% gain from unrecaptured depreciation on sale of a commercial building—$105,000

(c) 15% loss from sale of stock held as investment—$65,000

In this situation, taxpayer first offsets the $65,000 loss against the $4,000 gain. The remaining loss of $61,000 then offsets the 25% gain of $105,000. The remaining NLTCG of $44,000 is taxed at 25%.

    b. Short-term capital gains and losses are netted to produce a net short-term gain or loss.

        (1) If the result is a gain, the gain is used to absorb any net long-term capital loss. Any remaining short-term capital gain is taxed as ordinary income.

        (2) If the netting process results in a net short-term capital loss, the loss will offset available net long-term capital gain in the following order: 28% gains, 25% gains, and 15/0% gains. If a loss remains, up to $3,000 may be deducted as a deduction for AGI. Any additional loss is carried forward indefinitely.

        Example: If the taxpayer in the preceding example also had a net short-term capital loss of $15,000, the loss would offset the NLTCG of $44,000. The remaining $29,000 gain would be taxed at 25%.

        (3) Capital losses of individuals carry forward as either long-term or short-term depending on their origin. However, short-term losses are used first in calculating the $3,000 deduction.

4550.15 Net capital gains for corporations:

    a. Corporate capital gains are taxed as ordinary income.

    b. Before 1987, corporate capital gains received favorable tax treatment through an alternative tax.

4550.16 Net capital losses for corporations:

    a. Corporations are not allowed to deduct capital losses in excess of capital gains from ordinary income.

    b. Capital losses of a corporation can only be used to offset capital gains.

    c. All net capital losses carry back three years and forward five years as *short-term* capital losses.

4560 Taxation of Retirement Plan Benefits

4560.01 Roth IRAs:

    a. Distributions from a qualified Roth IRA will be tax-free and penalty-free if the distributions are made:

        (1) five years or more after the first contribution was made, and

        (2) on or after the date the taxpayer attains age 59-½, or

        (3) to a beneficiary as a result of the taxpayer's death, or

        (4) on account of the taxpayer's disability, or

        (5) for first-time homebuyer expenses ($10,000 limit).

    b. When distributions do not meet the criteria, amounts received in excess of contributions will be included in gross income and taxed. A 10% early withdrawal penalty will also apply to the taxable amount. Note that contributions are returned before any earnings are distributed with a Roth IRA.

    c. Setting up a Roth IRA:

        (1) Taxpayers may make nondeductible contributions of up to $5,000 each year to a Roth IRA.

        (2) Contributions from taxpayers age 70-½ or older are allowable.

        (3) Distributions before death are not required.

        (4) Contribution limits:

            (a) The annual $5,000 contribution limit is phased out proportionately in the year 2010 between the following AGI levels:

                i. Singles: $105,000–$120,000

                ii. Joint filers: $167,000–$177,000

            (b) The limit for total contributions to Roth IRAs and traditional IRAs combined is $5,000 (before phaseouts), not counting rollover contributions (see section **4560.02**).

            (c) Taxpayers age 50 before the end of the year may make an additional "catch-up" contribution of $1,000.

d. Rollover contributions:

(1) Funds in one Roth IRA can be rolled over tax-free to another Roth IRA.

(2) Funds in a traditional IRA (see section **4560.02**) can be rolled over penalty tax-free to a Roth IRA, but income tax must be paid on the distribution from the traditional IRA. However, the rollover is tax-free only if:

(a) the taxpayer's AGI for the year of distribution does not exceed $100,000 and

(b) the taxpayer is not married filing a separate return.

The $100,000 ceiling was waived for 2009. In 2010, the taxable amount can be split and reported half in 2011 and half in 2012.

4560.02 Retirement plans:

a. Self-employed persons may deduct up to $46,000 for contributions to a qualified retirement plan (Keogh plan).

(1) The deduction cannot exceed 25% of earned income.

(2) Earned income is income after the retirement contribution has been deducted. Consequently, the deduction is actually 20% of self-employment income.

(3) Additional earnings may be transferred to the plan with no resulting tax deduction (after tax).

b. Taxpayers may contribute (and deduct) up to $5,000 to a traditional individual retirement account (IRA), and this may equal up to 100% of their earned income. Included as acceptable investments are coins and bullion of gold, silver, and platinum, but not collectibles (e.g., stamps and antiques).

(1) For plans established to include a nonworking spouse, the deduction ceiling of $5,000 applies to both spouses. However, the contribution cannot exceed the sum of their earned incomes.

(2) Individuals, age 50 before the end of the year, may make an additional "catch-up" IRA contribution of $1,000. This brings their maximum contribution limit to $6,000.

(3) Alimony is treated as compensation for purposes of calculating allowable contributions to an IRA.

(4) Taxpayers who are active participants in an employer-sponsored retirement plan or Keogh plan face an IRA deduction phaseout.

(a) The phaseout takes place when AGI falls within these ranges:

		2010 AGI
1.	Single taxpayers and Heads of household	$56,000–$66,000
2.	Married filing jointly	$89,000–$109,000
3.	Married filing separately	$ 0–$10,000

(b) One spouse's active participation in an employer-sponsored plan will not disqualify the other spouse from making deductible IRA contributions.

i. A deduction phaseout does apply when AGI rises above $167,000.

ii. The phaseout is complete when AGI reaches $177,000.

(c) The maximum $5,000/$10,000 IRA deduction is phased out proportionately for each dollar of AGI that falls within the $10,000 phaseout range.

(d) Taxpayers with AGI above the phaseout range may still contribute up to $5,000/$10,000 to an IRA.

   i. These contributions will be *nondeductible.*

   ii. The earnings on such contributions will be tax-free until withdrawals are made from the IRA.

   iii. This program continues as an option to the Roth IRA.

(e) The limit for total contributions to all retirement IRAs combined is $5,000, before phaseouts, for each individual. This amount increases by $1,000 if "catch-up" contributions are involved.

(5) No deduction or contribution is allowed after age 70-½.

(6) Taxation of distributions:

(a) Distributions from a traditional IRA are generally taxable. However, taxpayers making nondeductible contributions to their accounts may withdraw these contributions tax-free using the rules for annuity proceeds (see section **4512.03**).

(b) Taxpayers receiving distributions before age 59-½ are subject to an additional 10% penalty on the taxable portion of the distribution. This penalty will not apply when the distribution is as follows:

   i. Due to a death or disability

   ii. Used to pay medical expenses in excess of 7.5% of AGI

   iii. Used by an unemployed person to buy health insurance

   iv. Used to pay qualified higher education expenses

   v. Used to pay expenses of a qualified first-time homebuyer

      a) There is a $10,000 lifetime limit.

      b) A first-time homebuyer is one who has not owned a principal residence in the past two years.

(c) Taxpayers must start withdrawing IRA funds no later than April 1 of the year after turning age 70-½.

c. SIMPLE retirement plan for small businesses:

(1) **The Savings Incentive Match Plan for Employers (SIMPLE)** simplifies complexities of retirement plans.

(a) Employees may elect to make a contribution to the plan, based on a percentage of compensation, of up to $11,500 and $14,000 for those age 50 or older each year.

(b) Following specified guidelines, employers are required to make contributions (deductible) to the plan.

(c) The plan can be either an IRA or Section 401(k) program.

(2) SIMPLE plans can be adopted by employers having 100 or fewer employees who received at least $5,000 in compensation from the employer in the preceding two years.

(a) The plan must be open to all employees who received $5,000 in compensation during the two previous years and who expect to receive $5,000 in the current year.

(b) The employee must not be part of another employer-sponsored retirement plan.

(c) All contributions are fully vested immediately.

(d) Employee contributions are deductible for AGI, and taxation on accumulations is deferred until distributed.

    d. **Caution:** Distributions before age 59-½ are subject to an additional tax of 10% (25% if taken during the 2-year period beginning on the date the individual first participated in any SIMPLE IRA plan of the employer). Exceptions include distributions for the following:

(1) Death

(2) Disability

(3) Medical expenses in excess of 7.5% of AGI

(4) Health insurance of an unemployed individual

(5) Qualified higher education expenses:

    (a) includes tuition, fees, books, supplies, equipment, and room and board for postsecondary education (includes graduate-level courses),

    (b) applies to taxpayer, spouse, children, and grandchildren, and

    (c) expenses are reduced by scholarships and similar excludible funding.

(6) First-time homebuyer expenses ($10,000 limit)

4570 Filing Status and Exemptions

4570.01 There are five filing statuses an individual can choose from: single, married filing jointly, married filing separately, head of household, and qualifying widower. The individual should choose the status that gives him or her the lowest tax.

4570.02 The single filing status is for individuals who are unmarried or legally separated on the last day of the year.

4570.03 The married filing jointly filing status is for individuals who are married and both spouses agree to file using the married filing jointly status. If both spouses receive income, they may want to figure the tax using the married filing separately status and married filing jointly status to get the lower combined tax available.

4570.04 The married filing separately status is for individuals who want to be responsible for only their portion of income, or if it results in less tax than filing jointly.

4570.05 The head of household filing status is for individuals who meet the following requirements:

    a. The individual is considered unmarried on the last day of the year.

    b. The individual paid for more than half the expenses of keeping a home for the year.

    c. The individual had a "qualifying person" living with them for more than half the year. If the "qualifying person" is a dependent parent, he or she does not have to live with the individual.

4570.06 The qualifying widower filing status is for an individual who had a spouse die in the last year for which he or she can file jointly. The individual can use this status for two years following the year of the spouse's death.

4580 Tax Computations and Credits

Tax Formula for Individuals

4580.01 The following tax formula is for individuals. Each step in the formula must be completed before the succeeding step is considered.

	Total income
−	Exclusions
=	Gross income
−	Deductions from gross income
=	Adjusted gross income
−	Larger of: Itemized deductions or standard deduction
−	Exemptions @ $3,650 in 2010
=	Taxable income
×	Tax rate
=	Tax liability before additions and credits
+	Additions to tax
−	Credits to tax
=	Final tax due (Refund)

4580.02 An expansion of the tax formula follows. It includes tax topics frequently encountered on the CPA Examination. This outline can be used as a quick review before the examination. However, keep in mind that the items in this expanded tax formula are "topics." Many of them are subject to specific provisions in the law that provide for exclusion, limitation, or special treatment. These are explained in the material that follows.

Tax Formula – Individuals
Topics to Review

Gross Income (But Not Limited To)
- Alimony
- Annuities
- Bargain purchases
- Dividends
  - Stock
  - Cash
  - Property
- Employee benefit programs
- Employer-paid adoption expenses
- Foreign earned income
- Gambling winnings
- Interest
- Life insurance
  - Proceeds
  - Dividends
- Gain on sale of residence
- Capital gains
- Unemployment benefits
- Social Security/railroad retirement
- Workers' compensation
- Prizes and awards
- Damages received
- Recoveries
- Group-term life insurance
- Scholarships

– Deductions From Gross Income
= Adjusted Gross Income
- Business expenses (Schedule C)
- Expenses of producing rent and royalty income (Schedule E)
- Capital loss deduction (Schedule D)
- Teachers' supplies (expired 12/31/2009; may be extended to 2010 by Congress)
- Contributions to retirement plans
  - Self-employed SEP, SIMPLE, Keogh IRA, 401(K)
- Student loan interest
- Qualified higher education expenses (expired 12/31/2009; may be extended to 2010 by Congress)
- Health Savings Account
- Qualified unreimbursed moving expenses
- 50% of self-employment tax
- Self-employed health insurance premiums
- Interest forfeited to bank on premature withdrawals
- Alimony paid
- Certain expenses of Reservists, Performing artists and fee-basis government officials
- Domestic production activities deduction

Adjusted Gross Income

ITEMIZED DEDUCTIONS
Medical expenses (7.5%)
Taxes
Interest expense
Contributions
Casualty and theft losses ($100/10%)
Miscellaneous itemized deductions:
    Gambling losses (limit: gambling winnings)
Unrecovered investment in pension
Impairment-related work expenses of a handicapped person
Miscellaneous deductions subject to 2% AGI limit:
    Unreimbursed employee expenses
      Travel
      Transportation
      Entertainment (50%)
      Meals (50%)
    Professional dues and subscriptions
    Union dues
    Special clothing
    Educational expenses
    Job hunting expenses
    Home office expenses
    Tax assistance fees
    Certain appraisal fees
    Hobby expenses (limit: hobby income)
    Investment expenses
2010 STANDARD DEDUCTIONS ($5,700/$11,400/$8,400)
Additions to the standard deduction ($1,100/$1,400)
    Age 65 married/single
    Blindness married/single
    Real estate property tax ($500/$1,000) (2009 only)
    Excise tax on new auto (2009 only)

– Greater of:
Itemized Deductions
or
Standard Deductions

– Exemptions

= Taxable Income

Taxpayer/spouse
Dependents
    Qualifying relatives
    Qualifying nonrelatives
    Qualifying children

Continued on following page...

Tax Tables
Rate Schedules
= Tentative Tax
- Married – joint return
- Surviving spouse
- Head of household
- Single
- Married – separate return

+ Additions
- Self-employment tax (Schedule SE)
- Household employment taxes (Schedule H)
- Alternative minimum tax

– Credits

= Income Tax
- Foreign tax credit
- Child/dependent care credit
- Credit for elderly or disabled
- American Opportunity Credit (formerly Hope credit)
- Lifetime learning credit
- Child tax credit
- Credit for adoption expenses
- General business credit:
    - Business energy tax credit
    - Credit for research and experimentation
    - Investment credit
    - Rehabilitation expenditures credit
    - Low-income housing credit
    - Disabled Access Credit
    - Certain mortgage interest credit
    - Credit for FICA tax on tips
    - Work opportunity credit
- Additional child tax credit
- Credit for employer provided child care facilities
- Credit for contributions to qualified retirement plans
- Earned income credit

Tax Credits

4580.03 **Tax credits** reduce the tax liability on a dollar-for-dollar basis. While most tax credits are limited to the income tax liability, some credits are further restricted as to the amount of the tax liability that they can offset. The general business credit is an example of such a restricted credit.

    a. General business credit.

        (1) Each of the business tax credits is computed separately and then combined to form a single "general business credit." A partial list of these credits follows:

            (a) Investment credit

            (b) Work opportunity credit

            (c) Research activities credit

            (d) Low-income housing credit

            (e) Disabled access credit

            (f) Employer-provided childcare credit

        (2) The deduction for the general business credit is limited to the lower of:

            (a) the excess of the taxpayer's regular tax liability over the tentative minimum tax for the year or

            (b) $25,000 plus 75% of the tax liability in excess of $25,000.

        (3) Any unused credit may be carried back one year and forward 20 years on a first-in, first-out basis.

    b. These credits and others are described as follows.

4580.04 **Investment credit (ITC):** This general business credit is based on the amount invested in qualified business properties during the tax year. While there are four separate credits currently included in the calculation of the ITC, only the rehabilitation credit will be discussed.

    a. **A rehabilitation credit** will be allowed to taxpayers for expenditures incurred to rehabilitate old commercial and industrial buildings and certified historic structures. No credit is allowed for personal use property.

    b. The credit is 10% of the expenditures incurred to rehabilitate buildings that were placed in service before 1936 and 20% for certified historic structures.

    c. The taxpayer is required to depreciate rehabilitated property using the straight-line method.

    d. The basis of rehabilitated buildings must be reduced by 100% of the rehabilitation credit taken.

    e. The rehabilitation credit is subject to recapture provisions if the building is disposed of prematurely or ceases to be qualified property.

    f. The rehabilitation credit is increased for qualified rehabilitation expenditures paid or incurred after August 27, 2005, and before January 1, 2009, on buildings located in the Gulf Opportunity (GO) Zone (core disaster area) as follows:

        (1) For pre-1936 buildings (other than certified historic structures), the credit percentage is increased from 10% to 13%.

        (2) For certified historic structures, the credit percentage is increased from 20% to 26%.

Note: The GO Zone (also called the core disaster area) covers the portion of the Hurricane Katrina disaster area determined by the Federal Emergency Management Agency (FEMA) to be eligible for either individual only or both individual and public assistance from the federal government. The GO Zone covers areas in the three states of Alabama, Louisiana, and Mississippi.

    g. **Midwestern Disaster Zone.** The rehabilitation credit is increased for qualified rehabilitation expenditures paid or incurred beginning on the applicable disaster date and ending on December 31, 2011, on buildings located in the Midwestern Disaster Area (core disaster area) as follows:

        (1) For pre-1936 buildings (other than certified historic structures), the credit percentage is increased from 10% to 13%.

        (2) For certified historic structures, the credit percentage is increased from 20% to 26%.

    Note: The Midwestern (Heartland) Disaster Area refers to the counties of 10 Midwestern states (Arkansas, Illinois, Indiana, Iowa, Kansas, Michigan, Minnesota, Missouri, Nebraska, and Wisconsin) that were declared to be major disaster areas by the president on or after May 20, 2008, and before August 1, 2008, because of floods, storms, and tornados.

4580.05 **Work opportunity credit** (a general business credit): Employers hiring employees from selected high unemployment groups are allowed a special credit.

    a. The credit is equal to 40% of the first $6,000 of first-year wages paid or accrued to each qualified employee who is hired during the year.

        (1) To qualify for the 40% rate, an employee must complete 400 or more hours of service.

        (2) Employees completing less than 400 hours of service, but at least 120 hours, qualify for a rate of only 25%.

    b. The work opportunity tax credit is elective. If taken, the employer's deduction for wages must be reduced by the amount of the credit.

4580.06 **Research activities credit** (a general business credit): To encourage technical research and development (R&D), a tax credit is available for qualified R&D expenditures. The credit is based on two research components.

    a. **Amount of credit.** The research credit is the sum of (1) 20% of the excess of qualified research expenses for the current year over a base period amount, (2) 20% of the basic research payments made to a qualified research organization, and (3) 20% of the amounts paid to an energy research consortium.

    b. **Base amount.** The base amount is determined by a special formula, but it may not be less than 50% of the qualified research expenses for the current year.

    c. The research activities credit may be claimed if the taxpayer expenses research expenditures or capitalizes them. However, the deduction for research expenditures must be reduced by the credit taken.

4580.07 **Low-income housing credit** (a general business credit): A tax credit may be claimed by owners of low-income rental housing units constructed, rehabilitated, or acquired after 1986.

    a. A credit may be taken in each of 10 years starting with the year the project is placed in service, or the next year if the taxpayer so elects.

b. The annual credit is equal to:

$$\begin{array}{r}\text{Qualified basis of low-income rental units} \\ \times \ \underline{\text{Specified percentage rate}} \\ = \ \underline{\text{Low-income housing credit}}\end{array}$$

(1) The qualified basis is that portion of the building's qualified cost that is attributable to low-income rental units.

(2) The applicable percentages are issued by the IRS for the month the building is placed in service.

c. An owner is required to recapture part of the credits taken if the owner disposes of the interest in the project or violates some aspect of the original entitlement any time within a 15-year period.

4580.08 **Disabled access credit** (a general business credit): Qualified taxpayers have available a nonrefundable tax credit that is based on the expenditures incurred to make their business accessible to disabled individuals.

a. The credit is equal to 50% of the eligible access expenditures for the year that fall between $250 and $10,250. Thus, the maximum credit available is $5,000 (50% × ($10,250 − $250)).

b. The credit is available to those small businesses that in the preceding tax year had either:

(1) gross receipts of $1 million or less or

(2) thirty, or fewer, full-time employees.

c. The credit is not available for expenditures paid or incurred on buildings placed in service after November 5, 1990.

d. The adjusted basis is reduced by the full amount of the credit taken.

4580.09 **Employer-provided childcare credit** (a general business credit): To encourage smaller businesses to provide childcare for their employees, a credit is available for childcare expenses paid by the employer.

a. A 25% credit is available for expenditures to acquire or prepare property for use as a childcare facility. The 25% credit also applies to:

(1) the operating costs of a childcare facility or

(2) the amount paid to a contracted childcare facility to provide childcare services to the taxpayer's employees.

b. A 10% credit is also available for expenses paid by the employer under a contract to provide childcare resource and referral services to the employees.

c. The total credit cannot exceed $150,000 per year.

d. Any credit based on the acquisition or improvement of property must be used to reduce the basis of that property. Likewise, any deductible expenses must be reduced by the related tax credit.

e. If a credit is claimed for a property acquisition or improvement, terminating the use of that property as a childcare facility within 10 years will trigger a recapture of some or all of the credit claimed.

4580.10 **Credit for the elderly and the permanently and totally disabled:** Individuals age 65 or over and individuals under 65 who are permanently and totally disabled have a special tax credit available.

- **a.** Individuals are permanently and totally disabled when they are expected to be unable to work for a period of 12 continuous months.
- **b.** This credit is equal to 15% of a base figure after certain adjustments.
    - (1) The base figure available to the taxpayer depends on the following factors:
        - (a) **Singles:**
            1. Age 65—$5,000
            2. Disabled—lesser of $5,000 or disability income
        - (b) **Married persons filing jointly:**
            1. Both 65—$7,500
            2. One 65—$5,000
            3. One 65, one disabled—lesser of $7,500 or $5,000 plus disability income
            4. One disabled—lesser of $5,000 or disability income
            5. Both disabled—lesser of $7,500 or sum of spouses' disability income
        - (c) **Married persons filing separately:**
            1. Age 65—$3,750
            2. Disabled—lesser of $3,750 or disability income
    - (2) Adjustments (deductions) to the base figure are required for the following:
        - (a) Social Security payments
        - (b) Railroad Retirement pensions
        - (c) One-half of adjusted gross income in excess of:
            1. $7,500 (single)
            2. $10,000 (married, filing jointly)
            3. $5,000 (married, filing separately)
- **c.** A married taxpayer filing separately may use the credit only if the couple has lived apart the entire tax year.

4580.11 **Foreign tax credit:** A taxpayer may apply income taxes paid to a foreign country or U.S. possession as a credit against United States income tax liability, or may use such taxes as an itemized deduction.

- **a.** This treatment is available for taxes paid to a foreign country on income that is taxable in the United States when no foreign income exclusion is taken.
- **b.** The election to use the credit or the deduction is made annually.
- **c.** The taxpayer cannot split foreign taxes between a credit and a deduction.

  d. The overall limit for the credit on taxes paid to *all* foreign countries is restricted to that portion of the U.S. income tax which relates to the taxable income from all foreign countries.

$$\frac{\text{Total foreign taxable income}}{\text{Total worldwide taxable income}} = \text{U.S. income tax}$$

  e. Excess credits may be carried back two years and forward five years.

4580.12 **Child and dependent care credit:** Taxpayers are permitted a nonrefundable tax credit for expenses incurred in caring for dependents so that the taxpayer(s) may be gainfully employed.

  a. The credit is available on a three-tiered basis as follows:

   (1) Taxpayers with an adjusted gross income of $15,000 or less will be entitled to a credit of 35% of dependent care expenses.

   (2) The credit will be reduced by one percentage point for each $2,000 of adjusted gross income, or fraction thereof, above $15,000.

   (3) For taxpayers with an adjusted gross income over $43,000, the credit will be 20%.

  b. The maximum amount of dependent care expenses that may be considered for the credit is $3,000 if there is one qualifying child or dependent and $6,000 if there are two or more qualifying dependents.

  c. Expenditures for dependent care cannot exceed the earned income of the low-income parent.

   (1) Special provisions apply where one of the spouses is a full-time student or is incapacitated, and the other spouse works. In this situation, the nonworking spouse is considered to have earned at least $250 per month, where one dependent requires care and $500 per month, where more than one dependent requires care.

  d. The dependent must be:

   (1) a child under age 13 or

   (2) an incapacitated dependent or spouse.

  e. Married taxpayers must file a joint return unless they live apart for the last six months of the year.

   (1) For divorced or separated parents, the credit is available to the parent having custody of the child for the longer period.

   (2) A custodial parent may claim the credit even though the child may not qualify as a dependent. However, two taxpayers filing separate returns cannot claim separate credits for the same child.

  f. Expenditures that qualify for the credit include amounts paid for both in-the-home care and out-of-the-home care.

   (1) In-the-home care may include expenditures for household services if they were partly for the well-being and protection of a qualifying individual.

   (2) Expenditures for out-of-the-home care are eligible for the credit only if incurred for:

    (a) a dependent under age 13 or

    (b) any other qualifying person who regularly spends at least eight hours each day in the taxpayer's household.

       g. Expenditures do not qualify for the credit if they were made to:

          (1) a relative who is a dependent of the taxpayer or

          (2) the taxpayer's child who is under age 19.

4580.13 **Credit for mortgage interest paid:** Qualified low-income homeowners who hold a mortgage credit certificate (MCC) may claim a credit for a portion of the interest paid on their home mortgage.

       a. MCCs are issued by the state to low-income taxpayers who plan to borrow money to purchase or improve a home.

       b. The portion of the mortgage interest that can be used as a credit is determined by the state, but it can range from 10% to 50% of the interest paid.

       c. If the percentage exceeds 20%, the taxpayer's maximum credit for the year is $2,000.

       d. Credits in excess of the tax liability may be carried over for three years.

       e. The taxpayer's itemized deduction for mortgage interest must be reduced by the amount of the credit claimed.

4580.14 **Earned income credit:** A special refundable tax credit may be available for low-income workers who have a principal residence in the United States. It represents a form of *negative income tax*—workers may receive money from the government even though they do not have a tax liability.

       a. The earned income credit (EIC) is equal to a percentage of a limited amount of earned income. Taxpayers with qualifying children receive greater benefits—a greater amount of income is eligible for a higher credit percentage.

       b. When the taxpayer's adjusted gross income (or earned income, if greater) exceeds a threshold amount, the EIC is phased out.

          (1) "Earned income" includes only taxable compensation; it does not include nontaxable employee compensation.

          (2) No credit is allowed to those with "disqualified income" (unearned income) in excess of $3,100 for 2010.

          (3) No credit is allowed for those failing to provide correct Social Security numbers for themselves, spouse, and qualifying child.

       c. The government provides an easy-to-use EIC table to determine the correct credit.

       d. **Qualifying children:** To be eligible for the earned income credit, parents must have children that can meet the following tests:

          (1) **Relationship:** The child must be a "qualifying child" (see section **4530.04.c**). The child may, however, provide over half of his or her own support.

          (2) **Residency:** The child must live in the taxpayer's residence over half of the year; foster children for the entire tax year.

          (3) **Age:** The child must be:

              (a) under age 19,

              (b) a full-time student under age 24, or

              (c) permanently and totally disabled.

e. Individuals without qualifying children may be eligible for this credit if:

   (1) they (or their spouse) are at least 25 years old, but not more than 64 years old, at the end of the year and

   (2) they cannot be claimed as a dependent by another taxpayer.

4580.15 **FICA tax credit on tips:** Proprietors of food and beverage establishments may claim a tax credit for a portion of the employer's share of FICA taxes. The credit is limited to those FICA taxes attributable to reported tips in excess of those treated as wages under the federal minimum wage laws. No deduction is permitted for any of the FICA expense claimed as a credit.

4580.16 **Credit for withholding and estimated tax payments:** A refundable tax credit is available to the taxpayer for withheld taxes and estimated tax payments.

4580.17 **Adoption credit:** In 2010, a refundable tax credit is available for qualified adoption expenses paid or incurred in the adoption of a qualified child. Expenses paid before adoption are claimed as a credit in the year the adoption is finalized. Health care reform legislation extended the credit through 2011, increased the maximum to $13,170, and made the adoption credit refundable.

   a. **Qualified expenses** include reasonable and necessary adoption fees, court costs, attorney fees, and other directly related expenses. Expenses up to $13,170 may be claimed as a credit. Adoption expenses for a child with special needs are considered to be $13,170, regardless of the actual amount expended. This credit begins to phase out if the taxpayer has modified adjusted gross income of $182,520 or more. If MAGI is $222,520 or more, then it is completely phased out.

   b. **Qualifying children** are those under age 18 or those who are physically or mentally handicapped.

   c. The credit allowable is phased out ratably as AGI rises from $182,520 to $222,520.

   d. Unused credits carry forward five years.

   e. Married taxpayers must file jointly, and the child's Social Security number must be reported.

4580.18 **Child tax credit:** Taxpayers may claim a $1,000 credit for each qualifying child under age 17.

   a. A qualifying child is defined as a "qualifying child" for purposes of the dependency exemption (see section **4530.04.c**). The under age 17 requirement still applies, however.

   b. The credit phases out at the rate of $50 per $1,000 (or fraction thereof) of modified AGI in excess of these thresholds:

   (1) $110,000 on a joint return

   (2) $75,000 for singles

   (3) $55,000 for married persons filing separately

   Generally, modified AGI is AGI before considering exclusions for foreign earned income and foreign housing costs.

   c. The credit is generally nonrefundable. However, if this credit exceeds the tax liability, the remaining credit is available for the "additional child tax credit." The additional child tax credit is refundable to the extent of 15% of the taxpayer's earned income in excess of $3,000.

4580.19 **Education tax credits:** Two tax credits available for students pursuing postsecondary college or vocational education are the American Opportunity credit and the Lifetime Learning credit. These credits are available for qualified educational expenditures of the taxpayer, spouse, and dependents.

    a. **American Opportunity credit (formerly Hope credit):** The Recovery Act of 2009 changed the name of the Hope credit and expanded the terms of the credit. Taxpayers may claim a credit of $2,500 per student for tuition, related expenses, and course materials (new) for each of the first *four* (new) years of postsecondary education.

        (1) The credit is equal to 100% of the first $2,000 and 25% of the next $2,000.

        (2) Students must be enrolled no less than half-time during at least one semester during the year.

        (3) Subject to an exception, 40% of the allowable credit is refundable.

    b. **Lifetime Learning credit:** This nonrefundable credit is equal to 20% of up to $10,000 of tuition expenses paid each year by the taxpayer. Expenses for which the American Opportunity credit is claimed do not qualify for this credit. In contrast to the American Opportunity credit, this credit:

        (1) does not vary with the number of students in the household,

        (2) is available for an unlimited number of years,

        (3) applies to undergraduate, graduate, and professional degree expenses,

        (4) applies to any course at an eligible institution that helps individuals acquire or improve their job skills, and

        (5) does not require half-time enrollment for one semester. (Thus, CPE credit courses and professional seminars provided by eligible educational institutions may qualify for the credit.)

    c. **Income limitations:** The sum of these credits is phased out proportionately between these AGI levels:

        (1) Singles: $80,000–$90,000

        (2) Joint filers: $160,000–$180,000

    d. **Other limitations:**

        (1) Married taxpayers must file jointly to receive these credits.

        (2) In a given tax year, only one of the following benefits may be claimed with respect to each student: (a) the American Opportunity credit, or (b) the Lifetime Learning credit. However, the American Opportunity or Lifetime Learning credit can be claimed in the same year as distributions from a Coverdell Education IRA (see section **4512.36**), provided that the proceeds from the distribution are not used to pay for the education costs used in claiming the American Opportunity or Lifetime Learning credit.

        (3) The credits are not available if the cost of the course may be deducted by the taxpayer as a business expense.

    e. The education credits were expanded for students attending an eligible educational institution located in a Midwestern disaster area. The American Opportunity credit for a student in the disaster area was increased to 100% of the first $2,000 in qualified education expenses and 50% of the next $2,000 of qualified education expenses for a maximum credit of $3,000 per student. The Lifetime Learning credit rate for such a student was increased from 20% to 40%. **Note:** This expanded credit was available for 2009, but terminated at December 31, 2009.

4580.20 Saver's credit for contributions to qualified retirement plans: A nonrefundable tax credit is available for contributions, or deferrals, to retirement savings plans.

    a. The credit applies to traditional and Roth IRAs and other qualified retirement plans such as 401(k) plans, 403(b) annuities, 457 plans, SIMPLE, and SEP plans.

    b. For 2010, the amount of the credit is based on filing status and AGI. The credit is determined by multiplying the contribution (not to exceed $2,000) by a percentage taken from the following table, which is based on AGI levels.

Joint Return		Head of Household		All Other Cases		Applicable %
Over	Not Over	Over	Not Over	Over	Not Over	
$ 0	$33,500	$ 0	$25,125	$ 0	$16,750	50%
33,500	41,625	25,125	27,000	16,750	18,000	20%
41,625	55,000	27,000	55,000	18,000	27,750	10%
55,000	—	55,000	—	27,750	—	0%

    c. The credit is in addition to any deduction or exclusion relating to the retirement plan contribution.

    d. Joint filers with AGI in excess of $55,000 receive no credit. For heads of households, the amount is $41,625, and for all others it is $27,750.

    e. The contribution eligible for the credit must be reduced by any distributions received from qualified retirement plans.

        (1) Such distributions include those paid out during (a) the current year, (b) the two preceding tax years, and (c) the period before the due date (including extensions) of the current return.

        (2) Distributions received by a spouse are considered as distributions to the taxpayer if a joint return is filed.

    f. Qualifying taxpayers must be at least 18 years old.

    g. Dependents and full-time students are not eligible for the credit.

4590 Alternative Minimum Tax

4590.01 Alternative minimum tax: A special alternative minimum tax is payable to the extent that it exceeds the taxpayer's regular tax before credits.

    a. **For 2009,** this tax was computed at a rate of 26% on alternative minimum taxable income (AMTI) in excess of $46,700 ($70,950 for joint returns and surviving spouses; $35,475 for married persons filing separately). The rate was 28% on the taxable portion of AMTI in excess of $175,000 ($87,500 for married persons filing separately). **For the 2010 tax year,** unless Congress passes legislation, the AMT exemption is set for $33,750 for single and head of household filers, $45,000 for joint filers and surviving spouses, and $22,500 for married filing separately filers. (**Note:** As of the publication date, legislation changing the 2010 tax information above had not been passed.)

b. Basically, the alternative minimum tax is computed as follows:

```
           Regular taxable income
  + or −   Adjustments
       +   Tax preferences
       =   AMTI
       −   Exemption amount
       =   AMT base
       ×   26% (28% on excess over $175,000)
       =   Tentative tax before foreign credit
       −   Foreign tax credit
       =   Tentative minimum tax
       −   Regular tax (less foreign tax credit)
       =   Alternative minimum tax
```

(1) Adjustments (plus or minus) include such items as the following:

   (a) Itemized deductions

   (b) Standard deduction

   (c) Personal exemptions

   (d) Excess ACRS deductions (accelerated depreciation)

   (e) Circulation expenditures (magazines and newspapers)

   (f) Research and experimental expenditures

   (g) Mining exploration and development costs

   (h) Passive activity losses

   (i) Certain installment sales

   (j) Long-term contracts

   (k) Incentive stock options

   (l) Alternative tax net operating loss

(2) Tax preferences may arise in the following areas:

   (a) Percentage depletion

   (b) Intangible drilling costs

   (c) Seven percent (7%) of excluded gain on qualified small business stock (See section **4512.39**.)

   (d) Accelerated depreciation

   (e) Certain tax-exempt interest

(3) **Exemption:** The AMT exemption available to the taxpayer for 2010 is based on filing status and income level as follows:

   (a) Filing status:

Married, filing jointly (surviving spouses)	$45,000
Single (head of household)	33,750
Married, filing separately	22,500

   (b) The exemption begins to phase out when the AMTI exceeds specified levels. The phaseout rate is 25 cents for every dollar of AMTI in excess of:

$150,000	for married persons filing jointly
$112,500	for singles
$ 75,000	for married persons filing separately

    c. An AMT tax credit may be available when regular taxable income is greater than AMTI. The regular tax liability, in this situation, may be offset by a credit representing minimum tax liabilities from prior years attributable to timing differences. The AMT credit carries forward indefinitely.

4590.02 **Self-employment tax** must be paid as an addition to the tax if net earnings from self-employment are $400 or more.

    a. Although the net self-employment earnings base changes annually, the tax rate remains constant at 15.3%. This is 12.4% for Old Age, Survivor, and Disability Insurance (OASDI) and 2.9% for the Hospital Insurance Plan (HIP). The maximum amount of income subject to this tax varies according to the type of insurance. In 2010, for the first time, no change was made due to a lack of inflation.

Type of Insurance		2010 Maximum Base
OASDI	at 12.4%	$106,800
HIP	at 2.9%	No Limit

        (1) The self-employment tax is computed as follows:

$$\begin{aligned}&\text{Qualifying net self-employment income} \times .9235 \times .124 = \text{OASDI tax}\\+\ &\underline{\text{Net self-employment income} \times .9235 \times .029 = \text{HIP tax}}\\=\ &\underline{\text{Self-employment tax}}\end{aligned}$$

        (2) An amount equal to one-half of the self-employment tax is available as a deduction from gross income.

    b. A special method for determining net earnings from self-employment is available for taxpayers in the following situations:

        (1) If gross self-employment income is $6,300 or less, the taxpayer may report two-thirds of gross income as net earnings, even though actual net earnings are less.

        (2) If gross self-employment is more than $6,300, the taxpayer may report actual net earnings. If net earnings are less than $4,200, however, the taxpayer may elect to report $4,200 as net earnings.

This page intentionally left blank.

Section 4600
Federal Taxation of Entities

4610 Similarities and Distinctions in Tax Reporting Among Business Entities
    4611 Formation
    4612 Operation
    4613 Distributions
    4614 Liquidation

4620 Differences Between Tax and Financial Accounting
    4621 Reconciliation of Book Income to Taxable Income
    4622 Disclosures Under Schedule M-3

4630 C Corporations
    4631 Determination of Taxable Income/Loss
    4632 Tax Computations and Credits, Including Alternative Minimum Tax
    4633 Net Operating Losses
    4634 Entity/Owner Transactions, Including Contributions and Distributions
    4635 Earnings and Profits
    4636 Consolidated Returns

4640 S Corporations
    4641 Eligibility and Election
    4642 Determination of Ordinary Income/Loss and Separately Stated Items
    4643 Basis of Shareholder's Interest
    4644 Entity/Owner Transactions, Including Contributions and Distributions
    4645 Built-In Gains Tax

4650 Partnerships
    4651 Determination of Ordinary Income/Loss and Separately Stated Items
    4652 Basis of Partner's/Member's Interest and Basis of Assets Contributed to the Partnership
    4653 Partnership and Partner Elections
    4654 Transactions Between a Partner and the Partnership
    4655 Treatment of Partnership Liabilities
    4656 Distribution of Partnership Assets
    4657 Ownership Changes, and Liquidation and Termination of Partnership

4660 Trusts and Estates
    4661 Types of Trusts
    4662 Income and Deductions
    4663 Determination of Beneficiary's Share of Taxable Income

4670 Tax-Exempt Organizations
    4671 Types of Organizations
    4672 Obtaining and Maintaining Tax-Exempt Status
    4673 Unrelated Business Income

4610 Similarities and Distinctions in Tax Reporting Among Business Entities

4611 Formation

4611.01 Subchapter C Corporation

a. The corporation is a creation of the state. The incorporated entity must be chartered under the laws of a specific state. Issuance of a certificate of incorporation by the secretary of state is the start of corporate existence.

b. Regular corporations report federal taxes under Subchapter C of the IRS Tax Code.

c. A C corporation is a tax-paying entity under federal tax laws.

d. The following diagram shows the activities that occur when a corporation is formed. Note that the incorporators do the paperwork with the state, while the promoters sell the stock.

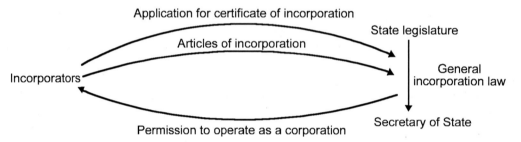

Charter: Old name
Certificate of incorporation: New name

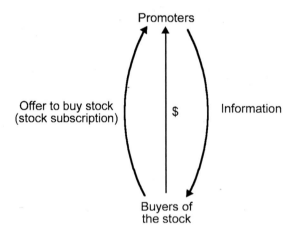

4611.02 Subchapter S Corporation

a. An S corporation is a creature of federal tax law.

b. An S corporation is treated as a regular corporation under state law; the S corporation elects special tax status for federal tax.

c. S corporations report federal taxes under Subchapter S of the IRS Tax Code.

d. It is a pass-through entity and does not pay federal income tax.

4611.03 General Partnership

a. A general partnership must meet the definition of a partnership: two or more persons working as co-owners of a business for profit.

b. A general partnership is not a taxable entity; tax attributes are passed through to the partners.

4611.04 Limited Partnership

a. The limited partnership has the same definition as a general partnership (two or more persons working as co-owners of a business for profit).

b. A limited partnership has at least one general partner and at least one limited partner.

c. Limited partnerships are authorized under the laws of a particular state.

d. Some states require the limited partnership to register with the state in order to be allowed to sell interests to limited partners.

4611.05 Limited Liability Company (LLC) (New Entity Format)

a. A limited liability company is an unincorporated entity formed under the LLC statute of a particular state.

b. None of the members bears personal liability for the debts of the LLC.

c. There is no uniformity among states.

4611.06 Limited Liability Partnership (LLP) (New Entity Format)

a. An LLP is a general partnership.

b. Partners may be protected from tort liabilities of other partners.

c. An LLP is now used often for legal, accounting, and other professional partnerships.

d. There is no uniformity among states.

4611.07 Sole Proprietorship

a. A sole proprietorship is a business entity with no separate identity from the owner.

b. There can only be one owner.

c. The entity can do business under an assumed name (dba).

4611.08 Formation of Entity

a. A sole proprietorship is simple to form. It starts up when an individual begins conducting business without incorporating or starting a partnership of any kind.

b. A corporation is also relatively simple to form:

(1) The incorporators must file articles of incorporation with the secretary of state where the entity is formed.

(2) Articles of incorporation can be generic or specific to the plans and objectives of the venture.

(3) A corporation generally is governed by a set of bylaws, which do not require approval by the secretary of state.

c. A general partnership can be formed by simple oral agreements; however:

(1) for their protection, new partners should prepare a partnership agreement in writing before a transfer of assets or a start of the business activities.

(2) since the acts of one partner can bind all of the partners, creating liabilities for them, partners should consult legal counsel for written partnership agreement.

(3) even without a written partnership agreement, the act of two or more persons carrying on a venture for profit may create a legally binding partnership under state law and for federal tax purposes.

d. Limited partnerships are more complicated than general partnerships:

(1) Limited partnerships must register with the state of formation.

(2) The partnership agreement must be filed with the state.

(3) Limited partners are often given preference in distributions and tax allocations.

(4) Special allocation to limited partnerships must have a business purpose and substantial economic effect. (IRC Section 704(b))

(5) The partnership agreement must contain provisions specified in IRS Regulation Section 1.704-1(b)(2).

(6) Each special provision makes the limited partnership more complex.

e. A limited liability partnership (LLP) is formed by filing articles of organization with the state.

f. A limited liability corporation (LLC) also must file articles of organization with the state. LLCs are governed by an operating agreement that looks much like a partnership agreement.

g. Buy-sell agreements for partnerships, LLCs, and closely held corporations (especially S corporations) are useful and important to provide for an orderly transfer of interests.

4611.09 Cost of Formation

a. Sole proprietorship cost of formation is minimal. Typically, there is no cost unless the name is registered.

b. Corporations (subchapter C) should be inexpensive to form.

(1) Corporate articles and bylaws should be very inexpensive.

(2) Attorney fees and state filing fees may not exceed a few hundred dollars.

c. The general partnership cost of formation varies with the complexity of the agreement.

(1) With equal sharing ratios for all the partners, a simple partnership agreement should cost no more than formation of a corporation.

(2) Often partnership agreements are more complex, with loss ratios different from profit ratios, leading to additional legal fees.

d. Limited partnership cost of formation rises with an increase in complexity.

e. LLC and LLP formation costs are affected by the complexity of the agreement. The cost may resemble that for partnerships. Articles of organization filed with the estate should not be an expensive document.

4612 Operation

4612.01 In the process of choosing the entity to use for the operation of a business, the need for limiting the liability of the owners of the business may be the most important factor to consider. The objective of this choice is to reduce or eliminate the exposure to personal liability for torts and claims against the entity.

4612.02 It would be advisable that any business where there could be a personal injury to a third party that would exceed the normal insurance coverage limits to conduct that business through a limited liability entity.

4612.03 Additional personal liability for the business owner could result from a variety of causes:
   a. Debts and expenses of the entity
   b. Personal or professional services provided
   c. Dangerous activities (construction, machinery, vehicles)
   d. Providing food service
   e. Environmental risks
   f. Actions of employees

4612.04 The limited liability company combines features of both partnerships and corporations.
   a. From the partnership form there is a complete pass-through of tax attributes generated by operations and great operational flexibility.
   b. From the state law, the LLC has the same limitation of personal liability as held by a corporation.
   c. Through the operating agreement there may be participation by all of the members, if that is desired.

4612.05 **Limited Liability Company Attributes**
   a. Liability protection for all members
   b. Legal entity created by state law
   c. LLC may own property, incur debts, enter into contracts, and sue or be sued.
   d. Members shielded from LLC's debts

4612.06 General partnerships offer no liability protection for general partners.

4612.07 Limited partnerships have liability protection for limited partners, but general partners have full liability.

4612.08 A limited liability partnership provides protection against torts by other partners, but no protection against general liability.

4613 Distributions

4613.01 Corporation's distribution of property to a shareholder:
   a. Property distributed to a shareholder has a fair market value in excess of the adjusted basis on the corporate books; a gain is recognized by the corporation (IRC Section 311(b)).

      b. The distribution to the shareholder is a dividend to the shareholder to the extent of the earnings and profits of the corporation. The difference between FMV and the basis in the corporation may be taxable to the shareholder.

4613.02 S corporation's distribution of property to a shareholder: When an S corporation distributes appreciated property, it also triggers a gain recognition at the corporate level. The gain is passed through to shareholders to be taxed at that level.

4613.03 Partnership's distribution of property to a partner:

      a. When a partner receives a distribution, it is only taxable to the extent that cash or securities exceed the partner's basis.

      b. Distributions of noncash appreciated property are tax free.

      c. The partner's basis in the partnership is reduced by the basis in the property, but not below zero.

      d. This treatment applies to general partnerships, limited partnerships, and LLCs taxed as a partnership.

4613.04 Nonliquidating distributions of a corporation:

      a. reduce the retained earnings of the corporation.

      b. are taxable as dividends to the shareholder if earnings and profits exist.

4613.05 Nonliquidating distributions of a partnership:

      a. are taxed as a capital gain to the partner only on the excess over the partner's basis.

      b. result in a reduction in the partner's capital account.

This tax treatment applies to general partnerships, limited partnerships, and LLCs taxed as partnerships.

4613.06 Nonliquidating distributions of an S corporation:

      a. are taxed as capital gain to the shareholder only on the excess over the basis held by the shareholder.

      b. reduce the S corporation's accumulated adjustments account balance.

      c. reduce the shareholder's stock basis.

4614 Liquidation

4614.01 Liquidating dividend from a corporation:

      a. The corporation (either C or S) recognizes a gain or a loss when a corporation is liquidated.

      b. The corporation recognizes gain or loss as if the property were sold at its fair market value.

4614.02 Liquidating distributions from a partnership:

      a. If a partner received cash or marketable securities in excess of the partner's adjusted basis, then gain is recognized on that excess.

      b. If no cash equivalents are distributed, no gain is recognized. (IRC Section 731(a)(1))

      c. If a partner receives cash, unrealized receivables, or inventory in a liquidating distribution, a loss may be recognized by the partner equal to the difference between FMV and the partner's basis. (IRC Section 732)

      d. If only other property is received, then no loss may be recognized.

4620 Differences Between Tax and Financial Accounting

4621 Reconciliation of Book Income to Taxable Income

4621.01 Required reconciliations:

    a. As part of the corporate tax return, corporations must reconcile the difference between taxable income and accounting income on Schedule M-1.

      (1) Some of the areas where differences may arise include depreciation, life insurance premiums and proceeds, tax-exempt income, expenses of tax-exempt income, capital losses, goodwill, and federal income taxes.

      (2) **Summary of Schedule M-1:**

```
              Net income per books (after taxes)
     Add:     Federal income tax
              Net capital loss
              Taxable income not recorded on the books
              Book expenses not deducted on the return
     Deduct:  Book income not subject to tax
              Deductions on the return not recorded on the books
       -      Taxable income (before net operating loss deduction and dividends-received deduction)
```

    b. Corporate taxpayers must also reconcile the opening and closing balances in retained earnings on Schedule M-2.

4622 Disclosures Under Schedule M-3

4622.01 Corporations with total assets of $10 million or more must reconcile financial statement net income to the net income or loss of the corporation reported for U.S. taxable income. (IRS Form 1120, Schedule M-3 is used instead of M-1.)

4622.02 Check-off of types of return for the corporation:

    a. Nonconsolidated return

    b. Consolidated return (IRS Form 1120 only)

    c. Mixed 1120/L/PC group

    d. Dormant subsidiaries attached

4622.03 Part 1, Schedule M-3: Type of report filed by the corporation:

    a. SEC Form 10-K

    b. Income statement that was:

      (1) certified audited and

      (2) nontax basis

c. Income statement that was:
   (1) not certified audited and
   (2) nontax basis.
d. Enter the date for the income statement period:
   (1) Has the income statement been restated?
   (2) Has the income statement been restated in the previous five periods?
e. Is any of the corporation's voting common stock publicly traded?
f. Enter the symbol for the corporation's stock that is:
   (1) the primary corporate stock,
   (2) is U.S. publicly traded, and
   (3) is voting common stock.
g. Enter the nine-digit CUSIP number of the corporation's stock that is:
   (1) the primary corporate stock,
   (2) is publicly traded in the United States, and
   (3) is voting common stock.

4622.04 Part 1, Continued: Reconciliation of statement income to taxable income:
a. Post the worldwide consolidated net income.
b. Check off the accounting standard used:
   (1) GAAP
   (2) IFRS
   (3) Statutory
   (4) Tax-basis
   (5) Other
c. Nonincludible foreign entities:
   (1) Net income
   (2) Net loss
d. Nonincludible U.S. entities:
   (1) Net income
   (2) Net loss
e. Net income or loss from other includible:
   (1) Foreign disregarded entities
   (2) U.S. disregarded entities
   (3) Other includible entities
f. Adjustments to eliminations of transactions between includible and nonincludible entities
g. Other adjustments

4622.05 Part II: Reconciliation of Net Income (Loss) per Income Statement of Includible Corporations with Taxable Income per Return—Income (Loss) items: Part II includes 38 lines for reconciling income items.

4622.06 Part III: Reconciliation of Net Income (Loss) per Income Statement of Includible Corporations with Taxable Income per Return—Expense/Deduction Items: Part III includes 38 lines for reconciling expense items.

4630 C Corporations

4631 Determination of Taxable Income/Loss

Note: Updates to corporation rules may be found in IRS Publication 542.

4631.01 Corporations are taxable entities—they must file tax returns and pay taxes.

  a. Other organizations taxed as a corporation include insurance companies, business trusts, associations, and joint stock companies.

  b. Generally, an unincorporated organization will be taxed as a corporation if it elects to be taxed as a corporation. The election is made on IRS Form 8832 (*Entity Classification Election*).

  c. Certain corporations are tax-exempt.

  d. Corporations not expressly exempt from income tax must file an annual tax return (Form 1120) on or before the 15th day of the third month following the close of their fiscal year.

4631.02 The following tax formula is for corporations. Each step in the formula must be completed before the succeeding step is considered.

```
  Total income
- Exclusions
= Gross income
- Deductions (other than charitable contributions and the dividends-received deduction)
= Taxable income before special deductions
- Charitable contributions
= Taxable income before the dividends-received deduction
- Dividends-received deduction
= Taxable income
× Tax rate
= Tax liability before additions and credits
+ Additions to tax
- Credits to tax
= Tax liability
```

4631.03 Gross income for the corporation is determined in approximately the same manner as for the individual.

  a. A corporation must include in gross income 100% of the dividends received from other corporations.

  b. No gain or loss is recognized on the sale or acquisition of the corporation's own capital stock.

  c. A corporation distributing appreciated property to its shareholders will be taxed on the appreciation.

4631.04 **Deductions from gross income** (other than contributions and dividends received) include expenses that are normally deducted from gross income by an individual. However, no deduction is allowed for capital losses in excess of capital gains.

    a. Losses can only be used to offset capital gains in carryover years.

        (1) Corporate capital losses carry back three years and forward five years as short-term capital losses.

        (2) Capital loss carrybacks and carryforwards are short-term.

    b. Net operating loss is calculated the same way as taxable income.

        (1) There is no deduction allowed for a carryback or carryforward from other years.

        (2) A dividends-received deduction may be taken without any limitation.

        (3) A 3-year carryback also applies to NOLs resulting from the following:

            (a) Casualty or theft

            (b) Presidentially declared disasters affecting small businesses and farmers

        (4) Small businesses are those whose average annual gross receipts in the last three years were $5 million or less.

4631.05 **Special deductions for corporations:**

    a. Charitable contributions:

        (1) The corporate limit for charitable contributions is 10% of taxable income computed before the deductions for contributions and the dividends-received deduction and before consideration of:

            (a) any net operating loss *carryback* and

            (b) any capital loss *carryback*.

        (2) Contributions in excess of the 10% limit may be carried forward five years.

            (a) The total contribution deduction for any year into which an unused contribution is carried is still limited to 10% of the applicable income figure for that year.

            (b) Carryovers are considered in the order in which they arise.

        (3) Accrual-basis corporations may accrue contributions if the contribution is paid within 2½ months after the close of the tax year.

        (4) Cash-basis corporations may deduct only those amounts actually paid out, increased by any carryovers that might be available.

    b. Dividends-received deduction:

        (1) A corporation may deduct a percentage of the dividends it receives from taxable domestic corporations. The amount of the dividends-received deduction is based on the shareholder corporation's percentage of ownership in the corporation making the dividend distribution. The percentage of the dividend received that is deductible is determined as follows:

Ownership	Deduction Percentage
Less than 20%	70%
20% or more, but less than 80%	80%
80% or more	100%

            (a) The deduction for shareholders that qualify for either the 70% or 80% deduction is further limited to 70% or 80% of taxable income computed before the deduction for dividends received and before any deduction for net operating loss carryforwards or carrybacks.

(b) This limit does not apply, however, if in deducting 70% or 80% of the dividends received, a net operating loss is either created or increased.

(c) If shareholders are entitled to both 70% and 80% deductions for dividends received from different companies, the 80% dividends-received deduction is calculated first. When calculating the 70% deduction limitation, the *total* amount of dividends received from 20% owned companies is subtracted from taxable income.

(2) The dividends-received deduction for dividends received from an affiliated company is equal to 100% of the dividends received.

(a) An affiliated group exists where:

i. a parent company owns at least 80% of the stock in at least one other corporation in the group or

ii. at least 80% of the stock of other companies in the group is owned directly by one or more companies in the affiliated group. (The 80% stock ownership test does not apply to nonvoting stock that is limited and preferred as to dividends.)

(b) Members of an affiliated group may elect to file a consolidated return if all members consent. In this situation, dividends paid among the members are eliminated from income.

4631.06 Tax rates for corporations:

a. Taxable corporations are subject to the following tax rate structure:

Taxable Income Over	But Not Over	Tax Rate
$ 0	$ 50,000	15%
50,000	75,000	25%
75,000	10,000,000	34%
10,000,000		35%

b. Corporations with taxable income in excess of $100,000 must pay an additional tax of 5% on the excess. The maximum additional tax is limited to $11,750. When taxable income reaches $335,000, the corporation pays a flat rate of 34% until taxable income exceeds $10 million.

c. Corporations with over $15 million of taxable income must increase their tax liability by the lesser of 3% of the excess or $100,000. Corporations pay a flat rate of 35% when taxable income reaches $18,333,333.

d. The tax rate for qualified personal service corporations is a flat 35% on all taxable income.

4632 Tax Computations and Credits, Including Alternative Minimum Tax

4632.01 Corporations are also subject to the alternative minimum tax. The tax is computed at a rate of 20% on alternative minimum taxable income (AMTI) in excess of $40,000. If this amount exceeds the corporation's regular tax, the excess is added to the company's tax liability.

4632.02 The corporate minimum tax is computed as follows:

	Taxable income (before NOL)
+ or −	Adjustments
+	Preferences
=	AMTI (before ACE adjustment and NOL)
+ or −	ACE adjustment
=	AMTI (before NOL)
−	NOL (limited to 90% of AMTI)
=	AMTI
−	Exemption ($40,000)
=	Tentative minimum tax base
×	20%
=	Tentative minimum tax before foreign tax credit
−	Foreign tax credit
=	Tentative minimum tax
−	Regular tax (less foreign tax credit)
=	Alternative minimum tax

4632.03 The corporate exemption is $40,000. It is reduced by 25% of AMTI in excess of $150,000.

4632.04 While many adjustments and preferences applicable to individuals (see section **4590.01**) also apply to corporations, the adjustment for adjusted current earnings (ACE) applies only to corporations.

  a. The ACE adjustment may be either positive or negative. The adjustment is 75% of the difference between ACE and unadjusted AMTI.

  b. The starting point for computing ACE is AMTI. To this figure certain positive and negative adjustments are made.

4632.05 Positive ACE adjustments (add items) include the following:

  a. Tax-exempt income

  b. 70% dividends-received deduction (DRD)—80% and 100% DRD are not affected

  c. Key employee insurance proceeds

  d. Deferred gain on installment sales

  e. Net income buildup on life insurance contracts

4632.06 Negative ACE adjustments (deduct items) include the following:

  a. Federal income tax

  b. Capital losses

  c. Disallowed travel or entertainment expenses

  d. Fines and penalties

  e. Excess charitable contributions

4632.07 Depreciation must be calculated using the alternative depreciation system (ADS) (see section **4430.02.d**).

4632.08 Small corporations are exempt from the AMT. Small corporations are those with gross receipts averaging less than $7.5 million annually for the preceding 3-year period.

4633 Net Operating Losses

4633.01 Net operating losses may be carried back 2 years and forward 20 years and used as a deduction toward AGI. For tax years beginning before August 6, 1997, the carryback is generally 3 years, and the carryforward is 15 years.

   a. A 3-year carryback also applies to NOLs resulting from the following:

   (1) Casualty or theft

   (2) Presidentially declared disasters affecting small businesses and farmers

   b. Small businesses are those whose average annual gross receipts in the last three years were $5 million or less.

   c. The 2009 American Recovery Act allows NOLs for years after 2007 to be carried back up to 5 years at the election of the taxpayer. The act also modifies the definition of a small business for the same period to include businesses with average annual gross receipts in the last three years to be $15 million or less.

4633.02 If the taxpayer's taxable income is a negative figure, no tax is due currently, and a net operating loss carryover may be available. To compute a net operating loss, the following adjustments must be made to the negative taxable income figure:

   a. Capital losses are deductible only to the extent of capital gains.

   b. No personal exemption deduction can be taken.

   c. No net operating loss deduction is allowed.

   d. Personal deductions can be used only to offset nonbusiness income.

   (1) Salary is considered as business income.

   (2) A casualty loss is treated as a business loss for net operating loss purposes.

   e. Contributions to a self-employment retirement plan are not allowed.

4633.03 A net operating loss is carried back to the earliest of the two (three) prior years, where it is first applied against taxable income to determine whether additional tax years will be affected.

   a. Any loss remaining after carryback to the second prior year must be reduced by the following:

   (1) Personal exemptions

   (2) Net capital loss of the second prior year

   b. Any loss remaining after the listed adjustments are made can be carried over to the next applicable year and the pattern again followed.

4633.04 The tax liability in carryover years must then be recomputed, giving consideration to the following items:

   a. The net operating loss will be treated as a deduction from gross income.

   b. The charitable contribution deduction is not affected by the carryback.

   c. Other deductions that are based on a percentage of adjusted gross income or taxable income must be recomputed after applying the carryback (e.g., medical expense).

   d. Tax credits computed in reference to the tax liability must also be redetermined.

   e. A refund is available to the taxpayer to the extent that the previously reported tax liability for a given year exceeds the recomputed tax liability for that year.

4633.05 Generally, a taxpayer can carry a net operating loss (NOL) back to the two tax years before the NOL year. However, the portion of an NOL that is a qualified Gulf Opportunity Zone loss can be carried back to the five tax years before the NOL year. In addition, the 90% limit on the alternative tax NOL deduction (ATNOLD) does not apply to such portion of the ATNOLD.

4633.06 For amounts paid or incurred on or after the disaster date within the Core Midwestern Disaster Area and before January 1, 2011, the 2009 American Recovery Act provides for a special 5-year carryback period for a "qualified Disaster Recovery Assistance (QRDA) loss" that includes NOLs to the extent of certain specified amounts related to a core Midwestern disaster area.

4633.07 The 2009 American Recovery Act adds a 5-year carryback for any small business NOL occurring in 2008 and 2009. The Act also changes the definition of "small" to average receipts of $15 million over the last three years.

4634 Entity/Owner Transactions, Including Contributions and Distributions

4634.01 Tax-free contributions to form a new corporation

   a. Property must be contributed by investors to the corporation.

   b. The investors must receive control of the corporation under the 80% rule.

   c. Control by the investors must exist immediately after the exchange.

   d. The investors must receive only stock in the corporation for their investment.

   e. An investor of property in the corporation receives no gain or loss if the investor receives only stock in the corporation in return. (IRS Section 351(a))

   f. If the stockholder receives cash or other property in the exchange, then gain is recognized up to the smaller of the boot received or the gain realized. (IRS Section 351(b))

4634.02 Recognition of gain resulting from boot

   a. If an investor is relieved of a liability or transfers property subject to a liability, that is considered boot equal to the amount of liability.

   b. Nonqualified preferred stock is treated as boot.

       (1) Nonqualified preferred stock includes redeemable stock.

       (2) Nonqualified preferred stock also includes stock where the dividend varies according to the movements of an outside index.

   c. Character of gain recognized when boot received under IRS Section 351 depends on the type of asset transferred:

       (1) Ordinary income if inventory is transferred

       (2) Capital gain if a capital asset is transferred

       (3) Section 1231 gain if there is gain on property used in a trade or business (after depreciation recapture)

4634.03 **Definition of corporate control**

   a. **Control** is defined by an individual or a small group of stockholders holding 80% of the total combined voting power of all classes of voting stock and 80% of the total number of shares of each class of nonvoting stock.

   b. The voting power test applies to all voting stock in the total. (IRS Revenue Ruling 59-259)

   c. The number-of-shares test is applied separately to each class of stock. (IRS Revenue Ruling 59-259)

   d. When using the control test, count only issued and outstanding stock. (IRS Regulation Section 1.351-1)

   e. A test for control of corporation must use only direct ownership.

   f. Constructive ownership or stock attribution rules cannot be used.

   g. Stock rights or stock warrants are not included with stock. (IRS Regulation Section 1.351-1)

4634.04 **Definition of property**

   a. Property includes the following:

   (1) Cash

   (2) Intangible assets such as stocks and patents

   (3) Tangible property such as buildings and equipment

   b. Property does **not** include the following:

   (1) Services

   (2) Indebtedness of the corporation

   (3) Interest on that debt

4634.05 **Can loss be recognized in a Section 351 transaction?**

   a. Originally, loss could never be recognized in a Section 351 transaction.

   b. **1998 Tax Act amendment:** If the transferor received only nonqualified preferred stock, a loss may be recognized.

4634.06 In a liquidation, the corporation generally disposes of its assets for cash and distributes the proceeds to its shareholders in exchange for their capital stock. The corporation may also distribute its assets directly to the shareholders in exchange for the stock. Problems arise in accounting for both the shareholder's treatment of such a transaction and the corporation's treatment of such an activity.

4634.07 **Shareholder concerns:**

   a. Cash or property received by shareholders in exchange for their capital stock will generally result in capital gain or loss to the shareholder. The basis of any property received is FMV.

   b. **Exception:** When a subsidiary distributes property to its parent corporation (80% ownership), no gain or loss is recognized by the parent. Generally, the property received by the parent has the same basis that it had in the hands of the subsidiary.

4634.08 Corporation concerns:

    a. Liquidating corporations are required to recognize a gain or loss on both liquidating sales and liquidating distributions.

    b. **Exception:** No gain or loss will be recognized by a liquidating subsidiary on the distribution of any property in a complete liquidation to an 80% corporate parent. However, distributions to minority interests will generally trigger gain recognition. Losses in this situation are not recognized.

4635 Earnings and Profits

4635.01 Earnings and profits (E&P) play a deciding role in the tax treatment of corporate distributions.

4635.02 General guidelines for distributions:

    a. Distributions are first considered to come from current E&P, which is allocated on a pro rata basis to all distributions made during the year. A taxable dividend results even if there is a deficit in accumulated E&P.

    b. Any distributions in excess of current E&P come from accumulated E&P, which is applied in chronological order to the distributions.

    c. Distributions in excess of both current E&P and accumulated E&P are considered to be a return of capital.

4635.03 A definition of earnings and profits is not specifically spelled out in the Internal Revenue Code.

4635.04 In determining earnings and profits, the effect of a specific transaction must be examined to determine whether the transaction increases or decreases the corporation's ability to pay a dividend.

4635.05 Current earnings and profits is similar to taxable income, but certain adjustments are required. Some of these adjustments include the following:

    a. Accelerated depreciation is not allowed in determining E&P. Generally, straight-line depreciation must be used.

    b. Accelerated cost recovery system deductions on pre-1987 property must be based on the straight-line method using the following extended periods:

        (1) 3-year property—5 years

        (2) 5-year property—12 years

        (3) 10-year property—25 years

        (4) 15-year property—35 years

        (5) Expensed property—5 years

        (6) If the taxpayer elects a longer recovery period, the reduction in earnings and profits is based on the longer period.

    c. For property placed in service after 1986, the alternative depreciation system is used for determining earnings and profits.

    d. Cost depletion is used to calculate E&P, even though percentage depletion is used for income tax purposes.

  e. Interest on state or municipal bonds is not taxable, but it does increase E&P. The expenses incurred to generate this income reduce E&P.

  f. Nondeductible capital losses reduce E&P.

  g. Federal income taxes reduce E&P.

  h. Charitable contributions in excess of the deduction limit reduce E&P. Carryover contributions increase E&P if and when a deduction is finally allowed.

4635.06 Accumulated earnings and profits may best be described as the total of all previous years' current E&P reduced by distributions considered to come from accumulated E&P.

4636 Consolidated Returns

4636.01 Election to file a consolidated corporate income tax return:

  a. IRC Section 1501 requires that:

   (1) all corporate members of the group must agree to be included for each tax reporting period,

   (2) all corporate members must agree to follow all the regulations issued concerning IRC Section 1502,

   (3) a consent form must be signed before the last day for filing the return,

   (4) the parent company must file copies of the consent form from all of the affiliated corporations in the group, and

   (5) a schedule must be attached listing all of the affiliated corporations in the group.

  b. IRC Section 1502 gives the Secretary of the Treasury the authority to issue and prescribe regulations for consolidated corporate tax returns. These are "legislative" regulations, meaning provided for in the statute, and not just "advisory."

  c. IRC Section 1503 states that the income tax liability of a consolidated corporate group will be determined by the regulations that exist on the last day for filing the return as provided by law.

  d. IRC Section 1504 defines the "affiliated group" that qualifies for the privilege for filing a consolidated corporate income tax return.

  e. IRC Section 1504 also identifies those qualified as "includible corporations."

  f. IRC Section 1552 defines the general rule for allocating the tax liability among the members of the affiliated group.

4636.02 What is the reason to elect to file a consolidated corporate tax return? Generally, the combined group will reduce the net taxable income and the tax due to a minimum by taking full advantage of the losses reported by some group members by offsetting the profits reported by other members of the group.

4636.03 Affiliated group requirements:

  a. The common parent directly owns at least 80% of the voting power of the stock of a corporation.

  b. The common parent directly owns at least 80% of the value of all of the stock of that corporation.

  c. The stock may be owned directly by one or more of the other corporations in the affiliated group.

4636.04 An includible corporation for consolidation purposes is described in IRC Section 1504(b), which says that any domestic corporation can be part of a consolidated group except for:

    a. a tax-exempt corporation under IRC Section 501,

    b. an insurance company under IRC Section 801,

    c. foreign corporations, except for some Canadian or Mexican corporations as listed in IRC Section 1504(d),

    d. corporations electing the possessions tax credit under IRC Section 936,

    e. regulated investment companies,

    f. real estate investment trusts,

    g. domestic international sales corporations (DISCs), and

    h. S corporations.

4636.05 An affiliated group is at least two corporations:

    a. One corporation must be the parent, owning one or more subsidiaries.

    b. One corporation must be a subsidiary at least 80% owned by the parent.

    c. This is a parent-subsidiary group.

4636.06 There is also a brother-sister controlled group, where two corporations are owned by five or fewer individuals, estates, or trusts.

4636.07 Consolidated return election:

    a. The election to file a consolidated return is a privilege.

    b. The parent company must file IRS Form 11222 in the first consolidated year as prescribed in IRS Regulation Section 1.1502-75(b)(1).

4636.08 Extension of time to file corporate income tax returns:

    a. File IRS Form 7004, *Application for Automatic Extension of Time to File Certain Business Income Tax, Information and Other Returns.*

    b. The extension is six months or October 15 for calendar-year corporations.

    c. Mark for the extension of IRS Form 1120 on the form.

4636.09 Relationship of parent and the subsidiaries concerning tax affairs:

    a. The common parent is the sole agent for each subsidiary in the group, authorized to act on all matters. (IRS Regulation Section 1.152-77(a))

    b. The common parent and each subsidiary of the consolidated group are severally liable for the consolidated tax liability of the entire group—for any taxable year that they are members. (IRS Regulation Section 1.1502-6(a))

4636.10 Consolidations: unique tax issues

    a. Accounting methods and periods

    b. Consolidated taxable income framework

    c. Separate return limitations year (SRLY)

4636.11 Accounting methods and periods

    a. Each subsidiary must adopt the common parent's annual period for the first year of consolidation. (IRS Regulation Section 1.1502-76(a))

    b. The subsidiary's original taxable year ends at the close of the day that it became a member of the consolidated group. The subsidiary must file a short-period return for the period ending that day. (IRS Regulation Section 1.1502-76(b)(1)(ii))

4636.12 The consolidated tax return will include the following:

    a. The common parent's tax items for the entire year:

        (1) Income

        (2) Gains

        (3) Deductions

        (4) Losses

        (5) Credits

    b. Each subsidiary's items are included for the part of the year that the subsidiary was a member of the group. (IRS Regulation Section 1.1502-76(b))

4636.13 Preparing the consolidated tax return:

    a. Compute each corporate member's separate taxable income.

    b. Use the member corporation's income to prepare the consolidated income and balance sheet.

    c. Eliminate the intercompany transactions from the consolidated return.

    d. Separate the items that are subject to special tax treatment:

        (1) Capital gains and losses

        (2) Section 1231 gains and losses

        (3) NOL deductions

        (4) Charitable contributions deduction

        (5) Dividends-received deduction

4640 S Corporations

4641 Eligibility and Election

4641.01 Certain domestic corporations may elect not to be taxed. Instead, the income is passed through to the stockholders, who are taxed on their share of the corporation's earnings.

    a. Stockholders are taxed on their share of the earnings even though the earnings are not distributed.

    b. In S corporations, FICA taxes apply only to designated salaries, and the corporation is responsible for paying the taxes. No FICA taxes are paid on the remaining ordinary income that passes to the owners.

c. S corporations must file Form 1120-S each year before the 15th day of the third month following the close of the taxable year.

   (1) Shareholders who held stock during the taxable year must consent to the election.

   (2) All shareholders on the date of the election must consent to the election.

   (3) The election will be considered timely if it is made within 2-1/2 months of the first day of its taxable year.

   (4) Filing Form 7004 will automatically extend the filing date for six months.

   (5) If estimated tax liability is expected to be $500 or more, an estimated tax payment must be paid.

d. S corporations may be part of an affiliated group, but a consolidated return is prohibited.

4641.02 The following requirements must be met before a corporation is eligible to elect S corporation status:

   a. S corporations are limited to a maximum of 100 shareholders. Family members can elect to be treated as one shareholder.

      (1) Family members include a common ancestor, his or her descendants, and the spouses (or former spouses) of the descendants.

      (2) The common ancestor cannot be more than six generations removed from the youngest generation of shareholders.

      (3) Husbands and wives are considered as one shareholder.

      (4) The individual, not the trust, is considered as the shareholder. This is considered when a trust is owned by an individual.

   b. All shareholders must agree to the S corporation election.

   c. Only one class of stock may be issued and outstanding. Differences in voting rights among shares of common stock will be allowed, however.

   d. Only individuals, estates, certain trusts, and charitable organizations may be shareholders.

      (1) Certain qualified retirement plan trusts and certain charitable organizations that are exempt from tax are eligible to be shareholders. The income from these will pass through to the shareholder as unrelated business taxable income.

      (2) A qualified Subchapter S trust (QSST) may be shareholder for two years beginning with the date of death of the owner.

   e. The election (Form 2553) may be made at any time during the prior year or on or before the 15th day of the third month of the election year. However, the IRS has the authority to waive this requirement.

   f. Only eligible domestic corporations may qualify. Ineligible corporations include the following:

      (1) Certain financial institutions

      (2) Most insurance companies

      (3) A current or former domestic international sales corporation (DISC)

      (4) A company electing the Puerto Rico and possessions tax credit

   g. Nonresident aliens are not allowed as shareholders.

4641.03 S corporation status may be terminated voluntarily or involuntarily.

    a. Voluntary termination may take place if shareholders owning more than 50% of the outstanding shares (including nonvoting shares) consent and file notice of revocation:

        (1) If the notice is filed on or before the 15th day of the third month of the taxable year, it will be effective for the entire year or as of some specified date.

        (2) If filed after this date, the revocation becomes effective the following year.

        (3) A new shareholder owning more than 50% of the voting stock may revoke S corporation status within 60 days of becoming a shareholder. This termination is effective on the day it occurs.

    b. Involuntary termination becomes effective on the day in which any of the following events takes place:

        (1) The number of stockholders exceeds the limit allowed by law.

        (2) More than one class of stock is outstanding.

        (3) A corporation or partnership becomes a shareholder.

        (4) A nonresident alien becomes a shareholder.

    c. Since involuntary termination is effective as of the date the corporation ceases to qualify as an S corporation, the result is ordinarily two short tax years.

    d. Generally, there is no passive investment income limitation for S corporations.

        (1) If an S corporation has C corporation (regular corporation) earnings and profits and more than 25% of its gross receipts for three successive years is from certain forms of passive income, S corporation status will be terminated as of the first day of the fourth year.

        (2) Excessive passive income can also result in a special tax levy on the corporation.

    e. If S corporation status is terminated, there is a 5-year waiting period, or consent of the IRS, before the S status may be reelected.

4641.04 An S corporation must generally use the calendar year as its tax year. A fiscal year may be adopted if the corporation can establish a sound business purpose for such a year or show that the tax deferral would not exceed three months.

4642 Determination of Ordinary Income/Loss and Separately Stated Items

4642.01 Generally, the S corporation is not subject to income tax. The company's taxable income or loss flows through to the shareholders and is reported by them on their individual income tax returns.

4642.02 Taxable income for the S corporation is determined in almost the same way as for a partnership. Allowable deductions are similar to those available to individuals, with the following exceptions:

    a. Itemized deductions

    b. Personal exemptions

    c. Net operating loss deductions

    d. Charitable contributions

- e. Foreign taxes
- f. Oil and gas depletion

4642.03 Certain items are not included in taxable income. They are listed separately and passed through to the individual shareholders. These items include the following:

- a. Tax-exempt income
- b. Section 1231 gains and losses
- c. Long-term and short-term capital gains and losses
- d. Charitable contributions
- e. Passive income (loss)
- f. Portfolio income (loss)
- g. Section 179 expense deduction
- h. Nonbusiness income or loss
- i. Intangible drilling costs
- j. Mining exploration expenditures
- k. Depletion
- l. Amortization of reforestation expenditures
- m. Discharge of indebtedness
- n. Investment income and expenses
- o. Recoveries of prior taxes, bad debts, and delinquency amounts
- p. Wagering gains or losses

4642.04 Also listed separately are the following:

- a. Tax credits
- b. Tax preferences and AMT adjustment items
- c. Foreign taxes

4642.05 Each shareholder must include on the personal tax return the share of the corporation's income or loss and special items from the corporate tax year that has ended with or within the personal tax year. Thus, income is recognized on a basis similar to that of partnerships.

- a. Where ownership has changed during the year, each owner must recognize a pro rata share of the income or loss allocated on a daily basis.
- b. Loss pass-throughs in excess of the taxpayer's basis in the corporation may be carried forward indefinitely and deducted when the taxpayer's basis has increased sufficiently to absorb the loss.

4643 Basis of Shareholder's Interest

4643.01 A shareholder's tax basis in an S corporation is increased by any stock purchases and capital contributions. The following items also cause an adjustment to basis. However, a shareholder's basis in an S corporation can never go below zero.

- a. Upward adjustments:
  - (1) Taxable income

(2) Separately stated income items

(3) Depletion in excess of the property's basis

b. Downward adjustments:

(1) Loss from operations

(2) Separately stated loss items

(3) Nontaxable distributions

(4) Nondeductible loss items

4644 Entity/Owner Transactions, Including Contributions and Distributions

4644.01 Distributions of cash and property are basically given the same treatment. Shareholders must recognize as a distribution the amount of cash and the fair market value of any property distributed.

a. The taxability of a distribution is determined by its source.

b. Distributions come from the following sources in the order listed:

(1) Distributions are first considered to come from an "accumulated adjustments account" (AAA).

(a) The AAA represents income earned after 1982 adjusted by any additions and subtractions that shareholders were required to make to the basis of their stock for this period. However, no adjustment is made for the following:

i. Tax-exempt income

ii. Corporate expenses not deductible in computing taxable income and not chargeable to a capital account

(b) Distributions from the AAA are nontaxable.

(2) Distributions are then considered as dividends to the extent of any accumulated earnings and profits (E&P).

(3) Beyond accumulated E&P, distributions represent a return of capital and then a capital gain.

c. If an S corporation distributes appreciated property to its shareholders, the transfer is treated as if the property had been sold to the shareholders at fair market value.

(1) A gain is recognized at the corporate level.

(2) The gain is subsequently passed through to the shareholders.

4645 Built-In Gains Tax

4645.01 When a regular C corporation converts to S corporation status, a tax (a built-in gains tax) may be imposed on the net appreciation that took place on the assets during the time they were held by the C corporation.

a. The tax will be imposed on the S corporation when it disposes of property at a gain within 10 years after the S election took effect.

b. The tax is levied on the pre-S corporation appreciation only. Independent appraisals of the assets should be obtained when converting a C corporation to an S corporation.

4645.02 When a C corporation using LIFO inventory converts to an S corporation, the C corporation must include in income the excess of FIFO inventory over LIFO inventory in the final C corporation return. The corporation now has a stepped-up basis for its LIFO inventory.

    a. The recapture should be included in the gross income for the C corporation and the tax paid in four equal installments.

    b. The first installment is due when the last C corporation tax return is due. The remaining three installments are due on the next three tax return due dates.

4650 Partnerships

4651 Determination of Ordinary Income/Loss and Separately Stated Items

Partnership Characteristics

Note: Updates to partnership rules may be found in IRS Publication 541.

4651.01 Partnerships are not taxable entities. They are reporting entities. Partnerships function as a conduit for income tax purposes.

    a. Ordinary income and losses along with special gain and loss items channel through the partnership down to the individual partners, who report these items on their personal tax returns.

    b. The partnership must report each partner's distributive share of the ordinary gain or loss as well as any specially treated items that the partner might use on an individual return.

    c. Self-employment taxes apply to all ordinary income passing to the owners.

4651.02 **A partnership** arises when two or more persons join together to conduct a business activity, the expected profits and losses of which will be shared in some manner by these persons.

    a. Organizations qualifying as a trust, estate, or corporation will not be treated as a partnership.

    b. Unincorporated entities that are eligible for taxation as a partnership also include the following:

        (1) Syndicate

        (2) Pool

        (3) Group

        (4) Joint venture

    c. In general, entities that qualify for partnership treatment also qualify for electing out of partnership treatment under the check-the-box regulations. If a business entity is not required to be treated as a corporation for federal tax purposes, it may choose its own classification. An entity with two or more members can be classified as either a partnership or an association taxed as a corporation. An entity with only one member can be classified as an association or can be disregarded as an entity separate from its owner and be treated as a sole proprietorship. A single-member limited liability company cannot elect partnership status. The default classification for a new entity with two or more members is a partnership, and the default classification for an entity with one member is a sole proprietorship.

4651.03 The partnership return (Form 1065) is strictly an informational return. Partnerships do not pay income taxes.

    a. This return is due on the 15th day of the fourth month following the close of the partnership's tax year.

    b. A return is required even though the firm has no gross income.

Reporting Partnership Income

4651.04 The ordinary gain or loss of a partnership must be computed and then allocated to the partners according to the agreed-upon method for distributing profits and losses.

    a. Gross income: Any item of gross income which receives special consideration on an individual's return must be excluded from ordinary gain or loss and shown as a separate item on Schedule K of Form 1065.

    b. Business deductions: Partnership deductions are basically the same as an individual's deductions toward adjusted gross income.

        (1) Any deduction that receives special consideration on an individual's return must be shown as a separate item on Schedule K. Such deductions do not enter the computation of ordinary gain or loss.

        (2) Included as allowable deductions are guaranteed payments to the partners for salaries and interest.

    c. Nonbusiness deductions: Partnerships do not include any nonbusiness deductions in the computation of ordinary gain or loss.

        (1) The standard deduction is not available to partnerships.

        (2) Deductions for personal exemptions are not allowed.

4651.05 Items receiving special treatment must be separately listed in Schedule K.

    a. Specially treated items in the partnership retain the same character on the tax return of the individual partners.

    b. Following are some of the partnership items that must be separately listed on Schedule K:

        (1) First-year Section 179 expensing deduction of business assets

        (2) Dividends, interest, and royalties

        (3) Net short-term capital gain (loss)

        (4) Net long-term capital gain (loss)

        (5) Net gain (loss) from casualty and theft

        (6) Net gain (loss) for sale or exchange of "Section 1231 assets"

        (7) Contributions

        (8) Foreign taxes

        (9) Income or loss from real estate rentals

        (10) Income or loss from other rentals

        (11) Expenses related to portfolio income

        (12) Tax-exempt interest

        (13) Recoveries of items previously deducted

(14) AMT preference items

(15) Nonbusiness and personal items

    c. In general, separate treatment must be accorded to any partnership item which, when treated separately, would result in a different tax liability than the partner would experience if the item had not been separately treated.

    d. Using a special schedule (Schedule K-1), the partnership must disclose each partner's distributive share of the Schedule K items. Guaranteed payments (salaries/interest) are also included.

        (1) The profit and loss sharing ratio is used to distribute these special items.

        (2) If the income ratio is different from the loss ratio, the special items are distributed accordingly, depending on whether the partnership has a profit or loss.

4651.06 Gains, losses, depreciation, and depletion on property contributed by a partner to a partnership must be allocated in a way that takes into account the difference between the partnership's basis for the contributed property and the property's fair market value at the time of contribution to the partnership. These items cannot be allocated to the partners in accordance with each partner's interest in the partnership.

4651.07 Partnership tax years:

    a. Reporting year: Each partner must include on the personal tax return a share of those partnership items from the partnership tax year that ends with or within the tax year.

        (1) Generally, the death, retirement, or withdrawal of a partner, the sale of a partnership interest, or the addition of a new partner will not terminate the partnership tax year. However, these events will close the tax year for the individual partner affected.

            (a) The partnership year will terminate with the sale or exchange of an aggregate interest of 50% or more in the partnership.

                i. The terminated partnership is deemed a liquidation with the assets and liabilities being distributed to the partners.

                ii. A new partnership is then created and the partners recontribute the assets and liabilities to the partnership with the possibility of a stepped-up basis.

            (b) Gift or inheritance of a 50% interest, however, will not cause the partnership year to end.

        (2) Income and losses will be allocated to a new partner only for that portion of the year during which the new partner was a member of the partnership. Allocation of income and losses will not be made retroactive to a period prior to the new partner's entry into the partnership.

    b. Establishing the tax year:

        (1) Generally, the tax year of a partnership must be determined by reference to the tax years of the partners.

            (a) If the majority partners (over 50% of the ownership) all have the same tax year, the partnership must adopt that tax year.

            (b) If the majority partners have different tax years, the partnership must adopt as its taxable year the tax year of the principal partners. Principal partners are partners with at least a 5% interest in capital or profits.

            (c) If neither the majority partners nor the principal partners have the same tax year, the partnership must adopt the calendar year as its taxable year.

(d) **Exceptions:**

  i. The partnership may establish that a business purpose exists for selecting another tax year.

  ii. If a partnership recognizes 25% or more of its gross receipts in the last two months of the same 12-month period for three consecutive years, it may adopt that 12-month period as its fiscal year.

(2) Partnerships may elect to use a different tax year than the one required if the income deferral is three months or less. In making this election, the partnership must make a noninterest-bearing deposit with the government to compensate it for revenue lost as a result of the tax deferral.

4652 Basis of Partner's/Member's Interest and Basis of Assets Contributed to the Partnership

4652.01 The basis of a partner's interest in a partnership must be computed without regard to the capital account balance as shown on the partnership books.

  a. A partner's basis is increased by the investment of property or cash.

  (1) The increase in a partner's investment for contributed property is limited to the basis in that property.

  (2) In addition, the basis of a partner's interest is increased by the distributive share of the following partnership items:

  (a) Taxable income

  (b) Tax-exempt income

  (c) Excess depletion deductions

  b. A partner's basis is decreased by the partner's withdrawals of money and by the adjusted basis of all other property distributed to the partner.

  (1) A partner's basis is further decreased by the distributive share of the following partnership items:

  (a) Partnership losses (including capital losses)

  (b) Nondeductible partnership expenditures

  (2) The basis of a partner's interest may not be decreased below zero.

4652.02 The basis of contributed property is the same in the hands of the partnership as it was in the hands of the partner who contributed it.

  a. As to the contribution of personal assets (nonbusiness property) to the partnership, however, the partnership basis will be the lesser of:

  (1) the adjusted basis of the contributing partner or

  (2) the fair market value at the time the property was contributed to the partnership.

  b. Generally, no gain or loss is recognized by either the partner or the partnership when a partner increases an investment through the contribution of property.

  (1) Income must be recognized by a partner who receives a capital interest in the partnership in exchange for services rendered.

  (2) The fair market value of the capital interest received shall be considered as compensation (ordinary income).

4652.03 Increases in the liabilities of the partnership are treated as though the partner contributed money for a share of those liabilities. The basis of the partner's investment increases accordingly.

   a. The assumption by the partnership of a partner's personal liability is treated as a distribution of money to the partner. The basis of the investment decreases by the amount of the liability assumed by the other partners.

   b. Generally, the ratio for sharing *losses* is used in the calculation to determine a partner's share of the partnership liabilities.

4652.04 Partnership losses reduce the basis of the partner's investment in the partnership.

   a. A partner may deduct the distributive share of partnership losses on a personal return only to the extent of the basis of the partner's interest in the partnership.

      (1) For purposes of computing a partner's loss absorption ability, the basis of a partner's investment will not include any partnership liability for which the partner has no personal liability.

      (2) This provision is designed to limit the loss that may be passed through to a *limited partner*. General partners are personally liable for the debts of the partnership, but limited partners are not liable beyond the amount of their contributed capital.

   b. Any disallowed loss remains available to the partner in future years when the basis has increased so as to absorb some or all of the loss.

4652.05 The withdrawal of money or property from the partnership decreases the basis of the partner's investment by the partnership's adjusted basis in that property.

   a. Generally, no gain or loss is recognized by either party when property is distributed in something other than the liquidation of a partner's interest. However, if a partner has contributed appreciated property to the partnership, the following rules may apply:

      (1) If the appreciated property is distributed within seven years to another partner, the contributing partner must recognize the precontribution gain as income.

      (2) If other property (other than cash) is distributed to the contributing partner within seven years, the contributing partner recognizes gain equal to the lesser of the precontribution gain or the excess of the distributed property's FMV over the partner's basis in the partnership.

   b. The basis of the property received by the partner is the same as it was while in the possession of the partnership.

   c. When the partnership's adjusted basis for the property distributed exceeds the basis of a partner's investment in the partnership, the basis of the property to the partner is limited to the basis of the investment in the partnership.

      (1) The basis of the partner's investment in the partnership is consequently reduced to zero.

      (2) The partnership's excess property basis will be treated as a basis decrease to the partner.

         (a) Distributions of unrealized receivables and inventory take the partnership's basis. Any shortfall is handled as described in (b) and (c) following.

         (b) The basis decrease is first allocated to property with unrealized depreciation to the extent that basis exceeds FMV. If insufficient basis is available to reduce the partner's basis by the full amount of depreciation, available basis is allocated to the properties in proportion to their respective amounts of unrealized depreciation (Basis − FMV).

(c) Any remaining decrease is allocated to the properties in proportion to their adjusted bases.

4653 Partnership and Partner Elections

4653.01 Special adjustments to the basis of partnership assets are available in certain situations.

    a. The partnership may elect to adjust the basis of its property for the benefit of a new partner.

        (1) Such an adjustment is possible under the following circumstances:

            (a) An established interest is sold, exchanged, or inherited

            (b) There is a difference between the new partner's *cost* for the interest and the partnership's basis for the share of the property

        (2) If the election is exercised, those partnership assets that are adjusted will carry a special basis strictly for the benefit of the new partner. The new partner's depreciation, depletion, and gain or loss will be determined separately on this special basis.

        Example: X, an equal partner in XYZ, sells his interest to W for $50,000. The partnership's basis for one-third of its assets is only $35,000, however. To avoid the inequities created by this situation, the partnership may elect to increase the basis of its assets by $15,000 for the sole benefit of W.

    b. A similar election is available to the partnership as a result of the complete or partial liquidation of a partner's interest.

        (1) Such an adjustment is available when money or other property is distributed to a partner so as to reduce or terminate the partner's capital interest in the partnership.

        (2) The adjustment is designed to reflect the difference between the basis of the partner's interest and the partnership's basis in the property used to terminate that interest.

4654 Transactions Between a Partner and the Partnership

4654.01 **Sale or exchange of a partnership interest:**

    a. The sale or exchange of a partnership interest is generally treated as the sale or exchange of a capital asset.

        (1) To the extent that the partner is disposing of a share of unrealized receivables and inventory, the gain associated with these items must be treated as ordinary income.

            (a) **Unrealized receivables** include the following:

                i. Receivables not previously included in gross income

                ii. Property holding ordinary income potential under the depreciation recapture provisions of the Internal Revenue Code

                iii. A franchise, trademark, or trade name

            (b) **Inventory** includes all noncapital assets other than Section 1231 assets.

        (2) In computing the ordinary income on the disposition of a partnership interest, a portion of the selling price must be allocated to the unrealized receivables and the inventory. In an arm's-length transaction, the portion that the buyer and the seller agree to allocate to such property will generally be regarded as correct.

(3) The remainder of the selling price is considered as the amount realized for the partner's capital interest in the partnership.

b. The capital gain or loss from the sale or exchange of a partnership interest will be long term or short term depending on the length of the period in which the seller had owned the interest in the partnership. Generally, this holding period will include the holding period of any property contributed by the partner.

c. If a partner sells the entire interest in the partnership, profits and losses up to the date of sale must be considered.

(1) If the partner withdraws the share of the earnings up to the date of sale, they are taxed to the partner accordingly.

(2) If these earnings are not withdrawn, the basis of the partnership interest will be increased by the profits not withdrawn. In addition, the partner must include a share of the profits up to the date of sale as ordinary income on the tax return.

4654.02 **Liquidation and retirement of a capital interest:**

a. Generally, no gain or loss is recognized by the partnership on the distribution of money or other property to a partner.

b. A partner realizes a gain on the liquidation of a partnership interest when the partnership's basis in the property distributed is more than the partner's investment in the partnership.

(1) A partner recognizes a gain only if the amount of cash received exceeds the basis of the partnership interest.

(a) If a gain is recognized, the basis of all other property received is zero.

(b) The gain recognized is capital gain, except to the extent of the unrealized receivables and inventory. The gain on these items is ordinary income.

(2) If the cash received is less than the basis of the partner's interest, no gain is recognized.

(a) If no gain is recognized, the basis of all other property received is equal to the basis of the partner's interest minus the cash received.

(b) This remainder is first allocated to any unrealized receivables and inventory items to the extent of their basis in the hands of the partnership. Basis is then allocated to other properties as follows:

i. To appreciated properties, basis is allocated up to the full extent of the appreciation. (Allocation of an amount less than the full appreciation requires a proportional allocation based on the respective amounts of unrealized appreciation.)

ii. If the basis increase has not been fully allocated, the remainder is allocated to all of the properties (other than the unrealized receivables and inventory) in proportion to the properties' respective fair market values.

c. A partner realizes a loss on the liquidation of the partnership interest when the partnership's basis in the property distributed is less than the partner's investment in the partnership.

(1) A partner recognizes a loss if cash, unrealized receivables, and inventory items are the only assets received for the partnership interest.

(a) In this situation, *inventory* refers to all inventory items, not just those that have appreciated in value.

- (b) The basis of the receivables and the inventory to the partner is the same as it was in the possession of the partnership.
- (2) Where the partner receives property other than cash, unrealized receivables, and inventory, no loss is recognized.
    - (a) The basis of the receivables and the inventory to the partner is the same as it was in the possession of the partnership.
    - (b) The basis of the other property received is equal to its basis in the partnership increased by the loss not recognized.

d. An exception to the general rule covering the distribution of property applies where a disproportionate distribution of unrealized receivables or substantially appreciated inventories takes place. Special rules provide for the possible recognition of a gain or loss to both the partner and the partnership in such a situation.

e. Certain future payments to a retiring partner may not qualify as proceeds from the sale of the partnership interest. These additional payments are taxable as ordinary income.

- (1) **Guaranteed payments:** If these future payments can be determined without reference to future income, they will be treated as guaranteed payments—ordinary income to the retiring partner and a deductible expense to the partnership.
- (2) **Distribution share:** If these future payments are going to be based on the partnership's future income, they will be treated as a distribution of partnership income—ordinary income to the retiring partner and a reduction in the distributive shares of the other partners.

f. Where payments are made to a deceased partner's successor, the successor generally "steps into the shoes of the decedent." Any amounts received by the successor are taxed in the same way they would have been taxed to the deceased partner.

g. Generally, the property distributed to a partner maintains the same character as it had in the partnership.

- (1) On the sale of noncapital assets received from the partnership, ordinary gain or loss treatment is limited to a period of five years, extending from the date of distribution.
- (2) Sales of noncapital assets taking place after five years produce capital gains and losses if these items are being held as capital assets by the former partner.

4654.03 **Sale of property to the partnership by a partner:**

a. Generally, the sale of a partner's property to the partnership will be recognized as an arm's-length transaction.

- (1) Gains and losses on such transactions will be recognized by the partner.
- (2) The basis of such property to the partnership is its cost to the partnership.

b. Exceptions include the following:

- (1) No loss is recognized in the following circumstances:
    - (a) A transaction between the partnership and a partner with more than 50% interest
    - (b) A transaction between two partnerships, each of which is more than 50% owned by the same person
    - (c) The disallowed loss remains available to the buyer to offset any recognized gain on a future disposal of the asset.

(2) Capital gain treatment is denied on the sale of IRC Section 1231 property (see section **4934** for a definition of IRC Section 1231 property) in the following circumstances:

(a) A transaction between the partnership and a partner with more than a 50% interest

(b) A transaction between two partnerships, each of which is more than 50% owned by the same person

4654.04 Merger or split-up of partnership:

a. Where two or more partnerships merge, the resulting partnership is a continuation of that prior partnership whose members own more than 50% of the capital and profits in the resulting partnership.

(1) If this test cannot be satisfied, the resulting partnership will be a continuation of that prior partnership providing the greatest dollar value of assets to the resulting partnership.

(2) If neither of these tests can be satisfied, all of the merged partnerships will be terminated and a new partnership will result.

b. Where a partnership is split up into two or more partnerships, the following guidelines apply:

(1) A resulting partnership will be a continuation of the original partnership if its members had more than 50% of the capital and profits in the original partnership.

(2) Any resulting partnership that cannot meet this test will be treated as a new partnership.

(3) If none of the resulting partnerships can meet this test, the original partnership will be terminated, and all of the resulting partnerships will be treated as new partnerships.

4655 Treatment of Partnership Liabilities

4655.01 Liabilities and Their Effects on Basis

a. A partner's share of the partnership's liabilities is added to the partner's capital account to calculate the partner's basis.

b. Liabilities recorded on the partnership's books are considered to be the obligations of the partners (the aggregate or conduit concept).

c. Any time the pool of liabilities increases, the partners are treated as having contributed money to the partnership because they obligate themselves to future payments (the aggregate theory). (IRC Section 752)

d. When partnership liabilities are reduced by repayment of loans or accounts payable, the partners are treated as having a distribution of money from the partnership, used to retire future debts.

e. When a partnership's liabilities increase, each partner's basis in his partnership interest increases in proportion to his respective share of such debts.

f. Correspondingly, each partner's basis decreases proportionally when the partnership's liabilities decrease.

4655.02 Types of Debt

a. **Recourse debt** is debt where the partnership and at least one partner is personally liable for the debt.

b. **Nonrecourse debt** is debt where there is no personal liability for the debt by the partnership or any partner. With nonrecourse debt, the lender must rely on repayment from the value of the pledged assets.

4655.03 Types of Partners

a. A **general partner** is personally liable for recourse partnership debts when the partnership cannot pay.

b. A **limited partner** is not liable for debts of the partnership beyond his or her partnership investment. This amount is increased by any future contributions the partner has agreed to.

4655.04 Partner's Basis

a. A general partner is allowed to increase partnership basis by his or her share of all recourse debt. The partner's share is calculated using the ratio for sharing losses.

b. A limited partner is allowed to increase partnership basis for their share of recourse debt if they share in partnership losses. A limited partner's share of partnership liabilities cannot exceed the total contributions the partner is obligated to make under the limited partnership agreement.

c. All recourse debt of the partnership is allocated to the partners in calculating the tax basis of their partnership investment.

d. If a limited partner is denied a share of recourse debt due to a lack of obligation, the general partner's allocation of debt must be adjusted upward to offset the limited partner's reduced allocation.

4656 Distribution of Partnership Assets

4656.01 Following are the types of nonliquidating partnership distributions:

a. Nonliquidating distributions of cash and other property that will not end in the liquidation of the distributee partner's interest

b. Disproportionate distributions, which affect the partner's share of ordinary income property of the partnership

4656.02 IRC Section 731: Gain or loss recognition

a. General Rule: No gain or loss is recognized by the partner or partnership in a distribution of cash or property.

b. Exception for cash distributions: If a cash distribution is received in excess of the partner's basis, then the amount that exceeds the basis is treated as a capital gain to the partner.

c. Beginning in 1995, marketable securities are treated as cash for purposes of IRC Section 731(a)(1). This applies to the calculation of a gain, but not to the calculation of a loss.

4656.03 IRC Section 732: Partner's basis in property received, distribution of property:

a. The partner receives the same basis in property as the partnership held.

      b. In a current distribution, the partner's outside basis is reduced by any money distributed and the basis of any other property distributed.

      c. The partner's basis cannot be reduced below zero.

4656.04 IRC Section 733: The partner's remaining basis in a partnership after these deductions:

      a. The partner's remaining basis in a partnership after these deductions reduces the partner's outside basis by the money distributed to the partner.

      b. The partner's remaining basis in a partnership after these deductions also reduces the partner's outside basis by the value of any property distributed to the partner.

      c. A distribution cannot reduce a partner's basis in the partnership below zero.

      d. Other effects of distributions:

          (1) Holding period: IRC Section 735(b) tacks on the holding period of the partnership so that it is included with the holding period of the partner.

          (2) The partnership recognizes no gain or loss on current or liquidating distributions to a partner.

          (3) The partner can have a gain or loss on a distribution that is considered the same as a gain or loss on sale of a partnership interest.

          (4) Actual interest: Even when distributions or allocation of partnership losses may reduce a partner's basis to zero, the partner still retains the same capital and profits interest in the partnership.

4657 Ownership Changes, and Liquidation and Termination of Partnership

4657.01 Liquidating Distributions

      a. Liquidating distributions are made to a partner in order to terminate the partner's entire interest in the partnership. (IRS Regulation Section 1.761-1(d))

      b. The forms of liquidating distributions can be:

          (1) cash distributions,

          (2) distributions in kind,

          (3) a lump-sum distribution, or

          (4) a series of distributions.

      c. The categories of liquidating distributions are:

          (1) general liquidating distributions and

          (2) distributions to retiring or deceased partners.

      d. Recognition of loss

          (1) Losses may be recognized with a liquidating distribution.

          (2) The distribution must consist solely of cash and Section 751 ordinary income assets.

          (3) Loss occurs if the partner's basis is larger than the total of the cash and Section 751 properties received. (IRC Section 731(a))

  e. Adjusted basis of property received

   (1) For liquidation distributions, the basis of property received is the adjusted basis less the cash received.

   (2) If two or more properties received, then the basis is allocated to the properties. (IRC Section 732 (c))

  f. **Allocation of basis.** Allocations are to be made under IRC Section 732(c) as follows:

   (1) Step 1:

    (a) Allocate to unrealized receivables and inventory items equal to the inside basis.

    (b) If there is any leftover outside basis, go to Step 2.

    (c) If there is insufficient outside basis to allow "hot assets" to receive basis equal to inside bases, allocate the deficiency as follows.

    (d) First, allocate in proportion to built-in losses.

    (e) Then, allocate to the hot assets in proportion to their adjusted bases.

   (2) Step 2:

    (a) Any basis left after Step 1(a) is allocated to cold assets (non-hot assets) equal to their inside basis.

    (b) If there is any leftover outside basis, go to Step 3.

    (c) If there is insufficient outside basis to allow all "cold assets" to receive an outside basis equal to the inside basis, allocate the deficiency as follows.

    (d) First, allocate to cold assets with an excess of basis over value, based on built-in losses.

    (e) Second, allocate to cold assets in proportion to the adjusted bases.

   (3) Step 3:

    (a) Any basis left over from Step 2(a) is allocated to cold assets based on the excess of fair market value over basis.

    (b) Any remaining outside basis is allocated under Step 4.

   (4) Step 4: The remaining basis is allocated to cold assets based on fair market value.

4657.02 Distributions to Retiring or Deceased Partners

  a. The death of a partner does not terminate the partnership.

  b. The deceased partner's successor in interest is a partner until the interest is liquidated.

  c. A retiring partner is recognized as a partner until his/her retirement is complete.

  d. Winding-down payments (IRC Section 736(a)):

   (1) These payments are treated as distributions of income or guaranteed payments.

   (2) Payments are taxable either to the retiring partner or deceased partner's successor in interest as ordinary income.

   (3) These payments reduce the other partners' distributive shares of income.

  e. Partnership interest payments (IRC Section 736(b)):

   (1) These are payments made for a partner's interest in partnership property.

   (2) These payments are for the interest in capital gain or loss properties.

4657.03   Partnership Terminations

a. A partnership exists for tax purposes until it is terminated (IRC Section 708(b)):

   (1) by the end of any business or financial operations.

   (2) by certain sales or exchanges of partnership interests in a 12-month period.

b. Cessation of business:

   (1) A partnership is terminated when no part of any business, financial operation, or venture is carried on by any of the partners.

   (2) When all partners agree to the state law dissolution of the partnership, it is terminated for tax purposes. (IRC Section 708(b)(1)(A))

   (3) Sale of a 50% partnership interest by one partner to the other 50% partner automatically terminates a two-person partnership. (IRS Regulation Section 1.708-1(b)(1))

c. Sales and exchanges: When there is a sale or exchange of 50% or more of the total interest in partnership capital and profits, the partnership is terminated for tax purposes. (IRC Section 708(b)(1)(B))

d. Using the special aggregation rule, all sales and exchanges made within a 12-month period are included, but the sale of the same interest is not counted twice. The period is for any consecutive 12-month period, not for a calendar year. (IRS Regulation Section 1.708-1(b)(2))

e. Under the aggregation rule, the following exchanges are included:

   (1) Transfer of a partnership interest to a corporation

   (2) Contribution of an interest in a partnership to another partner

   (3) Distribution of a partnership interest by a corporation or other entity

   (4) Acquisition of a partnership interest under a tax-free reorganization

f. The following exchanges are **not** included in the aggregation rules:

   (1) Gifts, bequests, or inheritance

   (2) Liquidation of a partner's entire interest in the partnership

   (3) Conversion of a general partnership interest into a limited partnership interest in the same partnership

g. If new partners contribute property in exchange for 50% or more of a partnership, then the partnership is not terminated. (IRS Revenue Ruling 75-423, 1975-1 CB 260)

h. Consequences to partners of terminated partnerships:

   (1) When a partnership is terminated due to a sale of 50% of the partnership interests, a new partnership is formed.

   (2) The old partnership tax year is closed for all partners.

   (3) The new partnership receives the assets of the old partnership with a carryover basis in the assets. (IRS Regulation Section 1.708-1(b)(4) and (5))

   (4) Holding period: For the assets of the new partnership, the holding period of the old partnership is tacked on and included in the holding period for the partnership.

   (5) Income bunching: Taxable income or loss for the old partnership is determined on the date of termination. This could cause a bunching of taxable income to the partners in their tax year. (IRC Section 706(c)(1) and IRS Regulation Section 1.706-1(c)(1))

(6) Deferred loss: Although unused losses are carried forward indefinitely, when the partnership is terminated, the deferred amounts cannot be used.

    i. The effects on the partnership:

       (1) The old basis is carried over to the new partnership.

       (2) The holding period for the assets includes the holding period of the old partnership. (IRC Sections 735 and 1223(2))

       (3) When the partnership is terminated, the elections made by the partnership are automatically terminated.

       (4) New elections must be made according to IRC Section 703(b).

4660 Trusts and Estates

4661 Types of Trusts

4661.01 There are five major types of trusts used in estate planning for a married person:

1. Marital trust, also called an "A" trust
2. Nonmarital trust
3. QTIP trust (qualified terminable interest property trust)
4. Estate trust
5. Life insurance trust

4661.02 **Marital trust** features:

a. Income produced by the trust must be paid out annually.

b. The surviving spouse must be entitled to all income from the trust.

c. The spouse must have a general power of appointment.

d. The power is exercisable in all events.

e. No person may have the power to appoint any assets to others.

g. The marital deduction applies to the transfer of all assets at the death of a spouse, resulting in a tax-free transfer.

4661.03 There are four major types of nonmarital trusts:

1. Bypass trust
2. Credit shelter trust
3. Family trust
4. "B" trust

4661.04 **Nonmarital trust** features:

a. The trust holds property transferred to the trust at the time of death of the spouse.

b. Often the amount transferred is equal to the amount of the marital deduction.

c. The trust is often used to receive property not allocated to the marital trust.

d. The trust will not be taxed on the death of the second spouse due to unified credit.

  e. The trust may provide income to the surviving spouse only, or to the surviving spouse or children of the decedent.

  f. An annual distribution of trust income is not required; the trustee may hold income for future distribution.

  g. The trust is most often used to provide income to the surviving spouse.

4661.05 Qualified terminable interest property trust (QTIP):

  a. The surviving spouse will receive a stream of income for life.

  b. Income must be distributed at least annually.

  c. Income may be paid only to the surviving spouse.

  d. The executor of the estate makes the election for a QTIP on the estate tax return.

  e. At the death of the second spouse, the property in the trust passes to a different heir.

  f. The heir was chosen by the first spouse.

  g. The value of the trust is included in the estate of the surviving spouse.

4661.06 Estate trusts:

  a. An estate trust provides income to the surviving spouse for life.

  b. The remainder of the trust must be payable to the estate.

  c. No interest passes to anyone else.

  d. This trust is used when the survivor does not need income.

  e. This trust is also used with assets not likely to appreciate in value.

4661.07 Life insurance trusts:

  a. These trusts are used for holding policies and receiving proceeds at death.

  b. The trusts may be inter vivos or testamentary.

  c. The trusts may be revocable or irrevocable.

  d. The trusts may be funded or unfunded.

  e. The use of this trust can prevent expenses and delays of probate.

  f. This trust reduces exposure to the beneficiary's creditors.

4661.08 Bypass trust:

  a. When the first spouse dies, the will of the decedent provides that a portion of the estate remainder (after estate taxes) is paid into a bypass trust for the surviving spouse.

  b. If the surviving spouse follows the rules provided by the IRS, estate tax will not be paid again on those funds.

  c. The surviving spouse must have only limited power to access the trust while alive.

  d. The surviving spouse must not have an unrestricted right to withdraw principal from the trust.

  e. The surviving spouse can be given the right to withdraw principal for health, education, maintenance, or support.

  f. The spouse may also be given the right to withdraw up to $5,000 of principal each year, or 5% of the total principal, whichever is greater.

- g. The spouse may also be given the right to withdraw all of the interest and dividends each year earned by the trust.
- h. Beyond the asset withdrawals listed above, the spouse cannot have the right to give trust assets to himself, his creditors, his estate, or his estate's creditors.
- i. The donor of the trust can name the person to receive the trust after the death of the spouse, or the donor can give the survivor a list of persons such as family members to choose to receive the assets.

4661.09 Credit shelter trust:

- a. A credit shelter trust is also referred to as a family trust, bypass trust, or Trust "B" in an "A-B plan."
- b. At death, an individual leaves an amount equal to the estate tax applicable exclusion amount to a credit shelter trust. The trust can be used to provide the surviving spouse with income for life and principal payments if needed to maintain his or her lifestyle.
- c. When the surviving spouse dies, the entire value of the trust, including appreciation, is passed to the heirs of the original spouse, free of federal estate tax.
- d. For the other assets of the surviving spouse, outside the trust, the estate tax exclusion is applied to the value of the estate. The result is that both applicable exclusion amounts are fully utilized.

4661.10 Family trust:

- a. A family trust is a trust designed to allow a parent to transfer assets to his or her children directly and prevent assets from being automatically inherited by a spouse.
- b. In this trust, the objective is to pass assets on to future generations instead of to the surviving spouse as shown in the bypass trust discussed in section **4661.08**.
- c. Expanded definition: A family trust is a trust created to benefit persons who are related to one another by blood, affinity, or law. It can be established by a family member for the benefit of the members of a family group. Family trusts act as an instrument to pass on the assets to future generations.

4662 Income and Deductions

4662.01 Estates and trusts are separate taxable entities. The taxable income from these entities, however, is taxed to either the entity or to its beneficiaries according to the income allocable to each party.

4662.02 IRS Form 1041 (*U.S. Fiduciary Income Tax Return*) must generally be filed if an estate's gross income is $600 or more. However, a trust files when it has either $600 of gross income or any amount of taxable income.

- a. The return is due by the 15th day of the fourth month following the close of the entity's tax year.
- b. Trusts must use the calendar year as their tax year. Estates may use either a fiscal or a calendar year.
- c. Estimated tax payments are generally required by both estates and trusts. However, an estate is exempt from making such payments during its first two tax years.

4662.03 **Gross income** for an estate or trust is basically the same as for an individual.

    a. Gains and losses will be recognized by estates and trusts when property is transferred to a beneficiary in lieu of cash to satisfy a specific cash bequest.

    b. No gain or loss will be recognized when specified property is transferred to a beneficiary under a specific bequest. However, the estate or trust may elect to recognize the gains and losses on all such distributions during the year.

    c. Income in respect of a decedent (IRD) is included in the gross income of the trust or estate. IRD is income that was earned by the decedent at the time of death but was not reportable on the decedent's final income tax return because of the accounting method utilized.

4662.04 **Deductions** for an estate or trust are similar to those of an individual.

    a. Expenses associated with income in respect of a decedent (IRD) that were not reported on the decedent's final income tax return may be claimed by the taxpayer receiving the IRD. Such expenses are deductible on both the estate tax return (Form 706) and on the income tax return of the recipient of the IRD.

    b. An estate may elect to claim administration expenses and casualty losses as either an estate tax deduction (Form 706) or as an income tax deduction (Form 1041). These expenses cannot be claimed on both returns.

    c. A personal exemption is allowed as follows:

        (1) $600 for estates

        (2) $300 for a trust that is required to distribute all of its income currently (simple trusts)

        (3) $3,500 for "qualified disability trusts"

        (4) $100 for all other trusts (complex trusts)

    d. An unlimited charitable contribution deduction is allowed to an estate or complex trust if the contribution is paid out of gross income.

        (1) No deduction is available for contributions paid from tax-exempt income.

            (a) The will or trust agreement may dictate the specific income source from which the contribution is to be paid.

            (b) Contributions not identified as to source are considered to be made proportionately from each element of income received by the trust or estate. Such contributions must be allocated between taxable and tax-exempt income.

        (2) No contribution deduction is available to simple trusts.

    e. Distributions of income to beneficiaries are allowed as a deduction to both estates and trusts. This deduction, however, cannot exceed distributable net income (DNI).

        (1) The DNI amount serves several roles:

            (a) DNI sets the limit on the amount of the distribution that is deductible by the estate or trust for the tax year.

            (b) DNI also determines the amount and character of the income to be reported by the beneficiaries.

(2) The DNI amount is basically the entity's taxable income before the distribution deduction with the following adjustments:

    (a) Additions:

        1. The personal exemption

        2. Net tax-exempt interest

        3. Net capital loss deduction

    (b) Subtractions:

        1. Net capital gains taxable to the entity

        2. For simple trusts, dividends allocable to corpus

f. Medical expenses and funeral expenses of a decedent are deductible on the estate's income tax return under the following rules:

(1) Medical expenses of a decedent that are paid within 12 months of the decedent's death are deductible on the decedent's final income tax return if they are not claimed as an estate tax deduction.

(2) Medical expenses that are not paid within one year of death are deductible only on the estate tax return (Form 706).

(3) Funeral expenses may be deducted on the estate tax return (Form 706).

g. Neither a capital loss nor a business loss sustained by a decedent may be carried forward and deducted on the estate's income tax return.

4662.05 Taxable income of estates and trusts is taxed at the following rates:

2010

Over	But Not Over	Rate
$ 0	$2,300	15.0%
2,300	5,350	25.0%
5,350	8,200	28.0%
8,200	11,200	33.0%
11,200		35.0%

4663 Determination of Beneficiary's Share of Taxable Income

4663.01 Beneficiaries are generally taxed on income distributions that they receive.

a. The character of the income distributed is the same to the beneficiary as it was to the estate or trust.

b. In a simple trust, beneficiaries are taxed on the income that is required to be distributed to them, whether or not it is actually distributed during the taxable year. The amount that is taxable, however, is limited to the trust's DNI.

c. Beneficiaries of estates and complex trusts must also pay taxes on the income required to be distributed currently (whether or not it is actually distributed) *plus* any other amounts that are paid, credited, or required to be distributed for the year.

(1) Distributions in excess of DNI are generally not taxable.

    (a) When a distribution from a complex trust exceeds the trust's DNI for the year, the beneficiary may be required to pay an additional income tax.

(b) This additional tax applies only when a complex trust has not distributed all of its DNI in prior years.

(c) The tax on this accumulation distribution is determined under special throwback rules.

(d) Beneficiaries of estates and simple trusts are not subject to the throwback rules.

(e) In general, special throwback rules apply to trust distributions made in tax years beginning before August 6, 1997. The throwback rules have been repealed for most trusts, but they continue to apply to trusts created before March 1, 1984, that would be treated as multiple trusts under IRC Section 643(f) and to foreign trusts and domestic trusts that were once treated as foreign trusts.

(2) When there is more than one beneficiary receiving a distribution from the trust or estate, DNI is divided between the beneficiaries using a two-tier system of allocation.

(a) First tier—DNI is allocated proportionately between all required income distributions.

(b) Second tier—Any remaining DNI is allocated proportionately between all other income distributions.

(c) Distributions from DNI are taxable. Additional distributions are generally not taxed.

(3) When there are multiple beneficiaries, the different income elements comprising DNI must be allocated to each beneficiary in proportion to the amount of DNI allocated to each.

4663.02 When an estate or trust terminates, several tax consequences should be noted:

a. No personal exemption may be claimed on the final income tax return of an estate or trust.

b. Unused carryovers of capital losses and net operating losses pass through to the beneficiaries who succeed to the estate or trust property. These carryovers will be used as deductions for AGI by the beneficiaries (individuals).

c. In the last tax year of existence, current deductions in excess of gross income will be allowed to the beneficiaries as miscellaneous itemized deductions.

4663.03 Special tax situations for trusts include the following:

a. When the grantor of a trust retains beneficial enjoyment or substantial control over the trust property or income, the trust is disregarded and the grantor is taxed on the trust income.

b. When appreciated property is transferred to a trust and subsequently sold at a gain within two years, a special tax applies. The gain (to the extent of the original built-in gain) will be taxed to the trust at the grantor's applicable tax rate for the year of sale.

4663.04 Crummey trusts allow a donor to transfer property to a minor. These types of trusts last for as long as the donor requests.

a. A Crummey trust transfer qualifies for the annual gift tax exclusion if the trust is properly structured where the beneficiary has the power to withdraw annual contributions.

b. The right to the trust income is only up to $13,000 per donor, per year.

4670 Tax-Exempt Organizations

4671 Types of Organizations

4671.01 The Internal Revenue Code includes legislation that exempts specified nonprofit organizations from taxation in most situations.

    a. The organization must qualify as one of the specified classes of exempt organizations provided for in the IRC.

    b. Examples of these organizations include charities, churches, educational institutions, social clubs, political organizations, employees' pension or profit sharing trusts, certain cooperatives, and private foundations.

4672 Obtaining and Maintaining Tax-Exempt Status

4672.01 Exemption from taxation is not automatic. An application for exemption must be filed with the IRS.

    a. If an exempt organization engages in a prohibited transaction, part or all of its income will be subject to tax. It may also lose its exempt status. Prohibited transactions include the following:

        (1) Failure to maintain qualification requirements

        (2) Attempting to influence legislation and participating in political campaigns (certain exempt organizations may engage in lobbying activities on a *limited* basis)

    b. Feeder organizations will be taxed. These are organizations that carry on a trade or business and turn over all of their profits to an exempt organization.

    c. Private foundations may be partially subject to tax.

        (1) Private foundations are exempt organizations that are not broadly supported by the general public. They are supported by and responsive to a limited number of donors.

        (2) Private foundations may be subject to the following taxes:

            (a) Tax on investment income

            (b) Tax on self-dealing

            (c) Tax on failure to distribute income for exempt purposes

            (d) Tax on excess business holdings

            (e) Tax on speculative investments that jeopardize the foundation's assets

            (f) Tax on expenditures that should not be made by private foundations

4672.02 Private foundations must file annual information returns. Other exempt organizations, except for churches, must file an annual information return if their gross receipts exceed $25,000 for the year. Churches are exempt from filing information returns.

    a. Returns must report the total annual contributions received and identify all substantial contributors.

    b. The return is due by the 15th day of the fifth month after the end of the accounting period.

4673 Unrelated Business Income

4673.01 Although these organizations are generally tax exempt, their unrelated business income may be taxed.

    a. Unrelated business income (UBI) is net income derived from:

        (1) the regular operation of a business activity that is unrelated to the organization's exempt purpose (includes earnings from ownership in an S corporation) or

        (2) debt-financed property.

    b. If the organization's UBI is taxed, trust rates apply if it is a trust and corporate rates apply if it is a corporation.

        (1) The first $1,000 of UBI is exempt from tax.

        (2) The tax does not apply to dividends, interest, royalties, capital gains, most rents, and similar items that are accepted as proper sources of income for a charity or trust. Income from debt-financed investments will be taxed, however.

        (3) Quarterly estimated tax payments for the UBI tax are required in the same manner as the estimated tax payments for regular corporations.

Index

A

Acceleration clause, 4232.51
Acceptance, 4221.41–.47
Acceptor, 4232.06 & .148
Accommodation indorser, 4232.07
Accord, 4224.14
Accounting
    vs. legal terminology, 4263.07
    for long-term contracts, 4343
    methods, 4340
    periods, 4330
Accredited investor, 4251.13
Accrual method, 4341.03
Accuracy-related tax penalties, 4326.03
ACRS, 4430.10–.11
Actual authority, 4212.06 & .12, 4264.03
Actuarial services, 4251.70
Adjusted gross income, 4530.03, 4580.01
Administrative
    relief, 4251.62
    sources (tax research), 4381.03
Admission of a new partner, 4264.06
Adoption
    assistance programs, 4512.35
    credit, 4580.17
Affiliated group, 4631.05
Age Discrimination in Employment Act (ADEA), 4252.64–.69
Agency, 4210
    authority of agents and principals, 4212
    creation of, 4211.15–.20
    duties and liabilities of agents and principals, 4213
    formation of, 4211
    purpose of, 4211.32
    termination of, 4211
Agent, 4211.07, .21–.25 & .30
    duties and obligations, 4213.01–.02
    liability, 4213.13–.16
    rights, 4213.06–.07
AGI, 4530.03, 4580.01
Agreement, 4221.22–.25, 4231.174
AICPA Statements on Standards for Tax Services (see also SSTS), 4112
Alimony payments, 4512.02, 4530.03
Alternative minimum tax (AMT), 4590, 4632
Alternative tax treatments, 4361
American common law, 4231.12
Americans with Disabilities Act (ADA), 4252.70–.77
American Opportunity credit, 4580.19
American Recovery Act, 4633.01 & .06–.07
Annuities, 4512.03
Answers to Questions on Returns (SSTS 2), 4112.03

Anticipatory repudiation, 4231.135 & .171
Antifraud provisions, 4251.48 & .55
Apparent authority, 4212.08, 4264.03
Articles of incorporation, 4262.17
Artisan's lien, 4233.42 & .51
Assessing tax sources, 4381.01
Assets
    basis of, 4420
    holding period of, 4420
    types of (property transactions), 4410
Assignment, 4222.41–.45
    for the benefit of creditors, 4241.28–.30
    of commercial paper, 4232.66–.67
    of contracts, 4222.41–.45
    of partnership interest, 4264.09
Attachment, 4233.09, 4241.04–.09
    of a security interest, 4233.09–.13
Auctioneer, 4211.22
Audit adjustments (tax), 4364
Authoritative hierarchy for tax research and communication, 4381
Authority
    of the agent to act for the principal, 4212
    certificate of, 4262.12
    of a partner, 4264.02
Authorized shares, 4263.05

B

Bailments, 4233.33
Bankruptcy, 4242
    chapters of the law, 4242.04
    plan, 4242.60–.65
Banks, 4232.193–.196
Bargain purchase, 4420.02, 4512.04
Basis of gifts, 4420.02
    gain/loss computation, 4420.02
    inheritance, 4473
Bearer, 4232.09
    paper, 4232.64–.65
Beneficiaries of warranties, 4231.127
Bid, 4221.32
Blank indorsement, 4232.70 & .82–.85
Board of directors, 4264.10
Bona fide occupational qualifications (BFOQ), 4252.58
Boot, and recognition of gain, 4634.02
Breach of warranty, 4231.185
Broker, 4211.22, 4251.14
Business
    entities and tax planning, 4363
    expense substantiation, 4325.02
    judgment rule, 4264.16
Business structure, 4260
    advantages, 4261
    capitalization, 4263

constraints, 4261
distributions, 4263
financial structure, 4263
formation, 4262
disadvantages, 4261
implications, 4261
operation, 4262
profit and loss allocation, 4263
rights, duties, legal obligations and authority of owners and management, 4264
termination, 4262
By operation of law, 4211.19, 4231.119
Buyer's
    actions and remedies, 4231.162–.177
    obligations, 4231.135
    remedies, 4231.163–.177
    rights on sales contracts, 4231.144
By operation of law, 4262.08
Bylaws, 4262.18
Bypass trust, 4661.08

C

C corporations, 4611.01, 4630
Canceled debt, 4512.06
Capital assets, 4410.04
Capital gains/losses, 4450.02–.09, 4530.06, 4550.05–.18
Cash method, 4341.02 & .05
Casual sales, 4251.45
Casualty and theft loss, 4440.02 & .04
Certain Procedural Aspects of Preparing Returns, (SSTS 3), 4112.04
Certificate
    of authority, 4262.12
    of deposit, 4232.21
Certification of a check by a bank, 4232.149–.150
Certified public accountant (CPA)
    and privileged communications, 4133.01–.04
    workpapers, 4133.05–.09
C. & F., 4231.110
Chapter 7 Bankruptcy, 4242.06–.08 & .77–.89
Chapter 9 Bankruptcy, 4242.90–.96
Chapter 11 Bankruptcy, 4242.97–.113
Chapter 13 Bankruptcy, 4242.114–.131
Charitable contributions, 4325.03, 4472.03, 4530.04
Chattel paper, 4233.18
Check, 4232.21
Check-the-box regulations, 4350.02
Child and dependent care credit, 4580.12
Child support, 4512.07
Childcare facilities, 4512.08
Child's interest and dividends, 4530.08
C.I.F., 4231.109
Circular 230 (Treasury Dept.), 4111
    duties and restrictions, 4111.11–.28

rules governing practice, 4111.01–.10
sanctions for violations, 4111.29–.32
Civil fraud penalties, 4326.04
Citizenship, corporation, 4262.16
Claims for refunds, 4327.03
Classification(s) of
    agents, 4211.21–.25
    collateral, 4233.14–.18
    contracts, 4221.02–.16
    guarantors and sureties, 4241.52
    principals, 4211.26–.28
Clean Air Act, 4252.156–.166
Clean Water Act, 4252.167–.173
Closely held, Closed, Close, 4261.07
Collateral, 4233.14
Collection between customers of
    different banks, 4232.195–.196
    the same bank, 4232.194
Commercial paper, 4232.02 & .04–.20, 4251.44
    clauses, 4232.51–.52
    functions, 4232.04
    ordinary contract rights, advantages over, 4232.05
    types, comparison of, 4232.23
Common law
    duties and liability, 4131
    lien, 4233.51–.54
Compensated agent, 4211.24
Compensatory damages, 4224.02
Completed contract method, 4343.02
Composition agreement, 4241.24–.27
Comprehensive Environmental Response, Compensation, and Liability Act (CERCLA), 4252.147–.155
Computation of gain, 4344.02
Computer technology rights, 4252.191–.213
Conditional indorsement, 4232.78 & .97
Confidentiality, 4133
Consideration, 4222.01, 4241.49
Consignment, 4231.68
Consolidated corporate tax return, 4636
Consolidated Omnibus Budget Reconciliation Act (COBRA), 4252.100–.109
Constitutional rights of a corporation, 4261.08
Construction bonds, 4241.57
Contingent fees, 4251.73
Contract(s), 4220, 4264.04
    breach, remedies for, 4224.01–.08
    carrier, role of, 4231.64
    creation of, 4221.48
    discharge of, 4224.09–.20
    formation of, 4221
    laws governing, 4221.18–.20
    long-term, accounting for, 4343
    performance, 4222
    price, 4344.02
    for sale of goods, law that applies to, 4231.12

sales, 4231
third-party assignments, 4223
Contractual capacity, 4222.19–.24
Copyrights, 4252.200–.213, 4550.08
Corporate
control, 4634.03
liquidations, 4634.06–.08
reporting, 4251.82
structure, major changes in, 4262.22
Corporation(s), 4262.11–.23
citizenship, 4262.16
classifications of, 4261.07
constitutional rights of, 4261.08
domicile of, 4262.13
by estoppel, 4261.07
foreign, 4262.12
formation of, 4262.13
improper use of, 4262.11
managers of, 4264.19
officers of, 4264.18
powers of, 4261.09
prohibited actions of, 4262.21
suing, 4262.19
termination of, 4262.23
Cost recovery (taxation), 4430
Course
of dealing, 4231.33–.36 & .72
of performance, 4231.33–.36
Cover, 4231.164
Coverdell Education Savings Accounts, 4512.36, 4580.19
Credit
rules (SEC), 4251.61
shelter trust, 4661.09
Creditor-debtor relationships, 4240
Creditor rights, duties, and liabilities, 4241
Credits (tax), 4580.03
adoption, 4580.17
child and dependent care, 4580.12
child tax, 4580.18
disabled access, 4580.08
earned income, 4580.14
education tax, 4580.19
elderly and disabled, 4580.10
employer-provided child care, 4580.09
FICA tax credit on tips, 4580.15
foreign tax, 4580.11
investment, 4580.04
low-income housing, 4580.07
mortgage interest paid, 4580.13
qualified retirement plans, 4580.20
rehabilitation, 4580.04
research activities, 4580.06
withholding and estimated tax, 4580.16
work opportunity, 4580.05

Criminal
penalties (taxes), 4326.08
proceedings against CPAs, 4132.18–.22
statutes, 4222.17
Crummey trust, 4663.04
Cumulative voting, 4264.21
Cure (U.C.C.), 4231.170
Customary authority, 4264.03

D

Damages (U.C.C.), 4231.171
De facto corporation, 4261.07
De jure corporation, 4261.07
Dealer, 4251.17
Death of
a customer, 4232.186
the principal or agent, 4212.18
Debt(s) not discharged by bankruptcy, 4242.66
Debtor-creditor relationships, 4240
Debtor
and bankruptcy, 4242.01
Chapter 7, under, 4242.06–.08
rights, duties, and liabilities, 4241
written notice to consumer, 4242.05
Decision making, role of taxes in, 4366
Deductions
and losses, 4530
miscellaneous, 4530.04
Default (U.C.C.), 4233.43–.48
Defenses of the parties, 4232.118–.119
Delegation of duties, 4222.46–.50
Demand instrument, 4232.158
Departures from a Position Previously Concluded in an Administrative Proceeding or Court Decision (SSTS 5), 4112.06
Depletion, 4430.06–.09
Depreciation
election (tax), 4350.03
recapture, 4430.10–.12
tax, 4430.01–.12
Directors
board of, 4264.10
liability of, 4264.15
loans to, 4264.14
Disability before age 65, 4252.03
Disallowed claims, 4242.53
Discharge, 4224.09, 4232.127
in bankruptcy, 4241.54
of a contract, 4224.09–.20
of debtor, 4242.67–.68
Disciplinary systems, 4120
Disclosed principal, 4211.26
Disclosure, 4251.18
Dishonor, 4232.160
Disparate discrimination

impact, 4252.57
treatment, 4252.56
Dissolution, causes of, 4262.08
District Court (U.S.), 4323.03
Dividends, 4264.17, 4512.10, 4631.05
Document of title, 4233.18, 4234
Domestic corporation, 4261.07
Domicile, corporate, 4262.13
Donee beneficiary, 4223.03
Draft, 4232.21
Drawee, 4232.10 & .148
Drawer, 4232.11 & .148
Due care, 4213.01
Due diligence, 4251.19
Duress, 4221.56–.63

E

Earned income credit, 4580.14
Earnings and profit, 4635
Elderly and disabled credit, 4580.10
Elements of a contract, 4221.21
Employee
    death benefit, 4512.11
    expenses, 4530.04
Employee Retirement Income Security Act (ERISA), 4252.91–.99
Employer and employee, 4211.12
Enforcement (SEC), 4251.82
English common law, 4231.12
English Sales of Goods Act in 1893, 4231.12
Entertainment expense, 4325.02
Entity, 4262.11
    distributions, 4613
    formation of, 4611.08–.09
    liquidation of, 4614
    operation of, 4612
    and owner transactions, 4634
Erroneous refund claims, 4326.05
Equal Pay Act (EPA), 4252.85–.90
Equity receivership, 4241.31–.33
Estate, 4242.21–.24, 4660
    beneficiary's share of taxable income, 4663
    deductions, 4662
    income, 4662
    taxes, 4470
    trust, 4661.06
    and trust income tax, 4662.01–.05
Estimated tax
    tax planning, impact on, 4365
    penalties, failure to pay, 4326.02
Estoppel, 4211.18
    corporation by, 4261.07
    nominal (ostensible)/partner by, 4262.02
    partnership by, 4262.02
Ethics in tax practice, 4110

Executive Order 112, 4252.61–.63
Executory, 4221.11
Exempt
    property, 4241.15–.18, 4242.25–.29
    securities, 4251.44 & .52
    transactions, 4251.45
Exemption(s), 4530.04
    SEC, 4251.44
Expert, 4251.21
Express
    authority, 4212.03
    powers (corporation), 4261.09
Express warranty, 4231.115
    by affirmation or promise, 4231.116
    by description, 4231.117
    by sample or model, 4231.118
Ex-ship, 4231.111
Extension clause (U.C.C.), 4232.52

F

Factor, 4211.22
Fair Debt Collection Practices Act, 4241.34–.44
Fair Labor Standards Act (FLSA), 4252.78–.84
False
    registration statements, 4251.47
    tax information and withholding, 4326.06
Family trust, 4661.10
Farming income, 4512.12, 4530.09
F.A.S., 4231.108
Federal Claims Court, 4323.04
Federal Court of Appeals, 4323.05
Federal
    securities regulation, 4251
    statutory liability, 4132
    tax legislative process, 4310
Federal tax procedures, 4320
    audit and appeals process, 4322
    disclosure of tax return positions, required, 4324
    due dates, 4321
    judicial process, 4323
    penalties, 4326
    statute of limitations, 4327
    substantiation requirements, 4325
Federal Unemployment Tax Act (FUTA), 4252.22–.31
FICA tax credit on tips, 4580.15
Fidelity bonds, 4241.57
Fiduciary duties, 4264.08
Filing status (tax, individuals), 4570
Financing statement, 4233.19–.23
Firm offer, 4231.14
Floating lien, 4233.49–.50
F.O.B., city
    of destination, 4231.106
    of shipment, 4231.105
    of shipment or destination, 4231.107

Foreign Corrupt Practices Act, 4251.63–.68
Foreign
    corporation, 4261.07, 4262.12
    tax(es), 4370.03
    tax credit, 4580.11
Foreseeability rules, 4131.19–.26
Forged indorsement, 4232.190
Forgery, 4232.189
Form and Content of Advice to Taxpayers (SSTS 7), 4112.08
Forms (SEC), 4251.90–.92
Franchiser and franchisee, 4211.14
Fraud, 4131.02
    in the execution, 4221.54–.55
    in the inducement, 4231.120
Fungible goods, 4231.08
Future goods, 4231.07

G

Gain, computation of, 4344.02
Gains and losses (see Taxes—Property Transactions)
Garnishment, 4241.19–.23
General partnership, 4611.03
Gift tax(es), 4472
Goods, 4231.01–.08
    title to, 4231.36
Government regulation of business, 4250
Gratuitous agent, 4211.23
Gross
    income, 4510, 4511.01, 4530.02, 4580.01
    negligence, 4131.03
Group-term life insurance, 4512.15
Guaranteed payments, 4654.02
Guarantor, 4241.48
    rights, duties, and liabilities, 4241.45–.57
    and surety, difference between, 4241.48
Guaranty, 4241.46

H

Head of household, 4530.04 & .06
Hierarchy for tax research and communication, 4381
Hochfelder, 4132.10
Holder, 4232.12 & .102–.103
    after a holder in due course, 4232.116
    in due course, 4232.14 & .104–.117
Hope credit, 4580.19
House of Representatives, 4310.01
Hybrid method, 4341.04

I

Illegal bargains, 4222.15–.18
Imperfect or defective title in the goods, 4231.41–.47
Implied
    authority, 4264.03
    powers (corporation), 4261.09
Implied warranties, 4231.119
    of fitness for a particular purpose, 4231.121
    of merchantability, 4231.120
Impossibility of performance, 4212.18, 4224.15, 4231.134
Incidental beneficiary, 4223.05
Income in respect of a decedent, 4512.33
Incomplete instrument, 4232.50
Incorporation laws, state, 4262.12
Incorporators, 4262.14
Indivisible, 4221.08
Indorsee, 4232.15
Indorsements, 4232.68–.81
Indorser, 4232.16
Initial issue of shares, 4263.04
Injunction (SEC), 4251.62
Insane person and partnerships, 4264.01
Insanity of the principal or agent, 4212.18
Insider, 4251.22
Insolvency, 4242
Inspection
    of corporate records, 4264.27
    of goods (U.C.C.), 4231.177
Installment sales, 4344
Insurable interest, 4231.65
Intangible personal property, 4233.18
Interest income, 4512.20
Internal Revenue Code (IRC), 4113
Internal Revenue Code (IRC) Section
    179 election, 4350.04
    351 transaction, 4634.05
    731 (gain or loss recognition), 4656.02
    732 (partner's basis in property received), 4656.03
    733 (partner's remaining basis), 4656.04
    1231 assets, 4410.07–.10
    1245 recapture, 4430.11
Internal Revenue Service (IRS) audit and appeals process, 4322
Interpretation
    of contracts, 4222.39–.40
    of sales contracts, 4231.33–.36
Intrastate offerings, 4251.45
Inventory valuation methods, 4342
Investment credit, 4580.04
Involuntary
    conversion, 4440.04
    petition, 4242.15–.20
Irrevocable offers, 4221.40, 4231.14
Issuer, 4251.23
Itemized deductions (Schedule A, individual tax), 4530

J

Joint
- conference committee, 4310.03
- contracts, 4224.21
- and several contracts, 4224.23
- tax returns, 4350.05
- ventures, 4261.03

Judicial
- bonds, 4241.57
- process (tax), 4323
- seizure, 4231.36
- sources (tax research), 4381.04

K

Knowledge of Error (SSTS 6), 4112.07

L

Leasehold improvements, 4512.18
Legal
- capacity of the parties, 4211.29–.31
- duties and responsibilities, 4130
- entity, 4261.01

Legislative sources (tax research), 4381.02
Letters of credit, 4232.197–.206
Liability(ies), 4121
- to clients under common law, 4131.01–.11
- and common law, 4131
- of directors, 4264.15
- federal statutory, 4132
- on a negotiable instrument, 4232.141–.145
- of the parties, 4232.146–.148
- partner's individual, 4264.04
- to third parties under common law, 4131.12–.15

Licensing systems, 4120
Life insurance
- proceeds, 4512.21
- trust, 4661.07

Lifetime Learning credit, 4580.19
Limited liability
- Company (LLC), 4261.04, 4611.05
- Partnership (LLP), 4261.05, 4611.06

Limited partnership, 4261.02, 4611.04
Liquidated
- damages, 4224.05, 4231.172
- debt, 4222.09

Liquidating distributions, 4657.01
Loans to directors, 4264.14
Local taxes, 4370.02
Long-term contracts, accounting for, 4343
Loss limitations (taxation), 4550
Low-income housing credit, 4580.07
Loyalty, 4213.01

M

MACRS, 4430.02
Main purpose doctrine, 4222.33
Maker, 4232.17 & .148
Managers of the corporation, 4264.19
Margin trading, 4251.60 & .82
Marital
- deduction, 4474
- trust, 4661.02

Market surveillance (SEC), 4251.82
Married filing
- jointly, 4570.03
- separately, 4570.04

Matched orders, 4251.24
Meal expense, 4325.02
Meals and lodging, 4512.22
Medicare, 4252.03
Merchants, 4231.09–.11
Merit system, 4252.58
Midwestern (Heartland) Disaster area, 4580.04 & .19, 4633.01
Minority of the principal debtor, 4241.54
Miscellaneous deductions, 4530.04
Missing indorsements, 4232.185
Mistakes, 4221.68–.72
Mitigation of damages, 4224.06
Money laundering, 4252.214–.216
Mortgage interest paid credit, 4580.13
Moving expense, 4530.03
Multijurisdictional tax issues, 4370
Mutual mistake, 4221.68

N

National Association of State Boards of Accountancy (NASBA), 4122.11
Negligence, 4131.04, 4231.186
Negotiability, 4232.24–.25
Negotiable instruments, 4232.21–.23
Negotiation of
- commercial paper, 4232.60–.65
- documents of title, 4234.13–.17

Net operating loss, 4631.04, 4633.01
Netting process, 4450
No-par shares, 4263.04
Nominal
- damages, 4224.03
- (ostensible)/partner by estoppel, 4262.02

Nonmarital trust, 4661.03–.04
Nonnegotiable commercial paper, 4232.02
Nonprofit corporation, 4261.07
Note, 4232.21
Notice of dishonor, 4232.161–.164
Novation, 4224.13

O

Obligations of drawee bank to holder of check, 4232.177–.179
Occupational Safety and Health Act, 4252.44–.52
Offer, 4221.26
Offering circular, 4251.25
Officers of the corporation, 4264.18
Open price terms in a sales contract, 4231.91
Option contract, 4221.38
Ostensible (nominal)/partner by estoppel, 4262.02
Overdrafts, 4232.188
Ownership rights in goods, 4231.35

P

Par value shares, 4263.04
Parol evidence rule, 4222.35–.38, 4231.175
Parol-extrinsic, 4222.35
Partially disclosed principal, 4211.27
Parties to commercial paper, 4232.06–.20
Partner(s)
    admission of new, 4264.06
    authority of, 4264.02
    duties of, 4264.08
    individual liability, 4264.04
    rights of, 4264.07
    types of, 4262.03
    who can and cannot be a, 4264.01
    withdrawal of a, 4264.05
Partnership(s), 4330.02, 4520.04, 4611.03–.04
    agreement, 4264.04
    capital, 4263.01
    creation of, 4262.01
    ending of, 4262.07
    by estoppel, 4262.02
    interest, assignment/transfer of, 4264.09
    limited, 4261.02
    limited liability (LLP), 4261.05
    priority of payments on dissolution of, 4262.09
    profits and losses, 4263.02–.03
    winding up, 4262.07
Pass-through entities, 4520
Passage of title from the seller to the buyer, 4231.37–.40
Passive losses, 4540
Patents, 4252.191–.199
Payee, 4232.18
Payment of an altered check, 4232.191
Penalties (tax), 4326
    on early withdrawal of savings, 4530.03, 4560.01
Percentage
    of completion method, 4343.03
    depletion method, 4430.07
Perfect title, 4231.41
Perfection of a security interest, 4233.24–.32

Personal
    defense, 4232.106 & .120
    service corporation, 4330.03
Policy of restraint (IRS), 4324.03
Power
    to appoint subagents, 4212.10
    of attorney, 4211.10
Preemptive right, 4264.24
Presentment warranties, 4232.168–.171
Primary
    offering, 4251.26
    party, 4232.19
Principal
    and agent, 4232.180
    and independent contractor, 4211.13
    liability, 4213.17–.21
    rights, 4213.08–.10
Privacy acts, 4133
Private placement, 4251.45
Privileged communications, 4133.01–.04
Prizes and awards, 4512.24
Professional corporation, 4261.07
Projection of tax consequences, 4362
Promissory estoppel, 4222.11
Proof of claim, 4242.47–.48
Property
    definition of, 4634.01
    transactions, taxation of, 4400
Prospectus, 4251.27
Proxy, 4251.28, 4264.22
    solicitation, 4251.59 & .82
    statement, 4251.29
Public Company Accounting Oversight Board (PCAOB), 4123.01, 4251.69
Publicly held corporation, 4261.07

Q

Qualified
    indorsements, 4232.90–.95
    subchapter S trust, 4641.02
    terminable interest property trust (QTIP), 4661.05
Quasi-public corporation, 4261.07

R

Ratification (of agency), 4211.17
Real defenses, 4232.107 & .121–.122
Recognition of
    gain or loss, 4550.03, 4634.02
    revenues and expenses, 4341
Records, inspection of corporate, 4264.27
Recoveries, 4512.26
Refund claims, 4327.03
Registration
    of securities, 4251.43 & .82

statement, 4251.43
Regulation D, 4251.45
Regulation
    of business by government, 4250
    of securities, federal, 4251
Regulatory agencies, requirements of, 4123
Rehabilitation credit, 4580.04
Related party transactions, 4460
Remedies
    for breach of contract, 4224
    of the guarantor or surety, 4241.56
Rents and royalties, 4512.25
Requisites for negotiability, 4232.24–.48
Research activities credit, 4580.06
Resource Conservation and Recovery Act (RCRA), 4252.174–.178
Respondeat superior, 4213.08, .11 & .14; 4261.09
Restitution, 4224
Restricted security, 4251.31
Restrictive indorsements, 4232.97–.100
Retirement plan benefits, 4560
Retraction, 4231.171
Right to setoff, 4242.30–.32
Rights of creditor, 4241.53
Risk of loss, 4231.47–.63
Rule 10b-5 (SEA '34), 4132.07–.11
Rule 3600T, Interim Independence Standards, 4251.73
Rule 3700, Advisory Groups, 4251.73

S

S corporations, 4261.10, 4330.02, 4350.06, 4611.02, 4640
Sale
    of goods, contracts, 4231.12
    of unregistered securities, 4251.46
Sales
    contracts, 4231
    and exchanges (taxation), 4440
Sanctions, 4251.49 & .62, 4252.31
Sarbanes-Oxley Act of 2002, 4123.02–.03, 4251.69–.71
Schedule M-3, 4622
Scholarships and fellowships, 4512.27
Scienter, 4132.10, 4251.32
SEC (Securities and Exchange Commission), 4251.78–.82
    required reports, 4251.53
    rules, making of (SEC), 4251.82
SEC Regulation A, 4251.43
SEC Rule
    10b-5, 4251.56
    144, 4251.87
    145, 4251.88
    146, 4251.45
    147, 4251.45
    240, 4251.43
    242, 4251.45 & .89
    246, 4251.43
    415, 4251.43
    504, 4251.45
    505, 4251.45
    506, 4251.45
SEC Section
    11, 4251.49
    11(A) (SA '33), 4132.01–.06
    12, 4251.48
    12(1) and 12(2), 4251.49
    17, 4251.48
    18 (SEA '34), 4132.12–.17
Secondary
    liability, 4232.147
    offering, 4251.33
    parties, 4232.20
Section (see Internal Revenue Code (IRC) Section and SEC Section)
Secured transactions, 4233
Securities
    exchange, 4251.34
    regulation of, 4251.10–.12
Securities Act of 1933, 4251.42–.49
    Section 11, 4132.01–.06
Securities Exchange Act of 1934, 4251.92
    Rule 10b-5, 4132.07–.11
    Section 18, 4132.12–.17
Securities and Exchange Commission (see SEC)
Security, 4251.35
    agreement, 4233.06
    interest, 4233.05
Self-employment tax, 4530.03, 4590.02
Seller's
    obligations on sales contracts, 4231.69
    remedies, 4231.157–.161
Senate, 4310.02
Separate maintenance payments, 4512.02
Several contract, 4224.22
Share(s)
    initial issue of, 4263.04
    no-par, 4263.04
    par value, 4263.04
    subscription, 4263.04
    types of, 4263.05
Shareholder(s), 4264.20–.27
    voting, 4264.21
Short-swing profit, 4251.36 & .57
Small
    business stock, 4512.39
    issues of securities, 4251.45
Social Security (FICA), 4252.01–.21
Sole proprietorship, 4261.06, 4611.07
Special
    agent, 4211.22

damages, 4224.04
    indorsement, 4232.86–.89
Specific performance, 4224.08
Stale check, 4232.184
Standard deduction, 4530.04
State
    boards of accountancy, 4122
    incorporation laws, 4262.12
    regulation of securities, 4251.01–.09
    taxes, 4370.02
Stated capital, amount of, 4263.08
Statements on Standards for Tax Services (SSTSs), 4112
    1, *Tax Return Positions*, 4112.02
    2, *Answers to Questions on Returns*, 4112.03
    3, *Certain Procedural Aspects of Preparing Returns*, 4112.04
    4, *Use of Estimates*, 4112.05
    5, *Departures from a Position Previously Concluded in an Administrative Proceeding or Court Decision*, 4112.06
    6, *Knowledge of Error*, 4112.07
    7, *Form and Content of Advice to Taxpayers*, 4112.08
Statute
    of frauds, 4222.25–.34, 4231.25–.26 & .85–.91
    of limitations, 4231.174, 4327
Statutory
    lien, 4233.55–.57
    powers (corporation), 4261.09
Stock
    corporation, 4261.07
    exchange, 4251.37
    on margin, buying, 4251.15
    options, 4512.29
Stop payment order, 4232.187
Straight voting, 4264.21
Subagent, 4211.25
Subrogation, 4241.56
Substantiation requirements (tax), 4325
Suing a corporation, 4262.19
Supplemental Security Income (SSI), 4252.03
Supreme Court, 4323.06
Surety, 4241.48
    bonds, 4241.57
    and guarantor, difference between, 4241.48
Suretyship, 4222.33
Surviving spouses, 4530.06

T

Tax Court, 4323.02
Tax credits, 4580.03–.20
Tax-exempt organizations, 4670
    unrelated business income, 4673
Tax-free
    exchange, 4440.03
    contributions (corporation), 4634.01
Tax practice, 4112.01
Tax return(s)
    elections, 4350
    preparer liability, 4131.10
Tax Return Positions (SSTS 1), 4112.02
Taxes—
    audit and appeals process, 4322
    business expenses, 4325.02
    business gifts, 4325.02
    capital losses, 4450.09
    casualty and theft losses, 4440.04, 4473.05, 4530.04, 4550.04
    charitable contributions, 4631.05
    check-the-box election, 4350.02
    communication with or on behalf of clients, 4382
    cost recovery (depreciation), 4430
    criminal penalties, 4326.08
    deductions and losses, 4530.03
    depletion, 4430.06–.09
    depreciation, 4430
    disclosure of tax return positions, 4324
    due dates, 4321
    education, 4512.28, .34 & .36; 4580.19
    employee expenses, 4530.04
    failure to deposit, 4326.07
    filing status, 4570
    franchise, 4430.05
    goodwill, 4430.05
    judicial process, 4323
    leasehold improvements, 4430.03–.05
    losses and credits from passive activities, 4540.01
    MACRS, 4430.02
    medical expenses, 4472.01, 4530.04, 4560.02, 4662.04
    miscellaneous deductions, 4530.04
    multijurisdictional issues, 4370
    net operating losses, 4633.01
    netting process, 4450
    passive activities, 4540
    penalties, 4326
    penalty on early withdrawal of savings, 4530.03
    personal exemption, 4633.03, 4642.02
    planning, 4360
    rental real estate, 4540.01
    research and communication, 4380
    research and development, 4580.06
    retirement plans, 4580.20
    self-employment tax, 4590.02
    standard deduction, 4530.04
    statute of limitations, 4327
    substantiation requirements, 4325
    trademarks, 4430.05
Taxes—Dependents, 4530.04, 4580.12

Taxes—Entities, 4610
   C corporations, 4631
   charitable contributions, 4631.05
   consolidated tax return, 4636
   corporate tax structure, 4631
   deductions from gross income, 4631.04
   dividends received, 4631.05
   earnings and profits, 4635
   entity/owner transactions, 4634
   gross income, 4631.03
   liquidations, 4634.06–.08
   S corporations, 4611.02, 4630
   Schedule M-3, 4622
   special deductions, 4631.05
   tax rates, 4631.06
   tax-exempt organizations, 4670
Taxes—Estate and trusts, 4473
   income taxes, 4473
Taxes—Exemptions, 4530.04
Taxes—Gift, 4471
Taxes—Individuals, 4580.01
   adjusted gross income, 4530.03
   adjustments and deductions, 4530
   adoption credit, 4580.17
   alimony and separate maintenance payments, 4512.02
   alternative minimum tax (AMT), 4590
   annuity proceeds, 4512.03
   bargain purchase, 4512.04
   bequests, 4512.05
   canceled debt, 4512.06
   child and dependent care credit, 4580.12
   child support, 4512.07
   child tax credit, 4580.18
   childcare, 4512.08
   computations, 4580
   Coverdell Education Savings Account, 4512.36, 4580.19
   credit(s), 4580.03
   credit for mortgage interest paid, 4580.13
   credit for the elderly, 4580.10
   damages collected, 4512.09
   dependents, 4530.04
   disabled access credit, 4580.08
   dividends of cash or property, 4512.10
   earned income credit, 4580.14
   education tax credit, 4580.19
   educational aid, 4512.28
   elderly and disabled credit, 4580.10
   employee death benefit, 4512.11
   exemptions, 4530.04
   farming income, 4512.12
   FICA on tips, 4580.15
   filing status, 4570
   foreign income exclusion, 4512.32
   foreign tax credit, 4580.11
   formula, 4580.01
   gambling winnings and losses, 4512.13
   gifts, 4512.14
   gross income, 4511.01, 4530.02 & .04
   group-term life insurance, 4512.15
   Hope scholarship credit, 4580.19
   illness or injury benefit, 4512.17
   improvements made by lessee, 4512.18
   income from illegal acts, 4512.19
   income in respect of a decedent, 4512.33
   income items, 4512
   interest, 4512.20
   investment credit (ITC), 4580.04
   life insurance proceeds, 4512.21
   Lifetime Learning credit, 4580.19
   low-income housing credit, 4580.07
   meals and lodging, 4512.22
   minor children, unearned income, 4530.07
   pensions, 4512.23
   prizes and awards, 4512.24
   rate schedules, 4530.06
   recoveries, 4512.26
   rents and royalties, 4512.25
   research activities credit, 4580.06
   retirement plan benefits, 4560
   scholarships and fellowships, 4512.27
   self-employment taxes, 4590.02
   stock options, 4512.29
   stock rights, 4512.30
   student loan interest, 4530.03
   table, 4530.05
   taxable income, 4530.04
   unemployment compensation, 4512.31
   withholding and estimated tax payments, 4580.16
   work opportunity credit, 4580.05
Taxes—Partnerships, 4650
   assets, distribution of, 4656
   basis of partner's interest, 4652.01
   characteristics of, 4520.04
   deceased partners, 4657.02
   elections, 4653
   liabilities, 4655
   liquidating distributions, 4657.01
   liquidation and retirement of partner's interest, 4654.02
   merger or split-up, 4654.04
   ordinary income/loss, 4651
   ownership changes, 4657
   property sale to partnership by partner, 4654.03
   reporting partnership income, 4651.04–.07
   retired partners, 4657.02
   sale or exchange of partner's interest, 4654.01
   separately stated items, 4651
   terminations, 4657.03
   transactions with partners, 4654

Taxes—Property transactions, 4400
   acquisition, method of, 4420.02
   assets, types of, 4410
   basis, 4420.01
   capital assets, 4550.07
   capital gains and losses, 4550.05–.18
   cost recovery, 4430
   depreciation and recovery allowance recapture, 4430.10–.12
   estate taxation, 4470
   gain or loss calculation, 4420.02
   gain or loss recognition, 4440
   gains and losses treatment, 4450, 4550.05–.18
   gift taxation, 4470
   holding period of assets, 4420
   involuntary conversions, 4440.02
   personal residence, 4440.05
   related party transactions, 4460
   sales and exchanges, 4440
   Section 1231 assets, 4410.07
   Section 1245, 4430.11
   Section 1250, 4430.12, 4450.05
   tax-free exchange, 4440.02–.03
   wash sale, 4440.02 & .06
Tenants' Corporation (1136), 4131.07
Tender
   of delivery, 4231.134
   offer, 4251.38, .58 & .82
Termination
   of the agency, 4212.13
   of the corporation, 4262.23
Terminology, accounting vs. legal, 4263.07
Third-party beneficiary
   contracts, 4223.02
   rule, 4131.16–.18
Tippee, 4251.39
Title VII (Civil Rights Act), 4252.53–.60
Title
   documents and title transfer, 4234
   to goods, 4231.36
Tolling, 4231.174
Tort, 4264.04
   of deceit, 4231.187
   of misrepresentation, 4231.188
Total gain, 4344.02
Transfer
   of commercial paper, 4232.53–.59
   of partnership interest, 4264.09
Transferee warranties, 4232.172–.176
Treasury Department Circular 230, 4111
   duties and restrictions, 4111.11–.28
   rules governing practice, 4111.01–.10
   sanctions for violations, 4111.29–.32
Treasury shares, 4263.05, 4264.21
Trust(s), 4660
   beneficiary's share of taxable income, 4663
   deductions, 4662
   income, 4662
   indorsement, 4232.97
   types of, 4661

U

Ultra vires, 4222.23, 4261.09
Ultramares, 4131.12–.15
Unaudited financial statement liability, 4131.27–.28
Unconditional instrument, 4232.29–.34
Unconscionable
   agreement, 4231.34
   contract, 4221.73–.75
Underwriter, 4251.40
Undisclosed principal, 4211.28
Undue influence, 4221.64–.67
Unearned income, 4530.07
Unenforceable, 4221.13
Unified credit, 4475
Uniform
   bankruptcy laws, 4242
   capitalization (UNICAP) rules, 4342.02
Uniform Commercial Code (U.C.C.), 4230
   documents of title and title transfer, 4234
   negotiable instruments, 4232
   principles, 4231.13
   sales contracts, 4231
   secured transactions, 4233
Uniform Sales Act, 4231.12
Unilateral mistake, 4221.69
Unliquidated debt, 4222.10
Unqualified indorsement, 4232.96
Usage of trade, 4231.33
Use of Estimates (SSTS 4), 4112.05
Usury, 4222.17

V

Void title, 4231.41
Voidable title, 4231.41, 4231.44
Voluntary petition (bankruptcy), 4242.09–.17
Voting
   cumulative, 4264.21
   shareholder, 4264.21

W

Wagering or gambling agreements, 4222.17
Warehouse receipts, 4234.06–.12
Warranties, 4231.113
Wash sale, 4251.41, 4440.06
Withholding and estimated tax credit, 4580.16
Work opportunity credit, 4580.05
Work
   delegated, that cannot be, 4213.19

illegal, 4213.19
  inherently dangerous, 4213.19
  inseparable from the principal's operation, 4213.19
Workers' compensation, 4252.32–.43
Workpapers, 4133.05–.09
Writ of execution, 4241.10–.14